THE OAU
AND THE UN

UNITAR STUDIES ON RELATIONS BETWEEN THE UNITED NATIONS AND REGIONAL INTERGOVERNMENTAL ORGANIZATIONS

THE RELATIONS BETWEEN THE COUNCIL OF EUROPE AND THE UNITED NATIONS (RS/1, 1972), A. H. Robertson

THE OAU AND THE UN: Relations between the Organization of African Unity and the United Nations (RS/2, 1975), Berhanykun Andemicael

GOVERNMENTAL CONTROL: A Prerequisite for Effective Relations between the United Nations and Non-United Nations Regional Organizations (RS/3, 1973), Sir Peter Smithers.

THE OAS AND THE UN: Relations in the Peace and Security Field (RS/4; PS/7, 1974), Aida Luisa Levin

PEACEFUL SETTLEMENT AMONG AFRICAN STATES: Roles of the United Nations and the Organization of African Unity (PS/5, 1972), Berhanykun Andemicael

The United Nations Institute for Training and Research was established by the Secretary-General as an autonomous institution within the framework of the United Nations for the purpose of enhancing, by the performance of the functions described hereafter, the effectiveness of the United Nations in achieving the major objectives of the Organization, in particular the maintenance of peace and security and the promotion of economic and social development.

The two functions of the Institute are training and research.

The Institute provides training at various levels to persons, particularly from developing countries, for assignments with the United Nations or the specialized agencies and for assignments in their national services which are connected with the work of the United Nations, the organizations related to it, or other institutions operating in related fields. These programmes can also include training for staff members of the United Nations and of the specialized agencies as well as training for special United Nations field assignments.

UNITAR's research programme has focused primarily on the structures and procedures of the United Nations which are relevant to the major objectives of the international organization. The Institute's studies and training activities are essentially practical and designed to facilitate action rather than formulate or test theory. Their aim is to facilitate objective appraisal and to clarify alternative modes of action. This by necessity leads to a multidisciplinary approach. Consequently the activities of the Institute are organized mainly in broad problem areas and not on lines of conventional academic disciplines.

THE OAU
AND THE UN

Relations between
The Organization of African Unity
and the United Nations

by Berhanykun Andemicael

A UNITAR Regional Study, No. 2

Published for the
United Nations Institute for Training and Research

by

AFRICANA PUBLISHING COMPANY

New York and London

Published in the United States of America 1976 by
AFRICANA PUBLISHING COMPANY
A Division of Holmes & Meier Publishers, Inc.
101 Fifth Avenue
New York, New York 10003

Published in Great Britain by
Holmes & Meier Publishers, Ltd.
Hillview House
1, Hallswelle Parade, Finchley Road
London, NW11 0DL

ISBN 0-8419-0186-4

LC 74-84658

PRINTED IN THE UNITED STATES OF AMERICA

Preface

The vital importance of developing a coherent and effective system of intergovernmental organizations at the global and regional levels has been stressed by successive Secretaries-General of the United Nations. They have shared the concern of many Governments about the centrifugal tendencies of several such organizations `and the need to make them fully' responsive to the requirements of the international community. UNITAR has, therefore, carried out a series of studies on relations between the United Nations and the major regional intergovernmental organizations outside the United Nations, of which the present study is a part. These studies seek to identify and analyze the areas of co-operation and the points of competition and other difficulties between the United Nations and regional organizations, and to evaluate the effectiveness of existing practices of co-operation. They also endeavor to formulate, where appropriate, proposals for improving existing relationships.

The project as a whole was initiated upon the suggestion of the Secretary-General of the United Nations, and after approval by the Board of Trustees of UNITAR. It was vigorously started during the period of office of my predecessor, Chief Simeon Adebo, and has continued to make active progress. The present study, by Dr. Berhanykun Andemicael, examines the respective roles and relationships of the Organization of African Unity (OAU) and the United Nations in all areas of mutual concern, in particular the peace and security sphere and the field of economic and social development. The existing literature devoted to the OAU and to African diplomacy provides a useful description of the structure and functioning of the OAU but it throws little light on how these relate to the objectives and role of the United Nations. The present study is, therefore, mainly designed to fill this gap. By carrying out a detailed empirical analysis of the initiatives taken by the OAU and the United Nations to solve the major African problems of the past decade, the author has made a special contribution which is of scholarly and practical value. Its utility is enhanced by the fact that he has drawn upon archives and documents which are not easily accessible to outside scholars and has obtained additional data from interviews with some national delegates and officials of the two organizations. His conclusions and proposals can, therefore, be expected to be realistic and to carry weight with policy-makers within both organizations.

Within the framework of his definition of African regionalism as it relates to the goals and priorities of the United Nations, the author has focused the study on three major areas of mutual concern to the United Nations and the OAU: peaceful settlement among African States; colonial and racial problems in Africa; and economic and social development. Addressing himself to the long-standing controversy over relative jurisdiction in the settlement of disputes within a region, he has not only ascertained the practice evolved in the African context but has also evaluated the effectiveness of the OAU as an organ of "first resort." This section is an updated version of a previously published monograph entitled: *Peaceful Settlement among African States: Roles of the United Nations and the Organization of African Unity* (UNITAR, PS No. 5, 1972). In the section relating to colonial and racial problems in Africa, the author has sought to clarify the constitutional limits of autonomous collective action by the OAU and has assessed the implications for both organizations of the present gap between OAU expectation of vigorous United Nations action in Southern Africa and the relatively modest response by the Security Council. In concluding this first part of the study concerning peace and security in Africa, he has proposed certain criteria for optimum allocation of tasks between the two organizations and has recommended steps for strengthening their co-operation.

In the second part, the analysis of relations in the economic and social field has brougth in sharp relief the problems of co-ordination between functional global agencies and multi-purpose regional bodies, as well as the difficulties arising from the creation of parallel regional structures by the United Nations and the OAU. On the basis of his analysis of the interplay of existing co-operative arrangements and the evolving tendencies for competition, especially between the United Nations Economic Commission for Africa (ECA) and the OAU, the author has put forth some bold proposals for reform.

The author of this volume, Dr. Berhanykun Andemicael, is a Research Fellow of UNITAR with specialization in international organization and African affairs. In preparing this study, he has greatly benefited from a review of the section on peaceful settlement among African States by an international panel and from written comments on other sections received from various diplomats, Secretariat officials and scholars. This assistance is deeply appreciated.

The views and conclusions put forward in this study are, of course, the responsibility of the author alone and do not necessarily reflect the opinions of the Board of Trustees or officials of UNITAR. While UNITAR takes no position on the views expressed by the authors of its studies, it does assume responsibility for determining whether a study merits publication and dissemination.

We are pleased to publish this UNITAR study by Dr. Andemicael.

Executive Director
Davidson Nicol

July 1974

CONTENTS

Part II. OAU-UN RELATIONS IN THE ECONOMIC AND
SOCIAL FIELD

CHARTS

Abbreviations

ADB	African Development Bank
AFCAC	African Civil Aviation Commission
ANC	Congolese National Army (Armée Nationale Congolaise)
BIS	Inter-African Soils Bureau
CCTA	Commission for Technical Co-operation in Africa South of the Sahara
CEAO	West African Economic Community (Communauté Economique de l'Afrique de l'Ouest)
CNL	National Liberation Committee (Comité National de Libération)
ECA	Economic Commission for Africa
ECLA	Economic Commission for Latin America
ECOS	Economic and Social Commission
ECOSOC	Economic and Social Council
EDC	Educational and Cultural Commission
EEC	European Economic Community
ESCHC	Educational, Scientific, Cultural and Health Commission
FAO	Food and Agricultural Organization
FRELIMO	Front for the Liberation of Mozambique (Frente de Libertação de Moçambique)
GAOR	General Assembly Official Records
GATT	General Agreement on Tariffs and Trade
HSNC	Health, Sanitation and Nutrition Commission
IAEA	International Atomic Energy Agency
IAPSC	Inter-African Phytosanitary Commission
IATA	International Air Traffic Association
IBAH	Inter-African Bureau for Animal Health
IBRD	International Bank for Reconstruction and Development
ICAO	International Civil Aviation Organization
IDEP	Institute for Economic Development and Planning
ILO	International Labour Organization
ITU	International Telecommunication Union
IUCN	International Union for Conservation of Nature and Natural Resources
NATO	North Atlantic Treaty Organization
NFD	Northern Frontier District
NGOs	Non-Governmental Organizations
OAS	Organization of American States
OAU	Organization of African Unity
OCAM	Organisation Commune Africaine, Malgache et Mauricienne
PAIGC	African Independence Party of Guinea and Cape Verde (Partido da Independência da Guiné e Cabo Verde)

SCOR	Official Records of the Security Council
STRC	Scientific, Technical and Research Commission
TRC	Transport and Communications Commission
UAM	Union Africaine et Malgache
UAMCE	Union Africaine et Malgache de Coopération Economique
UDEAC	Central African Customs and Economic Union (Union Douanière et Economique de l'Afrique Centrale)
UDEAO	Union Douanière des Etats de l'Afrique de l'Ouest
UNACAST	United Nations Advisory Committee on the Application of Science and Technology to Development
UNCTAD	United Nations Conference on Trade and Development
UNDP	United Nations Development Programme
UNESCO	United Nations Educational, Scientific and Cultural Organization
UNHCR	United Nations High Commissioner for Refugees
UNICEF	United Nations Children's Fund
UNIDO	United Nations Industrial Development Organization
UNITAR	United Nations Institute for Training and Research
UNRWA	United Nations Relief and Works Agency for Palestine Refugees in the Near East
UPU	Universal Postal Union.
WHO	World Health Organization

Acknowledgments

In writing this book as part of a larger UNITAR project, I have received invaluable advice and assistance from a number of diplomats, scholars, and international officials. With deep appreciation, I acknowledge the encouragement and support that I have received from Dr. Davidson Nicol, Executive Director of UNITAR, and from his predecessor, Chief S. O. Adebo. Throughout the project, Dr. Oscar Schachter, Director of Studies and Deputy Executive Director, gave me valuable guidance and criticism for which I am deeply grateful. I am indebted also to Sir Peter Smithers, a former Secretary-General of the Council of Europe, for his advice and suggestions in his capacity as Senior Fellow of UNITAR responsible for regional studies. My special thanks go also to Mr. Robert K. A. Gardiner, Executive Secretary of ECA, and Mr. Diallo Telli, then Administrative Secretary-General of the OAU, for the helpful interviews that I had with them and with members of their staff.

Special acknowledgment has already been made of the valuable panel review of an earlier version of Chapter III by participants, including several diplomats from Africa, whose names were listed in a previously published monograph on peaceful settlement of disputes among OAU member States. For their valuable criticisms and suggestions on various parts of the study, I owe special gratitude to many representatives to the United Nations, particularly Mr. Paul Blanc, Mr. Jay K. Katzen, Mr. Peter C. Petrie, and Mr. Kifle Wodajo; to Chief Justice T. O. Elias, Dr. Rosalyn Higgins, and Professors B. Boutros-Ghali, Arthur S. Lall, J. S. Magee, and Immanuel Wallerstein; to several OAU officials, especially J. D. Buliro, H. A. Dawood, D. Ouattara, G. Pognon, and M. M. Thiam; and to many of my colleagues at the United Nations and at UNITAR, particularly I. Andemicael, K. K. Apeadu, P. Civili, J. Colmar, K. K. S. Dadzie, S. I. Edokpayi, A. Elisha, Y. El-Ayouty, J. O. C. Jonah, G. L. Lardner, A. L. Levin, H. Millar-Craig, E. Nypan, R. Paw U, E. S. Reddy, J. Riby-Williams, T. R. Sutanto, A. Sylla, T. Tanaka, J. J. Therattil, F. M. Vendrell, and K. Venkata Raman. In addition, I am grateful to L. T. Kapungu and J. H. Mittelman for their research assistance at an earlier stage, to A. G. Moss and M. L. Quére-Messing for their help in checking references, and to N. Luciano for her efficient secretarial help.

While grateful for all the help that I have received, I remain solely responsible for the views expressed in this study and for any of its shortcomings.

B.A.

Author's Note

After the manuscript was sent for printing, there have been major developments concerning relations between French-speaking and English-speaking African States and between Arab and sub-Saharan Africa and concerning the situation in Southern Africa; but these developments do not significantly affect the main theme, the basic approaches and the conclusions of this study.

Eighteen months of intensive negotiations between the European Economic Community (EEC) and forty-six developing countries, of which thirty-seven are from sub-Saharan Africa, have brought about an agreement which will supersede the Yaoundé Convention of association with the EEC. The new Lomé Convention, signed on 28 February 1975, has now virtually removed the cleavage between the mainly Francophone membership of the Yaoundé Convention and the other sub-Saharan States. On the other hand, Afro-Arab relations within the Organization of African Unity (OAU) have been further strained over the volume and form of aid for sub-Saharan Africa from the oil-exporting members of the League of Arab States designed to compensate them for the damaging effects of the quadrupling of oil prices.

As regards Southern Africa, the demise of the colonialist regime in Portugal in April 1974 and the subsequent negotiations between the new Portuguese Government and the liberation movements concerned have brought about not only the independence of Guinea-Bissau but also the establishment of transitional self-government in Mozambique and Angola leading to independence in June and November 1975, respectively. These changes, combined with the intensification of the Afro-Asian policy of isolating South Africa which culminated in its exclusion from the twenty-ninth session of the General Assembly, appear to have induced a somewhat conciliatory attitude by South Africa on the Namibian question, though hardly on the issue of apartheid. These factors also appear to have induced constructive diplomatic initiatives regarding Southern Rhodesia, especially by the South African Prime Minister vis-à-vis the Rhodesian settler regime and by the Presidents of Botswana, Tanzania and Zambia and by the African leaders in Mozambique vis-à-vis the Zimbabwe liberation movements now united under the African National Council. A serious diplomatic effort is therefore being made for the first time in Southern Africa along the lines of the "Lusaka Manifesto." The OAU and the United

Nations may thus have an opportunity now to discourage backsliding and to facilitate peaceful change in the region. Of particular relevance in this regard are the approaches and suggestions outlined in Chapter V of this study.

General Introduction

The development of international organization has been accompanied by a continuing debate concerning the problem of regionalism, which has sometimes been mistakenly regarded as involving a choice between the concepts of regional and universal organization. In fact, since the time of the League of Nations, the two organizational concepts have received simultaneous application, and the real issues have concerned the balance and harmony of relationship between universal and regional organizations. At this point in the history of international organizations, when several Governments are concerned about the rapid multiplication of intergovernmental organizations and the concomitant issues of compatibility, control, and complimentarity, it seems especially important to deepen our understanding of the relationships between the United Nations and the major regional organizations.

It is the purpose of this volume to examine the relations of the United Nations with the Organization of African Unity (OAU) in all fields of mutual concern and, particularly, to evaluate the effectiveness of existing practices of co-operation and identify points of difficulty in order to suggest possibilities for strengthening the relationships. For convenience in analyzing the problems of co-operation, the subject has been divided somewhat arbitrarily into two major areas of relationship: the peace and security field (Part I) and the economic and social field (Part II). Since the relations of the United Nations with the OAU in both spheres of activity are essentially political in character, it is intended to avoid a dichotomy between the political and non-political spheres and instead to resort to a division based on more specific functional lines. Even then, certain subjects such as the refugee problem in Africa, though having significant implications for the maintenance of peace and security, have been dealt with mainly in Part II because of their greater relevance to relationships in the economic and social fields.

Bearing in mind the interdependence of multinational co-operation in the two fields of activity, an attempt is made below to outline, in the context of the United Nations Charter, the main problems and issues of relationship between the United Nations and the OAU which will be examined in detail in the two parts of this volume.

In Part I the focus of the study will be on relations in the peace and security field, mainly in terms of those parts of the United Nations Charter

1

which refer to regionalism. Like the Covenant of the League of Nations, the Charter of the United Nations regards the world organization and regional agencies and arrangements as partners in the maintenance of international peace and security. Chapter VIII of this Charter (Articles 52-54) not only recognizes the right of regional organizations and arrangements to exist but also stipulates principles for bringing them within the framework of the Charter. Article 52(1) states:

> Nothing in the present Charter precludes the existence of regional arrangements or agencies for dealing with such matters relating to the maintenance of international peace and security as are appropriate for regional action, provided that such arrangements or agencies and their activities are consistent with the Purposes and Principles of the United Nations.

The bases for determining whether a regional organization is a regional agency under Chapter VIII of the Charter are, therefore, (i) whether it plays such a role in the maintenance of international peace and security as is appropriate for regional action, including pacific settlement of disputes and enforcement action as authorized by the Security Council; and (ii) whether its objectives and activities are compatible with the purposes and principles of the United Nations (Articles 1 and 2 of the Charter).

It seems clear from the requirement of compatibility and the fact that the Security Council has primary responsibility for the maintenance of international peace and security that regional organizations were meant to be subordinated to the universal organization for this purpose. The over-all superiority of the United Nations is further confirmed by Article 103 which states:

> In the event of conflict between the obligations of the Members of the United Nations under the present Charter and their obligations under any other international agreement, their obligations under the present Charter shall prevail.

The OAU Charter is silent on the question of whether the OAU should be considered as a regional organization within the provisions of Chapter VIII of the United Nations Charter. It appears as if the founders of the OAU did not wish to commit themselves to such provisions. However, the fact that the OAU Charter presents as one of its principle goals the promotion of international co-operation, with due regard to the United Nations Charter, and that certain resolutions of the Security Council have, in harmony with the wishes of the OAU Members, encouraged the OAU to perform certain tasks in the context of Chapter VIII of the United Nations Charter, seems to indicate an increasing recognition of UN-OAU links in this sense.

Though the supremacy of the United Nations over regional organizations was established beyond question, no clear-cut principles were set up by the founders of the United Nations for the division of competence and responsibility between the two levels of international organization. With respect to disputes within a particular region, the Members of a regional organization were required to make every effort to achieve pacific settlement through such organization before referring them to the Security Council, and the Security Council was required to encourage such a development (Article 52(2) and (3)); at the same time, the Charter recognized both the right of any Member State to bring any dispute or situation that might lead to international friction to the attention of the Security Council or General Assembly, and the competence of the Council to investigate any such dispute or situation (Articles 52(4), 34 and 35). As regards situations calling for coercive action, the Charter has, on the one hand, recognized Member States' inherent right of individual or *collective* self-defense against armed attack, pending action by the Security Council (Article 51), and, on the other hand, permitted enforcement action by regional organizations only upon the authorization of the Security Council (with the exception of measures against aggressive acts of an "enemy" State in World War II—Article 53(1)). Since these provisions were the result of a compromise between the advocates of autonomous regionalism and predominant universalism, they were ambiguous enough to permit conflicting interpretations. Thus many crucial questions about division of labor between the United Nations and regional organizations remained unanswered. For instance, what matters relating to peace and security are "appropriate for regional action"; when should the Security Council be seized of a "local" dispute; where does collective self-defense end and enforcement action begin? The resulting ambiguity has, however, permitted flexibility in the development of patterns of regional-universal relationships in accordance with concrete political circumstances. As States need not, and do not, choose the regional or the universal approach to the exclusion of the other, the real question is how the two approaches should interrelate without undermining each other. Thus , as will be shown in Chapters III and IV, the issue is not which approach to adopt, but which to emphasize in solving specific problems of peace and security.

Given the pair of ambiguous combinations in the United Nations Charter—Article 52 with Articles 34 and 35, and Article 51 with Article 53—and the present tendency to regard the OAU as a regional organization in the meaning of Chapter VIII of the United Nations Charter, it is significant to study the nature of the relationships between the United Nations and the OAU that have emerged during the past decade as each organization tried to find solutions to political and security problems in Africa. Even though the OAU has not been involved in formal controversy concerning the division of competence and responsibilities between the United Nations and itself, an examination of the interplay between the two organizations in the peace and security field might make some contribution to a broader understanding of the problems of universal-regional relationships. More important, it would throw light on the political processes which determine or alter working relationships between the United Nations and the OAU and suggest ways in which co-operation between them may be strengthened. It should be noted that as the OAU is a multipurpose organization, its links with the United Nations under Chapter VIII of the Charter are only part of a larger network of relationships with all organs of the world body.

In studying UN-OAU relationships, it is useful to examine interorganizational relations as well as the relevant behavior of the OAU Members in both organizations, especially that of the parties to a dispute, and the attitudes of various influential members of the United Nations. In the context of Chapter VIII of the United Nations Charter, the main issues concerning relationships between the United Nations and the OAU in the peace and security field are the following:

1. To what extent are the aims and priorities of the United Nations and the OAU compatible and their institutions complementary?
2. In handling intra-OAU disputes or situations,
    (a) to what extent are the relative jurisdictions and actual roles of the United Nations and the OAU compatible?
    (b) under what circumstances is the OAU called upon by its Members and encouraged by the Security Council to settle disputes involving OAU Members before such disputes are referred to the Security Council or the General Assembly?
    (c) under what circumstances do the principal organs of the United Nations consider and act upon cases of pacific settlement of disputes concerning African States:
        —simultaneously with peace-making efforts of the OAU?
        —subsequent to an OAU attempt at peaceful settlement?
3. In handling situations involving OAU Members and other States,
    (a) what kinds of collective measures, if any, does the OAU take without authorization from the Security Council or without prior notification to it?
    (b) under what circumstances does it take such measures?
    (c) to what extent are such measures compatible with the relevant

provisions of the United Nations Charter?

4. What are the criteria for optimum allocation of tasks and the possibilities for strengthening collaboration between the two organizations?

An attempt will be made to answer the first question in Chapter II, the second set of questions in Chapter III, the third set in Chapter IV, and the last question in Chapter V. As a background for answering these questions, Chapter I will outline the main characteristics of African regionalism and identify the main problems of peace and security of common concern to the United Nations and the OAU.

In Part II, the focus of the study will be on the equally complex issues of UN-OAU relationships in the economic and social field. No specific provisions have been made in the United Nations Charter for relations with non-UN inter-governmental organizations in this area. But as the importance of the regional approach for postwar economic reconstruction and development became fully recognized in the early years of the United Nations, the progress that was made both toward geographical decentralization within the United Nations and toward the formation of non-UN regional bodies for economic and social co-operation has resulted in the rapid multiplication of inadequately co-ordinated regional structures. Within Africa, a major source of problem for the United Nations and the OAU has been the creation of parallel regional structures—the Economic Commission for Africa (ECA), established in 1958 as a subsidiary body of the United Nations Economic and Social Council (ECOSOC), and certain specialized commissions of the OAU, created in 1963 as subsidiary bodies under the OAU Charter.

The scope of this part of the study is limited to OAU's relations with the main organs and subsidiary bodies of the United Nations concerned with economic and social development and does not include relations with the United Nations specialized agencies and the International Atomic Energy Agency (IAEA). OAU's extensive relations with those agencies— which are themselves autonomous inter-governmental organizations linked with the United Nations by special agreements—are quite distinct and would deserve a separate study. However, reference will be made to interactions with those agencies whenever they are of direct relevance to UN-OAU relations.

It is the purpose of the study to explore ways for removing duplication or any wasteful overlapping of economic and social activities resulting from basic structural problems, deficiencies in co-ordinative mechanisms or organizational competition, especially between the OAU and ECA. The main issues of relationship to be examined are the following:

1. What is the extent of structural and functional overlapping and what measures are feasible for effective delimitation of responsibilities and division of labor?
2. How compatible and complementary are the policies and programs of the United Nations and the OAU in the economic and social field?
3. How effective are the existing forms, procedures, and practices of co-operation?
4. What are the possible remedies for deficiencies in existing mechanism and techniques of co-operation?

Since the relations between the United Nations and the OAU in the economic and social field are conducted essentially at the regional level, the main focus will be on OAU's relations with ECA. Accordingly, five chapters—VII through XI—will be devoted to those relations. These will be preceded by a chapter on OAU's relations with special global bodies of the United Nations in this field.

The conclusions for Parts I and II, which include suggestions for the strengthening of co-operation between the United Nations and the OAU, are given in Chapters V and XI, respectively.

Part I
OAU-UN Relations in the Peace and Security Field

Chapter I
African Regionalism and the United Nations

The raison d'etre of African regionalism is the attainment of peace and security, freedom and justice, and economic and social development through common efforts among the African States. As such, it seeks to promote within Africa the main purposes of the United Nations enumerated in Article 1 of the Charter. It is the purpose of this chapter to give a profile of African regionalism, and in that light to define the peace and security problems of common concern to the United Nations and the OAU.

A. MAIN FEATURES OF AFRICAN REGIONALISM

The main elements of African regionalism may be described in terms of the following basic attitudes of the African States which are embodied in the OAU Charter: (i) a unique inclination to combine Pan-Africanism with nationalism; (ii) a quest for autonomy in solving African problems; and (iii) a drive to liberate the entire continent from colonialism and racial discrimination.

1. Wellsprings of African Regionalism

During the decade preceding the establishment of the OAU, two major trends developed in the African political scene: a movement for the formation and consolidation of independent States within existing colonial boundaries and a Pan-African movement aspiring to knit together all such States or such groupings of them as were prepared to join forces for general or particular purposes. Though the two trends had the superficial appearance of being contradictory, it was widely agreed among African leaders that unity and solidarity would not only assure a common front to safeguard Africa's interests and give it a more effective voice in world affairs, but would also provide an antidote to the danger of fragmentation and remove some of the obstacles to rapid economic and social development on a broad and rational basis.[1] However, the question of what form such association or unity should take became a subject of great controversy.[2] For about six years, African inter-State relations underwent a gestation period characterized by groupings and countergroupings culminating in the establishment of the OAU in May 1963.

The thinking of the founders of the OAU appears to have been affected not only by the interplay of Pan-Africanism and nationalism but also by their evaluation of the efficacy of United Nations efforts before 1963 to solve African problems, especially the Congo crisis (1960-62) and the situation in Southern Africa.

As regards the Congo crisis, the African States were sharply divided in their opinions about the appropriateness and effectiveness of the role played by the United Nations. One group of African States (the so-called Brazzaville Group) maintained that the United Nations had intervened too much while a second group (the so-called Casablanca Group) felt that United Nations intervention was initially insufficient when help was being given to an undivided Congolese Central Government, but that subsequently it became prejudicial to the interests of the "genuinely" nationalist faction; only a small group of States (the so-called Monrovia/ Lagos Group, without the Brazzaville States in the Group) seemed to be satisfied with the role played by the United Nations throughout the crisis.*[3] Two important lessons were learned from the crisis. One was the realization of the fact that without solidarity among the African States, an African problem such as the Congo could hardly be solved by the United Nations. The second was the awareness of a danger that the cold-war and other divisive extra-African influences could easily spread over the continent whenever African solidarity was lacking. Thus, the need both to develop better cohesion among the African States and to avoid negative foreign influences in solving African problems seemed to have acted as a strong incentive for the establishment of a continental organization which could ensure the autonomy of the African region. The need for such an organization was specifically expressed as early as October 1961 when at the sixteenth session of the General Assembly Ethiopia called upon sister African States

> To join in the creation, under Article 52 of the United Nations Charter, of a regional organization of African States, the basic and fundamental task of which will be to furnish the mechanism whereby problems which arise on the continent and which are of primary interest to the region could, in the first instance, be dealt [with] by Africans, in an African forum, free from outside influence and pressure.[4]

The influence of the situation in Southern Africa was equally important. Although, by the time the OAU was established, 29 Territories in Africa had gained independence and two more were about to follow suit, the remaining fifteen Non-Self-Governing Territories included all the difficult cases of decolonization in Southern Africa.[5] The lack of positive results from the intensive initial efforts of the United Nations made the African

---

* The membership of the various Groups is given in Chart I.

States skeptical about the prospect of a just solution as long as they themselves failed to harmonize their policies at the highest possible level. They felt that the remedy would be to create an African organization and use it to exert maximum diplomatic pressure, within and outside the United Nations, on the major Powers, especially those maintaining friendly relations with recalcitrant regimes. The founders of the OAU believed that through their own organization they would be able to confront the latter Powers with a choice between "their friendship for the African peoples and their support of powers that suppress African peoples."[6] They thought that they would also be able to support national liberation movements in Africa more effectively.

Thus, while taking full advantage of their membership in the United Nations, the African States realized that in the final analysis the attainment of their collective aspirations would call for a larger measure of self-reliance which could be attained most effectively through the efforts of an African regional organization. In their view, such an organization could promote solidarity among them and render their collective relations with outside Powers more effective.

It was with these needs in mind that the Summit Conference of Independent African States decided in May 1963 to establish the OAU. Having before it the Charters of the Casblanca and Lagos Conferences,[6a] the proposals of President Nkrumah of Ghana for a Union of African States, and an Ethiopian draft Charter,[6b] the Preparatory Conference of Foreign Ministers selected the last-mentioned proposal as the basis for discussion. Little support was given at the Summit Conference for Nkrumah's proposal for the establishment of a "central political organization," consisting of a bicameral continental legislature with power to formulate a common African policy in foreign affairs, defense, economic development and monetary affairs. The vast majority of the "founding fathers" of the OAU preferred an association of sovereign States, without any supranational aspects, as recommended in both the Lagos Charter and the Ethiopian draft before the Summit Conference.

2. Main Characteristics of the OAU

The OAU is a comprehensive intergovernmental organization embracing all aspects of inter-State relationships, including political and security questions as well as economic, social, and related matters. Of the 43 independent States in Africa which are members of the United Nations, all except South Africa are members of the OAU.

a. OAU CHARTER AND OBLIGATIONS OF MEMBER STATES

One of the characteristics of the OAU is that it undertakes in Article

II(1) of its Charter "to promote the unity and solidarity of the African States." Although "unity and solidarity" are not defined in the Charter, the preamble refers to the common determination of the African Heads of State and Government "to promote understanding among [their] States in response to the aspirations of [their] peoples for brotherhood and solidarity, in a larger unity transcending ethnic and national differences." At the same time the Charter states that one of the purposes of the OAU is "to defend . . . [the] sovereignty . . . territorial integrity and independence" of the African States (Article II(1.c)—See Appendix I).

The obligation of the Member States under the OAU Charter is laid down in Article VI which states that they "pledge themselves to observe scrupulously the principles enumerated in Article III" consisting of the following: (i) sovereign equality of Member States; (ii) non-interference in the internal affairs of States; (iii) respect for the sovereignty and territorial integrity of each State; (iv) peaceful settlement of disputes by negotiation, mediation, conciliation, or arbitration; (v) unreserved condemnation of subversive activities; (vi) absolute dedication to the total emancipation of the dependent African territories; (vii) affirmation of a policy of non-alignment with regard to all blocs. More specific obligations are undertaken in Article XIX where the Member States "pledge to settle all disputes among themselves by peaceful means, and to this end, [undertake] to establish a Commission of Mediation, Conciliation, and Arbitration." According to the Protocol of this Commission, adopted by the OAU as an "integral part" of its Charter, recourse by Member States to arbitration is regarded as "submission in good faith to the award of the Arbitral Tribunal" (Article 28 of Protocol).[6c]

The resolutions of the OAU organs directed to the Member States are all recommendations. If such States fail to comply with them or even with the OAU Charter principles which they have pledged to observe, there seem to be no measures that the OAU could take against them. The OAU Charter does not provide for the suspension or expulsion of a Member State; cessation of membership can take place only at the request of the State concerned, which becomes effective one year from the date of written notification to the Administrative Secretary-General (Article XXXII of the OAU Charter).

b. MAIN CLEAVAGE PATTERN WITHIN THE OAU:
PROBLEM OF SUB-REGIONALISM

The establishment of the OAU represented an end to the sharp division among the African States that emerged from the first Congo crisis.

In 1961, the African States had formed two competing intergovernmental groupings—the Casablanca and Monrovia Groups—because of their divergent views on the handling of the Congo crisis, the conflict between France and the Algerian Liberation Front, the future of Mauritania, and the approach to African unity.[7] The Casablanca Group consisted of five West and North African States plus the "Algerian Provisional Government" which were generally regarded as being more radical than the other African States. The Monrovia Group consisted of twenty original members, including twelve French-speaking African States which were already members of the Union Africaine et Malgache (UAM), popularly known as the Brazzaville Group. Although the Casablanca and Monrovia Groups were abolished when the OAU was established, the Brazzaville Group remained, in one form or another.

The most significant division within the OAU is, therefore, between the former members of the Brazzaville Group and the other African States. Though the founders of the OAU were silent on the future of this group, its continued existence as a political grouping within the OAU became a major issue at the OAU's first Council of Ministers meeting (August 1963). As a result of pressure from the majority of the African States, a compromise was reached on the issue of sub-regionalism—one that emphasized the need for developing sub-regional groupings with a view to their adaptation to the Charter of the OAU, and recommended that any sub-regional grouping should meet the following criteria:[8]

(i) geographic realities and economic, social, and cultural factors common to the States;
(ii) need for co-ordination of economic, social, and cultural activities peculiar to the States concerned.

As its raison d'etre was shaken following the creation of the OAU, the UAM responded in March 1964 to pressure from the OAU and transformed itself into a purely economic and cultural structure under the name Union Africaine et Malgache de Coopération Economique (UAMCE). But as sharp differences emerged among the OAU Members later in 1964 and early 1965 over the general issue of interference in the internal affairs of States, and specifically with regard to the second Congo crisis, the new cleavage led to the retransformation of the UAMCE into a political organization, with a slightly enlarged membership, which became known as the Organization Commune Africaine, Malgache et Mauricienne (OCAM).[9] OCAM* was described by its founders as "a new African grouping whose aim, within the context of the O.A.U., is to reinforce co-operation and solidarity between Afro-Malagasy States, and to speed up their political,

---

* The membership is given in Chart I.

economic, social and technical, and cultural development." Although the political functions of OCAM became gradually de-emphasized, following the permanent solution of the Congo crisis later in 1965 and the various political changes that took place since then within several African States, the members of this organization still remain a closely knit political group within and outside the OAU. The continued existence of this group has, therefore preserved the main line of division within the OAU, that between the OCAM group and the remaining Members of the OAU.

As far as the sub-Saharan African States are concerned, this division coincides roughly with the cleavage between Francophone and Anglophone States. All the Francophone sub-Sahara States, except Guinea, Mali, Burundi, Mauritania (since June 1965), Zaire (since April 1972) and Congo (Brazzaville) (since 1973) are members of OCAM. Of these, all except Mauritius and Rwanda were former French Territories and maintain at present close cultural and economic relations with France. Many of them have also concluded defense arrangements with France. All the OCAM States along with Burundi, Mali, Mauritania, and Somalia are affiliated with the European Economic Community (EEC), under the Yaoundé Convention of Association (1963, 1969) and receive from the EEC development funds and special tariff preferences. (The members of the East African Community—Kenya, Uganda, Tanzania—as well as Morocco and Tunisia have subsequently signed association agreements offering less favorable terms).

The special ties of the former dependent Territories of France, Belgium and Italy with the EEC and of the former French colonies with France had been strongly opposed by several other African States, especially by the Anglophone ones which maintained no comparable cultural, economic, or political relations among themselves or with the U.K. through their Commonwealth association. Most Anglophone States not only tended to resent the tariff preferences given by EEC to their neighbors, which they regarded as detrimental to their own agricultural exports, but also argued that the Yaoundé Convention, and other association agreements would divide African States and impede African regional and sub-regional development. The more radical among the Anglophone and other non-OCAM and non-associated States have sometimes even employed the rhetoric of anti-imperialism and anti-neocolonialism in an attempt to embarrass the Francophone States about their connection with Europe. But with the enlargement of the EEC in 1972 (as a result of the admission of the U.K., Denmark, and Ireland) and the increase in interest among the remaining Anglophone African States to seek association, the division in sub-Saharan Africa is now rapidly declining.

In addition to the sub-Saharan Francophone and Anglophone States,

OAU membership includes the six Arabic-speaking North African States which are members of the League of Arab States.* The membership of the North African States in both the OAU and the League of Arab States has tended to create for those States tension between their policies of Pan-Africanism and Pan-Arabism and for the OAU a north-south division. But this situation has been increasingly alleviated by the political or ideological bonds maintained by most North African States with some sub-Saharan African States and by the growing solidarity of OAU Members with Egypt in opposition to Israeli refusal to withdraw from Egyptian territory occupied during the 1967 war.

These divisions have had significant implications for the role of the OAU in attempting to solve African problems. While most of the Franco-phone States have been inclined to favor a modest role for the OAU in handling internal and external problems of the OAU, the non-OCAM States on both sides of the Sahara have tended to advocate roles ranging from moderate to militant on both types of problems. As regards the north-south division, while the Arab Members of the OAU have sought to involve the OAU politically in the Arab-Israeli conflict, most of the other OAU Members have tended to oppose any involvement beyond a symbolic gesture of solidarity with the UAR, (Egypt). The opposing pulls resulting from the cleavages within the OAU have tended to limit its effectiveness in solving African problems, but current developments seem to suggest a reversal of this trend.

C. THE OAU AS COMPARED WITH OTHER REGIONAL ORGANIZATIONS

i. The OAU as an Instrument for Conflict Resolution among its Members but not for Collective Measures against Any of Them.

Like both the Organization of American States (OAS) and the League of Arab States, the OAU is distinguished from defense alliances such as the North Atlantic Treaty Organization (NATO) and the Warsaw Pact by its role as an agent for resolving conflicts and disputes among its own Member States. But in contrast to the OAS which, according to Article 7 of the Inter-American Treaty of Reciprocal Assistance, is required to take all necessary measures to re-establish or maintain peace and security between two or more Members of the OAS, or the League of Arab States which has the power under Article 6 of its pact to determine measures necessary to repulse aggression by any State against a Member State, the OAU is entrusted with no disciplinary power over any offending Member. The only

---

* During 1974, after this study was completed, Mauritania and Somalia became members of the League of Arab States.

power that it can use against a recalcitrant Member State is that of the opinions of other Members.

ii. As a Co-ordinator of African Policies on Regional Problems but not as a Defense Alliance

Unlike the OAS and the League of Arab States, the OAU can hardly be regarded as having elements of a defense alliance. The OAU Charter requires Member States to co-ordinate and harmonize their general policies regarding defense and security and provides for the establishment of a Defense Commission,[10] but its provisions have not been accompanied by a collective defense treaty such as the Inter-American Treaty of Reciprocal Assistance of the OAS or the Joint Defense and Economic Co-operation Treaty of the League of Arab States.[11]

Within the context of the United Nations, the OAU tends to act as the collective agent of its members in a more formal way than do the OAS and the League of Arab States in regard to their respective Member States: the African Group in the United Nations is regarded as a body of the OAU while the Latin American and Arab Groups have only informal links with their respective regional organizations.

iii. As an Agent for African Non-Alignment on East-West Issues

On global questions such as the reduction of international tension, including the problem of disarmament, the OAU seeks to define the general perspective of the African States within deliberative and negotiating international forums. In this regard the African States have explicitly affirmed as a cardinal principle of the OAU Charter the policy of non-alignment with respect to all blocs.[12] As in the case of the League of Arab States, but in contrast to the OAS, the OAU membership includes none of the Powers formally belonging to alliances with respect to the East-West ideological conflict. Virtually all its members have been full participants in the conferences of non-aligned States. But the extent to which they can follow an effective collective policy of non-alignment might largely depend on their ability to limit their individual dependence for development and, in some cases, for security on outside Powers, as well as to reduce cleavages and tension among themselves.

iv. As an Agency with Modest Capabilities

If we describe organizational capability in terms of material and political resources, the main components are administrative and financial resources as well as the capacity for independence and impartiality, for initiative in obtaining organizational discussion and for consensus in taking the necessary action. In material resources, the OAU is comparable to the League of Arab States but has far less capacity than the OAS. Being composed of small developing countries, the OAU has at its disposal a relatively small budget (about $3 million which is less than one sixth that of the OAS) and a small administrative staff; it has been plagued by recurrent arrears of dues and a recruitment problem. However, it has perhaps been better endowed than other regional organizations in political resources. Its salience for a third-party role is enhanced by the fact that it is free from the domination of any single country or group of countries. But existing cleavages have tended to inhibit both leadership and consensus on the more crucial issues of peace and security in Africa.[13]

Having described the main features of African regionalism and the characteristics of the OAU, we now turn to the major problems of peace and security of concern to both the OAU and the United Nations.

B. PEACE AND SECURITY PROBLEMS OF COMMON CONCERN TO THE UNITED NATIONS AND THE OAU

The interplay of three factors is crucial in the application of Chapter VIII of the United Nations Charter: first, the identity of the States involved in a dispute or situation (whether or not all the States, directly or indirectly involved, are members of the regional organization concerned); secondly, the intensity of the dispute or conflict between them (extent of potential or actual threat to international peace and security); and thirdly, the organizational capacity for effective response. When political problems do not involve disputes or other situations of tension—and hence do not raise the issue of relative competence and responsibility—organizational capacity combined with other factors such as the scale of priorities of the organization concerned tend to shape respective roles of the United Nations and a regional organization.

In terms of the identity of the States involved, the problem of peace and security in Africa can be divided into three categories; (i) disputes or situations involving only OAU members, (ii) situations involving OAU members and colonial or settler regimes; and (iii) situations arising from relations between OAU members and States outside Africa.

1. Disputes and Conflicts between OAU Members

The main problems involving only OAU Members are of two types: first, territorial or other disputes between neighboring States and, secondly, certain exceptional situations within individual African States brought about by ethnic, religious, political, or ideological differences which might create inter-State tensions or give rise to such problems as charges of foreign intervention and the outflow of refugees.

Territorial and boundary disputes between Members of the OAU have been the cause of numerous diplomatic incidents and hostilities in Africa.

Although examples of actual warfare are relatively few, many African States have potentially dangerous claims to ethnic groups and territories within the present boundaries of neighboring States or Non-Self-Governing Territories.[14]

Internal conflicts are normally considered to be outside the jurisdiction of both the United Nations[15] and the OAU[16] unless they have international repercussions of the nature mentioned above. In the main internal conflicts which became of great concern to both the United Nations and the OAU, there was alleged to be some form of intervention by other African States. While some of them became of concern to both the United Nations and the OAU mainly because of the mass flow of refugees, others involved conflicts with serious repercussions on international peace and security.[17]

2. Conflicts between OAU Members and Colonial and Racial Regimes in Africa

The second area of mutual political concern between the United Nations and the OAU has involved the danger of growing conflict along racial lines between the independent African States and the Governments or regimes in those countries in Africa which remain under colonial control or settler domination—especially Southern Rhodesia, South Africa, and Namibia (South West Africa) and, until recently, the Portuguese-administered territories of Angola, Mozambique, and Guinea-Bissau. The military preparations of Portugal, South Africa, and the minority regime in Southern Rhodesia have increased enormously within the last decade as have the repressive measures against African populations; and the African nationalists in exile have been trained in techniques of guerrilla warfare in order to liberate their countries. The unilateral declaration of independence by a minority group of European settlers in Southern Rhodesia has aggravated tension in that area. The confrontation between South Africa and most Member States of the United Nations over the former's policy of apartheid as well as South Africa's refusal to recognize the right of self-determination and independence for Namibia and its decision to break up that Territory into tribal governments under its tutelage have greatly exacerbated the situation in Southern Africa. That South Africa has acted in defiance of General Assembly resolution 2145(XXI) of 27 October 1966 terminating the mandate in South West Africa further aggravates the matter.

The main elements of the confrontation between the African States and the colonial and settler minority regimes in Africa are the following: the stubborn defiance of these regimes in violation of United Nations Charter provisions concerning human rights and self-determination of peoples, accompanied by repressive measures against nationalist movements; and the determination of the African States to use all means at their disposal to bring about political change, including the provision of assistance to nationalist movements in the dominated areas.

3. Certain Issues between OAU Members and Non-African States

The third area of mutual concern covers relations between the African States and States outside the continent. The aspects most relevant to the question of UN-OAU relations are the problem of intervention by non-African States in the internal conflicts of African States and that of the arms race in Africa.

a. INTERVENTION BY NON-AFRICAN STATES IN INTERNAL CONFLICTS OF AFRICAN STATES

When a civil strife occurring in an African country is regarded by local and foreign participants as part of a larger conflict of an ideological character, both regional and global peace and security may be threatened. The threat may be enhanced if one or both of the local parties in the conflict are determined and able to obtain external support in the form of weapons or troops or both. As the experience of the Congo crisis of 1960-62 has demonstrated, ethnic conflicts, leadership rivalries or secession movements, if conducted within the context of conflicting influences of external interests, can be of great concern both to the African States and the international community. In such cases, a major goal of both the United Nations and the OAU has been to discourage competitive external intervention in order to prevent transformation of the internal conflict into an international one.

b. ARMS RACE IN AFRICA

Although the level of armaments in most African States is still low, the pace of the arms race has been rapidly increasing, especially in Southern Africa, the Horn of Africa, North Africa, and parts of West Africa. This problem transcends the region not only because the arms suppliers are often non-African Powers with conflicting interests, but also because the tensions and conflicts associated with the arms race have implications for international peace and security.[18] The arms race is thus an issue which poses a challenge for both the United Nations and the OAU.

The concern over armaments in Africa is not limited to conventional weapons; it extends also to the potential danger of the spread of nuclear weapons into Africa. The denuclearization of Africa has been of great interest to both the United Nations[19] and the OAU.[20] It is an objective which can be attained only through collaboration between the United Nations and the OAU, once the few potential nuclear Powers in Africa and the Middle-East decide to adopt a policy of non-acquisition of nuclear weapons.

Within the context of these categories, based on the identity of the parties involved, we have identified four main issues of mutual concern to the United Nations and the OAU: acute internal conflicts of African States; disputes between OAU Members; confrontation with colonial and racial regimes; and intervention by non-African States in such situations, including military assistance. A rational division of labor between the United Nations and the OAU—one consistent with Chapter VIII of the United Nations Charter—would suggest that internal and inter-State disputes and conflicts of OAU Members should be settled, if possible, through the OAU, but that any tensions with colonial regimes and non-African States should be primarily handled by the United Nations. But the development of such complementary roles would depend upon the intensity of the tension or conflict and the capacity of each organization to respond effectively to a crisis. In view of the modest constitutional powers of the OAU and its limited material and political resources, one might expect that its capacity to handle internal and inter-State situations of Member States would be largely limited to low-intensity conflicts (externally supported insurgencies, inter-State tensions, and border clashes). In such situations, the OAU could effectively provide a forum for discussion and exhortation and arrange conciliation missions. But large-scale conflicts, internal or inter-State, which call for large field operations would at present seem to be beyond its capacity. In such situations, the OAU and its Member States might have to rely on the United Nations.

As regards the confrontation over colonial and racial issues, the OAU relies heavily upon the United Nations, but the latter's capacity to persuade recalcitrant colonial and settler regimes to bring about peaceful change is yet to be demonstrated. On the other hand, the United Nations appears to have a capacity for discouraging major Power intervention in African conflicts.

Irrespective of the identity of the parties concerned or the issues involved, if a situation deteriorates to such an extent that it is regarded by the Security Council as a threat to the peace, a breach of the peace, or an act of aggression, it becomes the primary responsibility of the Security Council under Chapter VII of the United Nations Charter.

CHART I

MEMBERSHIP OF AFRICAN COUNTRIES IN THE UN AND OTHER ORGANIZATIONS AND ASSOCIATIONS*

(AS OF SEPTEMBER 1974)

	Algeria	Botswana	Burundi	Cameroon	Central African Rep.	Chad	Congo (Braz.)	Dahomey	Egypt (UAR)	Ethiopia	Equatorial Guinea	Gabon	Gambia	Ghana	Guinea	Guinea-Bissau	Ivory Coast	Kenya	Lesotho	Liberia	Libya	Madagascar	Malawi	Mali	Mauritania	Mauritius	Morocco	Niger	Nigeria	Rwanda	Senegal	Sierra Leone	Somalia	South Africa	Sudan	Swaziland	Tanzania (Tanganyika)	Togo	Tunisia	Uganda	Upper Volta	Zaire (Congo D. R.)	Zambia
United Nations	X	X	X	X	X	X	X	X	X	X	X	X	X	X	X	X	X	X	X	X	X	X	X	X	X	X	X	X	X	X	X	X	X	X	X	X	X	X	X	X	X	X	X
UN Economic Commission for Africa (ECA)[1]	X	X	X	X	X	X	X	X	X	X	X	X	X	X	X	X	X	X	X	X	X	X	X	X	X	X	X	X	X	X	X	X	X	X	X	X	X	X	X	X	X	X	X
Organization of African Unity	X	X	X	X	X	X	X	X	X	X	X	X	X	X	X	X	X	X	X	X	X	X	X	X	X	X	X	X	X	X	X	X	X		X	X	X	X	X	X	X	X	X
African Development Bank	X	X	X	X	X	X	X	X	X	X	X	X	X	X	X	X	X	X	X	X	X	X	X	X	X	X	X	X	X	X	X	X	X		X	X	X	X	X	X	X	X	X
Non-Aligned Conferences (1964/1970/1973)[2]	X	X	X	X	X	X	X	X	X	X	X	X	X	X	X	X	X	X	X	X	X	X	X	X	X	X	X	X	X	X	X	X	X		X	X	X	X	X	X	X	X	X
Former Casablanca Group (1961-63)[3]	X								X					X	X						X			X			X																
Former Monrovia/ Lagos Group (1961-63)[4]				X	X	X	X	X		X		X					X			X	X	X			X			X	X		X	X	X					X	X		X	X	
Former Brazzaville Group (1960-64)				X	X	X	X	X				X					X					X			X			X			X										X		
Organisation Commune Africaine Malgache et Mauricienne (OCAM)[5]				X	X			X				X					X									X		X		X	X							X			X	X	

CHART I (continued)

	Algeria	Botswana	Burundi	Cameroon	Central African Rep.	Chad	Congo (Braz.)	Dahomey	Egypt (UAR)	Ethiopia	Equatorial Guinea	Gabon	Gambia	Ghana	Guinea	Guinea-Bissau	Ivory Coast	Kenya	Lesotho	Liberia	Libya	Madagascar	Malawi	Mali	Mauritania	Mauritius	Morocco	Niger	Nigeria	Rwanda	Senegal	Sierra Leone	Somalia	South Africa	Sudan	Swaziland	Tanzania (Tanganyika)	Togo	Tunisia	Uganda	Upper Volta	Zaire (Congo D. R.)	Zambia
Communanté Economique de l'Afrique de l'Ouest (CEAO)[6]								X									X							X	X			X			X										X		
Conseil de l'Entente								X									X											X										X			X		
Organisation pour la Mise en Valeur du Fleuve Sénégal (OMVS)																								X	X						X												
Lake Chad Basin Commission				X		X																						X	X														
River Niger Commission				X		X		X							X		X							X				X	X												X		
Union Douanière et Economique de l'Afrique Centrale (UDEAC)[7]				X	X		X					X																															
Conference of East and Central African States			X		X	X	X			X								X															X		X		X			X		X	X
East African Community																		X																			X			X			

Permanent Consultative Committee of the Maghreb[8]													x					
League of Arab States					x	x		x	x		x	x		x			x	
States Associated with the EEC[9]	x	x	x	x	x		x		x x		x x		x x		x	x x x x x		x	
Commonwealth	x					x	x		x		x	x		x	x x		x	x

*An earlier version of this chart was prepared in collaboration with James H. Mittelman.

1 South Africa has been suspended from ECA by the Economic and Social Council pending a change of its racial policies.

2 Malawi attended only the 1964 Conference. Dahomey attended the 1964 and 1973 Conferences. Botswana, Equatorial Guinea, Lesotho, and Swaziland, all of which became independent after 1964, attended the 1970 and 1973 Conferences. Gabon, Gambia, Ivory Coast, Madagascar, Mauritius, Niger, Rwanda, Upper Volta, and Zaire attended only the 1973 Conference.

3 Algeria was represented by the Provisional Government of the National Liberation Front; Libya attended the first Casablanca Conference but did not sign the Charter.

4 Libya and Tunisia attended only the Monrovia Conference; Congo (later Zaire) and Tanganyika (later Tanzania) attended only the Lagos Conference.

5 OCAM has succeeded the Union Africaine et Malgache de Coopération Economique which in turn replaced the Union Africaine et Malgache. Mauritania and Congo (Brazzaville) withdrew from OCAM in 1965 and 1973, respectively, but they as well as Mali participate in some of the specialized institutions. Zaire withdrew in 1973 and Cameroon, Chad, and Madagascar left in 1974.

6 CEAO has succeeded the Union Douanière des Etats de l'Afrique de l'Ouest (UDEAO).

7 Chad withdrew from UDEAC in 1968.

8 Libya withdrew in 1970.

9 Eighteen of these States are affiliated with the European Economic Community in accordance with the Yaoundé Convention of Association (1963 and 1969). The others have signed different agreements of association: the partner States of the East African Community—Kenya, Tanzania, and Uganda (1968); Morocco and Tunisia (1969).

Chapter II

The OAU and the UN: Objectives, Priorities, and Institutions

The present chapter examines the objectives and institutions of the OAU in relation to those of the United Nations. The scales of priorities of the two organizations will be examined in the light of the purposes and principles stipulated in their respective Charters. After the common objectives and points of possible divergence have been defined, we will attempt a comparative analysis of the institutional machinery of the two organizations in the peace and security field and a brief description of the means of co-ordination.

A. COMPARISON OF PURPOSES AND PRINCIPLES

The purposes and principles of the United Nations are to a large extent reflected in the Charter of thet OAU. Article II(1.e) of this Charter provides that one of the purposes of the OAU is "to promote international co-operation, having due regard to the Charter of the United Nations and the Universal Declaration of Human Rights." The phraseology of this Article is rather ambiguous as the words "having due regard" could be interpreted in two ways. They could either be regarded as introducing an element of discretion whereby the OAU could comply with or disregard the United Nations Charter, including its purposes and principles, or interpreted as implying that the OAU would promote international co-operation subject to the overriding constraints of the United Nations Charter and the Universal Declaration of Human Rights. In the absence of any specific provision in the OAU Charter on whether the OAU was intended as a regional organization under Chapter VIII of the United Nations Charter, the validity of either interpretation can be tested in terms of the Preamble of the OAU Charter and the special resolution on "Africa and the United Nations" (see Appendix II.1), adopted simultaneously with the signing of that Charter. In the Preamble, the African States assert as follows:

> persuaded that the Charter of the United Nations and the Universal Declaration of Human Rights, to the principles of which we reaffirm our adherence, provide a solid foundation for peaceful and positive co-operation among States.

In even stronger terms the resolution states that the African States reaffirm their "dedication to the purposes and principles of the UN Charter and [their] acceptance of all obligations" contained therein. There seems to be little doubt, therefore, that the second interpretation is more in line with the intention of the founders of the OAU—that the OAU was meant to operate within the framework of the UN Charter.[2]

The primary purpose of the United Nations—that of maintaining international peace and security (Article 1(1))—and the principles concerning the obligation of Member States to "refrain . . . from the threat or use of force against the territorial integrity or political independence of any State" (Article 2(4)) and to "settle their international disputes by peaceful means" (Article 2(3)) are reflected in Article III of the OAU Charter, In paragraphs 3 and 4 of Article III, the OAU Member States "solemnly affirm and declare their adherence" to the principle of "respect for the sovereignty and territorial integrity of each State and for its inalienable rights to independent existence" as well as to that of "peaceful settlement of disputes." In paragraphs 2 and 5 they pledge, in the spirit of the UN Charter, to observe the principle of "non-interference in the internal affairs of States" and undertake to condemn "all forms of political assassination as well as of subversive activities on the part of neighbouring States or any other State."

Although the OAU Charter does not go so far as the UN Charter in providing specifically for the taking of collective measures to prevent or remove threats to the peace and to suppress acts of aggression or other breaches of the peace (Article 1(1) of UN Charter), it makes a general provision in Article II(2.f) that the OAU Member States "shall co-ordinate and harmonize their general policies . . . for defense and security." The OAU Charter places great emphasis on the peaceful settlement of disputes. The forms of peaceful settlement to be used are largely similar to those enumerated in Article 33(1) of the UN Charter.

The second purpose of the United Nations—that of developing "friendly relations among nations based on respect for the principle of equal rights and self-determination of peoples . . ." (Article 1(2))—is reflected in OAU's purpose "to promote international co-operation" (Article II(1.e)) and "to eradicate all forms of colonialism from Africa" (Article II(1.d)). The OAU Member States have pledged themselves to end colonialism in Africa.

The purpose of achieving "international co-operation in solving international problems of an economic, social, cultural, or humanitarian character, and in promoting . . . respect for human rights," the third principal purpose of the United Nations, is embodied in the OAU Charter in the following general terms whereby the Organization undertakes "to coordinate and intensify . . . co-operation and effort to achiieve a better life for the peoples of Africa." The main elements of this broad objective have been elaborated in special resolutions[3] of the OAU adopted by the 1963 Summit Conference of Independent African States.

The obligations implied in the OAU purposes and principles are regarded by the African States as being applicable to relationships among themselves but not to relations with non-members of the OAU. The latter are, of course, governed by the obligations undertaken in the UN Charter, but the order of priorities of the African States would be influenced by the orientation of the OAU Charter. Since the OAU Charter is less categorical than the UN Charter with regard to the goal of maintaining international peace and security, but more emphatic on the eradication of colonialism and the prevention of flagrant violations of the right of racial equality, one might expect some conflict of priorities. Of course, in the event of a conflict between the obligations of the African States under the two Charters, it is the UN Charter obligations which should prevail (Article 103, UN Charter).

B. PROBLEM OF SCALE OF PRIORITIES

The founders of the United Nations declared in the Preamble of the Charter their determination first to "save succeeding generations from the scourge of war" and only secondly to "reaffirm faith in fundamental human rights, in the dignity and worth of the human person, in the equal rights of men and women and of nations large and small." Accordingly, in Article 1, they made the maintenance of international peace and security the first purpose of the United Nations, while giving second place to the purpose of developing "friendly relations among nations based on respect for the principle of equal rights and self-determination of peoples."

But in 1960, the impact of the membership of African States in the United Nations on the scale of values of the United Nations began to be felt when the newly independent African States were joined by some other States in articulating their special concerns and their demands on the international community. In the scale of priorities of these States, no question was more important than their commitment to secure a speedy and unconditional end of colonialism "in all its forms and manifestations" and the abolition of racial discrimination as a Government policy. This was reflected in the proceedings of their several summit conferences which as forerunners of the OAU had articulated the collective mandate of the African Group at the United Nations. The intensity of the concern of the African States with colonialism and apartheid is illustratde by the fact that more than half of their speeches at the General Assembly and its sessional

committees during 1960 and 1961 were on those two problems.[4] The aim
of the African States was to give special emphasis to the relationship between, on the one hand, the promotion of human rights and self-determination of peoples and, on the other, the maintenance of peace and security.
In their view, denial of human rights and of the right of self-determination
would jeopardize peace while their attainment would be instrumental in
the promotion of peace.

The process of making the uppermost objectives of the African States—
decolonization and the abolition of apartheid—goals of top priority
within the United Nations began when the General Assembly pronounced
certain principles which some observers regarded as constituting a reinter-
pretation of the UN Charter. The first is the Declaration on the Granting
of Independence to Colonial Countries and Peoples—resolution 1514
(XV), which was adopted by the General Assembly without opposition,
though with nine abstentions.[5] The Declaration sought to extend the obligations of the administering Powers under Article 73 of the UN Charter
from one of merely developing dependent Territories toward self-government to one of taking "immediate steps" in all Territories that had not yet
attained independence "to transfer all powers" to the peopes concerned,
without any conditions or reservations, "in accordance with their freely
expressed will and desire . . . in order to enable them to enjoy complete
independence and freedom." Not only did the Declaration seek to increase
the obligations of the administering Powers, but it also registered a new
notion about the relation between colonialism and the maintenance of
peace. Whereas Article 73 proclaimed that within the system of international peace and security the interests of the inhabitants were to be of
paramount importance in administering the dependent Territories, the
Declaration affirms that "the subjection of peoples to alien subjugation . . .
is an impediment to the promotion of world peace and co-operation" and
that the conflicts resulting from the denial of freedom to such peoples
would "constitute a serious threat to world peace." The Declaration expresses the belief that "the process of liberation is irresistible and irrever-
sible and that, in order to avoid serious crises, an end must be put to
colonialism and all practices of segregation and discrimination associated
therewith." These principles gained acceptance by additional States in
1961 when four of the nine States that had abstained on resolution 1514
(XV) voted in favor of the establishment of a Special Committee to review the implementation of the Declaration.[6]

In regard to the question of apartheid also, the efforts of the African
and Asian States since 1960 brought about a wide consensus against South
Africa's policy of racial discrimination. In April 1060, the Security Council
concluded that, if the situation in South Africa continued, "it might en-

danger international peace and security." In November 1962, the General Assembly adopted resolution 161 (XVII) which strongly deprecated "the continued and total disregard" by South Africa of its obligations under the UN Charter and "its determined aggravation of racial issues by enforcing measures of increasing ruthlessness involving violence and bloodshed," Moreover, it reaffirmed "that the continuance of those policies seriously endangers international peace and security."

Thus, before the establishment of the OAU in May 1963, it was widely recognized that solving the problem of colonialism and apartheid was a prerequisite for the maintenance of peace and security in the Territories concerned.

When the OAU was established, what was new was the idea of taking individual or collective measures to eradicate colonialism and apartheid. The year before, in 1962, India's argument after its forceful expulsion of Portugal from Goa that "colonialism is permanent aggression" was widely accepted among the Afro-Asian delegations in the United Nations.[7] Implicitly accepting this argument, the Summit Conference of Independent African States which created the OAU took a significant step in encouraging the use of force by African nationalists to fight colonialism and apartheid. In a resolution adopted simultaneously with the OAU Charter, the African Heads of State affirmed their collective "duty . . . to support dependent peoples in Africa in their struggle for freedom and independence" and undertook to lend moral, financial, and military support to national liberation movements in Africa, without themselves being engaged in a direct military conflict with the colonial powers.[8] Subsequently, the African Group at the United Nations, acting as an organ of the OAU, took every opportunity to attain recognition for the right to use force to hasten the end of colonial rule. In this light it sought to establish the legitimacy of the use of force by national liberation movements. In November 1966, it took advantage of a proposal made by Czechoslovakia for the establishment of principles for the "Strict Observance of the Prohibition of the Threat or Use of Force in International Relations and of the Right of Peoples to Self-Determination," and succeeded in securing wide acceptance in the General Assembly for the following doctrine:

> peoples subjected to colonial oppression are entitled to seek and receive all support in their struggle which is in accordance with the purposes and principles of the Charter.

In the resolution containing this doctrine, all States were urged strongly:

> to exert every effort and to undertake all necessary measures with a view to facilitating the exercise of the right of self-determination of peoples under colonial rule . . .[9]

The legitimacy of the use of force by liberation movement against forcible action by colonial rulers has been recognized by the vast majority of Member States, but several States have reservations about the legitimacy of military support for such movements. This issue, which was the subject of sharp differences during the preparation of the Declaration on Principles of International Law concerning Friendly Relations and Co-operations among States (1963-1970,[10] will be examined in more specific terms in Chapter IV.

The question of Non-Self-Governing Territories in Africa and that of apartheid have been persistently claimed by the colonial and settler regimes in southern Africa to be essentially within the domestic jurisdiction of the States concerned, and thus to be exempt from United Nations jurisdiction. But the majority of Member States maintain that these problems are of concern to the Organization not only because they involve fundamental human rights and the right to self-determination, but also because in certain circumstances they disturb international peace and security.

Just as the OAU Member States have been able to win wide support in the United Nations for the doctrine of the admissibility of intervention by the international community in the situation in southern Africa, they have been equally successful in their joint efforts with States from other regions designed to proscribe foreign intervention from the domestic affairs of small countries such as themselves. In December 1965, partly through the efforts of the African States, the General Assembly adopted without opposition[11] resolution 2131 (X) which became the "Declaration on the Inadmissibility of Intervention in Domestic Affairs of States and Protection of their Independence and Sovereignty." The Declaraltion affirmed that "no State has the right to intervene, directly or indirectly, for any reason whatever, in the internal or external affairs of any other State. . . ." It also indicated that both direct and indirect intervention constitute a violation of the United Nations Charter. The majority of States maintain that these restrictions do not apply to the efforts being made to end colonialism and racial discrimination, since all States are called upon in the Declaration to "contribute to the complete elimination" of both and as the Declaration is not meant to affect the application of United Nations Charter provisions regarding the maintenance of international peace and security contained in Chapters VI, VII, and VIII of the Charter.

The African States have brought to the United Nations the set of priorities initially adopted by their summit conferences and later embodied in the OAU Charter. They have persuaded the vast majority in the General Assembly to adapt the United Nations scale of values in terms of the African priorities. All the three declarations of the General Assembly—

that on decolonization, on the strict observance of the prohibition of threat or use of force, and on the inadmissibility of intervention in domestic affairs—define standards of conduct for Member States in a manner which conforms with the main interests of the OAU: the eradication of colonialism and racial discrimination as well as the prohibition of direct or indirect intervention in the affairs of small States.

C. COMPARISON OF MACHINERY FOR PROMOTING PEACE AND SECURITY

In trying to solve specific problems concerning peace and security, the role of the United Nations or a regional organization depends essentially on the nature of its purposes and principles and on the capacity of its institutional machinery. Having already outlined the general objectives of the two organizations, a comparison of their relevant institutions will provide a useful background to the examination, in the following chapters, of their respective roles in specific political and security problems concerning Africa. On the United Nations side, the relevant organs are the Security Council, the General Assembly (and their subsidiary bodies dealing with African problems), the International Court of Justice, and the Secretariat. On the OAU side, the principal institutions are the Assembly of Heads of State and Government, the Council of Ministers (and their subsidiary bodies), the Commission of Mediation, Conciliation, and Arbitration, and the General Secretariat.

1. The OAU and the UN Security Council

The OAU has no organ which could be regarded as a counterpart of the Security Council in terms of functions or powers. The Assembly of Heads of State and Government, though it is the supreme organ of the OAU, has been entrusted neither with a special responsibility for the maintenance of peace and security nor with a power to take legally binding decisions for such a purpose or to impose mandatory sanctions of a military or non-military character. It should, however, be pointed out that the normal practice of the OAU to limit its role to the promotion of pacific settlement of disputes through discussion and recommendations is similar to the deliberative role of the Security Council.

The relationship between this highest organ of the OAU and the Security Council is governed by the provisions of Chapter VIII of the United Nations Charter described in the Introduction.

2. The OAU Deliberative Organs and the UN General Assembly

The OAU Assembly may be regarded as the counterpart of the General Assembly. It is a comprehensive organ with two main functions:

(i) to discuss matters of common concern to Africa with a view to co-ordinating and harmonizing the general policy of the Organization; and

(ii) to review the structure, functions and acts of all the organs and any specialized agencies which may be created.

These functions resemble those of the General Assembly to discuss any questions or any matters within the scope of the United Nations Charter. The OAU Assembly, like the General Assembly, has the power only to make recommendations, but being the highest organ of the OAU, it is not subject to the type of limitation on recommendatory powers that constrains the General Assembly. The General Assembly may, under Article 11 (1 and 2), consider the general principles of co-operation in the maintenance of international peace and security and may discuss any specific questions brought before it; however, though it has an unqualified power to make recommendations with regard to the general principles involved, it may not, according to Article 12, do so with regard to a dispute or a situation while the Security Council is exercising its functions on the matter, unless the Council so requests. This difference between the recommendatory powers of the OAU Assembly and of the General Assembly is perhaps not very significant in practice, particularly in the light of the tendency of the General Assembly to exercise its functions in a manner that would effectively complement the primary responsibility of the Security Council for the maintenance of international peace and security.[12]

The functions of the OAU Assembly are less specific than those of the General Assembly, but specific content has been increasingly given to them in the light of the cases brought before the OAU. Since the OAU Assembly has the power to provide an authoritative interpretation of the OAU Charter,[13] it may develop the Charter systematically; it has thus an advantage over the United Nations principal organs, none of which may authoritatively interpret the UN Charter for the whole Organization.

The power of the OAU Assembly to make recommendations and to take decisions in connection with the above functions was neither specifically mentioned nor differentiated in the OAU Charter. But the rules of procedure of the OAU Assembly describe the results of deliberations of the the Assembly as "resolutions and decisions," without, however, defining either term. From the proceedings of the OAU Assembly, it appears that on issues concerning election and other important organizational matters such as budgetary questions the OAU Assembly, like the General Assembly, takes binding decisions by a two-thirds majority vote. However, since the OAU Charter, unlike the UN Charter, has not provided for such sanctions as the suspension or expulsion of a recalcitrant Member State, the OAU Assembly could not effect compliance with its decisions by the threat or use of such measures.

The second principal organ of the OAU, the Council of Ministers, is responsible to the OAU Assembly and is entrusted with the responsibility of, inter alia:

(i) preparing the conferences of the Assembly;
(ii) implementing the decisions of the Assembly;
(iii) co-ordinating inter-African co-operation in the fields of defense and security, politics and diplomacy, economic and social development, education and culture, health and nutrition, science and technology, in accordance with the instructions of the Assembly;
(iv) adopting the budget of the Organization;
(v) approving the regulations of the specialized commissions created under Article XX of the OAU Charter;
(vi) creating ad hoc committees and temporary working groups.[14]

In practice, the role of the Council of Ministers has grown to such an extent that most of the resolutions of the Council, adopted merely by a simple majority, are presented for immediate implementation without awaiting endorsement by the OAU Assembly. The OAU Assembly confirmed the appropriateness of this practice when it accepted the recommendation of its Institutional Committee that only in the case of a class of resolutions of the Council of Ministers defined by the Assembly as requiring its final approval should the implementation be delayed.[15] As the OAU Assembly has not subsequently defined such a category of resolutions, this limitation on the Council's power has not been applied in practice. After the first ordinary session of the OAU Assembly, the resolutions of the Council of Ministers have been reviewed in such a way that no formal resolutions of endorsement were considered to be necessary. Moreover, after its second ordinary session, the OAU Assembly began to limit its resolutions largely to subjects which it was requested by the Council of Ministers or a Member State to consider in the first instance, as well as to the perennial issues of colonialism and apartheid against which it was deemed necessary to employ the prestige and influence of the Assembly.

The functions and powers of the OAU deliberative organs are, therefore, comparable to those of the General Assembly (and those of the Security Council when it is exercising merely recommendatory powers).

3. Executive Machinery of the OAU and the UN

The executive machinery of the OAU tends to be far weaker than that of the United Nations. A Ghanaian proposal made during the first ordinary session of the OAU Assembly for establishing an Executive Council for the OAU through Charter amendment had failed to get sufficient support in the succeeding session of the Assembly.[16] Thus, for the implementation of its resolutions, the OAU continues to rely on a Council of Ministers which is composed of all Member States, and on an Administrative Secretary-General with only limited executive powers. The executive powers of these two organs fall far short of those entrusted by the UN Charter to the Security Council and the Secretary-General of the United Nations (hereafter referred to merely as Secretary-General).

The very name of the head of the OAU General Secretariat, "Administrative Secretary-General," indicates how anxious the founders of the OAU were to limit his powers. In the OAU Charter he is empowered merely to direct the affairs of the secretariat (Article XVI). The OAU Charter does not specifically provide as does the UN Charter (Article 98) for the role played by the Secretary-General in the meetings of the principal organs; nor does it specifically empower him to perform functions entrusted to him by such organs. However, according to the provisions of the "Functions and Regulations of the General Secretariat" of the OAU this organ is described as having a responsibility to "carry out the functions assigned to it by the Charter . . . , those that might be specified in other treaties and agreements among the Member States, and those that are established in [the] Regulations" (Rule 1). The Administrative Secretary-General is also described as having the power to act as a representative of the organization in performing such functions as reporting on the activities of the organization and its various organs, acting as depositary for agreements entered into among Member States and receiving notification of accession to or prospective withdrawal from the OAU Charter (Rules 2 and 11). Moreover, he is specifically required to "supervise the implementation of decisions of the Council of Ministers concerning all economic, social, legal and cultural exchanges of Member States" (Rule 2). These provisions, therefore, seem to entrust the Administrative Secretary-General with powers basically similar to those entrusted by Articles 97 and 98 of the UN Charter to the Secretary-General.

However, neither the OAU Charter nor the regulations of the General Secretariat empower the Administrative Secretary-General, as does Article 99 of the UN Charter in the case of the Secretary-General, to bring to the attention of the competent organ "any matter which in his opinion may threaten the maintenance of international peace and security." In the OAU, such an initiative is reserved for the Member States who alone may request the convening of an extraordinary session of the OAU Assembly or the Council of Ministers.[17] While the Secretary-General has been able, in the spirit of his prerogatives under Article 99, to conduct, on his own initiative, inquiries and investigations of potentially dangerous international developments, to engage in "preventive" diplomacy even before a situation is brought before the United Nations political organs, to intervene in their debates and propose a course of action, the Administrative Secretary-General has been limited to constitutional constraints in exercising diplomatic initiatives such as these.

Although the General Secretariat is one of the principal organs of the OAU, its head, the Administrative Secretary-General, is directly responsible to the Council of Ministers. He may be removed from office before the end of his four-year term by a two-thirds majority of the OAU Assembly whenever it is deemed necessary to do so "for the good functioning of the Organization."[18] This contrasts sharply with the absence of a provision in the UN Charter for removal of the Secretary-General before the completion of his term of office.

The fact that the Administrative Secretary-General lacks a constitutional prerogative for independent political initiative and for significant executive functions, combined with the unsuitability of the OAU Assembly and the Council of Ministers as executive organs (because of their entirely deliberative nature and unwieldy size) seems to indicate that the OAU has a far weaker machinery than the United Nations for exercising its responsibility on a continuous basis. It seems that the Administrative Secretary-General is in a less favorable position than the Secretary-General to develop his constitutional powers in order to compensate for any operative shortcoming of the deliberative organs.

Apparently, the limitations of the Administrative Secretary-General's role as a diplomatic and executive agent of the OAU and the absence of an effective executive council or committee under the deliberative organs are meant to be largely compensated for by the creation of a Commission of Mediation, Conciliation and Arbitration as the fourth principal organ and of specialized commissions as subsidiary bodies of the OAU.

4. Special Machinery for Pacific Settlement of Disputes

Not only does the OAU lack a counterpart to the Security Council but also to the International Court of Justice. It is significant that, of the means of peaceful settlement of disputes enumerated in Article 33 of the UN Charter, the founders of the OAU omitted judicial settlement. They were inclined to believe that a solution to African disputes should be sought through diplomatic rather than legal means.

The importance attached to peaceful settlement of intra-OAU disputes is reflected in the inclusion of Article XIX in the OAU Charter, whereby the African States

> pledge[d] to settle all disputes among themselves by peaceful means and, to this end decide[d] to establish a Commission of Mediation, Conciliation and Arbitration.

The special character of this Commission is marked by the fact that it was set up as one of the principal organs through a separate constitutional instrument—the Protocol—which became an integral part of the OAU Charter in accordance with Article XIX. The constitutional place of the Commission within the OAU structure resembles that of the International Court of Justice within the United Nations; but, of course, the former is not an institution for judicial settlement. Functionally, the OAU Commission of Mediation, Conciliation and Arbitration bears some resemblance to the United Nations Panel of Inquiry and Conciliation which was set up in 1949 upon the recommendation of the Interim Committee of the General Assembly, but whose services have never been called for by parties to a dispute.

According to its Protocol the main characteristics of the OAU Commission of Mediation, Conciliation and Arbitration are the following:[19]

   (i)   it consists of 21 members elected for five years by the OAU Assembly from a list of candidates with "recognized professional qualifications" nominated by Member States;
   (ii) it is administered by a Bureau comprising the President and the two Vice-Presidents of the Commission;
   (iii) its jurisdiction is limited to disputes between States only (a non-member State may avail itself of the Commission's services);
   (iv) it considers disputes brought to it jointly by both parties, by one party alone, provided that the other party accepts the Commission's jurisdiction, or by the OAU Assembly or the Council of Ministers;
   (v)   it has no compulsory jurisdiction with regard to a party not accepting the jurisdiction of the Commission either through a written commitment made in advance of any disputes or in respect of a particular dispute—the expectation is that persuasion and diplomacy applied by the OAU Assembly and the Council of Ministers might lead to a change of attitude;[20]
   (vi) the Bureau of the Commission consults with the parties to a dispute as to which of the three methods of settlement—mediation, conciliation, or arbitration—to apply, but leaves the decision on the choice to the parties;

(vii) the mediator(s) for a specific dispute are appointed by the President of the Bureau from among his colleagues while the Board of Five Conciliators is appointed partly by him and partly by the parties; but the Arbitral Tribunal is selected by the two parties (one arbitrator each) whose nominees in turn select the third arbitrator who would act as chairman. It is only if there is a deadlock over the selection of the chairman of the Arbitral Tribunal or a need is felt to increase the size of such tribunal that the Bureau designates arbitrators;

(viii) while the proposals resulting from mediation and conciliation are mere recommendations, the award made by an Arbitral Tribunal is binding on the parties that have accepted its jurisdiction; but no procedures or machinery exist to interpret, revise, or enforce the award.

In spite of the existence of a number of intra-OAU disputes, the Commission of Mediation, Conciliation and Arbitration has been remarkably dormant. Its significance in the present study is, therefore, only in terms of what it might be able to do in the future. So far there has been a marked reluctance to invoke its rather cumbersome and formalized procedures. In 1969, some OAU Members demanded that it should either be abolished or converted from a permanent to an ad hoc body while others joined the President of the Commission in opposing any changes. Upon the invitation of the OAU Assembly, the President of Dahomey submitted a proposel for amending the OAU Charter and the Protocol of the Commission, and on that basis the Commission has been converted to an ad hoc body relying on part-time instead of full-time service by the members of the Bureau—the President and the two Vice-Presidents.

Several intra-OAU disputes and situations that have arisen during the past decade have been handled by ad hoc bodies, namely: the Ad Hoc Commission on the Algerian-Moroccan Dispute; the Ad Hoc Commission on the Congo; the Ad Hoc Committee on Mercenaries; the Ad Hoc Consultative Committee on Nigeria; and the Committee of Good Offices on the Somali-Ethiopian Dispute. The OAU had also established an Ad Hoc Committee on the Israeli occupation of Egyptian territory in order to complement the Mission of the Special Representative of the United Nations Secretary-General in the post-1967 Middle East situation. These bodies, whose characteristics are given in Chart II, are not dissimilar to some of the special commissions created by the Security Council or the General Assembly to assist in the negotiation of African problems of an inter-State nature (e.g., Ruanda-Urundi, 1960) or in bringing about national reconciliation within an African country (e.g., Congo, 1961). But the OAU has so

CHART II

OAU

MAIN AD HOC BODIES FOR PACIFIC SETTLEMENT OF DISPUTES

(1963-1973)

Crisis	Ad Hoc Body and Years of Operation	Mandate From	Cease-Fire	Fact-Finding	National Reconciliation	Good Offices	Mediation	Others	Membership: Size, Level, and Composition
Algerian-Moroccan Dispute	Ad Hoc Commission on Algerian-Moroccan Dispute (1963-67)	Council of Ministers (ECM/Res. 1(I))		x			x		Seven Ministers (or their representatives): Ethiopia, Ivory Coast, Mali, Nigeria, Senegal, Sudan, Tanzania
Congo Civil War	Ad Hoc Commission on the Congo (1964-65)	Council of Ministers (ECM/Res. 5(III))			x		x		Prime Minister (Chairman) and nine Ministers: Cameroon, Ethiopia, Ghana, Guinea, Kenya, Nigeria, Somalia, Tunisia, UAR (Egypt), Upper Volta
Mercenary Activities	Ad Hoc Committee for the Expulsion of Mercenaries (1967-68)	Assembly of Heads of State and Government (AHG/Dec. 14(IV))		x				x	Ten Heads of State: Burundi, Central African Republic, Congo (Braz.), Congo (Zaire), Ethiopia, Rwanda, Sudan, Tanzania, Uganda, Zambia

Functions

(continued)

CHART II (continued)

Crisis	Ad Hoc Body and Years of Operation	Mandate From	Cease-Fire	Fact-Finding	National Reconciliation	Good Offices	Mediation	Others	Membership: Size, Level, and Composition
					F u n c t i o n s				
Nigerian Civil War	Consultative Committee (Mission) on Nigeria (1967-70)	Assembly of Heads of State and Government (AHG/Res. 51(IV), AHG/Res. 54(V), AHG/Res. 58(VI))	x		x	x			Six Heads of State: Cameroon, Congo (Zaire), Ethiopia, Ghana, Liberia, Niger
Somali-Ethiopian Boundary Dispute	Committee of Good Offices on Somali-Ethiopian Dispute (1973-)	Assembly of Heads of State and Government (AHG/Dec. 95(X))				x			Eight Ministers: Cameroon, Lesotho, Liberia, Mauritania, Nigeria, Senegal, Sudan, Tanzania
Middle East Situation	Committee on Israel; Occupation of Egyptian Territory; Mission of Inquiry (1971)	Assembly of Heads of State and Government		x					Ten Heads of State: Cameroon, *Congo (Zaire)*, Ethiopia, Liberia, Ivory Coast, Kenya, Mauritania, *Nigeria, Senegal,* Tanzania (members of Mission of Inquiry are in italics)

far not established any bodies such as the United Nations commissions on amnesty, repatriation, and true observation, or peace-keeping operations involving a multi-national police force.

5. Special Machinery for Promoting Political Independence and Racial Equality in Africa

Both the United Nations and the OAU have set up special committees and other bodies to promote national independence and racial equality.

The main special bodies of the United Nations and the OAU dealing with problems of decolonization in all African Non-Self-Governing Territories are: the United Nations·Special Committee on the situation with regard to the Implementation of the Declaration on the Granting of Independence to Colonial Countries and Peoples (Special Committee of Twenty-Four) and the OAU Co-ordinating Committee for the Liberation of Africa (Co-ordinating Committee). In addition, the United Nations organs have established the United Nations Council for Namibia and the Committee established in pursuance of Security Council Resolution 253 (1968) (Committee on Sanctions against Southern Rhodesia). The OAU had a Committee of Five on Southern Rhodesia, but this body has been inactive since the end of 1966. As in the case of Namibia and Southern Rhodesia, only the United Nations has a special body dealing with the problem of apartheid—the Special Committee on Apartheid.* The main characteristics of all these bodies are given in Chart III.

The OAU Co-ordinating Committee was created in 1963 by the founders of the OAU in order to harmonize the assistance given by African States to all national liberation movements and to administer a special fund which was set up for that purpose. The Committee provides political and financial aid to movements fighting against colonialism in Southern Rhodesia, Namibia, the Portuguese-administered Territories, and elsewhere in Africa, as well as against South Africa's policy of apartheid. Its functions are, therefore, quite different from the basically deliberative and investigatory functions of the Special Committee of Twenty-Four and the Special Committee on Apartheid whose end products are reports and recommendations to the General Assembly, the Security Council, and other bodies in the United Nations system. They are also different from the functions of the Committee on Sanctions against Southern Rhodesia to report on the implementation of the Security Council's decision, especially on any

---

* The full name of this committee was originally "Special Committee on the Policies of Apartheid of the Government of the Republic of South Africa," but was shortened to the form used here by a decision of the General Assembly on 8 December 1970. On 16 December 1974, by Resolution 3324D (XXIX), the General Assembly changed the name to "Special Committee Against Apartheid."

CHART III
OAU-UN
SPECIAL MACHINERY FOR PROMOTING POLITICAL INDEPENDENCE AND RACIAL EQUALITY (1963-1973)

	Issue and Special Body	Functions	Membership of African States	Remarks
OAU	*Decolonization* Co-ordinating Committee for the Liberation of Africa—est. in May 1963 by Summit Conference of Independent African States (CIAS/Plen. 2/Rev. 2. Res. A: Agenda Item II: Decolonization)	To accelerate decolonization —to co-ordinate financial assistance to national liberation movements —to co-ordinate military training and distribution of military equipment to such movements —to provide military advice through its ad hoc Committee of Experts —to reconcile rival liberation movements and assess their efforts	Eleven Members: Algeria Egypt Ethiopia Guinea Nigeria Senegal Somalia Tanzania Uganda Zaire (Congo, Dem. Rep.) Zambia	
UN	Special Committee on the Situation with regard to the Implementation of the Declaration on the Granting of Independence to Colonial Countries and Peoples (Special Committee on decolonization)—est. on 27 November 1961 under General Assembly Res. 1654(XVI); enlarged in 1962 from 17 to 24 by Res. 1810(XVII)	To help implement Declaration —to review application of Declaration and study obstacles —to conduct hearings at headquarters and elsewhere —to propose to General Assembly and Security Council measures for application of Declaration —to apprise Security Council of developments threatening peace and security	Seven out of 24 Members: * Congo (Braz.) Ethiopia Ivory Coast Mali Sierra Leone Tanzania Tunisia	

Southern Rhodesia				
UN	Committee Established in Pursuance of Security Council Resolution 253 (1968) (Committee on Sanctions against Southern Rhodesia)—est. on 29 May 1968 under Security Council Res. 253 (1968); enlarged in 1970 from 7 to 15	To oversee and report on the application of economic sanctions against Southern Rhodesia	2 or 3 out of the 15 members of the Security Council**	In 1965-66, the OAU Assembly had an Ad Hoc Committee on Rhodesia, comprising UAR (Egypt), Kenya, Nigeria, Tanzania, and Zambia, created to co-ordinate OAU measures to oppose unilateral declaration of independence by the settler regime and co-ordinate severance of diplomatic relations with the U.K. (AHG/Res. 39b(II))
Namibia				
UN	United Nations Council for Namibia—est. on 19 May 1967 under General Assembly Res.2248(S-V) as Council for South West Africa; name changed in 1968 by Res.2372(XXII); enlarged in 1972 from 11 to 18 by Res.3031(XXVII)	—To contact South Africa and lay down procedures for the latter's withdrawal from Namibia —To administer Namibia and prepare it for independence —To consult with representatives of Namibian people —To facilitate travel of Namibians abroad	5 out of 18 members:*** Burundi Egypt Liberia Nigeria Zambia	In 1970, the Security Council established an Ad Hoc Sub-Committee, comprising all Council members, to study ways and means for implementing the Council's resolutions on Namibia (Res. 276 (1970) and 283 (1971)). In February 1972, the Council formed a Group of three members which the Secretary-General was to consult in initiating contacts with all parties concerned regarding self-determination and independence for Namibia

	Issue and Special Body	Functions	Membership of African States	Remarks
	Apartheid			
UN	Special Committee on the Policies of *Apartheid* of the Government of the Republic of South Africa (Special Committee on Apartheid)— est. on 6 November 1962 under General Assembly Res.1761 (XVII); enlarged in 1970 from 11 to not more than 18 by Res.2671A(XXV)	To review racial policies of South Africa and measures against them —to conduct hearings —to send missions away from headquarters to consult with various organizations on means to concert anti-apartheid action —to report to General Assembly on non-observance by States of voluntary sanctions against South Africa	6 out of 16 members:**** Algeria Ghana Guinea Nigeria Somalia Sudan	

*The other members were: Afghanistan, Australia, Bulgaria, Chile, China, Czechoslovakia, Fiji, Indonesia, India, Iran, Iraq, Sweden, Syria, Trinidad and Tobago, USSR, Venezuela, and Yugoslavia.

**Since 1 October 1970, the Committee has comprised all members of the Security Council; the African members have been: Sierra Leone and Somalia in 1971, Somalia, Guinea, and Sudan in 1972, and Guinea, Sudan, and Kenya in 1973. (Previously, when it comprised members, it included Algeria in 1968-69 and Sierra Leone in 1970.)

***The other members were: Chile, China, Colombia, Guyana, India, Indonesia, Mexico, Pakistan, Poland, Romania, Turkey, Yugoslavia, and the USSR.

****The other members were: Haiti, Hungary, India, Malaysia, Nepal, Peru, Philippines, Syria, Trinidad and Tobago, and the Ukranian SSR.

possible violations, or from the task of the Council for Namibia to take over administration of the Territory from South Africa and prepare it for independence.

At the secretariat level, both the United Nations and the OAU have major departments or other units for decolonization and the campaign against apartheid. Such units are designed not only to service the corresponding special committee or other bodies but also to increase public awareness of the serious problems faced by peoples under colonial and racial domination.

D. MEMBERSHIP LINKS AND CO-ORDINATION

Within the United Nations, the essence of the UN-OAU relationship is the interplay between the demand of the OAU Members for the widest possible support for their scale of priorities and the resistance of some older Member States of the United Nations. A major actor in this interplay is the African Group at the United Nations, which is an organ of the OAU serviced by a branch of the OAU General Secretariat. This Group, comprising all African Permanent Missions to the United Nations, was entrusted by the founders of the OAU with a mandate to promote the objectives of the OAU Charter by ensuring "unity of action" on the part of its Members in studying problems, in determining policy and tactics, and in searching appropriate solutions within the United Nations. It is primarily an instrument of pressure on the rest of the United Nations membership, but to the extent that it helps to mediate between the global and regional perspectives in the search for solutions to common problems, its role may be regarded as having some co-ordinative elements as between the United Nations and the OAU.

At the level of limited-membership organs and subsidiary bodies of the United Nations, the main instruments for pressure as well as for co-ordination have been those African States serving on those bodies. In the Security Council, two to three of the fifteen members are now States from Africa. As the OAU Council of Ministers and the African Group at the United Nations do take an active part in nominating African candidates for membership in the Security Council, the African States thus nominated tend, upon their election by the General Assembly, to assume a role that combines national, regional, and international perspectives in dealing with problems before the Security Council. The co-ordinative aspect of the role of the non-permanent African members of the Security Council in regard to African questions is perhaps as significant as the aspect having to do with the promotion of African interests. The former aspect is facilitated by the existence of a second type of OAU "representation" in the Security

Council. The OAU Council of Ministers has developed a practice of sending special missions of African Foreign Ministers to speak on behalf of the OAU, technically as delegates of their respective countries. The Mandate of these missions has been to persuade the Security Council, especially its permanent members, to take effective action to solve African problems.

Chapter III
Relationships Concerning Disputes Among OAU Members *
A. INTRODUCTION

The purpose of this chapter is to examine the respective roles of the United Nations and the Organization of African Unity (OAU) and their relationships in the settlement of disputes and other differences between African States. Utilizing the case approach to research, it attempts to evaluate the relative effectiveness of the respective roles and to identify and analyze the areas of co-operation and any points of competition or jurisdictional conflict. It aims at drawing conclusions from which may emerge some suggestions for enhancing the effectiveness of the peace-making roles of both organizations in Africa.

A study of the present and potential roles and relationships of the two organizations in the field of peaceful settlement can most usefully proceed by reference to the options provided in two sets of provisions in the United Nations Charter: on the one hand, Articles 33 and 52(1, 2, and 3) as complemented by Article 37 and, on the other, Articles 34, 35, 36, 38, 52(4), as well as Articles 11 and 14. The OAU Charter contains no provisions governing OAU relationship with the United Nations; it merely states in Article II(1.e) that one of the purposes of the OAU is "to promote international co-operation, having due regard to the Charter of the United Nations. . . ."

Article 33(1) of the United Nations Charter requires the parties to any dispute, the continuation of which is likely to endanger the maintenance of international peace and security, to seek first a solution "by negotiation, inquiry, mediation, conciliation, arbitration, judicial settlement, resort to regional agencies or arrangements, or other peaceful means of their own choice." Article 52(2) places a special emphasis on regional settlement of disputes as it requires Member States of the United Nations which are also members of regional agencies or parties to regional arrangements to "make every effort to achieve pacific settlement of local disputes through such regional arrangements or by such regional agencies before referring them to

---

* This chapter is a slightly revised version of a previously published monograph by the same author entitled: *Peaceful Settlement Among African States: Roles of the United Nations and the Organization of African Unity,* UNITAR PS No. 5, New York, 1972.

the Security Council." For its part, the Security Council is required under Article 52(3) "to encourage the development of pacific settlement of local disputes through such regional arrangements or by such regional agencies either on the initiative of the States concerned or by reference from the Security Council." Should the parties to a dispute fail to settle their differences within a regional framework or by any of the other means indicated in Article 33, they are required under Article 37 to refer the matter to the Security Council; if the Council is convinced that the continuance of the dispute is in fact likely to endanger the maintenance of international peace and security, it is required either to propose specific procedures or methods of adjustment or to recommend appropriate terms of settlement.

Yet, in contrast to the foregoing provisions which imply that members of regional organizations must first seek regional remedies, Article 52(4) states that the provisions in the first three paragraphs of the same Article, shall in no way impair the application of Articles 34 and 35, namely, the right of the Security Council "to investigate any dispute, or any situation which might lead to international friction or give rise to a dispute" and the right of any Member State of the United Nations "to bring any dispute, or any situation of the nature referred to in Article 34, to the attention of the Security Council or of the General Assembly." In addition, Article 36 empowers the Security Council, at any stage of a dispute or a situation, to recommend appropriate procedures or methods of adjustment; in making recommendations it should take into consideration any procedures for the settlement of disputes (including regional ones) which have already been adopted by the parties. Furthermore, if all the parties to any dispute so request, the Security Council may under Article 38 make recommendations to them with a view to attaining a settlement of the dispute. Insofar as the Security Council is not exercising its functions with regard to a particular dispute or situation, the General Assembly may under Articles 11(2) and 14 make recommendations to the parties concerned.

The two sets of provisions represent the ambiguous compromise reached at San Francisco between the proponent of regionalist and universalist points of view; they provide alternative courses of action without giving any precise indication of the contemplated division of competence and responsibility between the United Nations and regional organizations. During the long history of controversy concerning the interpretation and application of those Articles, especially in the context of the Inter-American system, at least four types of claims have been made by Member States of the United Nations concerning the most appropriate spheres of jurisdiction of the United Nations and regional organizations:

(i) claims that the regional organization has exclusive jurisdiction;

  (ii) claims that it has exclusive initial jurisdiction (i.e., as a forum for initial consideration of a case);
 (iii) claims that it has concurrent jurisdiction with the Security Council;
 (iv) claims that the Security Council may terminate regional jurisdiction.

The OAU was created primarily to promote unity and solidarity among African States. Under Article XIX of the OAU Charter, Member States pledged themselves to settle all inter-state disputes by peaceful means and to this end decided to establish as one of the principal institutions of the OAU a Commission of Mediation, Conciliation and Arbitration. The fact that neither this Article nor the Protocol of the Commission refers to the jurisdiction of the United Nations in peaceful settlement seems to imply that the founders of the OAU preferred to seek settlement of inter-member disputes exclusively within an African framework, particularly through the machinery of the OAU. Since any claims to an exclusive jurisdiction of a regional organization or of the United Nations in the field of peaceful settlement would obviously be inconsistent with the provisions of the United Nations Charter, and would thus be hardly acceptable to most States, the central issue in the consideration of the relative competence and responsibility of the OAU and the United Nations is: whether, in practice, the OAU assumes undisputed jurisdiction as a forum for the initial consideration of a dispute, while the Security Council considers the matter only if those initial efforts do not succeed; or, whether the Security Council exercises concurrent jurisdiction with authority to terminate OAU jurisdiction in particular cases. An attempt will be made in this study to trace the evolution of the relationship between the United Nations and the OAU and to define as precisely as possible the division of competence and responsibility that has developed pragmatically. This will be done in the context of an examination of the relative effectiveness and compatibility of the respective roles of the two organizations.

The nature and extent of the roles played by the United Nations and the OAU in a dispute between African States and their compatibility would seem to depend upon a number of interrelated factors, namely:

  (i) the nature of the issues between the disputing parties;
 (ii) the disputants' notions about the respective constitutional or policy orientations of the United Nations and the OAU and their ideas about the probable outcome of deliberations on a particular issue in one forum or the other;
 (iii) the attitudes of fellow Members of the OAU and other Member States of the United Nations concerning the level (global or regional) at which settlement of a specific dispute should be effected;
 (iv) the type and effectiveness of the machinery for peaceful settlement

available within each organization; and

(v) the influence of norms concerning UN-OAU relationships—norms derived from the Charters of the United Nations and the OAU and evolved through the interaction of the above factors.

Under what circumstances, in what manner, and how effectively has the role of the OAU, which corresponds to the special emphasis given in the United Nations Charter to the need for prior attempts at regional settlement of local disputes, been exercised? An answer to this question together with an examination of any role played by the United Nations in the settlement of disputes or the regulation of other situations of tension in Africa will indicate the extent to which their roles have been compatible and complementary.

For this purpose, a study is made below of the efforts to settle the main disputes and other differences between African States arising during the first decade of the OAU. The cases, selected on the basis of their relevance to the respective roles of the United Nations and the OAU, may be classified into the following four categories:

Boundary disputes:
  (i) Algeria versus Morocco;
  (ii) Somalia versus Ethiopia and Kenya.

Differences over the future of neighboring Non-Self-Governing Territories:
  (i) French Territory of the Afars and the Issas;
  (ii) Spanish Sahara.

Friction between African States arising from internal conflicts:
  (i) Friction between Rwanda and Burundi;
  (ii) the Congo civil war (1964-65) and the mercenary problem (1967-68);
  (iii) the Nigerian civil war (1967-70).

Other situations of friction:
  (i) Ghana versus its neighbors (1965-66);
  (ii) Ghana versus Guinea (1966);
  (iii) Guinea versus Ivory Coast (1966-67).

Even though some of these cases have features falling under more than one category, they are classified here on the basis of their dominant characteristics.

B. PACIFIC SETTLEMENT OF BOUNDARY DISPUTES

Since the establishment of the OAU in 1963, several boundary disputes have occurred between African States, but the most serious ones were the Algerian-Moroccan dispute and Somalia's disputes with Ethiopia and Kenya. The present section is concerned with the efforts of third parties, especially the OAU, to settle those disputes. The three cases had the following characteristics in common:

(i) they were disputes between sovereign States;
(ii) they escalated into armed conflict, and thus became of particular concern to both the United Nations and the OAU;
(iii) they involved a claim by one party, on historical, cultural, ethnic, or religious grounds, to a segment of the territory presently under the jurisdiction of the other; a claim which the latter party regarded as a threat to its sovereignty and territorial integrity.

The preference of a party to the dispute for having the question considered by one organization rather than by the other seems to depend mainly on its expectation of a more favorable outcome from the former. Its notion of the relative constitutional orientations of the two organizations is thus an important factor in its choice of forum. The OAU Charter, in Article III(3), affirms the principle of "respect for the sovereignty and territorial integrity of each State and for its inalienable right to independent existence." In the absence of any Charter provision or policy within the OAU for the adjustment of existing boundaries, the States against whose territory a claim has been made, together with the majority of fellow Members of the OAU, have understood Article III(3) to have established a commitment to maintain the status quo on the question of boundaries. On the other hand, the States with a territorial claim have challenged this interpretation, but without being able in the context of the OAU Charter to make a case for the application of the principle of self-determination within the territory of a Member State of the OAU. Being aware of the fact that the provisions of the OAU Charter on the total emancipation of dependent territories were conceived exclusively in terms of dependent territories, the States with a territorial claim tend to hope that certain provisions of the United Nations Charter would lend themselves to a more flexible interpretation that would accommodate their claims; especially those provisions concerning the development of friendly relations "based on the principle of equal rights and self-determination of peoples."

1. Mediation of the Algerian-Moroccan Dispute

The Algerian-Moroccan dispute originated from the fact that only the northernmost sector of the boundary between Algeria and Morocco had been demarcated and that Morocco claimed a part of the Sahara on the ground that it was within its frontiers in precolonial times. The problem became further complicated when oil and other mineral resources were discovered in the disputed area. Upon gaining independence in 1956, Morocco refrained from concluding any boundary arrangements with France, preferring to await Algerian independence. In July 1961, the Moroccan Government concluded a secret agreement with the "Provisional Government of the Algerian Republic,"[1] recognizing "the territorial problem created by the delimitation imposed arbitrarily by France" and stating that the problem was to be resolved through negotiation between the Kingdom of Morocco and the Government of independent Algeria.[2] After independence, political differences between the Governments of the two countries not only prevented the envisaged negotiation but also increased tension between them to such an extent that a full-scale war broke out on 14 October 1963. The peace-making role of third parties became imperative when the two sides failed in their short-lived bilateral talks to end the armed conflict. A deadlock was reached on 18 October when Morocco insisted on negotiations on its territorial claims and Algeria insisted on the withdrawal of Moroccan forces from the positions they occupied as well as on the recognition of the borders existing at the time of Algerian independence.

Since the initiative taken by the League of Arab States on 19 and 20 October to conciliate the dispute had failed, both parties explored various other possibilities which led eventually to an agreement to seek a solution through the OAU. While Algeria sought consideration of the situation by the OAU Council of Ministers,[3] Morocco informed the Provisional Administrative Secretary-General of the OAU of the situation and explored possibilities for further direct negotiations.[4] In addition, on 26 October, Morocco informed the United Nations Secretary-General of the situation "in case circumstances should make it necessary for Morocco to refer it to the appropriate United Nations organ." The main relevant factors that could reasonably have been considered by the parties in their assessment of the relative appropriateness of the organizations concerned were the following. The fact that there was an armed conflict and that the involvement of non-African Powers seemed to be aggravating the situation were factors that might have made consideration by the Security Council appropriate. On the other hand, the not unreasonable expectation that several OAU Member States might favor the preservation of existing de facto boundaries might have made consideration by the OAU appear more suitable for the Algerian position.* As the parties weighed the various factors and their

---

* When Morocco ratified the OAU Charter, a month before the crisis with Algeria, it
attached to its signature of the Charter a reservation warning that its membership
in the OAU should not imply acceptance of existing boundaries or renunciation of its

implications, certain OAU Members encouraged them to seek a solution within an African framework and made suggestions for specific courses of action.

As it became clear that the good offices offered by certain North African Heads of State would not be mutually acceptable, the Emperor of Ethiopia and the President of Mali tried and succeeded in persuading the King of Morocco and the President of Algeria to meet with them on 29 October 1963 at Bamako, Mali, to conclude an agreement. It should be mentioned that as the Provisional Secretariat of the OAU was entrusted to the Government of Ethiopia, the Emperor of Ethiopia was able to offer his good offices not only in his personal capacity but also, in effect, on behalf of the OAU. The terms of the Bamako Agreement were:[5]

  (i) to effect a cease-fire from midnight on 1 November 1963;
 (ii) to establish a commission of Algerian, Moroccan, Ethiopian, and Malian officers to determine a demilitarized zone;
(iii) to invite Ethiopian and Malian observers to supervise the cease-fire and watch over security and military neutrality in the demilitarized zone;
 (iv) to request an extraordinary meeting of the OAU Council of Ministers in order to set up a commission that would determine responsibility for the outbreak of hostilities, study the frontier question, and make proposals for a settlement of the dispute;
  (v) to request Algeria and Morocco to cease all public and press attacks on each other as from 1 November and to observe strictly the principles of non-interference in each other's affairs and of settlement of all disputes between African States by means of negotiation.

But as fighting continued past the agreed cease-fire time, Morocco, according to press reports, brought the seriousness of the situation to the attention of the United Nations Secretary General, the Provisional Administrative Secretary-General of the OAU, and certain African Heads of State.[6] However, upon the achievement of a stable cease-fire on 4 November, with the help of the Bamako Commission, both sides began to concentrate on finding a solution through the OAU along the lines agreed at Bamako.

In mid-November, the OAU Council of Ministers met in an extraordinary session to consider the situation. It welcomed the Bamako Agreement and, after hearing the Moroccan claim of historical territorial rights and Algeria's insistence on the need to observe the OAU Charter principle concerniing territoriail integrity, it declared that all OAU Member States

---

rights. For the text of the reservation see *Maghreb* (Paris), March-April 1964 (Vol. 1, No. 2), p. 12.

should "scrupulously respect all the principles" enshrined in the OAU Charter and that they should settle all their differences "by peaceful means and within a strictly African framework."[7] In addition, in accordance with point four of the Bamako Agreement, the Council of Ministers created an Ad Hoc Commission of seven States to mediate the dispute.[8] The Bamako Commission, though not an OAU body, was encouraged to continue its work and to establish contact with the OAU Ad Hoc Commission. Its work was thus brought within the overall diplomatic effort of the OAU.[9]

The efforts of the OAU and those made within its framework were largely successful, even though the results were slow in coming. With some difficulty, the Bamako Commission succeeded on 20 February 1964 in facilitating an agreement between the Foreign Ministers of Algeria and Morocco to withdraw their troops to the positions they occupied before the outbreak of hostilities, thus creating a demilitarized zone along the border and the strategic highlands of the Figuig area.[10] With encouragement from the Council of Ministers, relations between Algeria and Morocco improved considerably during the next three months; in May 1964, the ambassadors of the two countries formed a joint committee and were able to reach agreement on a number of measures for normalizing relations, ranging from exchange of prisoners and of property seized during the hostilities to rehabilitation of the persons displaced as a result of the conflict. The Ad Hoc Commission was less successful in carrying out its difficult mandate: though it provided invaluable help in clarifying issues and narrowing down some areas of disagreement, it was not able to bring about a settlement of the dispute. However, the modest contribution that it had made before it adjourned indefinitely in 1967 appears to have facilitated progress in the subsequent bilateral negotiations on the border dispute which led to the conclusion in January 1969 of a general treaty of solidarity and co-operation between Algeria and Morocco. In May 1970, the two States concluded an agreement on the boundary question.[11] This agreement marked a significant achievement for OAU-encouraged bilateral negotiations between OAU Members and provided a possible model for the settlement of other boundary disputes.

The Security Council played no part in the attempts to settle the dispute because no interested Member State of the United Nations was decisively in favor of a United Nations role before an attempt could be made at the regional level particularly by the OAU. By giving the OAU role such an indirect support, the United Nations Members concerned helped to create a favorable psychological environment in which the OAU and the parties to the dispute could operate. This tended to strengthen the authority of the OAU and of its claim that African problems should, as far as possible, be settled within an African context. It can be regarded as a recognition of the

fact that effective regioinal solution of the dispute would advance the com-
'mon objective of the United Nations and the OAU—that of re-establish-
ing peace in the area concerned.

2. Diplomatic Efforts to Settle Somalia's Disputes with Ethiopia and Kenya

A precedent had already been established in the Algerian-Moroccan dispute to try the OAU first in settling disputes between African States when
the border disputes in the Horn of Africa flared up into an armed conflict.
When Kenya became independent in December 1963, hostilities broke out
between Kenyan troops and Somali-speaking groups in Kenya and led to
border incidents with Somalia. In January 1964, similar clashes between
Ethiopian troops and Somali-speaking groups in Ethiopia, which began in
1960, led to intensive conflict between the armed forces of Ethiopia and
Somalia.

The boundary disputes between Somalia and its two neighbors stem
from a claim by Somalia to large areas within present boundaries of those
States on grounds of historical, ethnic, and religious affinity.[12] These territories comprise the Ogaden and Haud regions of Ethiopia and the Northern
Frontier District (NFD) of Kenya. Somalia contends that the right of any
people to seek self-determination is enshrined in the Untied Nations Charter, the whole practice of the United Nations and, in particular, the resolutions of the General Assembly; and that, accordingly, the people in the disputed territories in Ethiopia and Kenya should be given an opportunity to
exercise this right.[13] On the other hand, Ethiopia and Kenya have rejected
Somalia's claims, stressing that the principle of self-determination does not
apply to territories within independent States and that to press such claims
would pose a threat to their sovereignty and territorial integrity contrary
to the principles of the United Nations Charter and those of the OAU
Charter.

On 9 February 1964, Somalia requested an urgent meeting of the Security Council to consider the "complaint by Somalia against Ethiopia
concerning acts of aggression infringing upon the sovereignty and security
of Somalia."[14] But before any action could be taken on this request, the
United Nations Secretary-General appealed to both parties to settle their
dispute peacefully and within an African framework. The Government of
the USSR also dispatched messages to both parties, supporting the message
of the Secretary-General.[15] Meanwhile Ethiopia and, later, also Somalia requested the OAU Council of Ministers to consider the matter at its second
extraordinary session scheduled to meet in February 1964 for a different
purpose. The border dispute between Somalia and Kenya was also placed
on the agenda of that session upon request of both of these countries.

Although Somalia had agreed to present the two cases for consideration by the OAU, it did not entirely abandon its original intention to have its dispute with Ethiopia placed before the Security Council. Thus, even though it had notified the United Nations Secretary-General that it was "the desire of the Somali Government not to raise the matter with the Security Council while the problem [was] in the hands of the OAU,"[16] Somalia still continued to send messages on developments to the President of the Security Council; it explained that the Council was "virtually seized with the Somali-Ethiopia question."[17]

When the OAU Council of Ministers considered the dispute between Somalia and its neighbors at Dar es Salaam it made it a point to express its conviction that "the solution to all disputes between Member States [should] be sought first within the [OAU]"[18]

The Council of Ministers' role in handling these two disputes was more modest than its role in regard to the Algerian-Moroccan case; no machinery was set up to mediate the two disputes. In the case of the Somali-Ethiopian dispute, the Council solemnly urged the two countries "to order an immediate cease-fire and to refrain from all hostile actions" and called upon all African States having official representation in the two countries "to assist in the implementation of the cease-fire."[19] In regard to this dispute as well as that between Somalia and Kenya, the Council urged Somalia and its two neighbors to refrain from further provocative actions and propaganda and to enter into direct negotiations to resolve their disputes peacefully.[20]

Since these resolutions had little effect in ending hostilities and reducing tension, the Council of Ministers at its second ordinary session later that month appealed for full implementation of its previous resolution and requested the parties concerned to report on their negotiations to the OAU Assembly of Heads of States and Government.

The role of the OAU Council of Ministers in the two border disputes had three aspects, including the one described above, namely, the application of pressure on the disputants to end hostilities and to start direct negotiations. The other two were: first, the discouragement at OAU meetings of debate on the merits of the disputes and the avoidance of direct OAU involvement in the restoration of peace and the settlement of disputes; and, secondly, the setting up of a norm applicable to the problem of border disputes.

The tendency to avoid direct OAU involvement can be illustrated by the attitude expressed by the majority of the African States at the second ordinary session of the OAU Council of Ministers—a reluctance to support either Ethiopia's request for OAU pressure on Somalia to renounce its claims and accept existing boundaries, or Somalia's request for direct OAU peace-making efforts such as the sending of observers to supervise the cease-fire.[21] At its third session, the Council of Ministers even went so far as to drop from the agenda that it was preparing for the OAU Assembly the question of the situation in the Horn of Africa; it did so when Somalia's strong protest against the signing of a defense pact between Ethiopia and Kenya led to a heated and somewhat divisive debate.[22] It seems clear that the OAU was reluctant to be further drawn into substantive issues of any particular dispute.

The role of the OAU in setting up a norm to govern border disputes began to emerge during the second ordinary session of the OAU Council of Ministers when reference was made for the first time to Article III(3) of the OAU Charter—"respect for sovereignty and territorial integrity" of Member States—as a principle which Somalia and Kenya should take into account in their negotiations.[23] It was, however, at the first ordinary session of the OAU Assembly, held in July 1964, that this norm was unequivocally stated and made to apply to all border disputes. In a resolution[24] approved by acclamation, the OAU Assembly expressed in the preamble the view that borders of the African States on the day of their independence constituted a tangible reality, and also that border problems constituted a grave and permanent factor of dissension. In the operative part of the resolution, the OAU Assembly reaffirmed the strict observance of Article III(3) of the OAU Charter and solemnly declared "that all Member States pledge themselves to respect the borders existing on the achievement of national independence."

Somalia, joined by Morocco, the other African State which sought a major change of boundaries in its favor, expressed reservation on the resolution and even indicated that it would not be bound by its terms. As it became quite clear for Somalia that it would receive little or no support for its claims within the OAU, its focus of diplomatic activity concerning its border disputes began to move decidedly toward bilateral negotiations. The OAU was thus left the option of playing only an indirect role—that of providing a suitable environment for contacts between the States in dispute and for mediatory initiatives by African statesmen.

This indirect role of the OAU was not a new one. As early as February 1964, the President of the Sudan offered Ethiopia and Somalia his good offices in the spirit of OAU resolutions and was able subsequently to help bring about an agreement for a cease-fire and for the demilitarization of the conflict area. Later, in December 1965, the same approach was followed by the President of Tanzania in helping to initiate negotiations between Kenya and Somalia at Arusha, Tanzania. Those mediatory initiatives were, however, not taken during the actual sessions of the OAU organs, and thus the role played by the OAU was very marginal.

While contact between Somalia and its neighbors was maintained during OAU meetings, it was at the fourth session of the OAU Assembly, held in September 1967, that the conference environment at the OAU had its full impact on the leaders of Somalia and its two neighbors. This was made possible in large measure by the installation in Somalia of a Government led by President Shermarke and Prime Minister Egal which had a new stance on the "Greater Somalia" issue—one that placed emphasis on the need to attain "by peaceful means" self-determination for the population in the disputed areas and on the need to normalize relations with the neighboring countries. When the Emperor of Ethiopia and the Prime Minister of Somalia met at the OAU conference, they were able to agree that they should initiate joint ministerial discussions with a view to finding a solution to the substantive aspects of the dispute. At the same time, the Vice-President of Kenya and the Somali Prime Minister were able to agree on a joint declaration, endorsed by the OAU Assembly, which stated that the two leaders "mutually and amicably expressed their desire to respect . . . [the] sovereignty and territorial integrity [of each other's country], to resolve any outstanding differences between them . . . and to refrain from conducting hostile propaganda against each other . . . ."[25]

These decisions by the leaders of the three countries resulted in a series of successful joint ministerial meetings between Ethiopia and Somalia[26] and of meetings between the leaders of Kenya and Somalia under the chairmanship of the President of Zambia.[27] Relations between Somalia and its two neighbors were normalized and even began to move in the direction of close cultural and economic co-operation, thus creating an atmosphere conducive to serious negotiation of the substantive issues of the border disputes. But since October 1969, when a military Government came to power in Somalia, the prevailing basic differences on the "major issues," accentuated by the reported discovery of oil on the Ethiopian side in the Ogaden, have posed a formidable obstacle to further progress. The détente between Somalia and Ethiopia has, therefore, given way to a further arms race and tension, culminating in a military confrontation during 1973. Upon the request of Somalia, the tenth session of the OAU Assembly has considered the crisis and has even established an eight-member Ad Hoc Committee to offer good offices, but its work has been hindered by differences over its terms of reference.

3. Conclusions

The first conclusion is that in the first year of the OAU, when the most critical stages of the three boundary disputes were reached, the foundation was laid for the application in Africa of two norms. The first, which has a direct bearing on the relationship between the United Nations and the OAU, concerned the need for settling by peaceful means and within a strictly African framework all disputes between African States. This need was recognized by the Member States and the Secretary-General of the United Nations who, without in any way suggesting exclusive jurisdiction for the OAU, encouraged application of the "try OAU first" approach. They tended to support the view that all possible reglonal means must first be tried. Whether or not the dispute would be appealed to the United Nations would depend upon the effectiveness of the efforts of the OAU.

The second norm concerned the application of the principle of *uti possidetis* as regards boundaries existing at the time of independence. It was designed to discourage boundary disputes from arising and, where such disputes had arisen, to provide a clearer meaning to Article III(3) of the OAU Charter regarding sovereignty and territorial integrity, thereby giving more weight to the peace-making efforts of the OAU.

Since the adoption of these norms, which were recommended by the first year's sessions of the OAU Council of Ministers and adopted in July 1964 by an overwhelming majority at the first ordinary session of the OAU Assembly (Somalia and Morocco expressed reservations about the second norm), no major new crises over territorial questions have occurred in Africa and the existing disputes have been contained within the bounds of peaceful negotiation. The apparently stabilizing influence of the above norms seems to have been enhanced by several factors, including the limited capability of the African Governments concerned to realize their claims by non-peaceful means, the determination of the African States to prevent negative external involvement in the disputes, and the restraint of non-African States from such involvement.

In considering the stabilizing effect of the two norms, it should be emphasized that they are highly interdependent. The norm of settlement of disputes by peaceful means within an African framework, taken by itself, might not sufficiently discourage States dissatisfied with the territorial status quo from relying on their power and influence in seekinig excessive concessions from their neighbors. Similarly, the principle of *uti possidetis* alone might, by freezing the existing territorial status quo, smother rather than settle existing boundary disputes. An application of this principle would need to take account of the fact that States with major territorial claims have emphatically indicated that they would not feel bound by it, a fact which would underline the need for negotiation of those frontiers which remain undefined or were not clearly defined during colonial times. Because of differences of interpretation of boundary treaties concluded during colonial times, in not a few cases, one could more appropriately speak of agreed boundary zones rather than agreed boundary lines. Adjustment by mutual consent may thus be necessary in the interest of permanent peace and stability. It would also be consistent with the widely felt need for evolving some new structure of frontiers to circumvent the disadvantages of the boundaries arbitrarily drawn in colonial times, a structure that could facilitate the working out of subregional and regional arrangements leading eventually to the establishment of larger political entities in Africa.

The second conclusion is that, except in the case of the Algerian-Moroccan dispute, the involvement of the OAU in the border disputes remained basically deliberative rather than one of direct mediation. Perhaps, in order to avoid arousing the resentment of any of its Member States, the OAU avoided the allocation of responsibility in any border clashes, except where it was expressly invited to do so by the parties as in the Bamako Agreement; even then the OAU organs were somewhat circumspect about this task. There seems to have developed a belief among the majority of the OAU Member States that African solidarity may be threatened more by an active involvement of the OAU in intermember disputes than by a modest role. Rather than itself discussing the substantive issues of the border disputes, the OAU has tended, after its experience with the Algerian-Moroccan dispute, to encourage bilateral negotiation of substantive issues and to rely more heavily on the role of selected African statesmen in an emergency situation. The role of such statesmen seems to compensate, at least in part, for the limitation of the OAU role attributable to the inoperative state of the OAU Commission of Mediation, Conciliation and Arbitration and the fact that the Administrative Secretary-General has, as his very title implies, been deliberately entrusted by the OAU Charter with no more than administrative functions.

Finally, regardless of the manner in which particular boundary disputes in Africa have been rendered quiescent within the African framework—through the OAU machinery, by individual mediation, by bilateral negotiation, or otherwise—the effect so far seems to have been to obviate the need for resort to the United Nations with regard to such disputes.

C. HANDLING OF DIFFERENCES OVER THE FUTURE OF NEIGHBORING NON-SELF-GOVERNING TERRITORIES

In contrast to the African boundary disputes which have been handled almost exclusively within the framework of the OAU, the problems arising from differences between African States over the future of neighboring Non-Self-Governing Territories have been handled more at the level of the United Nations than at that of the OAU, even if only in a marginal way. The Non-Self-Governing Territories which have been the subject of such differences are the French Territory of the Afars and the Issas (formerly French Somaliland*) and Spanish Sahara.

Populated by an almost equal number of Issa Somalis and Afars having kinship links with the Danakils of Ethiopia, the Territory has become the subject of rival claims between Somalia and Ethiopia, based on ethnic grounds. Moreover, both countries have brought historical arguments to strengthen their claims while Ethiopia has also stressed the importance of its economic interests in the port of Djibouti, one of its main commercial outlets. Somali-Ethiopian tension over the Territory increased following the 1966 riots in Djibouti and the subsequent promise for a second referendum[28] given by France to enable the people of the Territory to choose between political independence and continuation of association with France. Somalia appealed to the people of the Territory to opt for political independence in the referendum scheduled for March 1967, anticipating that, if they did so, they might subsequently decide in a plebiscite to unite with the Somali Republic. As an alternative, it suggested that the Territory be placed for two years under the administration of the United Nations in order to ensure the fairness of a subsequent plebiscite.[29] On the other hand, the Emperor of Ethiopia indicated in a statement to the press that "if they [the people of the Territory] were to choose independence there would arise ethnic and economic issues that could not be ignored and the question of association with Ethiopia would surge to the fore."[30] He also declared that Ethiopia "will never accept a solution . . . which is in contradiction to the interests and the rights of the Ethiopian people."[31]

Spanish Sahara has been claimed by both Morocco and Mauritania since 1960; until recently Mauritania itself had been claimed by Morocco. Both Morocco and Mauritania maintain that the majority of the population of Spanish Sahara is composed of nomadic tribesmen who spend part of the year in the Territory and the other part in Morocco, Mauritania, and Algeria and that the nomads should be entitled to express their wishes about the future of the Territory, just like the more settled population. With the discovery of rich phosphate deposits in 1964, the economic importance of the Territory became a significant factor in sharpening the competition and in intensifying Spain's desire for some form of continued association with the Territory.[32]

It has long been accepted by France and Spain that the Territories under their administration must achieve a status that is in conformity with the wishes of their peoples. But, though both of them adopted a policy of

---

* The new name of the Territory is "French Territory of the Afars and the Issas." This designation was introduced in United Nations terminology on 15 April 1968 at the request of the Administering Power (Terminology Bulletin No. 240 ST/CS/ SER.F/240)).

carrying out a referendum in their respective Territories, France did not allow the presence of impartial outside observers at its referendum, and Spain, while agreeing to accept any disinterested persons to conduct a referendum, has defined the composition of the population entitled to vote in such a manner as to exclude those nomadic tribesmen whom it regards as not belonging basically to the Territory, thereby virtually ruling out the possibility of an eventual merger of the Territory with Morocco or Mauritania.

Both the United Nations and the OAU have treated the two situations mainly as issues of decolonization, even though they were aware of the fact that the rival claims of the neighboring African countries constituted an obstacle to a permanent solution. Paradoxically, the OAU which often insists on having disputes between OAU Member States considered strictly within an African framework, seems to have made even less of an effort than the United Nations in encouraging reconciliation between the African States on those issues.

With regard to the French-administered Territory, the OAU has encountered a dilemma: on the one hand, it wished to see rapid progress toward independence and, on the other, it was concerned that France's immediate withdrawal might result in a serious confrontation between Somalia and Ethiopia. Hence, the majority of the African States could not support a Somali proposal calling upon the people of the territory to choose independence, criticizing French policy and demanding supervision of the referendum by the United Nations or the OAU. Nor could they support an Ivory Coast proposal merely taking notice of the French promise to hold a referendum. Consequently, a compromise resolution was adopted taking note of France's decision "to grant the people self-determination by means of a referendum" and expressing "the fervent desire that the voting may be conducted on an entirely free, democratic and impartial basis." Though it appealed to the people of the Territory to unite in confronting their destiny and assured them of OAU's "active solidarity, designed to bring about and consolidate . . . independence,[33] no appeal was made to Ethiopia and Somalia to resolve their differences. The General Assembly also refrained from addressing an appeal to Ethiopia and Somalia, but it demonstrated more readiness than the OAU to recommend a course of action that could ensure a freely expressed referendum—one that might hopefully provide the two States with a common basis for reconciliation. Thus it called upon France not only "to ensure that the right of self-determination shall be freely expressed and exercised by the indigenous inhabitants" but also to make appropriate arrangements, in consultation with the United Nations Secretary-General, for a United Nations presence before, and supervision during, the holding of a referendum.[34] It should be noted, however, that the

OAU Council of Ministers was almost as forceful as the General Assembly in criticizing France for having conducted the referendum without the presence of United Nations observers and in expressing reservations about the announced result that the majority of the people had decided to continue their association with France.[35]

In the Spanish Sahara case, the General Assembly went even farther in trying to ensure that the outcome of the referendum would be acceptable to the States with rival claims, but the OAU still refrained from taking such an initiative.[36] The Assembly tried indirectly to induce Morocco and Mauritania to reach a mutural understanding on the future of the Territory when it invited Spain in 1967 to determine, as early as possible, the procedures for holding a referendum under United Nations auspices and to do this not only in conformity with the aspirations of the indigenous population but also in consultation with the Governments of Morocco and Mauritania. It was not before 1969, however, that the chances of success of the envisaged consultations began to improve. During that year, Morocco and Mauritania established direct contacts which led to Moroccan recognition of Mauritania in September of that year and the establishment of diplomatic relations between them in January 1970. Six months later, the two States were able to conclude through bilateral negotiations a treaty whereby they agreed not only to respect each other's territorial integrity, but also to settle all their differences peacefully and to develop close relations. In addition, the Heads of the two States declared that the two countries will "co-operate closely to hasten the liberation of [Spanish Sahara], in accordance with the relevant United Nations resolutions."[37]

In both cases, since the Member States of the OAU have given much more prominence to the decolonization aspect of the problem than to the issue of rival claims of African States, the OAU has tended to duplicate the efforts of the United Nations on the former aspect while postponing, if not evading, consideration of the latter. By not concentrating on the issue of rival claims, which seems to be appropriate for intensive treatment within an African framework, the OAU is perhaps missing an opportunity for playing a role that could complement United Nations efforts. It would be worthwhile for the OAU to try to convince the States with rival claims to agree on the modalities of any future referendum and to commit themselves to the outcome in order to accelerate the process of decolonization in the two Territories. By doing so, it might succeed in removing any possible inconsistency between the application of the principles of self-determination to the two Non-Self-Governing Territories and the claims of the neighboring countries to such Territories.

D. HANDLING OF SITUATIONS OF FRICTION BETWEEN AFRICAN STATES ARISING FROM INTERNAL CONFLICTS

The roles played by both the United Nations and the OAU in solving problems arising primarily from internal conflicts have been largely limited by the reluctance of the Governments facing an internal challenge to their authority to permit international involvement in what they regard as a strictly domestic problem. But as most African countries have boundaries that cut across ethnic lines and as any major internal conflict is bound to cause an outflow of refugees and political exiles, an internal conflict often leads to tension with neighboring countries. It becomes of concern to international organizations not only because of humanitarian considerations but also for reasons of peace and security. The problems are compounded when an internal conflict develops into a war for secession.

The present section examines the respective roles of the United Nations and the OAU in handling situations of inter-State tension arising from internal conflicts in Rwanda, Burundi, the Congo (later Zaire)* and Nigeria. The problems created by these conflicts required the performance of two types of functions by international organizations: a humanitarian function of mobilizing emergency relief to the victims of the conflict; and a diplomatic one of reducing tension between the States concerned and, in the Congolese and Nigerian cases, also of facilitating conciliation between the two sides in the civil strife.

1. Friction between Rwanda and Burundi

The tension between Rwanda and Burundi passed through four stages comprising:

  (i) the insurgency of 1963 launched against the Rwanda Government, under the control of the Bahutu majority, by Rwandese (Batutsi) refugees in neighboring countries, especially Burundi; this was followed by Bahutu reprisals on the Batutsi population in Rwanda;

  (ii) the 1965 crisis in Burundi resulting from an attempt by some leaders of the Bahutu majority in that country to overthrow the monarchy which they blamed for having assisted in the perpetuation of Batutsi supremacy;

  (iii) the 1966 tension between Rwanda and Burundi allegedly resulting from subversive activities by refugees in Burundi;

---

* The designation "the Congo (Zaire)" refers to the Democratic Republic of the Congo (Republic of Zaire, since October 1971) while "Congo (Brazzaville)" will be used in referring to the People's Republic of the Congo.

(iv) the 1972 Bahutu uprising in Burundi and the Batutsi reprisals.

When conflict broke out in Rwanda in December 1963, the Rwandese Government charged Burundi with permitting several hundred Batutsi guerrillas to infiltrate into its territory in order to overthrow the Government. Denying the charge, the Burundi Government in turn accused Rwanda of conducting a "wide-scale slaughter" of the Batutsi population in Rwanda. Subsequently, the Burundi Government requested both the United Nations Secretary-General and the OAU Provisional Administrative Secretary-General to assist in putting an end to "provocations" from Rwanda.[38]

Both Secretaries-General appealed to Rwanda and Burundi to do all in their power to establish peaceful relations between them. In addition, the United Nations Secretary-General assured both parties that he wished "to be of maximum help . . . in alleviating the current difficulties."[39] Twice he dispatched the Officer-in-Charge of the United Nations Operations in the Congo to visit the two countries as his personal representative in order to assess the situation.[40] After examining the situation and consulting the Governments of the two countries, the Secretary-General's Special Representative, who was convinced that neither country wished to have United Nations observers or a commission of inquiry on its territory, was able to submit a set of recommendations to the two Governments. On the basis of those recommendations the two Governments were able to agree as follows: Burundi was to take continued measures to curb the activities of agitators among the refugees, the refugee burden on Burundi was to be alleviated through such measures as resettlement and, eventually, voluntary repatriation to Rwanda; Rwanda was to take all possible measures to prevent renewed reprisals against the Batutsi; and both Governments were to maintain regular contact with the Secretary-General's Special Representative.[41]

Faced with a request to assist in this complex situation only six months after its creation, and already burdened with the task of conciliating the Algerian-Moroccan dispute, the OAU was in no position to play a significant role. Therefore, in the absence of any prompt action by the OAU beyond the appeal of its Provisional Administrative Secretary-General, the United Nations Secretary-General felt it was "clearly the duty of the United Nations, and therefore [his] duty to be as helpful as possible in situations of this kind."[42] Accordingly, he sent his Special Representative to the two countries and invited the United Nations High Commissioner for Refugees (UNHCR) and relevant specialized agencies to provide emergency assistance to the refugees and to other victims of the conflict. The diplomatic efforts of the Special Representative combined with the relief and refugee resettlement activities of the various United Nations bodies, especially UNHCR, were instrumental in calming the situation. Subsequently, in February 1964, the second ordinary session of the OAU Council of Ministers discussed the refugee problem in Africa with particular reference to Rwandese refugees and established a ten-member commission, which included Rwanda and Burundi, to examine the whole problem and make recommendations. Though such recommendations were slow in coming, the Commission's occasional visits to the two countries reinforced the efforts of the United Nations and thus helped to keep down tension for over one year.

The second phase of the crisis between Rwanda and Burundi occurred in October 1965 when an abortive coup d'etat in Burundi conducted by a group of Bahutu military officers and politicians provoked a sporadic uprising by Bahutu peasants and precipitated considerable reprisals. A large number of Bahutu, including prominent politicians and labor leaders were reported killed, a situation which induced the International Labour Organization (ILO) and certain non-governmental organizations to protest on humanitarian grounds[43] and to send observers to Burundi in response to an invitation from the Burundi Government. But neither the United Nations nor the OAU played any significant role in the crisis. Though Rwanda was deeply concerned about the situation in Burundi and had opened its borders for any incoming refugees, it did not request intercession by either of the two organizations.

In the third phase, the OAU was able to play a significant role, while the United Nations remained in the background. In September 1966, Rwanda complained before the third session of the OAU Assembly stating that there was "dangerous tension" between the two countries, because of Burundi-based subversive activities of Rwandese refugees.[44] After hearing a similar complaint from Burundi about the activities of refugees in Rwanda, the OAU Assembly decided to request President Mobutu of the Congo (Zaire) to mediate between the two countries. The choice of President Mobutu was considered appropriate because, in August 1966, the Congo (Zaire) Burundi, and Rwanda had signed Joint Agreements on Mutual Security, Trade and Cultural Affairs (the Kinshasa Agreements). The three States had agreed to exclude from their respective territories individuals or groups of individuals who might be suspected of subversive activities against one of the other two parties.[45]

In response to the OAU Assembly's request and in the spirit of the Kinshasa Agreements, President Mobutu persuaded the Presidents of Burundi and Rwanda to meet with him in March 1967 in his country where they were able to agree on a number of measures to remove the possibility of subversive activities by refugees.[46] The main role of the OAU in the matter was one of encouraging and lending moral support to President Mobutu's task of mediation. There was obviously no need for the United Nations to be involved in this phase of the situation, apart from continuing the humanitarian activities of UNHCR.

The fourth phase, which occurred when another Bahutu uprising in Burundi in April 1972 provoked massive reprisals, was generally regarded by Member States as being primarily an internal crisis. There was, however, widespread international concern about the large-scale killings and a strong desire to ensure that all possible steps were taken to prevent further loss of life and to alleviate human suffering. Accordingly, the efforts of the United Nations Secretary-General were focused on mobilizing massive humanitarian aid and also on ensuring that such assistance reached all the victims in Burundi and the refugees abroad. However, the role of the OAU was limited to expressing satisfaction with the "saving action" being taken by the Burundi Government and the conviction that this effort would rapidly restore peace, national unity, and territorial integrity.

Apart from helping through an African statesman to bring about a specific settlement in phase three, OAU's main contribution has been to take action of a more general type to prevent the recurrence of tension between Rwanda and Burundi resulting from subversive activities by refugees. Through the efforts of the OAU Commission on Refugees, the African States were able to conclude in 1969 a Convention Governing the Specific Aspects of Refugee Problems in Africa, which requires signatory States to prohibit subversive activities by refugees.

2. The Congo Civil War and the Mercenary Problem (1964-68)

As a neighbor of Rwanda and Burundi and as a country which had been a dependency of the same administering Power—Belgium—the Congo has had relations with each of them that vacillated between highly positive and highly negative. The Kinshasa Agreements of August 1966 and the successful mediation by President Mobutu of the third phase of the Rwanda-Burundi situation in March 1967 represented major steps in the development of positive relationships among the three countries. Before that, the Congo crisis of 1964-65 had been a source of acute tension between the Congo (Zaire), on the one hand, and Burundi and Congo (Brazzaville), on the other, in addition to being a most divisive issue for the OAU. Afterwards, the problem of removing the last vestige of the civil war—that of expelling mercenaries from Central Africa—was to create tension between the Congo (Zaire) and Rwanda.

The Congo crisis of 1964-65 and the mercenary problem are perhaps the most instructive cases from the point of view of the respective roles of the

United Nations and the OAU in pacific settlement, since they were the subjects of extensive deliberations at both levels.

a. THE CONGO CIVIL WAR (1964-65)

This crisis had four main elements:

(i)   a civil war having an ideological character;
(ii) appointment of Moise Tshombé, the former secessionist leader of Katanga, as Prime Minister of the Congo;
(iii) employment of mercenaries by the Congolese Government;
(iv) alleged intervention by African and non-African States.

It was mainly because of the third and fourth elements—which were essentially the result of the second—that the 1964-65 crisis became of particular concern to both the United Nations and the OAU. As this crisis was indeed a new phase of a situation that became internationalized since its very beginning in mid-1960, any role played by the United Nations could be regarded as a continuation of its earlier involvement.

The turmoil in the Congo (Zaire) which had broken out in 1960 had never really ceased. Even though a government of national reconciliation had been established in August 1961 and the Katanga secession led by Moise Tshombé had been finally crushed by United Nations troops in January 1963, there still remained bitter rivalries among Congolese politicians and widespread dissatisfaction among the people. By September 1963, the situation had deteriorated to such an extent that the outbreak of sporadic disturbances precipitated the imposition of a state of emergency in the country. By the time the United Nations withdrew its troops from the Congo, that is, by June 1964, fighting had broken out in four provinces—Kwilu, Katanga, Orientale, and Kivu.

At this point, Prime Minister Adoula, who felt that he could no longer cope with the situation, resigned and was replaced on 10 July 1964 by Moise Tshombé; the latter had been claiming, while in exile in Spain, that he was the only politician who could restore order in the country. President Kasavubu's appointment of Tshombé as Prime Minister accentuated the ideological factor in the conflict to such an extent that the situation became transformed into a full scale civil war with considerable interference from abroad. Barely a month afterwards, insurgent forces extended their control over one-sixth of the country, including Stanleyville (later Kisangani), where they established a dissident "government."

The problem became of concern to most African States, since many of them were deeply distressed to see the man they identified with non-African interests assume leadership in the Congo (Zaire). The extent of their dislike for him was such that when it was learned that Prime Minister Tshombé was going to accompany President Kasavubu to the first session of the OAU Assembly (Cairo, 17-21 July 1964), many of them protested so strongly that Tshombé chose not to attend.[47] Their bitter disappointment over his accession to power developed into open criticism when it became known that his regime was not only receiving an increasing amount of military assistance from the United States, but was also recruiting foreign mercenaries, including some from South Africa and Southern Rhodesia, in order to regain the territory in the hands of the insurgents. On the other hand, some other States were disturbed by reports that the insurgents were receiving help from several African States as well as from the USSR and the Peoples Republic of China through the territories of Congo (Brazzaville) and Burundi. Congo (Brazzaville) was accused by Tshombé of harboring unfriendly elements—Christophe Gbenye and his National Liberation Committee (CNL)—and even of helping to arm and train them in camps in its territory; and Tshombé in return was accused of supporting the enemies of the new regime in Brazzaville who had been given refuge in Leopoldville (later Kinshasa). Burundi was accused of having allowed Gaston Soumialot, the leader of the rebellion in eastern Congo (Zaire), to establish his headquarters in its capital.

By September 1964, the situation in the Congo (Zaire) had deteriorated to such an extent that the Congolese Government requested the convening of an extraordinary session of the OAU Council of Ministers to consider the external aspects of the crisis. The Council of Ministers met for its third extraordinary session on 5-10 September 1964 and examined the Congolese problem as a whole: it discussed the internal conflict (with the acquiescence of the Congolese delegation) and its repercussions on the neighboring States and on the African scene at large. It prefaced its resolution[48] with a reaffirmation of its conviction concerning the responsibility and competence of the OAU "to find a peaceful solution to all the problems and differences which affect peace and security in the African continent." While refusing to grant Tshombé's request for military assistance from certain African States through the OAU, the Council of Ministers made the following appeals: to the Congolese Government to stop immediately the recruitment of mercenaries and to expel all those already in the country "as soon as possible" in order to facilitate an African solution; to all those fighting to cease hostilities; to all Congolese political leaders to seek national reconciliation with the help of the OAU; to all OAU Member States to refrain from any action that might aggravate the situation; and to all Powers which were intervening in the internal affairs of the Congo (Zaire) to end their interference. In addition, it established an Ad Hoc Commission of ten States,[49] under the chairmanship of Prime Minister (later President) Jomo Kenyatta of Kenya, to carry out the following mandate:

(i) to help and encourage the efforts of the Congolese Government in the restoration of national reconciliation; and

(ii) to help normalize relations between the Congo (Zaire) and its neighbors, especially Burundi and Congo (Brazzaville).

The resolution, though a remarkable compromise among the OAU Member States, tended to rely heavily on the good will of Tshombé for its full implementation. Though it had set up a Commission to assist in the restoration of national reconciliation and in the normalization of relations with the neighboring countries, it did not give any details as to the role envisaged for the OAU and did not provide for a machinery or for procedures to help attain a cease-fire or the expulsion of mercenaries. Responding to the sensitivity of the Congolese and some other Governments on the issue of national sovereignty, it authorized the Ad Hoc Commission "to help and encourage" the efforts of the Central Government rather than to mediate between the Government and its opponents.

In practice, however, the Ad Hoc Commission sought to carry out its mandate as if the offering of good offices was implied not only with regard to the normalization of the inter-State relations but also with respect to national reconciliation within the Congo (Zaire). When it met for its first session in Nairobi, on 18 September 1964, it sought in vain to persuade Tshombé to sit at the same table with the rebel spokesmen to discuss national reconciliation; Tshombé objected to the Commission's broad interpretation of its mandate, arguing that it would constitute interference in Congolese internal affairs. The Commission was thus able to hear only statements from Tshombé and the Foreign Ministers of Burundi and Congo (Brazzaville), all of whom emphasized their readiness to facilitate its visits to their respective countries and its contacts in carrying out its dual mandate. While refusing to meet with any of the leaders of the insurgency, Tshombé agreed to allow the Commission to hold talks with them in the Congo (Zaire). Subsequently, however, he refused to co-operate with the Commission when he discovered that not only had the Commission given the rebel leaders a sympathetic hearing in Nairobi after his departure but also that it was planning to send a delegation to the United States Government to request the suspension of the latter's military aid to the Congo (Zaire).[50] The Ad Hoc Commission's appeal for a cease-fire and for national reconciliation were thus not heeded and, in the face of strong protests from the Congolese Government, the Commission's efforts in Washington, D.C., remained fruitless. With the intensification of differences between the Commission and the Congo (Zaire) and the rising success of the mercenary-led Congolese army over the insurgents, the chances for a cease-fire declined sharply. As the Commission regarded the attainment of a cease-fire as a prerequisite for its dual mandate, it saw no point at that stage in visiting the Congo (Zaire) and its two neighbors. Instead, its attention was focused on a new task resulting from a desperate act of the retreating insurgents.

When the insurgents withdrew to their headquarters at Stanleyville they brought with them several foreign residents in the area, especially those of European and Asian origin, and held them as hostages. Prime Minister Kenyatta, the Commission's Chairman, offered his good offices and arranged negotiations at his home on 23 November 1964 between William Attwood, the United States Ambassador in Kenya, and Thomas Kanza, a representative of the insurgent regime. The Administrative Secretary-General of the OAU was also present. On the second day of negotiations when the Chairman was still trying to untangle a deadlock created by Kanza's insistence on a cease-fire as a minimum condition for the release of hostages and Attwood's insistence on limiting the discussion to the question of the safety of the hostages, the United States and Belgium, with British cooperation and with the consent of the Congolese Government, landed Belgian paratroopers in Stanleyville.

As the crisis reached a new height, the Ad Hoc Commission met on 27-28 November and recommended the convening of an extraordinary session of the OAU Assembly on 18 December to discuss all aspects of the Congo crisis and consider the Commission's proposals including one for the holding, under OAU auspices, of a round table conference of all Congolese leaders to arrange free elections.[51] Ethiopia sought to convene such a summit meeting but, in view of the opposition from about half of the OAU Member States, it decided not to press for it.

Thus, with the OAU Member States divided and the OAU Ad Hoc Commission deadlocked, the Chairman of this Commission himself urged that the Congo crisis should be brought before the United Nations organs. On 1 December, the day Belgium and the United States informed the Security Council of the completion of the rescue mission and the departure of the paratroopers from the Congo (Zaire), 22 States,[52] 18 of them from Africa, requested a meeting of the Security Council to consider urgently the situation created by the Stanleyville operation which they regarded as an intervention in African affairs and a threat to the peace and security of Africa.[53] Nine days later, the Congolese Government also requested the convening of the Security Council to examine what it described as the flagrant intervention in Congolese domestic affairs by Algeria, Sudan, Ghana, and the UAR as well as by the USSR and the People's Republic of China.[54]

The Security Council was convened to consider both complaints. After a long and bitter debate over the issue of foreign intervention, a compromise was finally reached, namely, to request all States to refrain from intervening in the domestic affairs of the Congo (Zaire). Neither the actions of Belgium and the United States nor those attributed to the four African States, the USSR, and the People's Republic of China were specifically condemned.

Two distinct positions on the issue of OAU-UN relationships were advocated during the debates in the Security Council. The first, presented by the spokesmen for the 18 African States that were critical of the Stanleyville operation, and supported by the USSR, maintained that the OAU should be encouraged to seek a solution to the Congo problem and that the Security Council should help in removing extra-continental factors which they felt were undermining the role of the OAU. The proponents stressed that the efforts of the OAU Ad Hoc Commission would have produced positive results had it not been for: (a) the lack of co-operation from Prime Minister Tshombé whose interest in a negotiated settlement declined as his hopes for a military victory were raised by the military assistance he was receiving from foreign Governments and from mercenaries; (b) the Stanleyville operation which they felt had frustrated the Nairobi negotiations and undermined the moral authority and prestige of the OAU.[55]

The second position, presented by the United States and Nigeria, supported by Brazil and the Republic of China and implicitly accepted by the Congo (Zaire), advocated the exercise of concurrent jurisdiction by the Security Council and the OAU. Without challenging the view that the Congolese problem could have been solved within the framework of the OAU, these States stressed that the matter had been mishandled by the OAU Ad Hoc Commission. Hence, they proposed that the Security Council should supplement the peace-making efforts of the OAU by sending a mission to the Congo (Zaire) to invesigate the matter of border complaints and bring to an end outside intervention in Congolese affairs. This was based on their belief that while the OAU should try to find new ways of applying the sound principles laid down by the Council of Ministers in its resolution of September 1964, the Security Council should consider what more it could do in collaboration with the OAU to assist the Congolese Government to solve its problems.[56]

The majority of the members of the Security Council were, however, of the opinion that the Congolese problem could best be solved within the framework of the OAU. After a long debate, the two African members of the Security Council, Morocco and Ivory Coast, introduced jointly a draft resolution incorporating the majority opinion while safeguarding the prerogatives of the Security Council under Chapter VIII of the United Nations Charter. As Morocco was inclined toward the position of the 18 African States while the Ivory Coast maintained a position somewhat similar to that of Nigeria and the United States,[57] the draft resolution provided a sound basis for a compromise. After making amendments resulting from consultations between the sponsors of the draft resolution and other States, especially the Congo (Zaire) and the 18 States, the Security Council adopted resolution 199 (1964)[58] which expressed a conviction that the OAU:

> should be able in the context of Article 52 of the Charter of the United Nations, to help find a peaceful solution to all the problems and disputes affecting peace and security in the continent of Africa.

Accordingly, the Security Council encouraged the OAU to pursue its efforts to help the Congolese Government to achieve national reconciliation in accordance with resolution ECM/Res.5(III) of the OAU. Moreover, it appealed for a cease-fire in the country in accordance with this resolution.

The Security Council thus endorsed the OAU's oft-repeated claim about its responsibility and competence to seek solutions to problems of peace and security in Africa. In encouraging the OAU to continue its efforts to bring about national reconciliation in the Congo (Zaire), the Security Council seemed to have confirmed the view expressed in the OAU resolution that the OAU's competence as a peace-maker was not to be limited merely to inter-States disputes but might be extended also to internal conflicts such as the Congo which had serious repercussions on peace and security in Africa. The Security Council did not, of course, recognize any right of exclusive jurisdiction for the OAU, but seemed to have adopted a policy that it would not interfere with the initial exercise of OAU jurisdiction. Of course, if the OAU failed to find a peaceful solution to the problem, the Security Council would resume its deliberations.

The main point of disagreement during the drafting of the resolution concerned the role of the United Nations Secretary-General. Should he:

(i) "follow the implementation" of the Security Council resolution as well as "follow the situation in the Congo"? or;

(ii) play a passive role while the OAU kept informing the Security Council, in accordance with Article 54 of the United Nations Charter, of any action it might take under the resolution?

Speaking on behalf of the 18 African States, Guinea indicated that any wording in the draft resolution such as that in (i) above which might imply supervision by the United Nations Secretary-General over the OAU peace-making efforts would be unacceptable because it would jeopardize the autonomy of the OAU.[59] This point of view was supported by the USSR, the only permanent member of the Security Council to express an opinion on the issue. On the other hand, Morocco and the Ivory Coast, the sponsors of the draft resolution, emphasized that the United Nations Secretary-General had a responsibility to follow any situation which might disturb international peace and that the Security Council must not shirk its responsibility and hand it over to a regional organization, however respectable it may be.[60] These two States seemed to imply that to limit the United Nations initiative on a regional question such as the Congo, which was already on the agenda of the Security Council, while awaiting reports from a regional organization on the implementation of the Security Council's own resolution would result in excessive autonomy for such regional organization.

The compromise that was finally reached was both: (a) to request the OAU to keep the Security Council fully informed of any action it may take under the resolution; and (b) to request the United Nations Secretary-General "to follow the situation in the Congo and report to the Security Council." Even though the most controversial phrase—that concerning following the implementation of the resolution of the Security Council—was left out, it could be inferred from the debates[61] that the Secretary-General would in any case be expected to follow the implementation of those aspects of the resolution for which OAU efforts alone would be insufficient, namely, the expulsion of mercenaries and the prevention of foreign intervention. On all aspects, of course, he was to exercise his responsibility of observing closely any developments in the Congo (Zaire), irrespective of the peace-making efforts of the OAU, and then to report to the Security Council. In practice, there was no problem of OAU-UN relationship regarding the implementation of the Security Council resolution: the United Nations Secretary-General remained vigilant of developments and was kept informed by the OAU secretariat of the OAU efforts.[62]

Having had the manner of its relationship with the Security Council and the United Nations Secretary-General thus clarified, the OAU resumed its diplomatic efforts. But as the organization itself was still deeply divided along political and ideological lines, it was not able to resolve the Congo crisis. The OAU Ad Hoc Commission, based on a negative balance—that is, composed mostly of States with strong partisan views on the question—was unable to mediate between the Congo (Zaire) and its two neighbors; it was also unable to bring about national reconciliation. It did not even leave Nairobi to study on the spot the situation in the three countries because the two sub-committees that it dispatched early in 1965 were unable to obtain sufficient co-operation from the three countries to ensure the safety of the Commission members.

However, despite the failure of its efforts, the OAU remained seized of the question. This was perhaps due to the fact that there was no serious deterioration of the situation—in the form of a new wave of foreign intervention or of an intensification of mercenary activities. At a time when the United Nations was facing a serious financial and constitutional crisis largely as a consequence of its deep involvement in the earlier rounds of the Congo crisis and in the face of insistence by most African States upon OAU handling of the problem, it became unlikely that the members of the Security Council would find it advisable to consider another complaint as long as the OAU continued its diplomatic efforts.

The Congo question was finally dropped from the OAU agenda when, in October 1965, the President of the Congo removed Prime Minister Tshombé from office and offered to expel the mercenaries and to seek reconciliation with neighboring countries.

Had it not been for the landing of Belgian paratroopers in Stanleyville, which more than half of the OAU Member States regarded as being detrimental to the diplomatic efforts of the OAU, perhaps the Congo crisis would not have been brought before the Security Council. The Congo's complaint against some African and other States followed rather than preceded the request of the 22 States for a meeting of the Security Council. Once the grievances regarding external intervention were fully aired, the key problem of national reconciliation and the dependent problem of rising tension with neighboring African countries were referred back for OAU mediation. The authority of the OAU to promote national reconciliation was enhanced by the Security Council resolution—a resolution which was accepted by the Congolese Government with its usual reservation against any acts that might infringe upon its domestic jurisdiction.

From the point of viey of clarification of the constitutional relationships between the United Nations and the OAU, the result of the Security Council consideration of the Congo question was to confirm the view that the OAU was a regional organization within the meaning of Chapter VIII of the United Nations Charter. The 'try OAU first' approach to pacific settlement of African disputes was underlined, without prejudice to the role of the United Nations Secretary-General in following developments in situations which might affect international peace and security.

b. PROBLEM OF EXPELLING MERCENARIES (1967-68)

Just as the presence of non-African mercenaries in the Congo (Zaire) in the service of the Tshombé Government was a cause of tension between that Government and those of many African States, the process of their expulsion from Central Africa became a major factor in the tension that developed between the new Congolese Government and Rwanda.

When General Mobutu assumed the Presidency of the Congo (Zaire) in November 1965 as a result of a military coup d'etat, he began after some delay to implement former President Kasavubu's promise to normalize relations with other African States and, in the first half of 1967, also the promise to expel mercenaries from the country. Until then, most of the mercenary corps left by Tshombé had been provisionally retained as an integral part of the Congolese national army (ANC). In September 1966, a complaint from the Congolese Government about illegal activities of mercenaries in the Congo was considered by the Security Council. But that situation involved a different group of mercenaries who had invaded a part of the Congo allegedly with the encouragement of certain non-African States and interests.[63] By the beginning of July 1967, responding to the long-standing appeals of the OAU and the Security Council and possibly sensing a potential threat to the Congolese Government from the mercenaries within the ANC (many of them were believed to be loyal to Tshombé who was back in exile), President Mobutu had already dismissed all except two units.

Early in July 1967, he was about to disband the remaining units when Tshombé was kidnapped to Algeria. On 5 July, the mercenary units in Bukavu revolted against the ANC and occupied the city with the help of a few hundred Congolese servicemen who had previously served under Tshombé's secessionist regime in Katanga. At the same time, according to the Congolese Government, two unknown aircraft parachuted groups of mercenaries at Kisangani (formerly Stanleyville).[64] The mutiny soon took a political turn when a rebel "government of public safety" was set up under a Congolese officer who was a close associate of Tshombé. The ANC encircled the well-entrenched and heavily armed mutineers and the siege of Bukavu continued for almost two months.

The case was brought by the Congolese Government both before the Security Council and the OAU Assembly. When the Security Council met on 6-10 July, the main issue was the reinforcement allegedly given by non-African States and interests to the mutineers. Without specifically mentioning those States which had been charged with complicity, the Security Council condemned States which gave assistance to the mercenaries and called upon Governments to ensure that neither the territories under their control nor their nationals were used for subversive activities against the Congo (Zaire).[65]

When the OAU Assembly met on 11-14 September for its fourth ordinary session at Kinshasa, the capital of the Congo, it condemned "aggression" by mercenaries against that country and demanded their immediate departure, "if necessary with the help of the competent international bodies." In the event that the mercenaries might refuse to leave, it called upon Member States "to lend their wholehearted support and every assistance in their power to the Government of the . . . Congo." It also called upon the United Nations "to deplore and take immediate action to eradicate . . . the illegal and immoral practices" of the mercenaries and appealed to all States "to enact laws declaring the recruitment and training of mercenaries in their territories a punishable crime and deterring their citizens from enlisting as mercenaries."[66] In a separate decision, the OAU Assembly established a ten-nation Ad Hoc Committee, under the chairmanship of President El Azhari of the Sudan, "to take all steps necessary for the evacuation of the mercenaries" in co-operation with the Assembly's Chairman-in-Office and with the assistance of the OAU Administrative Secretary-General.[67]

Upon the request of President Mobutu of the Congo, who was also the OAU Assembly's Chairman-in-Office, the International Committee of the Red Cross sought to arrange peaceful evacuation of the mercenaries from Bukavu. Red Cross emissaries sought to arrange the movement of the duly disarmed mercenaries, accompanied by an OAU security force, from Bukavu to Kemembe airport in Rwanda. But the mercenaries refused to co-operate and, after an unsuccessful armed clash with Congolese troops in late October and early November, they fled into Rwanda where they were eventually disarmed and detained by the Rwandese Government.

On 3 November, while the fighting was still going on, the Security Council was informed by the Congolese Government that a new band of mercenaries had invaded the country from Angola with Portuguese collusion and was requested to take the necessary measures to stop the "aggression." After discussing the problem on 8-15 November, the Security Council condemned Portugal for failing to prevent the use of Angolan territory as a launching ground for mercenary operations and called upon it to put an end to any assistance that was being given to them. It also urged all countries receiving mercenaries who had participated in the armed attacks against the Congo (Zaire) to take appropriate measures to prevent them from renewing their activities against any State and requested the United Nations Secretary-General to follow the implementation of the resolution.[68]

When the situation had calmed down following the flight of the mercenaries from the Congo (Zaire), the remaining problem was that of evacuating those detained in Rwanda, a task for which the OAU Ad Hoc Committee had sufficient mandate. In its first session, held later in November, the Ad Hoc Committee established a Five-Nation Commission of Inquiry[69] to identify the mercenaries detained in Rwanda as well as the States, organizations, or interested groups behind the mercenary activities. In addition, it decided that a just and equitable amount of reparations should be paid to the Congo (Zaire) by the mercenaries themselves or by the States or organizations to which they claimed to belong. Until such compensation was paid and written guarantees were given by the mercenaries or their Governments to ensure that they would never return to Africa to resume their "subversive activities," the Rwandese Government was requested to detain them "under the exclusive political authority and effective control of the OAU Ad Hoc Committee."[70]

Though the Ad Hoc Committee was able to persuade the Congolese Government to grant amnesty to returning Congolese servicemen who had joined the mercenaries, it was unable to proceed toward the evacuation of the mercenaries; this was due to a setback in the work of the Commission of Inquiry caused by differences between the Congo (Zaire) and Rwanda over the interpretation of the resolution of the OAU Assembly. Even though it had initially co-operated in faciliating investigation of the mercenaries, Rwanda objected to the various demands of the Commission and its line of questioning on the ground that they tended to infringe upon its domestic jurisdiction and to presume complicity between Rwanda and the detained mercenaries. Given this situation, the Ad Hoc Committee met again and decided to request Rwanda to transfer the mercenaries immediately to the Congo (Zaire) with the assistance of the Congolese and Burundi Governments in order that they might undergo full investigation by the Commission of Inquiry and trial in Congolese courts. But Rwanda could not agree to such a transfer which would obviously depart from the resolution of the OAU Assembly calling only for measures to evacuate the mercenaries from Africa. The Ad Hoc Committee had thus to find a less controversial course. In April 1968, its Chairman was able to persuade the Congolese Government to agree to an evacuation as requested by the OAU Assembly. At the same time, he was able to assure that Government against their return to Africa by obtaining written guarantees from the mercenaries themselves and their respective Governments. The mercenaries were finally evacuated from Africa with the help of the International Committee of the Red Cross.

The role of the OAU with regard to the mercenary question had thus evolved to a point where it gradually became more prominent than that of the United Nations. In 1964, both the OAU Council of Ministers and the Security Council had urged that the mercenaries should be withdrawn from the Congo (Zaire) as a matter of urgency. But as the mercenaries were serving the Congolese Government, the appeal for expulsion remained unanswered until President Mobutu had completed the task of restoring unity and order after Tshombé's departure. When the Congolese Government was challenged by the mercenaries and threatened by others from abroad, it became feasible for the OAU to offer more concrete assistance to discourage mercenary activities. Several factors seem to account for the intensification of the OAU role. First, most OAU Member States were eager to give the necessary assistance to President Mobutu to end the presence of mercenaries in his country—an attitude which was in sharp contrast to their refusal previously to meet Prime Minister Tshombé's request for African troops to replace the mercenaries. Secondly, as the link between the mercenaries and foreign Powers and interests was suspected but not yet proved, the OAU Ad Hoc Committee sought to strengthen the position of the African States at a future meeting of the Security Council by obtaining the necessary proof through a formal inquiry. In order to show that a fair and objective investigation had been conducted, the OAU invited the United Nations Secretary-General to send an observer to the proceedings of the OAU Commission of Inquiry. It should be recalled that the Secretary-General had a mandate to follow the implementation of various resolutions of the Security Council concerning the termination of mercenary activities. However, as the mandate of the Commission became the subject of sharp differences between Rwanda and the Congo (Zaire)[71] the Secretary-General refrained from sending an observer and thus left the task of inquiry entirely to the OAU. Thirdly, when the controversy between the two African States over the inquiry and the transfer of the mercenaries to the Congo became more prominent than that of their evacuation from Africa, it became logical for the OAU itself to find a compromise on the entire question.

3. The Nigerian Civil War (1967-70)

The Nigerian civil war was perhaps the gravest situation in independent Africa since the civil war in the Congo. The immediate origins of the conflict can be traced back to the interregional friction which emerged in Nigeria during the general elections of December 1964. The elections were based on the new census which by giving the Northern Region a clear majority in the country generated in the other regions fear of northern domination. Following bitter electoral campaigning, the main political parties in the Eastern and Western Regions decided to boycott the elections because of irregularities and lawlessness. The disturbances culminated in a bloody military coup d'etat on 15 January 1966: a group of junior officers, most of whom were Ibos, unleashed the coup which resulted in the assassination of the Federal Prime Minister, two Regional Premiers, the Federal Minister of Finance,[72] as well as many senior northern officers. A few days later anarchy was forestalled by the establishment of a provisional Military Government under the highest ranking Ibo officer, Major-General Johnson Aguiyi-Ironsi. General Ironsi's substitution of a unitary state for the federal system was strongly opposed by northern Nigerians who regarded the measure as a scheme for domination by Ibos. In addition, the fact that he and most of his advisers were Ibos and that he had not punished the officers responsible for the killings during the coup created such antagonism in the north that rioting broke out in northern cities and, on 29 July 1966, a group of northern soldiers carried out a counter-coup killing General Ironsi and many high-ranking Ibo officers. After a few days of crisis, Lieutenant Colonel (later General) Yakubu Gowon, a northern officer, was called upon to form and take command of a National Military Government. However, before the new Government could establish its authority, the communal riots resulted in the death of a large number of Ibos in the north and the flight of over a million others to the Ibo "homeland" in Eastern Nigeria.

Against this tragic background, the new Government reinstated the earlier federal system and declared that a constituent assembly would be convened and a referendum held to determine a widely acceptable system. After having convened in vain an ad hoc committee on constitutional reforms (September 1966), General Gowon met with the four Military Governors of Nigeria early in January 1967 at Aburi, Ghana, under the auspices of General Ankrah, the head of the Military Revolutionary Council of Ghana. It seemed as if a solution had been found, permitting the Eastern Region control of its security, some compensation for the loss of life and property of Ibos in Northern Nigeria and broad local powers, but implicitly ruling out the claim of that Region's leaders to a right to secede. Even then, there appeared differences of interpretation and, subsequently, Colonel Ojukwu, the Governor of the Eastern Region, halted payment of revenues to the Federal Government, complaining that the Ibos had not received the promised compensation. In retaliation, the Federal Government imposed economic sanctions. The two sides were on a collision course.

On 27 May 1967, the Federal Government promulgated a decree decentralizing the system of government and creating twelve states out of the former regions; for the Eastern Region this meant a division into one Ibo and two minority-run states. On 30 May 1967, after consulting a committee of representatives of the Eastern Region, Colonel Ojukwu declared the region an independent sovereign State to be named "Biafra." The Federal Government in Nigeria, which regarded the declaration as an act of rebellion, responded by mobilizing its troops and warning all countries not to interfere in the internal affairs of Nigeria. On 6 July 1967, fighting started between the troops of the Federal Government and "Biafra," and continued until the latter was completely defeated in January 1970.

For the OAU, the decision to discuss the Nigerian question was a difficult one to take. Initially, the Federal Government held firmly that any intervention even in the form of a discussion at the OAU or United Nations level would be in violation of the domestic jurisdiction clauses in Article III(2) of the OAU Charter and Article 2(7) of the United Nations Charter. On the other hand, the Biafran regime was constantly pressing for the internationalization of the issues of the conflict in order to involve international organizations in the matter. Pressure from African States for a cease-fire and for a negotiated settlement began to build up when a joint appeal was made on 8 July 1967 to the leaders of both sides by the Presidents of Kenya, Tanzania, Uganda, and Zambia and the Emperor of Ethiopia. But, in view of the insistence of the Nigerian Federal Government that the conflict was strictly an internal affair and should be solved by Nigerians themselves, it remained uncertain until the OAU Assembly met for its fourth session at Kinshasa on 11-14 September 1967 whether the OAU could take any initiative in the matter. Finally, Nigeria agreed to have the matter discussed on condition that no attempt would be made to interfere with its internal affairs. The resolution that was adopted took full account of Nigeria's preoccupation. In its preamble, it condemned secession in any Member States and recognized the situation in Nigeria as an internal affair, the solution of which was primarily the responsibility of the Nigerians themselves. The operative paragraph established a consultative mission of six Heads of State[73] whose task was "to assure" the Federal Government of Nigeria "of the Assembly's desire for the territorial integrity, unity and peace of Nigeria."[74] The resolution did not request a cease-fire or suggest a compromise, and did not even mention specifically good offices as part of the mission of the Committee. But since the Consultative Committee was by far the highest ranking ad hoc body created by the OAU, it was hard to imagine that it would do nothing more than demonstrate its solidarity with the Federal Government.

Had the Committee been able to visit Lagos on 27 September as originally scheduled, that is, at a time when no victory was in sight for either side, perhaps it might have been able to develop its role in such a way as to exercise good offices from the start. But when it visited Lagos two months later at a time when the "Biafran" forces were in retreat, the Committee was not left much leeway. By supporting the terms of the Federal Government for a return to peace and normal conditions in Nigeria—renunciation of secession and acceptance of the administrative structure of the Federation of Nigeria "as laid down by the Federal Military Government of Nigeria in Decree No. 14 of 1967"[75]—the Committee limited severely the possibility of its acting as an effective catalyst for negotiations. The Committee was able to persuade the Federal Government of the need to establish contact with the secessionists through one of its members in order to convey to them the text of the OAU Assembly resolution and the proceedings of the Committee's first session and to obtain their reaction. But no channels of communication could be established with the "Biafran" leaders, who condemned the Committee's endorsement of the Federal Government's position after consulting only one party to the dispute.

During the next four months the conflict was intensified partly as a result of the acquisition by both sides of additional arms from abroad; and the suffering of the population in war-stricken areas reached enormous proportions.

As the war of attrition continued, the "Biafran" military leaders began to press for mediation in a forum other than the OAU. As they had realized that the prospect for a United Nations diplomatic involvement was even less than that for OAU mediation, they started to explore possibilities for mediation by individual statesmen, and even proposed, in April, that each side in the conflict should nominate an African Head of State who would be asked to act as a co-mediator. By this time, the Federal Government had also begun to feel the need for negotiation. Both sides were thus able to agree early in May 1968 to start negotiations under the auspices of the Commonwealth Secretariat, as proposed by the Federal Government. But neither these talks, held in Kampala (Uganda) later in May under the chairmanship of the Commonwealth Secretary-General (and eventually also the co-chairmanship of Uganda's Foreign Minister), nor the various subsequent initiatives of the British Government could produce positive results. The "Biafran" insistence on a cease-fire and withdrawal of troops to prewar positions as a prerequisite to a negotiated settlement could not be reconciled with the Federal Government's demand for prior renunciation of secession.

The OAU was constrained to resume its diplomatic initiative for a number of reasons. First, the appalling suffering of the population in the conflict area aroused public opinion in Africa and elsewhere to such an extent that many African Heads of State, including the Members of the OAU Consultative Committee, felt that the OAU should not remain inactive. Secondly, with the shift of diplomatic initiative to the Commonwealth Secretariat (December 1967 to May 1968) and the British Government (June 1968), it began to dawn upon the African States that unless the OAU resumed its initiative, it might lose prestige and influence and become irrelevant to the major problems of African States. Thirdly, since the obstacle to initiating negotiation between the two sides had already been removed, there was now an opportunity for the OAU to play a mediatory role rather than a mere "consultative" one. Finally, when four African States—Tanzania, Gabon, Ivory Coast, and Zambia—recognized "Biafra" during April and May 1968, contrary to the policy of non-recognition implied in the

OAU's condemnation of secession, it became clear that there was a real danger of a split within the OAU which could cripple the organization.

The OAU Consultative Committee was, therefore, convened by the Emperor of Ethiopia, and, at its meeting in Niamey (Niger) in July 1968, it persuaded the two sides to begin immediate preliminary talks under the chairmanship of the President of Niger. It also persuaded them to resume peace negotiations as soon as possible in Addis Ababa under its auspices. Thus, having won the confidence of both sides, the Consultative Committee was able for the first time to offer its good offices. At the preliminary talks in Niamey, it was instrumental in bringing about an agreement on a three-point agenda for the Addis Ababa talks namely:

(i) arrangements for a permanent settlement;
(ii) terms for the cessation of hostilities;
(iii) proposals for the transport of relief supplies to civilian victims of the war.

Serious negotiations on the relief issue began at Niamey and were continued at the Addis Ababa talks where an agreement was reached in principle on the establishment of air and land "mercy corridors" for transporting relief supplies to the civilian victims of the war.

Five weeks of intensive negotiations took place at Addis Ababa under the chairmanship of the Emperor of Ethiopia, but no progress could be made even on the mutually agreed objective of setting up relief corridors. The prospect for any significant progress at Addis Ababa became minimal when it became known that General Gowon would be unable to participate personally in the negotiations—Colonel Ojukwu came to deliver a statement and then left the task of negotiation to his representative—and also when it became clear that neither side was inclined to make any concessions.

When, a few days later, the OAU Assembly met in Algiers for its fifth ordinary session, it gave emphatic support to the position of the Federal Government over the opposition of the four States that had recognized "Biafra." The Assembly's resolution[76] appealed to both sides to declare a cease-fire; to the secessionist leaders to co-operate with the Federal authorities "in order to restore peace and unity in Nigeria"; to the Federal Government to declare a general amnesty and to co-operate with the OAU in ensuring the physical security of all Nigerians; and to all concerned to co-operate in the speedy delivery of humanitarian supplies to the needy. Having rejected the thesis of the four States recognizing "Biafra" that unity should never be imposed by force but should stem only from consent, the OAU Assembly reaffirmed its policy of support for Nigeria and made more explicit its policy of opposition to the recognition of "Biafra." All Member

States of the United Nations and the OAU were, therefore, called upon "to refrain from any action detrimental to the peace, unity and territorial integrity of Nigeria."[77]

By reaffirming full support for Nigeria, the OAU virtually sealed the political fate of "Biafra," but this was done at the price of deepening the gulf between the majority of the African States and the four that had recognized "Biafra." When recognizing "Biafra," Tanzania had accused other African States of having "callously" watched "the massacre of tens of thousands of people" for the sake of upholding the territorial integrity of Nigeria. The other three States also emphasized the issue of "conscience." Nigeria had reacted immediately by breaking diplomatic relations with the four States. At Algiers, the debate on Nigeria became so acrimonious that the President of Algeria, an ardent supporter of the Nigerian position, went so far as to charge that the African "champions" of "Biafran" secession were being manipulated by imperialist Powers and foreign plotters aiming at destroying the foundations of an African State.[78] The antagonism between the majority and the minority was such that the President of Zambia refused nomination to become one of the Vice-Presidents of the OAU Assembly and even left the conference soon after the debate on Nigeria was completed. The rift could not be healed after "Biafra" was defeated when, in the context of the seventh session of the OAU Assembly at Addis Ababa, the Emperor of Ethiopia was able to reconcile the leaders of Nigeria and the four States.

Neither the four States' strong feeling of antagonism toward the policy of the majority nor the seemingly endless period of relative OAU inaction between the first and second attempts of the OAU Consultative Committee (November 1967 to July 1968) could induce any State supporting the "Biafran" cause to go so far as to make a formal request for the inscription of the Nigerian question on the agenda of a United Nations organ.[79] The "Biafran" strategy of delaying the advance of Nigerian troops "until the world's conscience [could] be effectively aroused against genocide" had considerable success with the mass media of a number of countries, but could induce only those Governments recognizing "Biafra" to draw the General Assembly's attention, during the general debate, to the possibility of human rights violation. Whatever chances there might have been initially of persuading other Governments to agree to a full-scale General Assembly consideration of this issue were removed when the "Biafran" charges of genocide were refuted in late 1968 by a team of observers representing the Secretaries-General of the United Nations and the OAU and the Governments of Canada, Poland, Sweden, and the United Kingdom; the team was invited by the Federal Government to observe the conduct of its troops as they advanced into "Biafran" territory.[80]

It is significant from the point of view of OAU-UN relationships that the United Nations Secretary-General had initially explored possibilities for exercising his good offices[81] and then decided to encourage the OAU to assist in the quest for a peaceful solution of the problem. When he spoke before the fifth session of the OAU Assembly, he stated that "the OAU should be the most appropriate instrument for the promotion of peace in Nigeria."[82] Again, in his speech before the sixth session, he emphasized that in the long run only the acceptance of the OAU recommendations could put an end to the crisis.[83]

If the United Nations organs did not play any direct peace-making role in the Nigerian situation, the role played by the United Nations Secretary-General and various bodies and agencies of the United Nations system with regard to the humanitarian aspect of the problem was of great significance. On 1 August 1968, with the concurrence of the Nigerian Government, the Secretary-General appointed a representative to assist in the relief and humanitarian activities for civilian victims of the hostilities in Nigeria. After assessing through him the extent and modalties of the humanitarian task, the Secretary-General encouraged the relevant United Nations bodies, especially UNICEF and the World Food Programme, to continue their efforts to mobilize large-scale relief operations for Nigeria with the help of the International Committee of the Red Cross which had agreed to co-ordinate the aid being given by all governmental and non-governmental agencies. On 11 January 1970, shortly before the defeat of the "Biafran" forces, the Secretary-General, who was then visiting West Africa, appealed to the Nigerian Government to show the greatest magnanimity and humaneness to all civilian population in the afflicted areas and requested it to issue instructions to all its forces to exercise the greatest restraint and civility. Upon receiving an invitation from the Nigerian Government, he visited Nigeria on 18 and 19 January and held consultations with General Gowon and with representatives of the various international agencies providing humanitarian assistance. Relief operations were intensified following the Secretary-General's meeting of 5 February at Headquarters with the heads of the United Nations agencies and programs and his senior colleagues.

4. Conclusions

In the foregoing situations arising from internal conflicts, the roles played by the OAU and the United Nations were highly complementary. In general the OAU has tended to assume primary responsibility for the political and diplomatic aspects of a situation while the United Nations has been inclined to limit itself to the humanitarian aspects. Any exceptions to this tendency can be explained either by the inability of the OAU to respond promptly to a Member State's request for help in a crisis or by the existence of factors in a conflict having wide international repercussions. Thus, the United Nations Secretary-General found it necessary in the first phase of the Rwanda-Burundi situation to play not only a humanitarian but also a diplomatic role to solve the problem, because at that time the OAU did not seem to have the capacity to play either role promptly. However, when the third phase was reached, the OAU was able to respond effectively to the needs of both countries for diplomatic assistance.

A comparison of the handling of the Congolese and Nigerian civil wars demonstrates the importance of certain factors of an internal conflict in shaping the nature of OAU and United Nations involvement. While both crises were primarily internal, that of the Congo had such an ideologically divisive character that it induced serious interference by certain African States and by non-African States and other foreign interests. The issue of domestic jurisdiction was, therefore, less of an obstacle in the Congo crisis than in the Nigerian one to a bold diplomatic initiative by either organization. It can be said that, having occurred in the wake of four years of deep United Nations involvement in the Congo, the new phase of the crisis started off as something more than a Congolese internal affair. It became internationalized when Tshombé was appointed Prime Minister and began suppressing the insurgents with the help of mercenaries and with military assistance from foreign Governments, thus provoking intervention by those African and non-African Governments which resented him the most. The issue of OAU competence in the crisis as a whole was waived at the outset when the Congolese Government itself brought the matter before the OAU and accepted the mandate of the Ad Hoc Commission on the Congo which included national reconciliation. Later, when the Commission encountered insurmountable difficulties and as the crisis became fully internationalized due to the Stanleyville operation, even the proponents of maximum autonomy for the OAU in peaceful settlement found it necessary to bring the case to the Security Council.

By contrast, in the Nigerian civil war, of which the central problem was secession rather than an ideologically inspired attempt to overthrow the central Government, the essentially domestic nature of the conflict could permit only a modest diplomatic role for the OAU. Being careful not to encourage or condone secession, and aware of the Federal Government's opposition to any OAU role that might constitute an infringement of Nigerian sovereignty, the OAU could not assume responsibility for national reconciliation. In the circumstances, it was significant that the OAU Assembly was able to take an initiative in discussing the Nigerian question and in setting up the Consultative Committee, even though Nigeria was believed to be reluctant to bring the matter before the OAU. It was even more significant that the Consultative Committee was able to develop its role from one of merely giving assurance of assistance to the Federal Government to one of providing good offices, and even mediation on such limited issues as relief for civilian victims. However, in spite of this development which took place without prejudice to the objective of the preservation of Nigerian unity and territorial integrity, the role of the OAU still remained rather modest and intermittent. Yet, as long as the OAU continued its diplomatic effort with full encouragement from the United Nations Secretary-General, Nigeria, supported by most African and other States,, was able to keep the question away from the United Nations; the matter thus remained within the framework of the OAU and, to a lesser extent, that of the Commonwealth Secretariat. Thus, even though little progress was made in the work of the Consultative Committee, it remained unlikely that any state supporting the "Biafran" cause would succeed in bringing the case before the United Nations.

As in the Congo case, the diplomatic efforts of the OAU were not successful in bringing about a negotiated settlement of the Nigerian conflict. Perhaps the most significant result of the OAU involvement was to set up a norm against the recognition of political entities in Africa created through secession. It can be expected that this norm, together with the norms for the prohibition of foreign intervention, including that by mercenaries, and of subversive activities by refugees, might in future exert a stabilizing influence in African countries facing a potential internal conflict.

E. HANDLING OF OTHER SITUATIONS
OF INTER-STATE FRICTION

1. Tension among Certain West African States (1965-67)

At different times, serious political quarrels or ideological differences created tension between certain African States which often led to mutual charges of subversion. It will be recalled that such differences constituted one of the main factors in the Congo crisis of 1964-65. In the West African cases examined below such differences may be regarded as the main cause of tension between the countries concerned. Although there were many instances of friction between various African States, the situation between Ghana and its French-speaking neighbors (1965-67) and Guinea's friction with Ghana and Ivory Coast (1966-67) have been selected here because they were of particular concern to the United Nations and the OAU; not only were these situations a source of ideologically motivated tension between States but were detrimental to the proper functioning of one or the other organization.

Before February 1966, Ghana's relations with some of its neighbors—the Ivory Coast, Niger, and Upper Volta—were constantly strained, in large measure due to sharp ideological differences between President Nkrumah of Ghana and the leaders of the other countries.[84] When Nkrumah was overthrown by a military coup d'etat and was granted political asylum in Guinea, tension developed between the Government of Guinea and those of Ghana and the Ivory Coast.

a. GHANA'S FRICTION WITH CERTAIN NEIGHBORS (1965-66)

As the Ghanaian question was a problem directly affecting the functioning of the OAU, it called for immediate action by the OAU.

For a number of years the Governments of the neighboring French-speaking countries had been criticizing the Ghanaian Government under President Nkrumah for granting asylum and support to opposition groups who left their home countries to continue resistance from abroad. Early in 1965, partly as a result of their rising tension with Ghana and their sharp differences with other African States over the Congo crisis, Ghana's French-speaking neighbors and other members of the former Brazzaville Group decided to re-establish the Union Africaine et Malgache (UAM), the political organization that they had abolished the previous year, under the new name of Organisation Commune Africaine et Malgache (OCAM). Since they felt that the OAU had been unable to meet their needs fully, these Francophone States set up OCAM as a supplementary instrument for reinforcing co-operation and solidarity among themselves and for speeding up their development. The most urgent task facing them then was the co-ordination of policies toward Ghana and the Congo: to oppose President Nkrumah's alleged support of subversive activities in Africa and to support the Congolese Government under Prime Minister Tshombé. Since the next session of the OAU Assembly was scheduled to take place in Accra, Ghana, eight members of OCAM—Ivory Coast, Niger, Upper Volta as well as Cameroon, Chad, Dahomey, Gabon, and Madagascar—joined by Liberia, threatened to boycott the session as a protest against Accra-based subversive activities.[85]

At the request of Nigeria, the OAU Council of Ministers held an extraordinary session in Lagos in June 1965 to attempt to resolve the situation between Ghana and its neighbors. Ghana agreed to expel from its territory for the duration of the OAU conference all persons and organizations considered subversive by OAU Member States. It further invited the OAU Administrative Secretary-General and the Chairman of the Council of

Ministers, Joseph Murumbi of Kenya, to visit Ghana and "ascertain the measures which [were] being taken towards the success of the Conference."[86]

Eight days before the OAU Assembly was convened, President Nkrumah met with Presidents Houphouët-Boigny of Ivory Coast, Hamani Diori of Niger, and Maurice Yameogo of Upper Volta in Bamako under the chairmanship of President Modibo Keita of Mali. However, even though the undesirable persons had been removed from Accra before the date of the Conference—a fact which was confirmed by the OAU Administrative Secretary-General—Nkrumah's promise to deport them from Ghana was not fulfilled and the three Presidents together with five other Heads of OCAM States boycotted the Conference. They explained that they did so not only "for reasons of security . . . , but also of dignity."[87]

The boycott revealed not only the intensity of the ideological differences but also the seriousness of the problem of subversive activities between African States. The Accra session of the OAU Assembly thus found it necessary to adopt a declaration on the problem of subversion. In the declaration, the OAU Assembly undertook solemnly in conformity with Article III(5) of the OAU Charter not to tolerate any subversive activities between African countries and to oppose collectively any form of subversion originating in foreign Powers and carried out with or without the collaboration of an African State.[88] Two months later, upon the initiative of African, Asian, and Latin American States, the General Assembly proscribed all forms of subversion when it adopted a declaration on the inadmissibility of intervention in the domestic affairs of States.[89]

b. GHANA VERSUS GUINEA (1966)

Political and ideological differences in West Africa reached a climax when, following his removal from power in Ghana, former President Nkrumah threatened to overthrow the new military regime with the help of the Government of Guinea.

On 10 March 1966, President Sekou Touré of Guinea reportedly announced that "20,000 Guinean ex-servicemen and 50,000 soldiers" would be marching to Ghana to "assist the people of Ghana" to overthrow the military regime.[90]

On 25 April, Ghana notified the President of the Security Council of the "intentions" of Guinea to invade Ghana, while Guinea denied the allegations.[91] But no attempt was made to convene the Security Council.

Later, in October, the Ghanaian Government detained the entire delegation of Guinea to the seventh session of the OAU Council of Ministers, when the plane carrying the delegation made an unscheduled landing in

Accra. The Ghanaian authorities announced that they would not release the delegation until Guinea had released the members of the Ghana Embassy in Conakry who were allegedly kept from returning home.[92] Earlier the Ghanaian Government had also demanded repatriation of Nkrumah by Guinea. The United Nations Secretary-General appealed to Ghana to release the Guinean diplomats and to Guinea to permit the International Committee of the Red Cross or any other acceptable international agency to investigate whether there were any Ghanaian political prisoners in Guinea. But his appeal was not heeded by either party.

Following an unsuccessful effort by a representative of the Ethiopian Government to obtain release of the Guinean delegation, the OAU Council of Ministers dispatched to Accra and Conakry a mission of three representatives of Member States—the Congo (Zaire), Kenya, and Sierra Leone—to negotiate the release of the Guinean diplomats as well as of any Ghanaians who might be detained in Guinea and also to help the two countries to normalize their relations. These OAU representatives also failed in the Ghanaian part of their mission, but were at least able to return from Guinea with the conclusion that there was no evidence of Ghanaians held there against their will.[93] It was not until the African Heads of State met for the third session of the OAU Assembly that a solution to the problem could be found. Within the conference environment, the Emperor of Ethiopia and the Presidents of Liberia, Mali, Tanzania, and the UAR (Egypt) were able jointly to persuade the Chairman of the Ghanaian National Liberation Council to release the Guinean diplomats.

In the Guinea-Ghana situation, the United Nations Secretary-General's role was largely limited to appeals reflecting the concern of the international community, while the OAU sought to mediate by sending to both Ghana and Guinea a delegation composed of high officials of Member States, none of whom could be characterized as being supporters or opponents of the Governments in dispute. The OAU further provided a forum within which African Statesmen commanding respect in both Ghana and Guinea could intercede personally.

Although the downfall of Nkrumah as President of Ghana was not a minor event, considering his influence and stature in many African countries, the OAU was able to avoid an ideological division over the Ghana-Guinea situation and to solve it in an impartial manner. On this clearly intra-OAU problem, it was apparently not deemed necessary to invite the services of an appropriate international agency as had been suggested by the United Nations Secretary-General.

C. GUINEA VERSUS IVORY COAST (1966-67)

Though there have been long-standing political and ideological differ-

ences between President Touré of Guinea and President Houphouët-Boigny
of the Ivory Coast, it was in March, 1966 that a real danger of conflict between their countries became apparent. Since the Ivory Coast lies between
Guinea and Ghana, the reported announcement by President Touré to
invade Ghana induced the President of the Ivory Coast to mobilize troops
to the frontier.

Even after the immediate danger of armed conflict had passed, tension
between Guinea and the Ivory Coast remained high and culminated in
an incident similar to that in the Ghana-Guinea case. Toward the end of
June 1967, the Ivory Coast Government detained Guinean officials returning from the fifth emergency special session of the General Assembly,
as well as a Guinean citizen serving with the Universal Postal Union, together with his family. It explained that its action was a consequence of
the prior "arbitrary arrest" by Guinea of several citizens and residents
of the Ivory Coast and the capture of a fishing trawler of the Ivory Coast.[94]
One citizen of the Ivory Coast was arrested allegedly for having plotted
to overthrow President Touré and the trawler was captured on suspicion
that its crew had plotted to kidnap former President Nkrumah.

Guinea addressed a letter to the United Nations Secretary-General
charging the Ivory Coast with "flagrant violation . . . of the Convention
on the Privileges and Immunities of the United Nations, of the Convention
on the Privileges and Immunities of the specialized agencies and of the
Vienna Convention on Diplomatic Relations."[95] Guinea drew the attention
of the Secretary-General to the special responsibility of the United Nations
in the matter. The Administrative Secretary-General of the OAU and
the representatives of five African States—Algeria, Mali, Mauritania, Tanzania, and Congo (Brazzaville)—felt that it would be appropriate for the
United Nations Secretary-General to handle the problem and thus requested him to intercede with the Government of the Ivory Coast in order
to secure the release of the detained delegation. The Ivory Coast also approached the United Nations Secretary-General and asked him to assist
in bringing about the release of the people detained in Guinea in exchange
for the release of the Guinean citizens.[96]

The United Nations Secretary-General held the view that the two
incidents should not be linked because "the detention of the Guinean
personalities was in contravention of international agreements to which the
Government of the Ivory Coast was a signatory, and had provoked international repercussions and even affected the responsibilities of the Secretary-
General" since he was required by General Assembly resolution 2202
(XXI) to consult urgently with Ambassador Achkar Marof, Chairman of
the Special Committee on the Policies of Apartheid, who was one of the
people detained.[97] However, he was willing to use his good offices in the

case of the nationals of the Ivory Coast arrested by Guinea. Accordingly, he sent José Rolz-Bennett, then Under-Secretary for Special Political Affairs, as his Personal Representative to the Presidents of Guinea and the Ivory Coast. Rolz-Bennett was joined later by I. S. Djermakoye, then Under-Secretary for the Department of Trusteeship and Non-Self Governing Territories. Since no progress was made after a month of intensive efforts by the Secretary-General's Personal Representatives, Guinea requested the Secretary-General to inscribe the matter on the agenda of the General Assembly or the Security Council. Accordingly, the Secretary-General requested inclusion of the question as an additional item on the agenda of the twenty-second session of the General Assembly.

In the meantime, the OAU Assembly at its fourth session requested President Tubman of Liberia, who had earlier offered his good offices, to renew his diplomatic efforts.[98] Before a decision was taken to include the problem in the General Assembly's agenda, the two Governments responded favorably to his appeals and agreed to release the detained nationals of each other.

The Guinea-Ivory Coast situation was initially handled by the United Nations rather than the OAU for the following reason. Guinea had made a strong case that the United Nations should be responsible for the release of the Guinean diplomats because the meeting from which they were returning was convened by the United Nations.[99] Having concluded that the Ivory Coast had violated section 11 of the Convention on the Privileges and Immunities of the United Nations and Article 40 of the Vienna Convention, the United Nations Secretary-General had asserted that, in the interest of the proper functioning of the United Nations, he would be "perfectly entitled to protest" on behalf of the Organization against such violations and "to seek to remedy the situation."[100] As the direct interest of the United Nations in the case of the detained Guinean citizens was obvious, the OAU itself, through its Administrative Secretary-General, encouraged intercession by the United Nations Secretary-General. As a matter of diplomacy, the United Nations Secretary-General decided to assist in seeking a simultaneous solution to the case of the Ivory Coast nationals detained in Guinea.

In view of the overriding interest of the United Nations in the matter, the OAU deferred to the role of the United Nations Secretary-General; only after an unsuccessful effort had been made by his representatives did it step in to encourage settlement through the good offices of an African statesman. As the OAU had hoped, a settlement was reached before the General Assembly started considering the question. Unfortunately, however, an acrimonious debate between Guinea and the Ivory Coast could not be avoided when the General Assembly and its Legal (Sixth) Committee considered the more general question of violation of treaties on diplomatic privileges and immunities.

In each of the West African cases discussed above, the problem had two dimensions: an incident constituting some form of reprisal; and an underlying political and ideological conflict expressing itself in subversive activities. The respective roles of the United Nations and the OAU and the nature of their collaboration in regard to the immediate problem were based on the extent to which each organization was directly affected by the incident. Thus, the impending boycott of the Accra summit conference of the OAU by Ghana's neighbors, being primarily an OAU affair, was handled by that organization itself; similarly with the case of the Guinean delegation to the OAU Council of Ministers detained in Ghana. On the other hand, the problem of the Guinean officials detained by the Ivory Coast, being of special concern to the United Nations, had to be handled first by the United Nations Secretary-General; only subsequently was it taken up by the OAU Assembly and mediated by an OAU-designated statesman.

Neither the OAU nor the United Nations was inclined to attempt reconciliation of the political and ideological differences, but both sought to discourage further subversive activities by issuing declarations that underlined the principle of non-intervention.

F. CONCLUSIONS

In the settlement of disputes and the adjustment of other differences between OAU Member States, relations between the United Nations and the OAU have largely conformed to the principle that a peaceful solution to all such problems should be sought through the OAU to the extent that it is able to provide effective diplomatic help. The nature and extent of the United Nations role in the solution of such problems would, therefore, depend upon the degree of success that the OAU may attain in solving or, at least, in containing those problems.

1. Application of the "Try OAU First" Principle

The "try OAU first" principle is based on Article 52(2) of the United Nations Charter which requires United Nations Member States, which are also members of a regional organization, to make every effort to achieve peaceful settlement of local disputes through such a regional organization before referring them to the Security Council. In none of the disputes or other differences between OAU Member States did the Security Council exercise its right to conduct an investigation under Article

34 of the United Nations Charter; to recommend, under Article 36, any method of adjustment other than the regional one; or to propose appropriate terms of settlement under Article 37. Similarly, in none of them did the General Assembly exercise its right to make recommendations under Articles 11 and 14. Whenever an OAU Member State tried to bring or did bring such a problem before the Security Council in accordance with Article 35 of the United Nations Charter, the OAU organs made it a point in their resolutions to emphasize the need to seek regional remedies first and sought to develop the principle in question in a way that could ensure for the OAU the widest possible jurisdiction. Thus, in considering the Algerian-Moroccan dispute the OAU Council of Ministers referred to "the imperative need" to settle all intra-OAU differences and expressed the determination of African States "always to seek" a peaceful solution within the framework of the OAU Charter. Later, when considering the Somali-Ethiopian dispute, the Council of Ministers re-emphasized the pre-eminence of the OAU within the African framework, but retracted from the wording used in the resolution on the Algerian-Moroccan case which seemed to imply a claim to exclusive jurisdiction for the OAU. By stating that a solution to all African disputes should "be sought first within the [OAU]" it seemed to claim for the OAU at most exclusive initial jurisdiction, that is, as a forum for the initial consideration of a case. But, in the Congo case, it sought again to widen OAU jurisdiction by refraining from implicitly suggesting a distinction between initial and ultimate responsibility. Moreover, by affirming that the OAU had responsibility and competence "to find peaceful solutions" not only to disputes between OAU Member States but also to other "problems" which affected peace and security in Africa, it sought to cover as wide an area as that indicated in Article 52(1) of the United Nations Charter (i.e., "such matters relating to the maintenance of international peace and security as are appropriate for regional action").

In view of this uneven development of an OAU approach to OAU-UN relationships, it was at the Security Council that the "try OAU first" principle was crystallized. Though, significantly, the Security Council confirmed that the OAU had competence to seek peaceful solutions not only to disputes among its Member States but also to other problems affecting peace and security in Africa, it introduced three qualifications to the principle of relationship as formulated by the OAU in the Congo case. First, what the Security Council expressed was a conviction that the OAU "should be able . . . to help find a peaceful solution" rather than, as indicated in the OAU resolution, a conviction that the OAU had competence "to find" such a solution. The wording seems to reflect the view that the Security Council should defer to the OAU machinery on pragmatic grounds (ability) rather than on formal jurisdictional grounds (competence). Secondly, by referring to OAU capability "to help find" rather than "to find" a solution, the Security Council stressed the auxiliary nature of the OAU role not only vis-à-vis the role of the parties to a dispute but also as regards the Council's function. Finally, by indicating that the capability of the OAU was to be conceived in the context of Article 52 of the United Nations Charter—there was no mention of this Article in the OAU resolution—the Security Council made it clear that the role of the OAU was to be understood in terms of its function as a forum for initial consideration of a dispute.

This formulation of the principle concerning OAU-UN relationships, which was fully acceptable to the OAU Member States, was supported by virtually all members of the Security Council, including most of its permanent members. France abstained on the relevant resolution because it believed that the application of the principle to the Congolese case would be contrary to the rule of non-intervention in domestic affairs; but it was not opposed to the "try OAU first" principle as such.[101] The favorable attitudes of the Republic of China, the United Kingdom, and the United States on this issue was largely consistent with their positions in regard to the respective roles of the United Nations and the Organization of American States (OAS) in disputes or situations arising in Latin America. What was new, and thus significant, was the attitude of the USSR which was in sharp contrast to its position regarding the handling of Latin American disputes or situations. The USSR's encouragement of peaceful settlement of disputes through the OAU was as emphatic as its advocacy of the rights and competence of the Security Council vis-à-vis the OAS. The favorable attitude of the Soviet Union toward regional autonomy in Africa can be explained partly by the fact that the OAU follows officially a policy of non-alignment with regard to all blocs and is not, unlike the OAS, subject to disproportionate influence of a rival major Power. It ought to be mentioned also that, evidently, the role to be played by the OAU under its Charter would remain within the limits of the peaceful settlement field, unlike that of the OAS which could possibly involve measures such as those stipulated in Chapter VII of the United Nations Charter, the application of which would require authorization from the Security Council.

In practice, the "try OAU first" principle has been applied by and large in three of the four categories of cases examined above—that is, in the boundary disputes, the situations of friction arising from internal conflicts, and the situations of friction in West Africa arising from political or ideological differences. The main exception, which will be examined later, pertains to the fourth category—situations arising from differences over the future of neighboring Non-Self-Governing Territories.

In two of the three boundary disputes—the Algerian-Moroccan case and that of Somalia and Ethiopia—the parties with territorial claims had apparently explored possibilities for convening the Security Council to consider their complaints, but they were encouraged by other African States, by certain permanent members of the Security Council, and, in one case, also by the United Nations Secretary-General to seek a solution within an African framework. In the third boundary dispute and in two of the three crises involving internal conflicts—the Somali-Kenyan dispute and the cases of Rwanda-Burundi and of Nigeria—no attempt seems to have been made by any of the States concerned or other interested States to convene the Security Council or to inscribe those questions on the agenda of the General Assembly. Even though the suffering of the victims of fighting in the Nigerian civil war had aroused widespread concern in countries beyond Africa, it was normally the deliberative organs of the OAU and, at a certain stage, also the Commonwealth Secretariat and the British Government, which were induced to provide diplomatic assistance.

Even the consideration of the Congo crisis by the Security Council was not an exception to the "try OAU first" principle. The Congo question was brought to the Security Council essentially because of the extracontinental factors in the crisis. In requesting a meeting of the Security Council, the African States were neither bypassing the OAU nor "appealing" a case from the OAU to the United Nations. Even the Congo which was not satisfied with the role being played by the OAU and its Ad Hoc Committee did not challenge the competence of the OAU to continue its efforts in regard to the intra-African aspects of the conflict. At the Security Council, the debate tended to focus more on extracontinental intervention than on friction between the Congo and other African States. Far from replacing the OAU in the quest for a solution to the crisis, the Security Council adopted a resolution that encouraged continuation of the OAU peace-making effort.

As regards the situations of friction in West Africa arising from basic political or ideological differences, in only the Guinea-Ivory Coast dispute, which was of particular interest to the United Nations, was there a distinct possibility of deliberations by an organ of the United Nations rather than of the OAU. However, when the matter was about to be considered by the General Assembly following the unsuccessful efforts of the Personal Representatives of the United Nations Secretary-General, the OAU Assembly, which happened to be in session, hastened to seek a solution within an African framework.

Only in the two cases of rival claims to neighboring Non-Self-Governing

Territories did the OAU Member States seem more inclined to utilize a United Nations deliberative organ than an organ of the OAU. Thus, while hardly mentioning in OAU meetings the need for reconciliation of the rival claims, they have generally supported the General Assembly's attempts in the Spanish Sahara case to draw Morocco and Mauritania into parallel consultations with the administering Power regarding a referendum—consultations which could conceivably lead to an eventual dialogue between the two African States. Some possible reasons for this apparent exception in the application of the "try OAU first" principle are, on the one hand, the tendency in the OAU to give lower priority to the issue of rival claims, as these are less significant as a source of tension than other fundamental disputes existing between the same African States; and, on the other hand, the tendency to subordinate the issue of claims to the more immediate problem of decolonization in the two Territories, a proper solution of which might hopefully obviate the need for reconciling the rival claims.

The "try OAU first" principle has been applied in regard to OAU relationships with the Security Council and the General Assembly, but not with the United Nations Secretary-General. The proceedings of the Security Council on the Congo have shown that the principle does not include the Secretary-General's role of watching developments in any dispute or situation, even while OAU organs were trying to find a solution. Realizing that the effectiveness of the OAU in the Congo crisis had hitherto been undermined by an ideological split among the African States, the members of the Security Council and at least half of the African States encouraged him to follow the situation closely, presumably to enable him to offer diplomatic assistance whenever necessary. In his Introduction to the Annual Report of the Secretary-General on the Work of the Organization, covering the period June 1970-June 1971, U Thant has explained the nature of his political role as follows:

> . . . in order to exercise his right under Article 99, the Secretary-General must necessarily have all the powers, including those of inquiry, to reach a reasoned and independent opinion on whether or not a particular matter may threaten international peace and security. He may also endeavor, through the exercise of good offices, to play a part in 'preventive diplomacy' designed to ensure that a matter does not become a threat to international peace and security.[102]

On some occasions, the United Nations Secretary-General himself has taken diplomatic initiatives before the OAU organs could meet to handle the problem, because he felt that it was his duty to be as helpful as possible in such situations. In the Ghana-Guinea case, he addressed an appeal and a suggestion to the parties concerned before the OAU Council of Ministers sent a mission. Sometimes he made appeals for a negotiated settlement even while the OAU was attempting to find a solution; such appeals were, however, regarded by the African States as a manifestation of moral support for OAU efforts and as a proper expression of the concern of the international community rather than as an indication of rivalry. Finally, where no prompt action could be taken by the OAU, as in the first phase of the Rwanda-Burundi situation, the United Nations Secretary-General responded promptly to the request for diplomatic and material assistance to reduce tension.

Where, as in the Guinea-Ivory Coast case, there was a special reason for requesting diplomatic assistance from the United Nations in the first instance but also the risk of an acrimonious ideological debate, the tendency of the African States has been to invite the United Nations Secretary-General rather than the Security Council or the General Assembly to provide diplomatic assistance.

Apart from the political aspect of the United Nations Secretary-General's role, which has been complementary to the role of the OAU, his efforts at organizing within the United Nations large-scale relief operations in conflict areas and at resettling refugees have served a vital need—a need which could hardly be met by the OAU but which contributed indirectly to its peace-making efforts.

It was mentioned in the introduction to this chapter that, barring exclusive jurisdiction for a regional organization or for the United Nations, both of which alternatives are obviously inconsistent with the United Nations Charter, the central issue in the consideration of the competence and responsibility of the United Nations and the OAU, respectively, is: whether, in practice, the OAU has assumed undisputed jurisdiction as a forum for the initial consideration of a dispute, while the Security Council considers the matter only if those initial efforts do not succeed; or, whether the Security Council exercises concurrent jurisdiction while the matter is being considered by the OAU. There seems to have been a marked tendency, both among African States and other Member States of the United Nations, to adopt the "try OAU first" approach on pragmatic grounds. In a legal sense, adoption of such an approach could not constitute recognition of any right of exclusive jurisdiction for the OAU; the right of the Security Council and of individual Member States to involve the United Nations organs at any stage of a dispute remains unimpaired under the provisions of the United Nations Charter. However, adoption of this approach would seem to indicate that as a matter of policy there would be no consideration by the Security Council until the OAU machinery has been fully tried. In this practical sense, the application of the "try

OAU first" principle would seem to create no jurisdictional conflict between the OAU and the United Nations.

At the same time, the United Nations Secretary-General would continue to exercise his function under Article 99 of the United Nations Charter. Not only would he be able to play a role complementary to that of the OAU but would also be able to follow developments that might eventually pose a threat to international peace and security; he may, if necessary, bring the crisis to the attention of the Security Council. Such a situation could possibly arise if he is convinced that the role being played by the OAU in a particular situation is not effective enough to remove such a threat.

2. Effectiveness of the OAU in Peaceful Settlement

In assessing the effectiveness of the OAU in handling differences between its Member States, it is necessary to distinguish between the normalization of relations and the final settlement of disputes. The main achievement of the OAU has been in regard to the former, where it was able to act as an effective instrument for reducing inter-State tension without necessarily solving the problems that caused tension.

Unless tension rises to a crisis stage and, normally, unless a Member State brings a complaint before the OAU, its organs tend to refrain from being involved in the search for a solution to the problem. As was mentioned before, this perhaps explains partly why the OAU has been reluctant to take an initiative in reconciling the rival claims of certain African States to neighboring Non-Self-Governing Territories. By its reluctance to go into such a problem, the OAU may be missing an opportunity to resolve situations that aggravate existing tension between those States as well as to facilitate United Nations efforts to help bring about decolonization of the Territories concerned.

In handling disputes or situations between its Member States, the OAU has utilized a combination of methods, both direct and indirect, with varying degrees of success. The direct methods which involved formal action by the OAU consisted mainly of: the establishment or reinforcement of norms for inter-State relations in regard to specific problems; the channeling of appeals to the States in dispute to reduce tension between them and to seek agreement through negotiation, bilaterally or with the help of a mediator; and the establishment of a mediation commission or the designation of an individual mediator. The indirect method is mainly that of providing a convenient environment for bilateral diplomatic contacts and for the development of mediatory initiatives on the part of African statesmen.

Let us first evaluate the application of the direct methods by the OAU While discouraging debates on the merits of the respective positions of the States in dispute and carefully avoiding the task of identifying the "guilty" party in a crisis, the OAU Assembly has been quite effective in enunciating principles to regulate different kinds of disputes or situations. For the boundary disputes, it adopted the principle that Member States should respect the borders existing on their achievement of national independence. As regards situations of tension arising from subversive activities by refugees or by political exiles, it has adopted the principle that the OAU will not tolerate any subversion against a Member State originating in other Member States or elsewhere and has endorsed the convention on refugee problems in Africa which requires States to prohibit subversive activities by refugees. Finally, it has elaborated the principle of respect for the sovereignty and territorial integrity of States in such a way as to prevent secession in any Member State. As declarations of the highest OAU organ. these principles are expected to inhibit African States from pursuing irredentist policies, from conducting, encouraging, or tolerating subversive activities, and from supporting secessionist movements against other OAU Member States.

The method of addressing appeals to States to normalize relations and to seek a peaceful solution to their differences through negotiation has been successful only in some cases. This method, used frequently by the Council of Ministers in its extraordinary as well as ordinary sessions, was helpful in bringing about a cease-fire and eventually a reduction of tension between Somalia and its two neighbors, but did not produce similar results in the Congo civil war. During the Nigerian crisis, the OAU Assembly itself appealed repeatedly for a cease-fire and for a peaceful solution of the problem, but its efforts produced no positive results.

On several occasions, the OAU sought to settle disputes or other differences through ad hoc mediation bodies. Although the OAU Charter had called for the establishment of a Commission of Mediation, Conciliation and Arbitration, this permanent machinery could be established only after a special Protocol was approved by the OAU Assembly in July 1964 and after the 21 members of the Commission were elected in October 1965. Even then the Commission remained idle, since neither the parties to a dispute nor the OAU deliberative organs were inclined to utilize its elaborate machinery. Instead, they continued to devise more flexible ad hoc bodies of varying sizes (ranging from eight to ten), levels of national representation (ranging from senior civil servants to Heads of State), and scope of responsibilities. The most successful were those composed of Heads of State and which had relatively easy tasks. Thus, the Ad Hoc Committee on the Congo mercenary problem, which consisted of the

Heads of State of ten countries in East and Central Africa, was able to bring about an agreement between the Congo (Zaire) and Rwanda on the expulsion of mercenaries from central Africa and to secure guarantees against their return. While the OAU mission of three Ministers to Guinea and Ghana had failed to secure the release of the detained Guinean diplomats, five influential Heads of State were able later to attain this objective.

On the other hand, the Ad Hoc Consultative Committee on Nigeria, though composed of six influential Heads of State, was unable to bring about reconciliation between the Nigerian Federal Government and "Biafra." Initially, its mandate was so limited—that is, merely to consult the Nigerian Federal Government in a manner that would help the cause of peace and unity in Nigeria—that it found it difficult at crucial moments to offer its good offices to the two sides. By the time it was able to overcome this difficulty, it became virtually impossible to attain meaningful negotiations in view of the expected military victory of the Federal Government, which in reality proved to be more remote and costly than had been envisaged.

The ten-member Ad Hoc Commission on the Congo, which had at least as difficult a task as the Ad Hoc Consultative Committee on Nigeria, failed completely in its mandate. Even though it was entrusted with the task of bringing about a cease-fire and a reconciliation between the ideologically opposed Congolese leaders as well as of normalizing relations between the Congo (Zaire) and its neighbors, it was organized just at the ministerial level, though under the chairmanship of a Prime Minister, and was unwisely composed mostly of States with strong partisan views.

The seven-member Ad Hoc Commission on the Algerian-Moroccan dispute, which had a less difficult task than the ad hoc bodies set up for the Congo and Nigeria, was partially successful in its mission. Composed of officials at or just below the ministerial rank, it was able to clarify the issues of the border dispute and to narrow down some areas of disagreement, once the two sides had implemented the agreement for a cease-fire and the withdrawal of troops brought about at Bamako with the help of two Heads of State. Its modest contribution seems to have facilitated progress in the bilateral negotiations which eventually brought about a final settlement.

In the mediating bodies created both to handle the immediate crisis and to solve the problems causing the crises, it appears that, irrespective of the variations in size, the chances of success have tended to improve with the inclusion of Heads of State as members of those bodies and also with the increase in the degree of impartiality of the team of mediators as a whole. In all cases, the role of the chairman was crucial; whatever positive results that were attained were due in large part to his special efforts.

In the Ad Hoc Commission on the Algerian-Moroccan dispute—the only body created to mediate only substantive issues of the dispute—it was felt that there was no need to have Heads of State act as mediators in the long and detailed negotiations; perhaps the Commission might have been able to make a greater contribution toward the final settlement had it been presided over by a prominent African statesman.

One of the most successful methods of conflict resolution among OAU Member States has been the designation of an individual Head of State by the OAU as sole intermediary in a dispute. The effectiveness of this method was amply demonstrated in the third phase of the Rwanda-Burundi situation and the Guinea-Ivory Coast case, which were resolved with the help of individual Heads of State from neighboring countries who enjoyed the confidence of the parties concerned.

If the designation of an individual mediator by the OAU has been a significant aspect of the direct role, the services given by individual statesmen upon their own initiative have been a major aspect of the indirect role of the OAU. The indirect role stems from the capacity of the OAU to serve as a forum and as a source of guiding principles. The OAU Assembly's sessions have provided a suitable environment for contact between leaders of States having a dispute and for the emergence of third-party initiatives. Either during the sessions or at other times, individual statesmen have taken such initiatives in the spirit of the OAU Charter; they have been able to exercise their good offices on several occasions, particularly in the conflicts between Algeria and Morocco, Somalia and Ethiopia, and Somalia and Kenya, as well as in some cases that were not brought before the OAU, such as the dispute between Chad and Sudan and that between Uganda and Tanzania.[103]

Another equally important feature of the indirect services of the OAU stemming from its capacity as a forum has to do with the opportunity given to a Member State to express its grievances publicly in order to direct African opinion against its adversary. Awareness of such a possibility seems to have exerted a restraining influence on Member States with the result that the lid has been put on some incipient disputes.

On the whole, both the direct and indirect roles of the OAU in peaceful settlement have been considerably successful in handling crisis situations; they have often helped in reducing tension and occasionally in solving disputes. However, these roles would need to be strengthened if possible before a dispute develops into a crisis and, if not, after the crisis has subsided. Some suggestions in this regard will be made in Chapter V.

Chapter IV
Relationships Regarding Colonial and
Racial Problems in Africa
A. INTRODUCTION

The main concern of this chapter is the relationship between the United Nations and the OAU in dealing with colonial questions and the problem of apartheid. There are three main aspects which bear upon the questions of compatibility and complementarity between the two organizations: United Nations responsibility versus OAU autonomy in the recommendation of collective measures;[1] OAU pressure to influence United Nations policies and to bring about further collaboration for more effective action; and the problem of reporting to the Security Council any measures planned or undertaken by the OAU. The first two aspcts will be examined in this chapter while the third will be discussed in Chapter V as part of the problem of co-ordination in the peace and security field.

The degree of autonomy enjoyed by a regional organization in taking collective measures is governed essentially by the provisions of Article 53 of the United Nations Charter, but Article 51 is also relevant. Article 53(1) states:

> The Security Council shall, where appropriate, utilize such regional arrangements or agencies for enforcement action under its authority. But no enforcement action shall be taken under regional arrangements or by regional agencies without the authorization of the Security Council. . . .

Article 51 was introduced at the San Francisco Conference not merely in order to preserve the exception to the prohibition of "the threat or use of force" by Member States "against the territorial integrity or political independence of any State . . ." (Article 2(4)) but also as a means of resolving a dilemma precipitated, on the one hand, by fears that Security Council authorization for effective regional action might be blocked by a veto in the Council and, on the other, by fears that the necessity of universality in this vital field—peace and security—might be undermined if too much latitude were given to regional organizations. This Article, whose concept of "collective self-defence" enables regional organizations or other groupings of States to take initial action against armed attack on their own responsibility, states:

> Nothing in the present Charter shall impair the inherent right of

individual or collective self-defence if an armed attack occurs against a Member of the United Nations, until the Security Council has taken measures necessary to maintain international peace and security. Measures taken by Members in the exercise of this right of self-defence shall be immediately reported to the Security Council and shall not in any way affect the authority and responsibility of the Security Council under the present Charter to take at any time such action as it deems necessary in order to maintain or restore international peace and security.

Thus while "enforcement action" by a regional organization requires Security Council authorization, "collective self-defence" in response to an "armed attack" need not have such authorization, but must be immediately reported to the Security Council. But since the Charter does not provide a definition of "enforcement action," the limit of regional authority under Article 53 remains unclear. The scope of the right of collective self-defense is also less than clear as it would depend upon the meaning given to "armed attack" as well as on other criteria of self-defense.

As regards "enforcement action," the main issues bearing upon the authority of a regional organization such as the OAU are the following:

   (i) whether the term refers to measures involving the use of force, as described in Article 42, as well as to the non-military measures enumerated in Article 41, namely, the severance of diplomatic and economic relations and the interruption of all forms of transport and communication with a State that threatens or breaks international peace and security;

  (ii) whether the term applies to non-mandatory measures as well as to mandatory measures;

 (iii) whether it encompasses such regional collective measures as material assistance to liberation movements for the purpose of restoring self-determination and independence.

The measures so far adopted by the OAU or taken within its framework against colonial or settler regimes include the following: urging Member States to sever diplomatic and economic relations and all forms of communication with those regimes; requesting Member States to provide moral and material assistance, including financial aid, military training, and transit facilities, to national liberation movements already fighting against those regimes; and providing co-ordinative services in both respects through the OAU Co-ordinating Committee for the Liberation of Africa and the Sanctions Bureau of the OAU secretariat. These measures have been taken neither upon the authorization nor with the encouragement of the Security Council. The possibility of any juridical conflict between any of these OAU measures and the purposes and principles of the United Nations Charter or the provisions of any specific Article would seem to arise if the answer to any of the foregoing questions is in the affirmative.

With regard to the first question—whether "enforcement action" refers both to military and non-military measures—the *travaux préparatoires* of the United Nations Conference on International Organization, while not providing a categorical answer, seem to support the view that the term was intended to apply to all measures that the Security Council would decide to take under both Articles 41 and 42.[2] In practice, some States, including the USSR,[3] have continued to support this broad interpretation of the term, while some others, including the U.K. and the U.S., have given the term a more restrictive interpretation which would exclude non-military measures that individual States could legally take in exercising their national sovereignty.[4] With regard to the latter argument, it would seem to follow that any State which did not wsih to join fellow members of a regional organization in taking any recommended non-military measures would remain free not to do so. In two cases involving this issue brought before the Security Council—the Dominican case (1960) and the Cuban case (1962)—the Council by majority vote expressed its unwillingness to question the competence of the Organization of American States (OAS) to take diplomatic and economic measures agreed upon among its members, thus lending substantial weight to the interpretation that such measures did not amount to "enforcement action."[5] The Security Council has not considered this issue in terms of the economic and diplomatic measures recommended by the OAU against recalcitrant colonial and settler regimes, but, as will be spelled out in subsequent sections, the vast majority of Member States in the General Assembly have tended to regard those measures as not requiring authorization from the Security Council.

As regards the second question—whether "enforcement action" under Article 53 refers to non-mandatory as well as mandatory regional measures—there seems to be some ground for the argument that measures based on recommendations are precluded. The argument is based mainly on a reasoning by analogy from the distinction drawn between Security Council measures that are obligatory and thus constitute "action" and measures that are mere recommendations of the Council or the General Assembly. Under Article 11(2) of the United Nations Charter, the General Assembly may make recommendations on any questions relating to the maintenance of international peace and security, except while the Security Council is exercising its function in respect of the same questions; but the Assembly is required to refer to the Council any such questions on which "action" is necessary. It has been argued in connection with the adoption of the Uniting for Peace resolution in 1950 that "action" referred to "enforcement action" which, in turn, meant mandatory action.[6] The international Court of Justice has expressed a similar opinion and has stated that the word "action" in Article 11(2)

> must mean such action as is solely within the province of the Security Council. It cannot refer to recommendations which the Security Council might make, for instance under Article 39, because the General Assembly under Article 11 has a comparable power.[7]

But the limitations of the analogy should be recognized in applying an interpretation concerning the relative powers of two organs of the same organization to define the relative powers of two separate organizations. Such recognition is particularly essential in spelling out the relative powers of regional organizations in taking measures involving the use of force. Under the Uniting for Peace resolution, the General Assembly would step in to recommend collective measures, including military action, in the case of a breach of the peace or an act of aggression, only after the Security Council had had an opportunity to take action and failed to do so, thereby ensuring the continued effectiveness of the United Nations to achieve its objective of peace and security. On the other hand, if a regional organization recommends the use of military force, other than for defense against armed attack, without Security Council authorization, it would probably be expanding its powers beyond the permissible limits of action by individual Members as sovereign States under the United Nations Charter, particularly the limits on non-use of force imposed by Article 2(4). It may raise serious doubts as to whether its action would be justified as legitimate collective self-defense or enforcement action. Thus it may be argued that insofar as the collective measures taken through a regional organization do not involve the threat or use of force against a State and are based on recommendations rather than on mandatory decisions, they would be within the discretionary powers of the individual States concerned and would, therefore, not be subject to the limitations stipulated in Article 53. The diplomatic and economic measures recommended by the OAU fall clearly under this category. As for the issue of the "use of force," the following paragraphs will provide some clarification.

Turning to the third question raised above—whether material assistance given to national liberation movements upon the recommendation and with the co-ordinative support of the OAU constitutes "enforcement action"— if the answer is in the affirmative, then the role of the OAU may have violated Article 53 for having been taken without Security Council authorization. If the answer is in the negative, would the OAU role violate any other provisions of the United Nations Charter? It would seem that such a role would be inconsistent with Article 2(4) only:

  (i) if it involves a "threat or use of force against the territorial integrity or political independence of any State" in situations which could not be justified as collective self-defense under Article 51;
  (ii) if it is "in any other manner inconsistent with the Purposes of the United Nations."

In the first place, a distinction should be made between the utilization by the OAU of the military forces of its Member States and the use of force by nationalist movements with financial and other indirect assistance from those States. As long as the OAU does not assume the former role in order to enforce a decision relating to the maintenance of international peace and security, it is difficult to see how its present indirect role could constitute "enforcement action" and thus reguire Security Council authorization. As regards the compatibility of this "facilitative" role of the OAU with the spirit of Article 2(4), it should again be stressed that no armed forces of OAU Members are being used "against the territorial integrity or political independence of any State." It is the national liberation movements that are using force in their own Territories with moral and material assistance from OAU Members and other States. It has been observed that such a struggle for freedom and independence and such external assistance could hardly be regarded as being inconsistent with Article 2(4), if they are seen in the light of the "Declaration on Principles of International Law concerning Friendly Relations and Co-operation among States in accordance with the Charter of the United Nations," adopted in October 1970 by the General Assembly (resolution 2625(XXV) and Annex). Under two of the seven principles elaborated—non-use of force and equal rights and self-determination of peoples—the Declaration proclaims that:

> Every State has the duty to refrain from any forcible action which deprives peoples . . . of their right to self-determination and freedom and independence.

It adds under the latter principle that:

> In their actions against, and resistance to, such forcible action in pursuit of the exercise of their right to self-determination, such peoples are entitled to seek and to receive support in accordance with the purposes and principles of the Charter.

Because of the addition of the last phrase as the result of a compromise, the exact meaning of the paragraph remains unclear. When the General Assembly adopted the Declaration by consensus, some delegations expressed reservations on the majority view concerning certain elaborations of the seven principles. One point of difference was the meaning of "support" for the struggle of oppressed dependent peoples. The majority of Member States did not exclude military support or armed assistance. Several States maintained that where the rights of peoples to self-determination, freedom, and independence are suppressed by force, the type of support being given by Governments to liberation movements directly or through organizations such as the OAU could not be subject to that aspect of the principle of non-use of force which prohibits "the organization of irregular forces or armed bands . . . for incursion into the territory of another State.[8] Some other States, including France, the U.K., the U.S.,[9] as well as Portugal and South Africa, stressed that such forms of assistance would not be permissible. In addition, Portugal reiterated its own version of self-determination which omitted the distinction made in the Declaration between the territory of a colony or other Non-Self-Governing Territory and that of a State administering it; in that light it welcomed the prohibition of external assistance to terrorist groups in another State.[10] For its part, South Africa stressed that, contrary to the implication in the Declaration, the inviolability of the territorial integrity of other States was absolute and thus should definitely apply where a State was regarded by other States as not possessing a government representing the whole people.[11]

If the moral and material support presently given to liberation movements within the OAU cannot be equated to the threat or use of force referred to in Article 2(4), then it would hardly be relevant whether the African States were exercising through the OAU their right of collective self-defense under Article 51.[12] This issue would seem to arise only if the armed forces of the OAU Member States were actually used to threaten or attack the territorial integrity or political independence of another State.

As will be spelled out in the cases examined below, most States consider the facilitative role of the OAU in the struggle against recalcitrant colonial and settler regimes as not being inconsistent with the purposes and principles of the United Nations. This role has in fact been widely recognized as legitimate and has been actively encouraged by the General Assembly and, in certain situations, by the Security Council.

At present, the real problem of relationship facing the United Nations and the OAU is, therefore, not so much the possibility of jurisdictional conflict but rather the difficulty of reconciling the policies of the Security Council and the OAU on how best to achieve their common objectives. Since the OAU exerts maximum pressure on the United Nations organs in order to influence them into adopting effective collective measures, there has emerged a major discrepancy between the scope of OAU demands and the Security Council responses, with important implications for the effectiveness of OAU-UN relations.

B. EFFORTS AGAINST COLONIALISM AND APARTHEID

By May 1963, when the OAU was established, the preoccupation of the United Nations with questions of colonialism and apartheid had come to include not only the promotion of moral, political, and legal rights of peoples in the Territories concerned but also the removal of any danger to international peace and security resulting from an absolute denial of those rights. The OAU Member States and their many supporters at the United Nations have tried to persuade the United Nations organs to move from the stage of adopting merely exhortative resolutions to that of imposing mandatory economic sanctions and, in certain cases, even the use of force. But the differences that have emerged among United Nations Member States, especially between the African States and some permanent members of the Security Council, as to the extent of the danger to peace and the measures required to remove such danger have tended to create points of incongruence in OAU's relations with the Security Council. The extent of agreement (or disagreement) over the two issues—imminence of the threat to peace and the collective measures required—varies from case to case.

The following sections will summarize the efforts made by the OAU and the United Nations in the past decade to solve the main colonial and racial problems in Africa and will evaluate their roles and relationships in each case in terms of the following indicators of extent of agreement on the two issues within the United Nations, especially between the "spokesmen" for the OAU and those members of the Security Council having the veto power:

(i) maximum agreement: a unanimous vote (no abstention) or a consensus without formal vote in the Security Council; a positive vote in the General Assembly by all except the recalcitrant Governments;

(ii) wide agreement: a positive vote in the Council, supported by a large majority, but with one or two permanent members abstaining; an Assembly vote, supported by more than two-thirds of those present, but without all large, middle, and small Powers joining the majority;

(iii) minimum agreement: a positive vote in the Council, with three or more permanent members abstaining; an Assembly vote that barely meets the constitutional requirements, but with unduly numerous abstentions;

(iv) no agreement: a negative vote in the Council or the Assembly.

OAU's relations with the General Assembly, which are characterized by full agreement between their resolutions in virtually all cases, will be discussed in less detail and mainly in the context of OAU-Security Council relations, except where the General Assembly has adopted resolutions with particularly relevant elements for contrast. Because of the voting strength of the African States and their supporters in the General Assembly, far-reaching resolutions reflecting the OAU position on colonial and racial issues have been adopted by the Assembly by votes far in excess of the required two-thirds majority. However, unanimity has been ruled out in all cases by the constant opposition of South Africa and Portugal, the frequent negative votes and occasional abstentions of France, the U.K., the U.S., and some of their allies, and the frequent abstentions of some non-Afro-Asian States. The far-reaching resolutions of the General Assembly often serve as the basis for many draft resolutions proposed in the Security Council by African States and their supporters on colonial issues—proposals which are eventually "watered down" considerably in order to avoid a veto by a permanent member of the Security Council. Since the resolutions of the General Assembly are similar in substance to those of the OAU, the discrepancy between the positions adopted by the Assembly and the Security Council is nearly as wide as that between the positions of the OAU and the Security Council. The implications of this discrepancy for relations between the United Nations as a whole and the OAU, and for the functioning of each organization, will be examined in the concluding section.

1. Main Cases of Decolonization

When the OAU was established, the first wave of decolonization in Africa had virtually run its course after having advanced with remarkable speed. The second wave, though given considerable impetus by the OAU, has been blocked by formidable obstacles raised by the remaining colonial and settler regimes. The colonial problems of greatest concern to both the United Nations and the OAU have been those relating to: the Portuguese-administered Territories which have now attained or are about to attain independence; Southern Rhodesia (Zimbabwe); and Namibia (South-West Africa). The following cases will focus mainly on the Territories in Southern Africa where the problem has been most serious; only an occasional reference will be made to Guinea-Bissau, which is in West Africa, since the issues involved were similar to those concerning the Portuguese-administered Territories in the South.

a. THE QUESTION OF PORTUGUESE-ADMINISTERED TERRITORIES

During the three years preceding the establishment of the OAU, the United Nations was already deeply concerned with the situation in the Territories under Portuguese administration, especially Angola. In December 1960, Portugal opposed the General Assembly's classification of the Portuguese-administered Territories as Non-Self-Governing[13] and refused to comply later with resolution 1514(XV)—the Declaration on the Granting of Independence to Colonial Countries and Peoples.

Early in 1961, an uprising by nationalists in Angola against Portuguese oppression induced Portugal to apply such strong repressive measures that, for the first time, the matter was brought by Liberia before the Security Council. Since the Security Council was unable to adopt a resolution when it met in March 1961, it was again convened late in May upon the request of 44 Afro-Asian States. This time it adopted resolution 163 (1961), without opposition but with France and the U.K. abstaining whereby it described the situation as one the continuation of which was "likely to endanger the maintenance of international peace and security" and called upon Portugal to desist from "the large-scale killings and the severely repressive measures." Upon considering detailed reports on the Portuguese-administered Territories, the General Assembly concluded in December 1962 that the colonial war in Angola and Portugal's non-compliance with United Nations resolutions constituted "a serious threat to international peace and security." It, therefore, recommended that (i) all Member States should deny Portugal any support which may be used by it to suppress Angolans and should in particular terminate arms supplies to that country; and that (ii) the Security Council should "take appropriate measures, including sanctions, to secure Portugal's compliance" with the United Nations resolutions.[14] The General Assembly thus set the stage for a vigorous campaign in the Security Council against Portuguese colonial wars in Africa.

One of the first acts of the OAU following its establishment in 1963 was to send a delegation of four African Foreign Ministers—from Liberia, Madagascar, Sierra Leone, and Tunisia, the last three of which were members of the United Nations Special Committee on decolonization—to draw the Security Council's attention to the explosive situation arising from Portugal's colonial policies and South Africa's policy of apartheid. At the request of the members of the African Group at the United Nations, the Security Council met in July and December 1963 to consider the situation in the Portuguese-administered Territories as a whole and determined in its July meeting that the situation was *"seriously disturbing peace and security in Africa"* (emphasis added). But in spite of the requests of the African States and the 1962 recommendations of the General Assembly for the application of appropriate measures, including sanctions, the Council was able to reach agreement only on the urgent need for negotiation about independence between Portugal and the political parties within and outside the Territories and on a recommendation to all States to prevent the sale and supply of arms and military equipment that would enable it to continue its repressive action (resolutions 180 (July 1963) and 183 (December 1963)). In view of Portugal's uncooperative attitude and the intensification of its repressive measures, the Security Council met again in November 1965 at the request of the African States. In addition to indicating the broader international implications of the situation—that it *"seriously disturbs international peace and security"* (emphasis added)—the Council recommended in resolution 218 (1965) the broadening of the arms embargo to include termination of the supply of any materials for the manufacture and maintenance of arms and ammunition by Portugal.

Although there were no negative votes on the three resolutions, the U.K. and the U.S. voted only for the resolution of December 1963 which did not specifically mention the implications to peace and security, while France abstained on all three. France remained unconvinced that the situation was at least a *potential* threat to peace in Africa and thus continued to question the jurisdiction of the Security Council in the matter.[15] However, the U.K. and the U.S. appeared to accept implicitly such assessment of the situation when they agreed in December 1963 to support the recommendation for an arms embargo. When they abstained in November 1965, they did not express any reservations on the paragraph referring to the disturbance to peace and security; by voting for an amendment that toned down the wording of the paragraph when they could have abstained on grounds of disagreement with the substance, they appeared to have tacitly accepted the assessment. Their abstention on the resolution as a whole seemed to be based mainly on their reservations about the resolution's emphasis on measures of pressure against Portugal instead of on the resumption of peaceful negotiations.[16]

Negotiation between Portugal and OAU Member States for a peaceful implementation of United Nations resolutions had already been tried and failed. In September 1963, in accordance with a general mandate given to him by the Security Council resolution of July 1963, the United Nations Secretary-General arranged a brief dialogue between Portugal and representatives of the African Group at the United Nations. But the talks, which were arranged through a personal representative of the Secretary-General to the Portuguese Government—Mr. G.K.J. Amachree, Under-Secretary for Trusteeship and Non-Self-Governing Territories—ended unsuccessfully because Portugal refused to accept the principle of self-determination as laid out in the resolutions of the General Assembly.[17]

It was upon the failure of those talks that the African Group resumed its emphasis on the need to apply diplomatic and economic measures— measures which the OAU, like the General Assembly, had been recommending since its establishment.[18] In November 1965, when the African States failed to win sufficient support in the Security Council for diplomatic and economic sanctions against Portugal, particularly from the permanent members of the Council (except for the USSR), they turned to the General Assembly. On 21 December 1965, the Assembly adopted resolution 2107(XX)—by a vote of 66 to 26, with 15 abstentions—which recommended not only such sanctions but also the provision of "moral and material support" by all States to the peoples of the Portuguese colonies" for the restoration of their inalienable rights."[19] Several of the States that voted against or abstained on the resolution explained that they were opposed to the paragraph calling for sanctions because they believed that the General Assembly, unlike the Security Council, did not have competence under the United Nations Charter to recommend such measures.[20] Of particular significance was the fact that, apart from the question of competence, three permanent members of the Security Council which had either voted against or abstained on the Assembly resolution—France, the U.K., and the U.S.—did not agree with the majority that the situation in the Portuguese-administered Territories was an actual threat to international peace and security and thus justified the application of any measures under Chapter VII of the United Nations Charter; nor did they agree with the assumption that Portugal was using in Africa military equipment received from its NATO allies.[21]

In the next two years, some progress was made in the General Assembly toward the wider acceptance of diplomatic and economic measures against Portugal,[22] but this was made possible largely by the substitution of a recommendation to the Security Council to apply sanctions for the Assembly's own call upon States to take such measures. Subsequently, the African States and their supporters sought to reduce further the margin of opposition and abstention but were able to do so only at the price of considerably "watering down" their proposals. Thus, in resolution 2507 (XXIV) of November 1969, the General Assembly was able to approach maximum agreement—97 votes in favor, 2 against (Portugal and South Africa), with 18 abstentions[23]—by avoiding reference to resolution 2107 (XX), by refraining from characterizing the situation as an actual threat to international peace and security, and by altering the Assembly's recommendation to the Security Council from a specific call for the imposition of diplomatic and economic sanctions to a more general one for the taking of effective steps in accordance with the relevant provisions of the United Nations Charter. Subsequent Assembly resolutions have reinstituted the stronger tone of the pre-1968 resolutions, but with no significant gain in support for sanctions. It ought to be mentioned that the Assembly's appeals to Member States and to organizations within the United Nations family to provide, in co-operation with the OAU, moral and material assistance to nationalist movements in Territories under Portuguese administration have been more widely supported than its calls for the application of economic sanctions.

For its part, the OAU sought since 1965 to ensure that its own Members should strictly apply diplomatic and economic sanctions against Portugal. In accordance with a 1964 resolution of the OAU Assembly, the OAU secretariat set up a bureau of sanctions to facilitate co-ordination of effort by compiling information on the application of sanctions by States inside and outside Africa.[24] But the efforts of this Bureau have had relatively little influence in bringing about a total African boycott; some of the States have not fully complied with the OAU recommendations and a few have strengthened their ties with Portugal. Such non-compliance appears to have undermined the prospect of obtaining significant co-operation from non-African States in carrying out measures against Portugal. A more significant form of pressure on Portugal has been OAU's encouragement and support of national liberation movement in Portuguese-administered Territories. Through its Co-ordination Committee for the Liberation of Africa, the OAU has continued to give modest financial and other material assistance to all such movements which were "in fact fighting" and has made arrangements for them to utilize the Territories of OAU Member States for military training and for transit.[25] The OAU has also encouraged all "freedom-loving countries" outside Africa to give moral and material assistance to the liberation movements. Since the effectiveness of the struggle against Portugal was being undermined by rivalry between factions of the liberation movements, especially in Angola, a major task of the Co-ordinating Committee was to bring about the formation of common fronts for each Territory. After several years of persistent effort by this Committee and by successive special commissions to reconcile the rival movements in Angola, significant progress is now being made to solve the problem of disunity. In Mozambique and Guinea-Bissau where the division in the ranks of the liberation movements was not as serious, the struggle for liberation was much more successful.

Far from weakening Portugal's determination to continue its colonial rule in the three Territories, the political, material, and strategic support organized by the OAU for the national liberation movement had in fact induced Portugal for several years to use its armed forces to conduct raids within the African countries bordering the Territories under its administration. The situation thus intermittently deteriorated from a potential threat to peace to an actual breach of peace across international boundaries. Initially, the OAU response was to encourage those of its Members subjected to Portuguese attacks to seek redress through the Security Council.

On several occasions since 1963, the Security Council considered complaints by Senegal, Guinea, and Zambia, and on all occasions it adopted, without any opposition, resolutions which condemned the incursions by Portuguese military forces into their respective territories and urgently called upon Portugal to desist from such actions. But only the earlier resolutions on Senegal (178 (1963) and 204 (1965)), which did not refer to the implications for peace and security, and those resolutions on Guinea, which did not specifically identify Portugal as the source of the attacks (289 (1970) and 295 (1971)), were adopted without any abstentions. On all the other resolutions, reservations were expressed usually for the reason that not enough evidence had been submitted to justify the Council's conclusions.[26] As was discussed in some detail in the preceding chapter, the Security Council also considered complaints of the Congo (Zaire) about Portuguese use of Angola and Cabinda as bases for the operations of European mercenaries designed to overthrow the Congolese Government and unanimously called upon Portugal to desist from supporting the mercenaries.[27] But none of these resolutions appear to have inhibited the recurrence of Portuguese attacks.

A new stage was reached in November 1970 when the Security Council met to consider Guinea's charges of armed attack by Portugal against Guinea's capital, using naval units, commando troops, and mercenaries. The operation was of such a magnitude that the Council treated it differently from previous attacks against African States which were regarded as isolated incidents and were, at best, characterized merely as potential threats to international peace. Upon ascertaining the facts of the situation through a special mission to Guinea, the Security Council declared in December that such armed attacks against African States and, indeed, the presence of Portuguese colonialism in Africa constituted *"a serious threat to the peace and security of independent African States"* (emphasis added). The Council went beyond condemning Portugal for its invasion of Guinea and warned it that in the event of any repetition of armed attacks against African States, the Council "shall immediately consider appropriate effective steps" in accordance with the relevant provisions of the United Nations Charter.[28] In addition, it requested Portugal to pay compensation for the damages and urged all States to refrain from providing Portugal with any military or material assistance enabling it to continue its repressive actions against the people under its domination and against African States. But the resolution was not acceptable to France, the U.K., the U.S., and Spain, which abstained because they believed that the resolution went beyond the findings of the special mission in the direction of defining the situation in a manner that could call for Security Council action under Chapter VII of the United Nations Charter.[29]

Even though the Security Council had declared Portuguese colonialism in Africa to be a serious threat to the peace and security of African States—and had thus defined the situation in a somewhat similar manner as had the OAU and the General Assembly—there still remained a wide gap between, on the one hand, the OAU request and the General Assembly recommendation for the application of mandatory diplomatic and economic sanctions against Portugal and, on the other, the Council's vague response about possible future steps. None of the more recent resolutions of the Security Council advanced beyond condemning Portuguese acts of violence and calling upon Portugal to stop them, and only occasionally were they supported by the U.K. and the U.S. while France supported only those concerning Senegal's complaints. These permanent members of the Security Council, whose active co-operation was necessary if any measures recommended by the Council were to be effective, continued to advocate peaceful negotiation with Portugal and seemed to be unwilling to support any measure going beyond a voluntary partial arms embargo involving only those types of arms and ammunition used by Portuguese troops in Africa. Thus, the gap between the OAU request (as endorsed by the General Assembly) and the courses of action fully acceptable to the three States was so wide that even in cases of armed incursions by Portugal into the territories of African States, the latter came to realize that they could not count on the Security Council alone for effective support.

It can be concluded that as it became clear by the end of 1965 that the Security Council was not likely to apply any sanctions against Portugal, the OAU began to intensify its own collective measures outside the framework of the Council. This tendency seemed to have been strengthened by the continued discrepancy in the Security Council between the trend toward a wide agreement as regards the existence of a danger to peace and security in Africa, if not beyond Africa, and the lack of agreement on appropriate measures. The OAU thus continued to co-ordinate its Members' diplomatic and economic boycott of Portugal and to encourage and support national liberation movements fighting against Portuguese authorities. Both measures received the endorsement of the General Assembly which itself began to urge all States to apply them; but they were never endorsed by the Security Council.

b. THE QUESTION OF SOUTHERN RHODESIA

In contrast to the case of the Portuguese-administered Territories, the question of Southern Rhodesia is one on which there has been, since December 1966, full agreement in the Security Council as regards the existence of a threat to international peace and security and a wide agreement as to the measures to be taken by international organizations. As the first situation where the Security Council was able to call for mandatory economic sanctions, and thus to respond favorably to a large part of the OAU request, it has been a test case of the capacity of the United Nations to take effective action in a crisis involving OAU Member States and colonial or settler regimes in Africa.

In Southern Rhodesia, less than a quarter of a million economically dominant European settlers exercise political power over almost five million Africans. Before the OAU was established, the Southern Rhodesian question had already been considered by the General Assembly which determined in 1962, upon the insistence of African and Asian States and on the basis of the recommendation of its Special Committee of Seventeen on decolonization (later Special Committee of Twenty-Four), that Southern Rhodesia was a Non-Self-Governing Territory within the meaning of Articles 73 and 74 of the United Nations Charter and General Assembly resolution 1514(XV).[30] The majority of Member States supported this position on the ground that the Territory was not a sovereign independent State and that the U.K., which retained certain residual powers in domestic affairs and more in foreign relations, was not exempted from the provisions of Article 73. But the U.K. rejected this decision arguing that Southern Rhodesia had acquired in 1923, and further in 1961, constitutional rights and privileges which "naturally and inevitably curtailed the powers and functions of the British Government" to such an extent that its status remained outside the conventional sphere of the Non-Self-Governing Territories under the Charter.[31]

It was against this background of British rejection of the competence of the United Nations on the question of Southern Rhodesia that in May 1963 the Summit Conference of Independent African States adopted a two-pronged policy:[32]

(i) to hold the U.K. fully responsible for the situation in Southern Rhodesia and urge it "not to transfer the powers and attributes of sovereignty to foreign minority governments imposed on African peoples by the use of force and under cover of racial legislation," and

(ii) to declare solemnly that "if power in Southern Rhodesia were to be usurped by a racial white minority government [the African

States] would lend their effective moral and practical support to any legitimate measures which the African nationalist leaders may devise . . . [to transfer it] to the African majority . . ."

In its first year, the OAU concentrated on the first line of policy and sought in vain through the Security Council to discourage the U.K. from transferring the military force of the defunct Central African Federation to Southern Rhodesia.[33] It began seriously assisting the African liberation movements in Southern Rhodesia only after the British Labor Party, which returned to power in October 1964 after thirteen years in opposition, gave a hint in April 1965 that the British Government intended to meet a unilateral declaration of independence (UDI) solely by economic sanctions, thus ruling out the use of military force. By then, the minority regime in Southern Rhodesia was campaigning for a mandate from the electorate to carry out UDI while intensifying its repressive measures against African nationalist leaders.

In these circumstances, following the failure of a Sub-Committee of the Special Committee of Twenty-Four to secure from the U.K. a firm guarantee against UDI, the Security Council was convened upon the request of the African States and adopted its first resolution on Southern Rhodesia. The resolution requested the U.K. to take all necessary action to prevent UDI and to grant independence only in accordance with the aspirations of the majority of the population and called upon the U.K. and all other Member States to deny recognition to any illegal entity that might be brought about through UDI. In contrast to the resolutions of the OAU organs and the General Assembly and its Special Committee, this resolution was quite moderate, yet it was adopted by only seven votes to none, with four abstentions.[34]

In October and early November 1965, the signs of an imminent UDI caused intensive diplomatic activity at both the OAU and the United Nations. The OAU Assembly warned that if UDI was not prevented it would reconsider all diplomatic and economic relations of African States with the U.K. and use all possible means including force to oppose UDI. It even established a Committee of Five to co-ordinate African efforts in this regard. At the same time, it requested the U.K. to suspend the 1961 Constitution of Southern Rhodesia and "to take all necessary steps including the use of armed force" in order to resume the administration of the Territory, to release all political prisoners, and to convene a constitutional conference.[35] Two weeks later the General Assembly incorporated these recommendations in its own resolution and for the first time endorsed the OAU's request to all States "to render moral and material help to the people of Zimbabwe [i.e., Southern

Rhodesia] in their struggle for freedom and independence . . ."[36] Though refraining from participating in the voting, the U.K. stated during the debate that it was determined to continue its policy of firm assurance, clear warning, and persistent negotiations as regards the minority regime but that it would not use force to suppress UDI—an approach stressed also by many of the States that voted against or abstained on the resolution.[37]

On 11 November 1965, the settler regime's act of declaring independence unilaterally induced the General Assembly to adopt almost unanimously a resolution which invited the U.K. to end the rebellion and requested the Security Council to consider the situation "as a matter of urgency."[38] Meeting the next day at the request not only of the African and Asian States but also of the U.K., the Security Council called upon all States not to recognize the "illegal racist minority regime" and to refrain from rendering any assistance to it.[39]

It is significant that in supporting the resolution the U.K. assumed a new position on the issue of jurisdiction concerning Southern Rhodesia. It explained that once UDI was declared, the only lawful Government of Southern Rhodesia was the British Government and that it was "clearly and unmistakably a British responsibility to re-establish the rule of law in Southern Rhodesia. . . ." It acknowledged the interest of the United Nations by stating that the attempt to establish in Africa an illegal regime based on minority rule was "a matter of world concern." Besides, as the British Foreign Secretary emphasized in his statement to the Security Council, if the measures that were being taken by the U.K. to end the rebellion were to have an impact, the goodwill, co-operation and active support of other Member States would be required.[40] Thus UDI brought the U.K. constitutional position somewhat closer to the position long held by the General Assembly that the U.K. was legally responsible for events in Southern Rhodesia and that the United Nations had a legitimate concern.[41] This change made it possible for the Security Council to assume the central role on this issue.

The relationship between the OAU and the United Nations expressed itself essentially in terms of an interplay between, on the one hand, the far-reaching demands of the African States, some of whom had been officially designated by the OAU to speak on its behalf, and, on the other, the more modest proposals for action set forth by the U.K. The African demands, which were fully reflected in the recommendations of the United Nations Special Committee of Twenty-Four, were usually endorsed with little modification by the General Assembly. At the Security Council, however, the more limited proposals of the U.K. provided the minimum common denominator on which any decision could be based if a veto was to be avoided.

The main OAU demands as reflected in the resolutions of the OAU Assembly and the United Nations General Assembly can be summarized as follows:[42]

   (i) to obtain from the U.K. effective measures, including the use of force, to end UDI and to prevent any supplies, including oil and petroleum products, from reaching Southern Rhodesia;

 (ii) to obtain in the Security Council the necessary enforcement action. starting with comprehensive mandatory sanctions under Chapter VII of the United Nations Charter;

(iii) to condemn Portugal and South Africa for their support to the illegal regime;

(iv) to condemn the activities of foreign financial and other interests which were supporting the illegal regime and to invite the States concerned to end such activities;

 (v) to condemn any arrangements between the U.K. and the illegal regime resulting in a transfer of authority to the latter contrary to the principle of universal suffrage; and

(vi) to secure moral and material support for the people of Southern Rhodesia in their struggle for independence.

At the level of the Security Council four major resolutions were adopted at different stages in the Rhodesian crisis, but none of them fully met African demands. On 20 November 1965, the Council adopted unanimously resolution 217 determining that the situation resulting from UDI was "extremely grave" and that its continuance in time would constitute "a threat to international peace and security"; calling upon the U.K. "to quell this rebellion" and to take all other appropriate measures to eliminate the authority of the minority regime; and calling upon all States not to recognize the illegal regime and to deny it any assistance or encouragement and, particularly,

> to desist from providing it with arms, equipment and material, and to do their utmost in order to break all economic relations with Southern Rhodesia, including an embargo on oil and petroleum products.

The Afro-Asian plea for mandatoy sanctions did not at this stage receive sufficient support in the Council. Significantly, however, the resolution contained a paragraph most pertinent to the relationship between the United Nations and the OAU. Paragraph 10 called upon the OAU

> to do all in its power to assist in the implementation of the . . .

resolution, in conformity with Chapter VIII of the Charter of the United Nations.

For the first time, the Security Council called upon the OAU to carry on diplomatic and economic sanctions by OAU Members against a political entity outside the membership of the OAU. One might argue that this constituted both an indirect endorsement of the measures that the OAU had already been taking against the minority regime in Southern Rhodesia and an authorization for the continuation of those measures.

With this encouragement, the Council of Ministers and the Committee of Five of the OAU set out to help implement the Security Council resolution on non-mandatory sanctions as well as the resolutions adopted by the OAU organs. The measures recommended by the resolutions of the sixth extraordinary session of the Council of Ministers (ECM/Res. 13(VI) and 14(VI)) were much more far-reaching than those contained in the Security Council resolution. They included: breaking off by OAU Members of all communications and commercial and financial connections with Southern Rhodesia; severance of diplomatic relations between African States and the U.K. in the event the latter failed to "crush the rebellion . . . and to prepare the way for majority rule in Rhodesia" before the 15th of December 1965; mobilization of military and other assistance for the liberation movements in Southern Rhodesia; and planning of military or other contributions by Member States to meet any emergency arising from an attack by Southern Rhodesia on a neighbouring OAU Member State.[43]

However, the limitations of the OAU role became apparent at the outset when Member States began to realize that they had over-committed themselves. The OAU hope of obtaining a change in British policy through the threat of breaking Member States' diplomatic relations with the U.K. vanished when only nine States[44] actually carried out their threat. After the Committee of Five had, with the help of military advisers from several African States, carefully examined the feasibility of mobilizing force against Southern Rhodesia, it became convinced that it would be unwise for the African States to take direct military action. The African States, most of whom had very small armies, realized how difficult it would be to organize an effective composite expeditionary force against Southern Rhodesia's small but highly modern military establishment which was increasing rapidly and was likely to be reinforced by Portuguese and South African troops. Against such odds, therefore, the OAU limited itself to increasing its support in funds, materials, and military training to the rival liberation movements, whose effectiveness was undermined by their failure to comply with OAU's recommendation for the formation of a common front. The African economic boycott of Southern Rho-

desia was equally ineffective since most African countries had little or
no trade with that country. Far from crippling the economy of Southern
Rhodesia, the economic measures taken by African and other States
against that country created such a hardship for neighboring Zambia,
whose economy was heavily dependent upon Southern Rhodesia, that the
OAU Council of Ministers decided to establish a Committee of Solidarity
for Zambia to co-ordinate assistance from African and other States. However, in spite of the efforts of this Committee and subsequent appeals by
the Security Council to all States to extend assistance to Zambia, the
Zambian Government has had to bear "all the costs with only a little help
from the British Government at the start of the emergency."[45]

Realizing the limitations of its own role, the OAU shifted to a policy
of diplomacy and persuasion toward the U.K. and began to concentrate
on efforts to induce the Security Council to take more effective action.
Some progress was made toward the enforcement of the recommended
sanctions when the Security Council, convened in April 1966 at the request of the U.K., called upon the British Government to prevent, "by the
use of force if necessary," the arrival at Beira (Mozambique) of tankers
reasonably believed to be carrying oil destined for Southern Rhodesia.[46]
But no further steps could be taken in the Council to expand the scope
of the measures against the illegal regime until the U.K. had exhausted
prospects for negotiation with that regime. Contrary to OAU's appeal to
the British Government to consult only with the African political parties,
the British Labor Government intensified its efforts in the second half
of 1966 to conclude an agreement with the illegal regime on the basis of
the following six principles, the first five of which were originally enunciated by the previous Conservative Government:[47]

  (i) unimpeded progress to majority rule, already enshrined in the 1961
      Constitution;
 (ii) no retrogressive amendment of the Constitution;
(iii) immediate improvement in the political status of the African popu-
      lation;
 (iv) progress toward ending racial discrimination;
  (v) acceptability of any proposal for independence to the people of
      Southern Rhodesia as a whole; and
 (vi) regardless of race, no oppression of majority by minority or of
      minority by majority.

During the talks between British Prime Minister Harold Wilson and Ian
Smith the leader of the illegal regime, aboard the HMS *Tiger* (2-3 December 1966), concrete proposals made by the former narrowed down the
differences between the two sides, but the jointly drafted proposals for

a settlement were rejected by the illegal regime.[48] On 20 December, Prime Minister Wilson informed the House of Commons that he was withdrawing all previous proposals for a settlement and accepted a principle which had long been advocated by OAU Member States: that there would be no "independence for Southern Rhodesia before majority rule" ("NIBMAR").

Upon the failure of the talks, the British Government also decided to recommend a major step in the Security Council: the imposition of mandatory sanctions upon Southern Rhodesia with regard to certain key products, under Chapter VII of the United Nations Charter. The Council met on 8 December upon the request of the U.K. and, after one week of intensive debate, decided for the first time to apply mandatory economic sanctions. Resolution 232 (1966), which was adopted without opposition but with four States abstaining (Bulgaria, France, Mali, and the USSR), determined that the situation in Southern Rhodesia constituted a threat to international peace and security and decided that all Member States of the United Nations "shall prevent":

(i) importation into their territories of nine vital exports of Southern Rhodesia—asbestos, iron ore, chrome, pig iron, sugar, tobacco, copper, meat and meat products, as well as hides, skins, and leather;

(ii) shipment in vessels or aircraft of their registration of any of those commodities;

(iii) any activities by their nationals or in their territories promoting the export of those commodities from Southern Rhodesia;

(iv) any activities by their nationals or in their territories promoting the sale or shipment to Southern Rhodesia of arms, ammunition, military and other aircraft, military and other motor vehicles, and equipment and materials for their manufacture and maintenance; and

(v) participation in any form in the supply of oil or oil products to Southern Rhodesia.

The resolution reminded Member States that failure by any of them to implement the resolution "shall constitute a violation of Article 25" of the United Nations Charter. Although some minor amendments proposed by the African States were incorporated in the final resolution, the OAU demands for comprehensive sanctions and other far-reaching measures failed to receive sufficient support in the Council.[49]

The climax was reached one and a half years later when the Security Council met upon the request of the African States, which had become gravely concerned over the failure of the selective mandatory sanctions and the deterioration of the situation in Southern Rhodesia. Although the OAU demands for military sanctions against the illegal regime were not met, the Council adopted on 29 May 1968 resolution 253 whereby it decided to apply mandatory sanctions with regard to all trade, investment, and travel and called upon Member States to report the measures taken by them to the United Nations Secretary-General. A committee was established to examine the Secretary-General's reports on the implementation of the resolution and to seek from any State Member of the United Nations or of the specialized agencies such further information regarding the trade of that State or any activities by its nationals or within its territory that may constitute an evasion of sanctions.[50] For the first time, the Council recognized, as did the General Assembly two and a half years earlier, the legitimacy of the struggle of the people of Southern Rhodesia to secure their rights of freedom and independence and urged Member States to render "moral and material assistance" to them in their struggle.

Thus, the long-standing plea of the OAU to the Security Council for mandatory comprehensive sanctions against Southern Rhodesia and for legitimization of the support being given to the liberation movements there were finally met. But the demand for more radical measures to end UDI remained to be realized.

It soon became quite clear from the reports of the Security Council's Committee that the measures being taken would not have the desired effect as long as there remained such extensive violations and evasions. To remedy this situation, the OAU Council of Ministers specifically instructed the African Group at the United Nations to intensify its efforts to attain through the Security Council: (i) interruption of all existing means of transportation and communication to and from Southern Rhodesia; (ii) extension of the mandatory sanctions to Portugal and South Africa; and (iii) use of military force by the U.K. against the rebel regime.[51] When the Security Council was convened in June 1969 by 60 African, Asian, and other States, the five Afro-Asian members of the Council submitted a joint draft resolution advocating the application of those measures, but their proposals failed to obtain the required majority.[52] When the Council met again in March 1970 in the wake of the illegal proclamation of a republican status for Southern Rhodesia by the rebel regime, it had before it resolution 2508(XXIV) of the General Assembly drawing its attention to the urgent necessity of applying the very same measures. But the proposal was again rejected by the Council—this time due to a veto by both the U.K. and the U.S., the latter casting its first negative vote in the Council. With the rejection also of a U.K. draft resolution—which called merely for non-recognition of the republican status—the Council became so deadlocked that the African States found it necessary to settle for a compromise resolution proposed by Finland. The proposal which was adopted as resolution 277 (1970) by a vote of 14 to none, with one abstention (Spain), made the withdrawal of consular and trade representatives in Southern Rhodesia mandatory and required Member States to interrupt any existing means of transportation to and from that Territory. But it exempted other means of communication and refrained from recommending measures against Portugal and South Africa or the use of British force against the illegal regime.

The compromise resolution marked the dead end of the consideration of the Southern Rhodesian question by the Security Council. With the accession of the British Conservative Party to power in June 1970, which had a commitment to the electorate to seek a "realistic basis" for a settlement of the Rhodesian problem, the OAU's concern became one of finding ways to discourage the conclusion of any agreement with the illegal regime and of preventing any erosion of the sanctions being taken. During 1971. a serious blow was given to the OAU position first when the U.S. Congress enacted a legislation which would allow the importation of Southern Rhodesian chrome and then when the U.K. concluded an agreement with the rebel regime proposing independance under a constitution that would theoretically permit gradual progress toward majority rule.[53] The "proposals for a settlement" were, however, contingent upon the fulfillment of the fifth of the six principles laid down by the U.K.—that the British Government would need to be satisfied that the proposals were "acceptable to the people of Rhodesia as a whole." It was for this purpose, as agreed with the rebel regime, that the British Government appointed a "Commission on Rhodesian Opinion," under the chairmanship of Lord Pearce, with a mandate to ascertain the response of all sections of the population of Southern Rhodesia and to report to the British Government. Many observers then expected that this Commission might merely whitewash the agreed formula and serve as a face-saving device for the British Government. Thus upon the insistence of the African States, the General Assembly rejected the "proposals for a settlement" indicating that it regarded them as "a flagrant violation of the inalienable rights of the African people of Zimbabwe to self-determination and independence."[54] However, the Security Council, because of a veto by the U.K., repeatedly failed to adopt Afro-Asian draft resolutions which would have rejected the "proposals for a settlement" and would have requested the U.K. not to transfer to the minority regime in Southern Rhodesia any powers of sovereignty.[55]

It was significant that, within Southern Rhodesia, the Pearce Commission carried out its mandate with such competence and impartiality that it became the focus for African nationalist activity through a newly formed

African National Council and facilitated the rejection of the proposals by the African majority and the acceptance by the British Government of the validity of this rejection. Thus it became clear that no appropriate solution could be found unless the interests of the African majority were fully represented in any efforts for a settlement. The British Government, therefore, decided that the next stage should be discussion within the Territory "between the racial groups" and that any further arrangements must be within the agreed principles. In the meantime, it decided that the status quo, including sanctions, should be preserved. In the United Nations, both the Security Council and the General Assembly have since been repeatedly calling upon States to take more effective measures to ensure full implementation of the sanctions and urging the U.S. to co-operate fully in this respect, particularly as regards its importation of chrome ore from Southern Rhodesia.[56]

A comparison of the handling of the question of Southern Rhodesia with that of the Territories under Portuguese administration shows that the discrepancy between the OAU demands and Security Council response has been much smaller in the former case than in the latter. In response to OAU demands and with the concurrence of the U.K., the Security Council has categorized the situation in Southern Rhodesia as a threat to international peace and security and has raised the vigor of the measures against the rebel regime from selective non-mandatory sanctions to comprehensive mandatory sanctions. Furthermore, it has confirmed the legitimacy of the support given by African and other States to the Southern Rhodesian struggle for freedom and has even encouraged United Nations Member States to increase their assistance to them. Even though the OAU requests for an extension of the sanctions to Portugal and South Africa and for the use of force by the U.K. have not been met by the Security Council, the approval by the latter of the less far-reaching measures have made it possible for the OAU to intensify its own measures of pressure against the rebel regime without provoking any arguments about the possibility of conflict between the two organizations.

C. THE QUESTION OF NAMIBIA (SOUTH WEST AFRICA)

In the case of Namibia (South West Africa), the level of agreement among United Nations Member States, including the permanent members of the Security Council, both as regards the imminence of a threat to peace and the need for taking collective measures, has been rather low until the beginning of 1972. In view of the special responsibility of the United Nations for the future of the Territory, the large discrepancy between the "ambitious" demands of the OAU and the "modest" steps taken so far by the Security Council seems to have been the cause of perhaps the greatest dissatisfaction for the OAU.

Namibia, or South West Africa as the Territory was called until June 1968, has been a problem for the United Nations since 1946, when South Africa, the Mandatory Power of the Territory under Article 22 of the Covenant of the League of Nations, refused to enter into a trusteeship agreement with the United Nations under Article 79 of the United Nations Charter, arguing that its responsibility for the Territory was only to the League of Nations. South Africa sought to ward off any criticism of its policies within the Territory by arguing that Article 2(1) of the Mandate had specifically entrusted it with full administrative and legislative powers over the Territory "as an integral part of the Union of South Africa."[57]

But the General Assembly could not accept South Africa's interpretation of the Mandate and the issue was submitted several times in the 1950s to the International Court of Justice for advisory opinion. The Court endorsed repeatedly the position of the General Assembly that the United Nations is the successor of the League of Nations in relation to the supervision of surviving mandates and that the mandate status persisted and continued to govern the rights and duties of South Africa as Mandatory.[58] But since South Africa kept ignoring those opinions, contending that they were political rather than legal in character, two African States which were members of the League of Nations—Ethiopia and Liberia—initiated in 1960 a litigation against South Africa on the ground that the latter had consistently violated the terms of the Mandate as a result of the application of the policy of apartheid in the Territory. They did so in response to a decision of the 1960 Summit Conference of Independent African States and with financial help from all those States.

The juridical phase of the problem came to an end on 18 July 1966 when the International Court of Justice dismissed the case of South West Africa by the narrowest possible majority—a 7 to 7 tie decided by the casting vote of the President. It ruled that the plaintiffs, Ethiopia and Liberia, "could not be considered to have established any legal right or interest appertaining to them in the subject-matter of [their] . . . claims."[59] By declining to give effect to the claim of the African States, the Court frustrated not only their expectation of a restatement of its earlier advisory opinions in binding form but also their hope for a binding instruction to South Africa to cease forthwith the alleged violations of the terms of the Mandate—especially the introduction of apartheid into South West Africa contrary to the Mandatory's obligation to promote the well-being of the inhabitants.[60] In response, the OAU began a campaign through the African Group at the United Nations to find a political solution to the problem.

On 27 October 1966, as a result of the intensive efforts of the African and Asian States, the General Assembly adopted resolution 2145 (XXI) which terminated South Africa's mandate and entrusted the United Nations with direct responsibility for the administration of South West Africa to enable the people to achieve independence.[61] A 14-member Ad Hoc Committee was established "to recommend practical means by which South West Africa should be administered."

Since the Ad Hoc Committee comprised a cross section of the United Nations membership,[62] an examination of the various proposals made within the Committee helps to reveal the contrasting attitudes of the different groups toward the respective roles of the United Nations and the OAU with regard to South West Africa. On the one hand, the USSR proposed that the General Assembly should confer wide powers on the OAU, in its capacity as a regional organization, so that the latter could help the national liberation movements in the Territory to organize elections. The OAU was to inform the United Nations of the steps taken to achieve those aims and indicate the steps which it considered the United Nations might take to implement its decision on the Territory. The Soviet Union, therefore, recommended an unprecedented delegation of power to the OAU and an unclear role for the United Nations in the expulsion of South African authorities from South West Africa. Together with Czechoslovakia, it opposed the idea of establishing a United Nations body to assume direct administrative responsibility in the Territory.[63] But this proposal was unacceptable to the majority which maintained that it was the responsibility of the United Nations to perform this difficult task, a task which would in any case be beyond the limited capabilities of the OAU.

In sharp contrast to the Soviet proposal, the four African members of the Ad Hoc Committee—Ethiopia, Nigeria, Senegal, and the UAR (Egypt)—acting under directives from the African Group, submitted with the concurrence of Pakistan and Finland a proposal for the creation of a United Nations Council for South West Africa. The new body would administer the Territory with the assistance of a Commissioner in order to prepare the people for independence. It would have at its disposal a United Nations police force for the maintenance of law and order. Any action by South Africa which frustrated or obstructed its task would be regarded as an act of aggression against the people and the territorial integrity of South West Africa, which would call for enforcement action by the Security Council under Chapter VII of the United Nations Charter. Solution to the South West African problem was, therefore, to be sought exclusively through the United Nations.[64]

But the three Western Powers in the Committee—Canada, Italy, and the U.S.—though emphasizing the special responsibility of the United Nations could not support the establishment of a provisional United Nations administration in the Territory. Instead, they proposed that the General Assembly should appoint a three-member Council and a Special Representative for South West Africa which would perform the following functions: survey the economic and political situation in the Territory; establish all contacts which the Special Representative would consider necessary; consult with all representative elements about the establishment of a nucleus of self-government; and determine the necessary conditions that would enable the people to achieve self-determination and independence. Any form of alien administration of the Territory was to be ruled out.[65]

In an effort to bring about a compromise, the two Latin-American members of the Committee, Chile and Mexico, together with Japan proposed a plan resembling the six-Power proposal, but without any mention of an international police force or enforcement action by the Security Council.[66] But its emphasis on consultations with South Africa was not acceptable to the majority.

Since no agreement could be reached in the Ad Hoc Committee, all four proposals were referred to the fifth special session of the General Assembly. The six-Power proposal, which had already been endorsed by the OAU Council of Ministers,[67] was accepted by the General Assembly with minor modifications. It was adopted as resolution 2248(S-V) by a vote of 85 to 2 (Portugal and South Africa), with 30 abstentions.[68] Although virtually all of the African, Asian, and Latin-American States voted in favor, most of the States that were capable of exerting some influence on South Africa were among those abstaining, thus casting some doubt upon the effectiveness of the envisaged United Nations Council for South West Africa.

A problem of immediate concern for the Council for South West Africa was the action being taken by South Africa to implement the proposals of its 1964 Odendaal Commission which recommended transfer of the main legislative and administrative powers from the territorial government in South West Africa to the South African Government and for the creation of ethnic-based separate "homelands" with nominal self-government for the non-white population. This action involving forcible relocation of large numbers of people was accompanied by the arrest and sentencing of several South West Africans alleged to have participated in guerrilla activities in Ovamboland, the area designated to become the first "homeland."[69] South Africa ignored the repeated demands of the General Assembly to desist from applying its new policy and to release immediately the prisoners, in spite of the Security Council's warning that unless the prisoners were promptly released the Council would urgently meet "to determine upon effective steps or measures in conformity with the relevant provisions of the Charter . . ." (resolution 246 (1968)).

The demand of the OAU for effective United Nations measures became increasingly intensive when, in February 1968, South Africa sentenced to death 33 of the 37 prisoners on charges of terrorism and, two months later, frustrated an attempt of the Council for South West Africa to enter the Territory. On 11 June 1968, the General Assembly adopted resolution 2372(XXII), which, in addition to renaming the Territory "Namibia," declared that the continued occupation of the Territory by South Africa "constitute[d] a grave threat to international peace and security" and recommended to the Security Council urgently "to take effective measures in accordance with the appropriate provisions of the Charter . . . to ensure the immediate removal of the South African presence" from the Territory. The resolution also called upon all States "to take effective economic and other measures" against South Africa.

It was not until March 1969 that the Security Council responded more fully by addressing itself to all aspects of the problem and then adopting resolution 264 (1969) (by a vote of 13 to 0, with France and the U.K. abstaining) whereby it recognized not only the termination of the Mandate but also the fact that the United Nations had assumed direct responsibility for the Territory until independence. Responding to the long-standing requests of the OAU, the Security Council called upon South Africa to withdraw from the Territory and decided that, in the event of refusal by the latter to comply with the resolution, the Council would "meet immediately to determine upon *necessary steps or measures* in accordance with the relevant provision of the Charter . . ." (emphasis added). France and the U.K. abstained partly because they questioned the legality and wisdom of the General Assembly decision to withdraw unilaterally the Mandate from South Africa and to assume the task of administering the Territory. They stressed that the United Nations, as heir to the League of Nations could not, in matters concerning the Mandate, overstep the authority invested in the League. Both also felt that it was unwise for the Security Council to continue the course adopted by the General Assembly and to adopt resolutions which were bound to remain ineffective.[70] Five months later, the Security Council met again to consider South Africa's refusal to co-operate and adopted on 12 August its strongest resolution on Namibia, resolution 269 (1969), by a vote of 11 to 0, with 4 abstentions (Finland, France, the U.K., and the U.S.). It declared that the South African occupation of the Territory "constitute[d] an aggressive encroachment on the authority of the United Nations" and a violation of the territorial integrity of Namibia and decided that, if South Africa failed to withdraw from the Territory before 4 October 1969, the Council would "meet immediately to determine upon effective measures in accordance with the appropriate provisions of the relevant chapters of the United Nations Charter." In addition, the Council recognized the *legitimacy of the struggle of the Namibian people* against foreign occupation and requested all States to increase their *moral and material assistance* (emphasis added). Although, the resolution does not specifically refer to Chapter VII of the Charter, as has been persistently requested by the OAU, the taking of measures under that Chapter seems to be implied. The U.K. and the U.S. indicated that they could not agree to any commitments under Chapter VII against South Africa,[71] and France maintained that the United Nations must take a realistic view of the situation and must suit its actions to its own capabilities.[72] Finland, the fourth abstaining State, expressed the view that since it was obvious that agreement could not be reached on a proposal to resort to enforcement action because of lack of support from all permanent members of the Council, the Council should adopt a course based on the existing area of agreement—one that would be backed by the full weight of the Council's undivided authority.[73]

However, even though South Africa has continued to defy the Security Council's decision beyond the October 1969 deadline, the Security Council has been unable for lack of agreement to take any measures against South Africa. In its meeting of January 1970, it merely established an Ad Hoc Sub-Committee to recommend ways and means by which the relevant resolutions of the Council can be effectively implemented. Six months later, in accordance with the recommendation of the Ad Hoc Sub-Committee, it decided to request the International Court of Justice to give an advisory opinion on the legal consequences for other States of the continued presence of South Africa in Namibia. At the same time it called upon all States to terminate existing diplomatic, consular, and other relations with South Africa so far as these apply to Namibia. However, even though these resolutions[74] contain none of the strong language used in the Security Council resolution of August 1969, France and the U.K. continued to abstain. From the OAU standpoint, therefore, there was a slight retrogression in the position of the Security Council concerning Namibia without a corresponding increase in the number of favorable votes in the Council.[75]

Although there was little enthusiasm among the OAU Members for the Security Council's request for an advisory opinion of the International Court of Justice—they had reservations due to their bitter disappointment over the 1966 judgment on the South West Africa case—the OAU decided to take a new offensive in the Security Council when the Court delivered the following opinion on 21 June 1971:

(1) that, the continued presence of South Africa in Namibia being

illegal, South Africa is under obligation to withdraw its administration from Namibia immediately and thus put an end to its
occupation of the Territory;

(2) that States Members of the United Nations are under obligation
to recognize the illegality of South Africa's presence in Namibia
and the invalidity of its acts on behalf of or concerning Namibia,
and to refrain from any acts and in particular any dealings with
the Government of South Africa implying recognition of the
legality of, or lending support or assistance to, such presence and
administration;

(3) that it is incumbent upon States which are not Members of the
United Nations to give assistance, within the scope of subpara-
graph (2) above, in the action which has been taken by the
United Nations with regard to Namibia.[76]

The eighth session of the OAU Assembly welcomed the advisory opinion
and urged the African Group at the United Nations to request an urgent
meeting of the Security Council to consider ways and means of implementing past resolutions of the United Nations organs in the light of the
legal obligations referred to in the Court's advisory opinion. In order to
make a maximum impact on the proceedings of the Security Council, the
OAU Assembly dispatched to the September/October session of the
Security Council on Namibia a delegation composed of its Chairman,
President Ould Daddah of Mauritania, and the Foreign Ministers of
Chad, Ethiopia, Liberia, Nigeria, and Sudan.[77] Although there was not
sufficient support in the Council for the OAU's request for the application
of the provisions of Chapter VII of the United Nations Charter, the Council adopted an Afro-Asian draft resolution whereby it endorsed the Court's
advisory opinion and declared that any further refusal by South Africa to
withdraw from Namibia "could create conditions detrimental to the maintenance of peace and security in the region." In addition, it requested its
Ad Hoc Committee on Namibia to review and report on all treaties and
agreements with South Africa which were contrary to the provisions of
the resolutions calling upon all States to refrain from any relationships
implying recognition of South African authority over the Territory. But
France and the U.K. abstained once again, indicating that they were not
persuaded by the reasoning advanced in the Court's advisory opinion that
the General Assembly's resolution terminating the Mandate had any validity and could not, therefore, support the provisions of the draft resolution
before the Council.[78] For them, the appropriate course would be to call
upon South Africa to fulfill its obligation to negotiate in good faith with
the United Nations for the establishment of an international regime enab-

ling the people of Namibia to exercise their right of self-determination. They felt that it was by dialogue rather than confrontation that progress could be made in promoting the interests of the Namibians and safeguarding the prestige of the United Nations.[79] Accordingly, France suggested that the Security Council should give careful attention to the appeal of the OAU Chairman for an initiative by the Council with the assistance of the Secretary-General and should respond by inviting South Africa to get in touch with the Secretary-General in order to negotiate an agreement on the setting up of a provisional international regime to enable the people of the Territory to exercise its right of self-determination.[80] The essence of this idea was taken up by other delegations and was subsequently presented by Argentina in the form of a draft resolution. Since South Africa had indicated its readiness to invite the Secretary-General to visit the Territory, the question remained whether the idea would be acceptable to the spokesmen of the OAU and their supporters at the Security Council.

When the Security Council met in Addis Ababa, Ethiopia, from 28 January to 4 February 1972, in response to a request of the OAU Council of Ministers for the holding of a special session on African questions in an African capital, the new approach was adopted concurrently with a draft resolution sponsored by OAU Member States and their supporters. Upon the initiative of Argentina, the Security Council adopted, by a vote of 14 to 0, with the People's Republic of China not participating in the voting, resolution 309 (1972) whereby it invited the Secretary-General, in consultation and close co-operation with the representatives of Argentina, Somalia, and Yugoslavia,

> . . . to initiate as soon as possible contacts with all parties concerned, with a view to establishing the necessary conditions so as to enable the people of Namibia, freely and with strict regard to the principle of human equality, to exercise their right of self-determination and independence, in accordance with the Charter of the United Nations . . .

and it called upon South Africa to co-operate fully with the Secretary-General. Only China was unable to support the proposal since it felt that the draft resolution did not envisage immediate independence for Namibia, free from any outside interference. Naturally, France and the U.K. gave the resolution strong support since it conformed with the approach that they had been advocating. The OAU Member States decided to support it apparently because they believed that if unanimity could be attained, a diplomatic offensive by the Secretary-General under a mandate of the Council would be worth trying. The fact that a new Secretary-General, Kurt Waldheim, had come upon the scene may have provided an additional impetus to try the new approach; if his efforts failed to produce positive results, the experience might at least serve to clear the ground for an eventual intervention by the Council. In addition, they considered the resolution to be complementary to another resolution sponsored by the three African members of the Security Council and Yugoslavia. The latter resolution, which contained some provisions that went even beyond the Council's previous resolutions, was adopted as resolution 310 (1972) by a vote of 13 to 0, with 2 abstentions (France and the U.K.). In addition to declaring that the defiant attitude of South Africa "undermines the authority of the United Nations," this resolution states that the *continued occupation* of Namibia *"creates conditions detrimental to the maintenance of peace and security in the region"* (emphasis added) and that, in the event of further non-compliance by South Africa, the Security Council would meet immediately to determine upon "effective steps or measures." However, unlike the resolution of October 1969, it did not include a provision calling upon all States to increase their moral and material support to Namibians in their struggle against South African occupation.

The proceedings of the Addis Ababa session of the Security Council on Namibia marked a considerable progress in the sense that the spokesmen for the OAU found common ground with France and the U.K. in trying out a new approach to the problem—one that would give priority to methods of peaceful settlement over those of confrontation. This approach involved consultations with the Namibian people as well as negotiations with South Africa for the purpose of creating the necessary conditions for self-determination and independence of Namibia.

In accordance with his mandate from the Security Council to initiate contacts in close collaboration with the Group of Three of the Council, the Secretary-General visited Africa and Namibia from 6 to 10 March 1972 and had extensive discussions with the Prime Minister and Foreign Minister of South Africa and representatives of ethnic and political groups in Namibia. The Secretary-General's visit and subsequent consultations by his Special Representative, Alfred M. Escher, have clearly confirmed that

> the overwhelming majority of the opinions consulted . . . were in favour of the immediate abolition of the 'homelands' policy, withdrawal of the South African administration from the Territory, Namibia's accession to national independence and the preservation of its territorial integrity. . . .[81]

However, his contacts with the South African Government—personally, through his Representative and through diplomatic channels—have not produced "complete and unequivocal clarification of South Africa's policy" in regard to self-determination and independence for Namibia. While expressing an intention to respect fully the wishes of the whole population of the Territory and not to impose any constitutional system, South Africa has continued to carry out its "homelands" policy. Far from contemplating immediate withdrawal from the Territory, it has indicated that, on the basis of "present developments," the population as a whole might need as long as ten years to be ready to exercise its right to self-determination. In view of the meager progress made in response to his intensive efforts, the Secretary-General has concluded that should the Security Council decide to renew his mandate for the fourth time, it should bear in mind that "time and protracted discussions would be required if any progress is to be achieved."[82] The fact that as the contacts were going on South Africa had officially proclaimed two "homelands" (Ovamboland and Kavangoland) as "self-governing areas" and that it had created an "advisory council" for the Territory, predominantly comprising members of the "homelands" administrations and excluding representatives of Namibian political parties, has convinced not only OAU Members but also several other States that further continuation of those contacts might be detrimental to the interests of the Namibian people. Since they have seriously questioned the good faith of South Africa in the "dialogue" with the Secretary-General, they have once again reverted to methods of "confrontation." Accordingly, the OAU Assembly as well as the United Nations Council for Namibia and the Special Committee of Twenty-Four have urged the Security Council to terminate those contacts and to adopt effective measures to secure South Africa's withdrawal from Namibia.[83]

2. The Problem of Apartheid

For the OAU and for the majority of States in the General Assembly, the solution to the problem of Namibia depends upon the determination of Member States to impose economic sanctions against South Africa. In their view, such action can be further justified in terms of the need to stop South Africa from undermining the effectiveness of the economic sanctions against Southern Rhodesia as well as the need to remove the danger to international peace and security posed by South Africa's policy of apartheid which is spreading beyond its borders. As in the case of the Portuguese-administered Territories, the situation arising from apartheid is one on which an agreement has been reached among the majority of Member States as to the imminence of the danger that it poses for international peace and security, while there is much less agreement on the required collective measures.

Although the problem of South Africa's racial policies has been considered by the General Assembly, in one form or another, since 1946, it was only after the Sharpeville Incident of 1960—the large-scale shooting of peaceful anti-apartheid demonstrators—that its implications for international peace and security have become recognized by the United Nations. In April 1960, three years before the establishment of the OAU, the Security Council met at the request of the African and Asian States and adopted resolution 134 (1960) (by a vote of 9 to 0, with France and the U.K. abstaining) declaring that the situation in South Africa "is one that has led to international friction and if continued might endanger international peace and security." It was then that the Security Council itself overrode for the first time South Africa's arguments that its apartheid policy was a matter of domestic jurisdiction.

Since then the goal of the African States has been to persuade the Security Council to define the situation, even in the absence of further tragic shootings, as constituting a threat to international peace and security and, consequently, to apply sanctions under Chapter VII of the United Nations Charter. In November 1962, the General Assembly adopted resolutions 1761(XVII) (by a vote of 67 to 16, with 23 abstentions),[84] which closely resembled one adopted by the Conference of Independent African States, held in June 1960.[85] The resolution requested Member States, separately or collectively, to apply diplomatic and economic sanctions as well as an arms embargo against South Africa. It also established a Special Committee to keep the apartheid policies of South Africa under review. Upon the establishment of the OAU, an early meeting of the Security Council was requested by the African Group at the United Nations with the hope that the Council would apply the same measures as those recommended by the General Assembly.

The Security Council met twice in 1963 and once in 1964 to consider the situation arising from apartheid but was not reconvened until 1970 on this problem, partly because the main preoccupation had shifted during 1965/1966 to Southern Rhodesia and South West Africa.

At the Security Council, in August 1963, the non-permanent members from Africa and a delegation of four African Foreign Ministers from the OAU sought not only to ensure that the Council would call upon the South African Government to abandon its policy of apartheid and release all political prisoners—demands which could easily win wide support among the permanent members—but also to ensure that the Council would call upon all States to take the following measures against the recalcitrant Government:

    (i) an arms embargo, including a halt of all assistance to South Africa's growing armaments industry;
    (ii) severance of diplomatic, consular, and other official relations with South Africa;

(iii) comprehensive mandatory economic sanctions, including cut-off of all transport and communications.

But the OAU delegation was able to win support from the majority of the members (France and the U.K. abstained) only for a resolution calling upon all States to stop the sale and shipment of arms, ammunitions, and military vehicles to South Africa (resolution 181 (1963)),[86] a non-mandatory ban which was expanded in December 1963 to include equipment and materials for the manufacture and maintenance of armaments (resolution 182 (1963)).[87] Resolution 182, which was adopted unanimously, reaffirmed that the situation was *"seriously disturbing international peace and security,"* but rather than calling for diplomatic and economic sanctions, it recommended the establishment of an expert group to examine peaceful methods for solving the South African problem (emphasis added).

When the Security Council met again in June 1964, the most it could do—apart from endorsing the main conclusion of the Expert Group that "all the people of South Africa should be brought into consultation and should thus be enabled to decide the future of their country at the national level"—was to establish an expert committee consisting of the Security Council members[88] to undertake a technical and practical study of the feasibility, effectiveness, and implications of measures which could be appropriately taken by the Council under the United Nations Charter.[89] In February 1965, the Expert Committee reported that it had been unable to reach full agreement. The majority in the Committee—Bolivia, Brazil, the Republic of China, Norway, the U.K., and the U.S.—concluded that while South Africa would not be readily susceptible to economic measures, it was not immune to damage from such measures. The degree of effectiveness of economic measures would, according to them, depend directly on the universality of application and on the manner and duration of enforcement. On the other hand, the minority—Ivory Coast, Morocco, Czechoslovakia, and the USSR—maintained that sanctions of an economic and political nature against South Africa would unquestionably be feasible and would induce the South African authorities to abandon their racial policies.[90] The report of the Expert Committee was never considered by the Security Council; apparently, the Committee's failure to recommend common conclusions had undermined any chances for a consensus at the level of the Council.

Later that year, the OAU Assembly renewed its request to OAU Members to apply economic sanctions against South Africa. Independently of the Security Council, but in line with previous General Assembly resolutions, the OAU Assembly proceeded through the OAU secretariat's Bureau of Sanctions, to co-ordinate the application of economic sanctions by African States against South Africa and to promote a campaign for similar efforts by "friendly" countries. Through the African Group at the United Nations, it sought to persuade the General Assembly to single out the major trading partners of South Africa, particularly, the U.K., the U.S., the Federal Republic of Germany, Japan, Italy, and France, and to urge them to sever their economic relations with that country.[91] Finally, in order to influence in its favor the proceedings of the Security Council dealing with South Africa, it sought without much success to promote the election to the Council of States which supported effective action against apartheid.[92]

At the General Assembly, the African Group carried out its mandate with considerable success. In December 1965, the Assembly adopted resolution 2054A(XX) declaring that universally applied economic sanctions under Chapter VII of the United Nations Charter were the only means to achieve a peaceful solution to the apartheid problem and appealing to the major trading partners of South Africa to end their economic ties with it. The Assembly decided to enlarge the Special Committee on Apartheid from 11 to 17 in order to include those States with primary responsibility for the maintenance of peace and security and those having a large share of world trade. The African States had placed special emphasis on the enlargement of this Committee hoping that they could constantly engage the trading partners of South Africa in a "serious discussion" over the question of economic sanctions. The resolution was adopted by a vote of 80 to 2 (Portugal and South Africa), with 16 abstentions;[93] most of the States that voted against resolution 1761(XVII) in 1962 preferred to abstain while the majority of those that had abstained previously voted in favor of the resolution. Among the 16 abstaining States were some of South Africa's main trading partners, including three permanent members of the Security Council—the U.K., the U.S., and France. None of them were willing to apply the recommended sanctions and none were inclined to serve on the Committee.

Subsequent resolutions of the General Assembly became increasingly strong in their condemnation of South Africa and their criticism of its main trading partners, as well as in their advocacy of effective measures to induce political change in South Africa. Resolution 2396(XXIII) of the General Assembly, adopted in December 1968 by a vote of 85 to 2 (Portugal and South Africa), with 14 abstentions,[94] described apartheid as a "crime against humanity" and called for the exercise by the people of South Africa of "their right to self-determination" in order to "attain majority rule based on universal suffrage." In addition, it stressed that South Africa's illegal occupation of Namibia and its policy of extending the application of apartheid to that Territory, as well as its assistance to the illegal regime in Southern Rhodesia, had created a situation in the whole of Southern Africa which constituted "a grave threat to international peace and security." It drew the attention of the Security Council to this grave situation and requested the Council to resume urgently the consideration of the question of apartheid "with a view to adopting, under Chapter VII of the Charter . . . effective measures to ensure the full implementation of comprehensive mandatory sanctions against South Africa." In addition, the resolution called upon all States "to provide greater moral, political and material assistance to the South African liberation movement in its legitimate struggle" and declared that all "freedom fighters" who were taken prisoner by South Africa should be treated as prisoners of war under international law. Furthermore, it recommended an intensification of the international campaign against apartheid and, to this end: authorized the Special Committee on Apartheid to hold sessions away from Headquarters or to send a sub-committee on a mission to consult any specialized agencies, regional organizations, States, and non-governmental organizations; and requested the Secretary-General, the specialized agencies, and all States to intensify the dissemination of information on the evils of apartheid.

As a result of pressure from the OAU Members, therefore, the position of the vast majority of States in the General Assembly advanced so far ahead of the position on which the Security Council had previously been able to reach an agreement that there was hardly any possibility of obtaining support for the envisaged measures from all the permanent members of the Council. When the question of South Africa was brought before the Security Council in July 1970, it became difficult even to maintain the level of agreement on measures against South Africa reached in 1963. The Council was convened at the request of forty States, including thirty-six OAU Members, to consider the problem of violations of the arms embargo against South Africa in force since 1963, and particularly the declared intention of the U.K. to export to South Africa certain limited categories of arms for maritime defense. The acrimonious debate between the African States and the major Western Powers over alleged violations of the arms embargo by the latter, especially France and the U.K., revealed that the 1963 consensus on the arms issue had long been eroded. In the spirit of a qualification that it had expressed in 1963—to reserve the right to apply the arms embargo in the light of any future requirements for common defense with South Africa—the U.K. had actually exempted arms intended for the "external defense" of South Africa and had thus applied the ban only to arms which might be used for internal repression.[95] France also had applied the ban only to the latter type of arms, in accordance with a policy it had explained previously.[96] However, even as those two States emphasized the limited nature of the recommended suspension of arms trade, the OAU Members and Asian States in the Security Council sought to strengthen the embargo. Although the Security Council was able to adopt without opposition a resolution along the lines advocated by the African and Asian States, France, the U.K., and the U.S. abstained. The Security Council adopted resolution 282 (1970) which strongly condemned all "violations of the arms embargo called for" in previous resolutions and called upon States to implement it "unconditionally and without reservations whatsoever." In addition, it urged States to strengthen the arms embargo: by withholding the supply of all vehicles, equipment, and spare parts for the use of the armed forces and paramilitary organizations of South Africa; by revoking all licenses and military patents granted to South Africa for the manufacture of arms, ammunition, and military vehicles; by prohibiting economic investment, technical assistance, and training for military purposes in South Africa; and by ceasing all other forms of military co-operation with South Africa. Even though there were no negative votes on the resolution, France, the U.K., and the U.S. abstained.

This lack of active support from the three States was regarded by the OAU Members as a major setback at a time when there was an urgent need not only for an arms embargo but also for economic sanctions against South Africa. However, this setback was alleviated during the Addis Ababa session of the Security Council in January/February 1972 when a five-Power draft resolution relating to apartheid (sponsored by Guinea, Somalia, Sudan, India, and Yugoslavia) was adopted as resolution 311 (1972), with the support of the U.K. and the U.S.—but not of France, which continued to abstain. After expressing in the preamble of the resolution its grave concern that the situation in South Africa "seriously disturbs international peace and security in Southern Africa," the Security Council expressed for the first time in an operative pargraph its recognition of "the *legitimacy of the struggle* of the oppressed people of South Africa in pursuance of their human and political rights as set forth in the Charter of the United Nations and the Universal Declaration of Human Rights" (emphasis added) and urged Governments, organizations, and individuals to contribute generously to the United Nations Fund used for humanitarian and training purposes to assist the victims of apartheid. It also called upon all States "to observe strictly" the arms embargo but refrained from reiterating its recommendation of 1970 that they cease all forms of military co-operation with South Africa. As far as the arms embargo is concerned, therefore, there has been some backsliding from the

Security Council's position of 1970; but even this has not brought about unanimity in the Council.

3. Quest for an Integrated Solution to the Problems of Southern Africa

It may be concluded from the foregoing four cases that although the United Nations organs and the OAU are in full agreement over the objectives to be attained, there is a great difference between the Security Council and the OAU over the measures that should be taken to realize these objectives. This is partly due to differences over the assessment of the extent of threat posed by each situation to international peace and security and the measures needed to solve each problem. In analyzing the possible effects of these differences on OAU-UN relationships it is convenient to regard the developments in Africa during the first decade of the OAU as forming two stages, with the end of 1968 as the dividing line. In the 1963-1968 period the OAU tended to follow a diversified approach to the four situations, with the result that it sought maximum Security Council involvement in those cases where active support from all the permanent members of the Council seemed possible while relying upon its own initiative and resources as regards other cases. But since 1969, the OAU has, for a number of reasons to be mentioned later, tended to regard the four situations as parts of a single problem of Southern Africa and has maintained that, in the absence of a revolutionary change in any of those countries, an integrated solution would have to be found in close collaboration with the United Nations.

In the first stage, the OAU decided to rely on its own initiative in regard to the question of Portuguese-administered Territories. It assumed responsibility for liberating those Territories, partly because there was no support from France, the U.K., and the U.S. for Security Council measures, other than a limited voluntary arms embargo against Portugal. A second reason for the OAU initiative was that the Portuguese-administered Territories were more vulnerable than Southern Rhodesia and South Africa to an African economic boycott and to pressure from OAU-supported activities of liberation movements, because of their common borders with a number of the OAU Member States. Finally, since the liberation movements in each of the Portuguese-administered Territories were already fairly well organized, the OAU was convinced that it could, through concerted effort and with adequate assistance from its Members, help to expel Portugal from its colonies.

On the other hand, the OAU regarded the solution of the Southern Rhodesian problem as being the responsibility of the U.K.; it was when the latter found itself unable to prevent UDI that the OAU sought to mobilize effective action through the Security Council. Not satisfied with the non-mandatory economic sanctions recommended by the Council, yet using as a starting point the Council's encouragement of OAU collaboration in regard to those measures, the OAU organs explored every possibility of taking effective action against Southern Rhodesia, including the use of force independently of the Security Council. Since the liberation movements in Southern Rhodesia were too weak and disunited to serve as the principal means of pressure on the settler regime, the OAU focused its attention on the possibility of direct use of armed forces. However, upon realizing the difficulty of mounting a military operation against Southern Rhodesia (which could probably be organized only through Zambia, thus exposing it to massive retaliation), and bearing in mind the uncertainty of many Member States as to the legality of such a move and their awareness of the weakness of African solidarity as revealed by the 1965 fiasco about breaking diplomatic relations with the U.K., the OAU once again decided to press for more vigorous action through the Security Council. When an agreement was reached at the Security Council in December 1966 to define the situation as a threat to international peace and to apply non-military sanctions under Article VII of the United Nations Charter, the Council assumed the principal role on the question of Southern Rhodesia.

As regards South Africa, it was agreed among all members of the Security Council as early as December 1963 that the situation in that country was seriously disturbing international peace and security, but nothing more than a partial arms embargo, that is, arms for internal use, could command their unanimous support. In regard to Namibia, not even the same degree of agreement on the implications to international peace could be reached in the Security Council. Yet, in view of South Africa's invulnerability to any measures of pressure from the OAU and the belief that the solution of the Namibian question was primarily the responsibility of the United Nations, the African States sought persistently to mobilize United Nations collective measures against South Africa.

In the second stage, the OAU moved toward greater dependence on the United Nations for the solution of the problems of Southern Africa as a whole. This came about as a result of a number of setbacks to the efforts of the OAU during 1967 and 1968, especially the following. First, South Africa seemed to have succeeded in weakening the OAU campaign against it by sowing discord among the OAU Member States through its new policy of establishing friendly relations with those independent African States in Southern Africa which depended heavily on its good will for their economic survival.[97] Through pressure or economic inducements, it appears to have succeeded in obtaining the consent of Malawi, Lesotho,

Swaziland, and, to a lesser extent, Botswana that they would observe a policy of strict non-interference with regard to its racial policies. Even though none of the leaders of these countries have indicated that they would condone such policies, the establishment of formal diplomatic relations between South Africa and Malawi on 10 September 1967 was a major blow to African solidarity and to the struggle against apartheid and colonialism in Southern Africa. Secondly, the intensive guerrilla activities of the national liberation movements in 1966 and 1967 encountered formidable obstacles: on the one hand, the OAU failed in its efforts to persuade the rival liberation movements to form effective common fronts, and, on the other, Portugal and the illegal regime in Southern Rhodesia embarked on vigorous counterattacks which brought about a stalemate in the fighting. In addition, Portugal began increasing the number of raids by its troops within the territories of African States bordering its colonies as well as encouraging mercenary activities. Thirdly, South Africa, the strongest and wealthiest country in Southern Africa, sought vigorously to ensure continued white rule in Southern Rhodesia, Angola, and Mozambique through a policy of military and economic assistance. It was with the help of South African troops that the regime in Southern Rhodesia suppressed the guerrilla campaigns of August 1967 and March 1968. It was also with their help that Portugal had been able to guard the site of its major hydroelectric and irrigation project in Mozambique from guerrilla attacks. As regards economic assistance, the illegal regime in Southern Rhodesia has been able to withstand economic sanctions largely because of the determination of South Africa and until recently Portugal to keep open trade channels and even strengthen their economic ties with that regime in defiance of the Security Council's decision. As the colonial wars in Angola, Mozambique, and Guinea (Bissau) became too costly by Portuguese standards, Portugal encouraged foreign investments in its colonies and received a generous response, especially from South Africa and Southern Rhodesia. Since most of the finance for the Cabora Bassa Dam project in Mozambique was from South Africa and Southern Rhodesia and since a large part of the investment in the Cunene River Scheme in southern Angola was from South Africa, the white regimes in Pretoria and Salisbury developed an economic stake in continued Portuguese rule.[98] As the most influential power in the area, South Africa seemed to be establishing a system of alliance under its control against any inroads by African nationalism.

Late in 1968 the OAU had explored possibilities for collective self-defense by African States: it had declared that "any aggression on any OAU Member State by the colonialist and facist regimes of Portugal, South Africa and Rhodesia is regarded as an aggression on all Members of the OAU,"[99] and had accordingly sought to revive the OAU Defence Commission which had been dormant since 1965. But as the magnitude of the foregoing obstacles was fully realized, the OAU organs decided in 1969 to adopt a United Nations-based dual strategy on Southern Africa: to try a peaceful approach toward the recalcitrant regimes and, if that failed, to obtain wider support for measures of military and economic pressure.

In September 1969, the OAU Assembly took a significant diplomatic initiative when it endorsed a Manifesto on Southern Africa which was originally proclaimed by the Fifth Summit Conference of East and Central African States (Lusaka, April 1969).[100]

The "Lusaka Manifesto," which was welcomed by the twenty-fourth session of the General Assembly,[101] expressed the dedication of the African States to the full liberation of Southern Africa and their preference to achieve this goal without violence, as far as possible. It explained their support to liberation movements in Africa under the aegis of the OAU in the following terms:

> While peaceful progress is blocked by actions of those at present in power in the States of Southern Africa, we have no choice but to give to the peoples of those territories all the support of which we are capable in their struggle against their oppressors.

They explained that it was because of the failure of the Security Council to take effective measures to ensure peaceful progress in the area that they had to resort to such a non-peaceful course of action. They emphatically stated that they would be prepared to urge the liberation movements to desist from their armed struggle and to resort to procedures of peaceful change if the following conditions were met: if the U.K. undertook to reassert its authority in Southern Rhodesia and to bring about peaceful progress to majority rule and independence; if the United Nations enforced its decision to take over the administration of Namibia; if South Africa and Portugal were made to change their attitudes toward the principle of self-determination, and the latter also to change its racial policies.

But far from eliciting a positive response from the white regimes in Southern Africa, the African diplomatic initiative induced political and military counteroffensives by Portugal and South Africa. Portugal rejected the Lusaka Manifesto, explaining that it regarded the document merely as an "apologia" for the military activities of the liberation movements and for the aid being given to them by African States,[102] and subsequently intensified its military activities.

In rejecting the Lusaka Manifesto, South Africa argued in the General Assembly that the sections referring to it were based on a misconception of its racial and other policies, which it regarded as being outside the jurisdiction of the United Nations and other organizations. While categorically rejecting the idea of a dialogue designed to influence its racial policies, it announced that it would continue to engage in dialogues with Governments which were "genuinely interested in informing themselves on conditions in South Africa and on its policies."[103] In Southern Africa, not only did it continue its efforts to establish a system of black and white "client" States, but it also began to increase the number of armed incursions into Zambia from the Caprivi Strip of Namibia, ostensibly in pursuit of Namibian freedom-fighters.[104] Zambia, it should be noted, was the only OAU Member in Southern Africa opposing white supremacy which rejected categorically South Africa's advances under the so-called outward-looking policy of "dialogue" on South Africa's terms. Since South Africa tried to influence the foreign policy of Zambia and sought even to persuade African States farther north of the advantages of accepting its version of "dialogue," the whole idea of peaceful negotiation with the recalcitrant regimes became so controversial that the OAU Council of Ministers found it necessary in June 1971 to issue a declaration on the question of dialogue. It reaffirmed that the Lusaka Manifesto was "the only objective basis for any meaningful solution to the problem of apartheid and colonialism in Africa" and that any notion of dialogue with South Africa which was not designed to obtain the elimination of apartheid was inconsistent with the objectives of the Manifesto. Describing South Africa's proposal for a "dialogue" as a manoeuvre "to divide African States, confuse world public opinion, relieve South Africa of international ostracism . . . and obtain acceptance of the status quo," the Council of Ministers indicated that "any form of dialogue should appropriately be commenced only between the minority racist regime of South Africa and the people they are opposing, exploiting, and suppressing."[105]

Immediately after the formal rejection of the Lusaka Manifesto by South Africa and Portugal, the OAU Members concluded that there was no basis for a meaningful dialogue and thus decided to revert to their policy of confrontation. In fact, the same session of the General Assembly which welcomed the Manifesto was prevailed upon by the African States and other strongly anti-colonial Powers to adopt two measures which they had long been advocating. The first was a recommendation to the Security Council to extend the sanctions being taken against Southern Rhodesia to South Africa and Portugal.[106] The second was a recommendation to the specialized agencies and other bodies within the United Nations system to take measures aimed at discontinuing any collaboration with and assistance to the recalcitrant regimes in Southern Africa as well as to give all possible assistance to the peoples struggling to liberate themselves from colonial rule and in particular to work out, within the scope of their respective activities and in co-operation with the Organization of African Unity and, through it, with the national liberation movements, concrete programmes for assisting the oppressed peoples of Southern Rhodesia, Namibia and the Territories under Portuguese administration.[107]

By requesting all the organizations concerned not only to introduce for this purpose maximum flexibility in their procedures but also to make special arrangements with the OAU, the General Assembly sought to involve the entire United Nations system in the campaign against colonialism as well as to give impetus to the role of the OAU in promoting the struggle for liberation. A distinction is made in practice between military assistance and non-military aid to the liberation movements. The OAU has been arranging both types of assistance with the help of African and some non-African States, but the organizations within the United Nations family which took steps to implement the resolution have, within their respective areas of competence, been providing assistance for non-military objectives, especially the following: education and training, employment and rural settlement, both for the people residing in the "liberated areas" and those living abroad as refugees, and legal defense for those persecuted under repressive and discriminatory legislation in Southern Africa and humanitarian relief to their dependents.[108]

In 1970, in connection with the tenth anniversary of the Declaration on the Granting of Independence to Colonial Countries and Peoples, the Committee of Twenty-Four worked out a program of action, with special emphasis on Southern Africa, for adoption by the General Assembly. After intensive consultations with the OAU secretariat and with representatives of African liberation movements recognized by the OAU, a working group of the Special Committee prepared an integrated program of action which carried forward all the measures against the recalcitrant regimes recommended by previous sessions of the General Assembly, employing, however, language which seemed to suggest that Member States had an obligation to ensure the taking of effective measures for the full implementation of the Declaration on decolonization. The program, based entirely on the sanctionist approach, was adopted by the General Assembly as resolution 2621 (XXV). But even though 89 States, that is, over two-thirds of the membership, voted for the resolution, the fact that five States voted against it while 16 others abstained marked a deepening of the gulf between, on the one hand, the African and other strongly anti-colonial States and, on the other, those Powers which had exclusively been advocating methods of peaceful settlement. Whereas ten years earlier the

Declaration on decolonization itself had been adopted without any opposition and with only nine States abstaining, the new program of action for the full implementation of the Declaration was opposed by Australia, New Zealand, the U.K., the U.S., as well as South Africa (Portugal did not participate in the voting). In addition, such staunch anti-colonial States as the Scandinavian countries and Austria found themselves unable to support the program and had to abstain along with the Benelux countries, Canada, Italy, France, Japan, as well as Malawi and Swaziland. Several of the States that voted against or abstained on the resolution were of the opinion that many of the paragraphs were extreme in their formulation.

The magnitude of the gap between the sanctionist approach of the vast majority, including OAU Members, and the non-sanctionist approach of a significant minority, including three permanent members of the Security Council that were also administering Powers of Non-Self-Governing Territories—France, the U.K., and the U.S.—can be easily seen from the following juxtaposition of the main elements of the approved program of action and the main points of an Italian proposal[109] made on behalf of Italy, Norway, the U.K., and the U.S. but which failed to obtain support from other members of the Special Committee of Twenty-Four.

The most basic difference between the two approaches concerned the recognition of the legitimacy of the activities of liberation movements in Africa and the encouragement of such activities by the United Nations. Without denying the right of colonial peoples to resort to any means at their disposal, including violence if necessitated by armed suppression on the part of a colonial Power, the supporters of the Italian proposal and the other States which refused to support the adopted program, felt that a general endorsement and encouragement of such violence by the United Nations—an organization dedicated to peace—could hardly be reconciled with the provisions of the United Nations Charter. Furthermore, those States maintained that the adopted program failed to make a clear distinction between the various forms of colonialism and thus tended to lump together the problems of small and isolated colonies with the grave problems of Southern Africa. They were also critical of the program on the ground that, in sharp contrast to the substance and tone of the Lusaka Manifesto, it recommended extreme courses of action which could not command universal support, thereby removing itself from any likelihood of effective implementation.[110] Thus, when seventeen U.S.-proposed amendments were rejected, several of those States drew the conclusion that future activities of the United Nations based on the adopted program would be most unconstructive. Three of them—Italy, the U.K., and the U.S.—subsequently withdrew their membership from the Special

Program of Action Under Resolution 2621(XXV)		*Program of Action Proposed by Italy (on behalf of Italy, Norway, the U.K., and the U.S.)*
Member States:		Member States:
reaffirm the inherent right of colonial peoples to struggle by all necessary means at their disposal against colonial Powers which suppress their aspirations for freedom and independence.	1. Legitimacy of liberation movements	undertake to refrain from any forcible action contrary to the principles and purposes of the Charter which might impede the exercise of the right to self-determination, freedom and independence.
shall render all necessary moral and material assistance to the peoples in the colonial Territories in their struggle to attain freedom and independence.	2. Assistance to colonial peoples	agree to render, as they deem appropriate, moral and material support, consistent with the purposes and principles of the Charter, to the peoples of the Non-Self-Governing Territories in Southern Africa in their efforts to attain freedom and independence.
shall wage a vigorous campaign against all military activities by colonial Powers in their colonies, shall oppose collaboration among recalcitrant régimes and shall do their utmost to secure urgent consideration by the Security Council of the question of imposing fully and unconditionally, under international supervision, an arms embargo on South Africa, Southern Rhodesia and Portugal.	3. Arms Embargo	agree to condemn the use of military force to suppress the aspirations of colonial peoples and to consider the promotion of effective measures to prevent the sale or supply of arms to colonial régimes intended for such repression.

Program of Action Under Resolution 2621(XXV)		*Program of Action Proposed by Italy (on behalf of Italy, Norway, the U.K., and the U.S.)*
Member States:		Member States:
shall do their utmost to promote the adoption by the Security Council of effective measures against recalcitrant régimes, and particularly to widen the scope of the sanctions against Southern Rhodesia and to consider imposing sanctions upon South Africa and Portugal.	4. Effective measures by United Nations bodies including sanctions	agree to ensure that the Security Council keeps under review the situation in Southern Africa; and undertake to promote in the General Assembly and in other bodies of the United Nations, as appropriate, resolutions designed to facilitate decolonization, bearing in mind the need for their effective implementation.
shall intensify their efforts to end all forms of aid received by the recalcitrant régimes which enables them to persist in their colonial policies and shall consider taking steps to discourage their nationals and all companies under their jurisdiction from engaging in any activities that benefit those régimes.	5. Cut-off of economic collaboration	shall take steps to discourage and limit the activities of those foreign economic interests operating in Non-Self-Governing Territories which may impede the process of decolonization.
shall take measures for carrying out more vigorous public information campaign to enhance public awareness of the need for active assistance in the achievement of complete decolonization.	6. Public information campaign	undertake to extend assistance for the development of an informed public opinion in the Territories concerned and for the spread of knowledge about the range of choices open to their peoples in exercise of their right of self-determination.

Committee of Twenty-Four, having already had serious reservations about the practical value of its work and of their contributions to it.

These developments have led to an even greater reliance by the OAU on the Security Council, where an automatic involvement of France, the U.K., and the U.S. would be assured. The convening of a special session of the Security Council on African questions at an African capital (Addis Ababa, January/February 1972) in response to an OAU request has underlined both the importance attached by the OAU to the role of the Security Council and the need to find an integrated solution to colonial and racial problems of Southern Africa.

C. IMPLICATIONS FOR OAU-UN RELATIONSHIPS

Two main questions were raised in the introduction to this chapter: (i) whether any collective measures planned or taken by the OAU infringe upon the jurisdiction of the Security Council; and (ii) whether the pressure exerted by the OAU on the United Natiions to obtain support for OAU policies creates any incompatibility between the two organizations.

1. Issue of Regional Autonomy in Recommending Collective Measures

Article 53 of the United Nations Charter prohibits regional enforcement action without the authorization of the Security Council; Article 51 lifts this restriction if the measures taken, whatever their nature, are in collective self-defense against "'armed attack," pending appropriate action by the Security Council. The issue of compatibility of OAU's non-binding collective measures with the provisions of Articles 51 and 53 was briefly examined in the introduction to this chapter. It was observed then that the majority of Member States maintain that since OAU's appeals to its Members to provide moral and material assistance to African liberation movements and its own contribution of financial aid and co-ordinative services to those movements can hardly be regarded as a threat or use of military force by the OAU (or by its Member States) to enforce a decision against any State, these OAU activities do not seem to constitute "enforcement action" requiring authorization from the Security Council. It was also observed that, since the diplomatic and economic measures recommended by the OAU against the colonial and settler regimes in Southern Africa do not involve the use of military force and are in any case non-binding, they also have hardly been regarded as "enforcement action." The practice of the United Nations organs with regard to the hitherto intractable problems of colonialism and racial discrimination in Southern Africa seems to confirm this conclusion. While the issue of whether any collective measures recommended by the OAU should constitute enforcement action requiring prior Security Council authorization seems never to have been raised within the United Nations organs, the OAU Members have behaved, with the active support or acquiescence of other States, as though those measures would not constitute enforcement action. Upon the request of the African and other strongly anti-colonial States, both types of measures—diplomatic and economic sanctions and assistance to liberation movements—have been endorsed by the General Assembly in a series of resolutions which directly or indirectly support these forms of OAU intervention in Southern Africa. At the Security Council, the African States raised the question of those measures not in order to obtain authorization from the Council but rather to persuade it to urge all Member States of the United Nations to apply them as recommended by the General Assembly. The Security Council has not sought to play the role of giving or denying authorization for the autonomous activities of the OAU in this regard. When the Security Council called upon the OAU to assist in the implementation of an arms embargo and non-mandatory economic sanctions in the context of Chapter VIII of the United Nations Charter, it did not indicate that it was performing an authorizing function. In addition to asking for OAU help, it appeared to be taking cognizance of the course of action that the OAU had been taking independently. When, a few years later, it requested United Nations Member States to give "moral and material assistance" to the Southern Rhodesians and Namibians struggling for the independence of their respective countries, the Council strengthened the authority of similar General Assembly resolutions and can be said to have given an indirect endorsement of the assistance being given by the OAU.

Only in the case of Southern Rhodesia immediately after UDI (November 1965) was there a real possibility of jurisdictional dispute between the OAU and the Security Council. This was when the OAU contemplated direct use of force by its Members against the illegal regime in the spirit of Article 51 of the United Nations Charter, that is, without Security Council authorization. Although there was no actual "armed attack" against any OAU Member State to precipitate the invocation of the right of individual or collective self-defense, many OAU Members believed that the rebellion carried out in Southern Rhodesia by the hostile illegal regime was a threat to the security of neighboring African States, especially Zambia, which had welcomed African refugees and nationalists struggling against the regime's oppressive policy of racial domination. Though the OAU decided then not to recommend direct military action by its Members, it did not rule out the possibility of such action in the future as an act of collective self-defense against the illegal regime. Later, the OAU sought to prepare the ground for possible use of military force prior to any action by the Security Council and without the Council's authorization. It did so by declaring that any "aggression" against an OAU Member State by a colonial or settler regime would be considered an "aggression" against all Members and pledging in specific cases to provide "immediate and complete assistance" of a technical, financial, and military character to the victim.[111] Implied is a claim by the OAU to recommend and co-ordinate, if feasible, the use of military force by its Member States in defense against "aggression," that is, in defense against a wider range of hostile actions by the colonial and settler regimes than an "armed attack," the type of aggression referred to in Article 51 of the United Nations Charter. The OAU seems to have adopted a broader interpretation of the "inherent right of individual and collective self-defense" referred to in Article 51, thus raising the issue of whether any military action taken within the framework of the OAU in response to a threat to peace or an act of aggression not amounting to an armed attack might not constitute enforcement—which requires Security Council authorization—rather than collective self-defense. However, as it is at present unlikely for the OAU to recommend such a course of action, the issue of possible jurisdictional conflict with the Security Council remains hypothetical.

At present, no jurisdictional or other legal conflict would seem to arise between the OAU and the United Nations from the measures being taken under OAU auspices against colonial and settler regimes. Those measures might be regarded as permissible regional action relating to the maintenance of peace and security which, according to Article 52(1), would apparently not be precluded by any provision of the United Nations Charter.

It seems clear that the increasingly militant role of the OAU in recommending and co-ordinating measures against the recalcitrant regimes stems not from any desire for OAU autonomy in the pursuit of regional objectives but rather from despair about the relative ineffectiveness of the United Nations in achieving the common objectives in Southern Africa. Since its own resources are very limited, the OAU has in fact been eager to induce the Security Council to take greater initiative regarding the problems of Southern Africa.

2. Problem of Discrepancy Between OAU Demands and Security Council Response

The OAU has requested the United Nations to regard the situation in the whole of Southern Africa as constituting a threat to international peace and security and to meet the threat by applying economic sanctions under

Chapter VII of the United Nations Charter and by recommending moral and material support for the national liberation movements in Africa. While the General Assembly has adopted such request with overwhelming support, those Powers which are themselves administering Powers and which have defense arrangements or substantial economic relations with South Africa and Portugal have opposed extension to these countries of the sanctions being taken against Southern Rhodesia. Since three of those States have the power of veto in the Security Council, the Council has been unable to approve any measures that would be unacceptable or intolerable to them. Thus the Council has been able to take only the following measures: comprehensive mandatory sanctions against Southern Rhodesia, comprising the severance of all economic and transportation links and an embargo on all arms, but excluding certain means of communication for humanitarian reasons; a non-mandatory embargo on arms for South Africa and encouragement of moral and material support for Namibians struggling for independence from South Africa; and a non-mandatory arms embargo against Portugal. The wide discrepancy between OAU demands and the response of the Security Council appears to have had a negative effect on some aspects of United Nations functioning. In addition, it has been responsible for certain policies which pose a challenge to the concept of universality of membership in the United Nations and that of settlement of differences by peaceful means.

a. GENERAL EFFECT ON UNITED NATIONS FUNCTIONING

The OAU has continued the trend initiated by previous African summit conferences to ensure acceptance of the uppermost objectives of the African States—the abolition of apartheid and the promotion of decolonization and development—as goals of top priority in the United Nations. The United Nations itself has provided an environment which enhances the impact of the OAU. The commitments of United Nations Member States to the broad purposes and principles of the United Nations Charter provide moral and legal justification for most of the OAU demands and have made it possible for the OAU to exert pressure on United Nations Member States to live up to their Charter obligations. But since there could be no unanimous agreement on the order of priorities brought to the United Nations by the African States, an escalation of the OAU demands has led to a hardening of the resistance by a significant minority of States, including the three permanent members of the Security Council, with the result that the gap between the positions of the General Assembly and the Security Council regarding measures against colonialism and apartheid in Southern Africa has been widening at the same rate as that between the positions of the OAU and the Security Council. This development seems to have compounded the long-standing jurisdictional issue between the Security Council and the General Assembly with regard to the maintenance of international peace and security. This widening gap seems also to have undermined the possibility of developing a United Nations strategy on Southern Africa which could win not only the support of the overwhelming majority in terms of votes but also the commitment of those States and the collaboration of all States having commercial ties with Southern Africa. Such commitment and co-operation would be indispensable for implementing measures against the recalcitrant regimes. The authority of the United Nations as a whole seems to have been undermined on the one hand by the annual repetition in the General Assembly of large numbers of strongly worded resolutions which are known to have little prospect of effective implementation and, on the other, by the continual adoption in the Security Council of resolutions which are too weak to have any impact upon the recalcitrant regimes. Moreover, as has often been stated, existing rivalry among the various departmental units of the United Nations Secretariat concerned with Southern Africa seems to have made concerted action somewhat difficult. The net result has been a further decline of the image of the United Nations as a problem-solving mechanism in the peace and security field, accompanied by mutual recrimination and antagonism between the strongly anti-colonial majority, including the African Group, and the major trading partners of the regimes in Southern Africa.

Within the General Assembly, the sharp differences on problems of colonialism and apartheid have led to increasing disengagement by the latter Powers from United Nations activities relating to such problems. When the General Assembly decided in 1965 to expand the membership of the Special Committee on Apartheid by adding six States, including those with primary responsibility for the maintenance of international peace and security and for world trade, fifteen of the nineteen States approached by the President of the Assembly, including France, the U.K., and the U.S., declined membership.[112] Since only the USSR expressed an unconditional willingness to serve on the Special Committee, the membership remained the same until a second effort made five years later resulted in the appointment of five additional members, none of which were permanent members of the Security Council. In 1967, when the Council for South West Africa was established, France, the U.K., and the U.S. were among those that declined membership—the first two because of their reservation about the legality of resolution 2145(XXI) and the U.S. because of its disagreement with the terms of reference of the Council. By the beginning of 1971, in the wake of the adoption of a new program of action on decolonization, the U.K., the U.S., and Italy even came to discontinue their membership in the Special Committee of Twenty-Four.[113] The absence of France, the U.K., and the U.S. from the two Special Committees and the Council for Namibia will most probably remove any possibility of developing those bodies into a mechanism for consultation and negotiation in the drafting of recommendations to the General Assembly and the Security Council which can bridge the gap between the present forceful declaration of intention and the low level of actual implementation.

Of course, those three Powers do encounter the problems of Southern Africa in the Security Council, since the OAU Members have been increasingly directing these problems to the Council. It is undoubtedly only through this organ that the United Nations can expect to overcome the resistance of the recalcitrant regimes. But it should be recalled that the Security Council is responsible only for the international peace and security aspects of the problems of Southern Africa rather than for the whole range of complex problems involved in the attainment of freedom and independence, in Southern Africa or elsewhere. The present non-involvement of those Powers in the work of the three subsidiary bodies of the General Assembly may therefore reduce the effectiveness of these bodies and their parent organ in developing a strategy that might induce those Powers having some leverage on the recalcitrant regimes to re-examine all aspects of their present policies toward Southern Africa.

b. ISSUE OF SUSPENSION OR EXPULSION OF RECALCITRANT STATES FROM THE UNITED NATIONS

A significant problem for United Nations-OAU relationship has been the OAU demand for the suspension or expulsion of South Africa and Portugal from membership in various international organizations. Through a policy of systematic exclusion from international sports and other voluntary social activities, the Afro-Asian States and anti-apartheid groups have quite successfully induced some change in South Africa's racial practices regarding those areas. It should, however, be noted that the nature and implications of such social and political pressure are qualitatively different from the envisaged diplomatic exclusion of South Africa from universal intergovernmental organizations.

In July 1963, the Economic and Social Council, responding to the demands of the African States submitted in 1962 through a resolution of the Economic Commission for Africa (ECA), expelled Portugal from membership in ECA and suspended South Africa from the same body pending a change in its racial policies.[114] Since then South Africa has, under pressure from African and other anti-colonial States, withdrawn from the International Labour Organization (ILO) and the Food and Agricultural Organization (FAO)—it had withdrawn from UNESCO in 1956—while its voting rights in WHO have been suspended pending a change in its racial policies.[115] In addition, its delegation was expelled from the 1969 session of the Congress of the Universal Postal Union (UPU) and from the 1965 Plenipotentiary Conference of the International Telecommunication Union (ITU) of 1965 and has been excluded from ITU's regional conferences for Africa.[116] A campaign was being made by the OAU Members to exclude not only South Africa but also Portugal from the specialized agencies and from some of the permanent subsidiary bodies of the General Assembly. But in most of the organizations concerned, constitutional problems have been encountered: in some of them, complete severance of links with the Governments of South Africa and Portugal could be effected only through a modification of their constitutions and, in others, only after the United Nations itself would have first acted to suspend those Governments from the rights and privileges of membership.

The case of the United Nations Conference on Trade and Development (UNCTAD) illustrates the magnitude of the latter problem. In February 1968, an attempt by the OAU Members and several Asian States to obtain the expulsion of South Africa from the second conference of UNCTAD almost led to a breakup of the conference. The debate between the supporters and opponents of the measure centered on political as well as constitutional issues. Although the OAU Members were able to win the support of the majority at the Conference for a recommendation to the General Assembly to suspend South Africa from future conferences, they failed later to attain an amendment by the General Assembly of the provisions on membership of UNCTAD.[117]

The legal opinion presented by the Legal Counsel of the United Nations during the debate on the issue concludes that

> Procedures for the suspension of a Member State from an organ open to the general membersip are laid down exclusively in Article 5 of the Charter, which. permits suspension only through joint action by both the Security Council and the General Assembly.[118]

But the African States have continued to argue that it is within the powers of the General Assembly to amend the terms of reference of UNCTAD, including the provisions on membership. For the African States, the issue has not yet been resolved.

The main goal of the OAU Members in their drive to isolate South Africa is to exclude it from the United Nations as a whole. But a Member State may be suspended or expelled by the General Assembly only upon the recommendation of the Security Council. In November 1970, the General Assembly, in response to the requests of OAU Members, decided not to accept the credentials of South Africa's representatives to its twenty-fifth session, but the President of the Assembly interpreted this decision as being a solemn "warning" rather than an act affecting South Africa's rights and privileges of membership. If further attempts by OAU Members to exclude the South African delegation from successive sessions of the General Assembly succeed in winning sufficient support, the present confrontation between the OAU Members and the States opposed to any kind of measures against South Africa may develop into a constitutional dispute between the General Assembly and the Security Council centered on the issue of suspension of membership.

An intensification of tension between the two organs of the United Nations might be detrimental to the effectiveness of the Organization. The result would undoubtedly be disillusionment on the part of the vast majority of States that have had confidence in the Organization and relief on the part of the recalcitrant regimes in Southern Africa that they would have nothing to fear from the world body. In addition, the present limited conflict in Southern Africa would most likely escalate into a "race war" which might attract competitive interventions by major non-African Powers.

It appears that the only promising alternative for the future—one that could possibly effect peaceful change in Southern Africa, restore confidence in the United Nations, and strengthen relations between the United Nations and the OAU—is an approach that would place greater emphasis on a diplomacy of persuasion and consensus and less reliance on the adoption of resolutions that would be ignored by the very States whose co-operation is necessary for effective implementation. The focus of such an approach would have to be on negotiations between the spokesmen for the OAU and those major Powers that normally vote against or abstain on United Nations resolutions concerning Southern Africa but whose active co-operation is necessary to influence the policies of the recalcitrant regimes. The main features of such an approach will be examined in the next chapter.

Chapter V

Possibilities for Strengthening Relationships
in the Peace and Security Field

The United Nations and the OAU share the objectives of peace, the promotion of human rights and fundamental freedoms, and economic and social development in Africa. In seeking to attain these objectives, the African States have been engaged within the United Nations and the OAU in a three-tiered structure of diplomatic activity: involving relations among themselves; with colonial and settler regimes; and with extra-continental Powers. In these relations, they have been guided, respectively, by their commitment to Pan-Africanism, the immediate liberation of African peoples from all forms of foreign domination, and the policy of non-alignment in global ideological conflicts.

It has been shown in Chapter III that on the whole the OAU Members have been strongly inclined to seek solutions to disputes among themselves within an African framework and have accordingly stressed the need for the primacy of the OAU over the United Nations on such matters. The United Nations itself has encouraged the initial consideration of such disputes by the OAU. By handling such problems effectively, the OAU might be able to crystallize its autonomy in this regard while at the same time contributing to the attainment of the objectives that it shares with the United Nations. To the extent that its capabilities—authority, functions, structure, and personnel—are inadequate to effect regional solutions, it would seem to be in the interest of both organizations to devise ways to strengthen them and to remedy any remaining shortcomings by an appropriate United Nations role.

The problem of rear-guard colonialism and gross racial discrimination in Southern Africa is, as indicated in Chapter IV, of particular concern to both the United Nations and the OAU. As an organization devoted to the maintenance of international peace and security, as well as to human progress, including the promotion of human rights and fundamental freedoms, the United Nations has a special responsibility to prevent war in Southern Africa by helping to bring about peaceful change in the area. For this purpose, it would need to devise ways for enhancing the effectiveness of its machinery for peaceful adjustment of the explosive situation in the area with the full support of its Member States, especially those that have a special interest or responsibility in the situation—the OAU Members and the permanent members of the Security Council.

An important aspect of the extracontinental diplomacy of the OAU aims, on the one hand, at preventing divisive external intervention in the disputes or other differences between its Members and, on the other, at securing effective external assistance, especially from the major Powers, for eradicating colonial rule and racial domination in Africa. To attain both objectives fully, the OAU would depend heavily on United Nations assistance.

A. CRITERIA FOR OPTIMUM ALLOCATION OF AUTHORITY

In considering possibbilities for strengthening United Nations-OAU relations in the peace and security field, it is important to consider first the criteria for optimum allocation of competence between the United Nations and a regional organization. A scholar who has examined this question on a comparative basis[1] has suggested that, since most issues of peace and security in the interdependent world of today have a tendency to affect all the members of the world community, the United Nations should retain ultimate authority for the maintenance of peace and security. He suggests that it should itself consider situations in which:

  (i) the decisions to be taken affect States both within and outside a regional organization;
 (ii) the effectiveness of such decisions would be enhanced by the inclusion of the major Powers in the decision process; or
(iii) a broadly based decision rather than a regional one is likely to reflect the common interest of the international community.

The problems of colonialism, racial discrimination, and impermissible intervention by external Powers in disputes and conflicts between African States would obviously be among the situations envisaged. These criteria are, of course, consistent with the primary responsibility of the Security Council for the maintenance of international peace and security.

Within this framework, the same scholar suggests that on pragmatic grounds the United Nations should encourage the efforts of regional organizations in situations in which:

  (i) the interests at stake are primarily regional;
 (ii) the regional machinery offers more effective conflict management; and
(iii) the parties genuinely prefer resort to a regional forum.

The present study would tend to confirm that disputes and other differences among OAU Members would be covered by these criteria, provided that the last one is modified to refer also to situations in which a party which is initially reluctant to resort to a regional forum is likely to be persuaded to do so.

The two sets of criteria are useful as a general guide in the allocation of authority between the Security Council (or the General Assembly) and the organs of a regional organization, but they would need to be supplemented and elaborated for practical application in each region. The main shortcoming is that they do not give any guidance with respect to situations in which neither the Security Council nor the competent deliberative organ of a regional organization is likely to act effectively while the Secretary-General of the global and, possibly, the regional organization might be able to play a useful role. They also do not seem to provide for the consideration by the United Nations of certain serious problems, such as a civil war, in which the interests at stake may be primarily national and regional but for which a regional organization alone is unlikely to find a solution. It would thus seem appropriate to add the following points to the suggested criteria:

(i) that in situations in which ideological or other divisive factors are likely to prevent effective action by the principal intergovernmental organs of a regional organization or the United Nations, the Secretary-General of the United Nations or, possibly, of the regional organization might consider offering his good offices or other supportive services;

(ii) that whenever a serious problem of a basically regional character defies all peace-making efforts of a regional organization, the United Nations organs might, as appropriate, organize moral and political support for such efforts or play a complementary diplomatic role.

Having tentatively outlined criteria for optimum allocation of authority between the United Nations and the OAU in the peace and security field, it is important to seek answers to the following questions which are basic to the strengthening of relations between the United Nations and the OAU. First, how could the existing procedures and practices of co-operation be improved? Secondly, and more fundamentally, what could be done: (a) to strengthen the role of the OAU in the settlement of inter-Member disputes; (b) to enhance the role of the United Nations in promoting peaceful change in Southern Africa?

B. EXISTING PROCEDURES AND PRACTICES
OF CO-OPERATION

The process of co-operation between the Security Council and the OAU can be evaluated in terms of its effectiveness in facilitating the basic objective of Chapter VIII of the United Nations Charter—the encouragement of regional efforts in the maintenance of international peace and security under the authority of the Security Council. At this level, the essence of the relationship is accountability to the Security Council. The relationships of the OAU with other organs of the United Nations, which are essentially of a reciprocal nature, are based on resolutions of the General Assembly and the OAU Assembly.

1. The OAU and the Security Council

Representation and reporting. The main feature of the relationship between the Security Council and the OAU has been a quest on the part of the OAU to utilize the Security Council in internationalizing certain measures already being taken by the African States under the auspices of the OAU. For this purpose, the OAU has set up a new practice for effective presentation of its plea to the Security Council. In the absence of a practice of direct representation of regional organizations in the deliberations of the Security Council, it has become common for a non-permanent member of the Security Council to speak not only for itself but also, unofficially, on behalf of the group of States in its own region. Such a role has been played by the African members of the Council which have often acted as though they represented the interests of the OAU. A further step has been taken by the OAU in strengthening the representation of its interests by dispatching small groups of African Foreign Ministers to the Security Council with a mandate to request the Council to adopt effective measures against the recalcitrant regimes in Southern Africa. Although procedurally the Foreign Ministers concerned have been invited by the Security Council as representatives of their respective States to participate in its proceedings without the right to vote, their role as spokesmen for the OAU has been recognized in practice.

Since the non-permanent members of the Security Council are elected by the entire membership of the General Assembly and not merely by the regional group to which they belong, they are expected to represent the inclusive interests of the international community and not merely their narrow national or regional interests. Dispatching a mission of Foreign Ministers to the Security Council provides the OAU with an opportunity to have its interests represented directly by persons who actually participate in the meetings of its main policy-making organs (rather than less directly through the Permanent Representatives of African States members of the Security Council and ambassadors of other States selected by the African Group at the United Nations). At the same time, it makes it easier for the African members of the Security Council to emphasize the role which they share with the other members of the Council—that of finding solutions transcending national or regional interests. It would seem to be mutually advantageous for the two organizations to continue this practice.

According to Article 54 of the United Nations Charter, regional organizations have an obligation at all times to keep the Security Council fully informed about activities for the maintenance of international peace and security which they are contemplating or have already undertaken. In practice, this duty does not seem to have been satisfactorily met by the OAU. The OAU does not usually report to the Security Council its activities concerning disputes or other differences between its Members. In addition, while following a practice of regularly communicating to the Security Council OAU resolutions concerning the problems of colonialism and apartheid and other situations involving OAU Members and other States, the OAU does not report to the Council any decisions or activities of its Co-ordinating Committee for the Liberation of Africa or of its Defence Commission. If the Security Council is to be given an opportunity to exercise a more meaningful control over the activities of the OAU affecting international peace and security, it would seem important for the Council to require fuller reporting. But any stress by the Council on the need for full reporting, if it is not to become an instrument of negative control, should be accompanied by some assurance that the Council itself would be willing to consider taking effective measures. Pending improvement of the practice of formal reporting, it might be useful for both the United Nations and the OAU to enlarge the present intersecretariat exchange of information on problems of peace and security in Africa and to continue the African visits of those Special Committees of the United Nations concerned with colonial and related issues. Such exchanges and visits would enable the United Nations Secretary-General to follow developments in Africa that might pose a threat to peace and security so that he may decide in what manner he might complement the role of the OAU and when to bring particular developments to the attention of the Security Council.

2. The OAU and Other United Nations Organs Concerned with Peace and Security

OAU's co-operation with the United Nations organs other than the Security Council is based on parallel resolutions of the General Assembly and the OAU Assembly. In its resolution 2011(XX) of 11 October 1965, the General Assembly requested the United Nations Secretary-General not only to invite the OAU Administrative Secretary-General to attend sessions of the General Assembly as an observer but also "to explore, in consultation with the appropriate bodies of the [OAU], the means of promoting co-operation between the two organizations." Two weeks later, the OAU Assembly adopted resolution AHG/Res. 33(II) whereby it requested the Administrative Secretary-General not only to invite the United Nations Secretary-General to attend sessions of the OAU organs and their subsidiary bodies as an observer but also "to do his utmost to ensure that . . . co-operation [with the United Nations] be as close as possible and cover all fields that interest both organizations."

No formal agreement has been concluded on relationships between the United Nations as a whole and the OAU, but the two Secretaries-General have mutually agreed, in the spirit of the above resolutions, that the co-operation between their respective organizations should consist not merely of "the courtesy of exchanging observers and other formalities" but also of "positive, dynamic co-operation and mutual assistance,"[2] subject only to "real procedural, administrative and budgetary limitations." This understanding has been officially expressed in the form of a report of the United Nations Secretary-General presented to the General Assembly.[3]

Reciprocal representation. There seems to have been no problem in the application of the procedures of reciprocal representation between the United Nations and the OAU. It has been the practice of the United Nations Secretary-General to respond to the invitations of the OAU Administrative Secretary-General by personally attending or arranging high-level representation at the sessions of the OAU Assembly. He has personally attended a number of sessions and has delivered major addresses.

On the OAU side, there have been three forms of representation in the meetings of the General Assembly and its subsidiary bodies. First, in accordance with the above-mentioned resolutions, it has been common practice for the OAU Administrative Secretary-General and his representatives to participate without a vote in the discussions of several sessional committees and special bodies of the General Assembly in whose work the OAU is particularly interested, particularly the Special Political Committee, the Fourth Committee, the Special Committee of Twenty-Four, the Special Committee on Apartheid, and the Council for Namibia. Whenever any of the special bodies conduct their meetings in African capitals, the OAU secretariat participates in their proceedings and offers proposals. A second form of representation has been provided by the African Group in the United Nations whose chairman-of-the-month acts as the spokesman for the Group—hence for the OAU—in many United Nations meetings. The third form comprises visits by African Heads of State to deliver special messages to the General Assembly or the Security Council in their capacity as Chairmen of the OAU Assembly.

Recommendation of items for the agenda. According to the rules or procedure of the General Assembly, regional organizations are not entitled to request directly inclusion of an item in the agenda of the Assembly. But the OAU has not encountered any problem in this regard. Since most of the items of interest to the OAU are in any event regularly placed in the provisional agenda prepared by the United Nations Secretary-General, the occasions on which the OAU wished to propose additional items have been relatively few. On such occasions, the OAU has utilized the African Group in the United Nations as its channel. It was upon the joint request of the African States that the items on the denuclearization of Africa and on co-operation between the United Nations and the OAU were included in the agenda of successive sessions of the General Assembly.

Intersecretariat liaison. Liaison between the secretariats of the United Nations and the OAU is facilitated by the existence of an OAU office in New York and by the fact that Addis Ababa is the seat of the headquarters of both the OAU and ECA, the principal United Nations office in Africa. Consultations and exchange of information may thus be carried out on a day-to-day basis. The liaison between the two organizations has been quite effective, especially since, on the one hand, the strengthening of the OAU New York Office by the appointment of an Executive Secretary of ambassadorial rank and, on the other, the arrangements within the United Nations Secretariat to ensure that the appropriate departments would carry out their respective co-operation with the OAU in consultation with a centrally placed senior official, until recently the Chef de Cabinet and presently the Under-Secretary-General for Inter-Agency Affairs and Coordination.

The only aspect of the liaison arrangements which seems not to have been implemented with satisfactory reciprocity is that concerning the exchange of documents. Though the OAU secretariat has had access to most of the documents of the United Nations, the United Nations Secretariat has difficulty in obtaining OAU documents on a regular basis. A major problem in this regard is that all the records and other documents of the OAU Assembly and the Council of Ministers, except the resolutions, are regarded as confidential documents designed only for limited circulation. In the interest of more effective exchange of information, perhaps serious thought should be given by the OAU to the possibility of narrowing the category of confidential documents or making them available on a confidential basis.

Technical co-operation. The principle of mutual assistance in the recruitment, training, and exchange of administrative, conference, and general service staff and other personnel has been accepted by the Secretaries-General of the two organizations, subject to such considerations as the availability of staff, recruitment difficulties, and the prior obligations of each to meet the requirements of his own organization. Specific possibilities of such assistance have been dealt with as they arose.

In addition to continuing such assistance to the OAU secretariat, the United Nations might find it desirable, in the interest of promoting peace and security in Africa, to study the possibility of strengthening the role of the OAU in peaceful settlement of disputes. The OAU secretariat might benefit from the considerable experience of the United Nations in handling disputes and situations of different kinds and from the fund of knowledge on techniques of peaceful settlement accumulated by the United Nations Secretariat and UNITAR. Although the OAU Protocol of Mediation, Conciliation and Arbitration does not seem to provide for the inclusion of non-Africans in a Board of Conciliators or an Arbitral Tribunal set up for a case, thought might be given to the possibility of obtaining through the United Nations Secretary-General assistance from outside Africa for use in circumstances where the talent of non-African diplomats and their experience with relevant cases of pacific settlement in other regions may be of particular value. Consideration might also be given to the possibility of reciprocal utilization of the members of the OAU Commission of Mediation, Conciliation and Arbitration by the United Nations for diplomatic functions outside Africa.

A precedent on United Nations technical assistance for the OAU in a specific political field of common concern was established by the General Assembly in 1965 when it adopted a resolution requesting the United Nations Secretary-General "to extend to the [OAU] such facilities and assistance as may be requested" in order to help it to carry out studies and other necessary measures for the implementation of the OAU Declaration on the Denuclearization of Africa.[4] A similar policy with regard to the subject of pacific settlement of disputes in Africa might be mutually beneficial for the United Nations and the OAU.

C. STRENGTHENING RESPECTIVE ROLES AND RELATIONSHIPS

1. Disputes Among OAU Members

The OAU has often been successful in bringing about a reduction of tension between those of its Members engaged in hostilities, especially when the conflict in question emerged from a clear-cut inter-State dispute, but it has seldom been able to resolve the underlying disputes. In the major internal conflcits brought before it, it has been unable even to bring about a cease-fire. It would seem to be desirable to strengthen the respective roles of the OAU and the United Nations in helping to end conflict between, as well as within, African States and in providing diplomatic assistance in settling the. disputes.

A civil war situation is problematical for both the United Nations and the OAU from the point of view of jurisdiction. If such a situation is likely to endanger the maintenance of international peace and security, then the Security Council may take appropriate steps under Chapters VI or VII of the United Nations Charter. But no such steps would be expected without an agreement among the permanent members of the Security Council and a substantial majority of other United Nations Member States. If, on the other hand, the situation could not be defined in such terms, the United Nations or the OAU may interpose only with the consent of the legally constituted Government. Sometimes it is difficult to identify the legitimate Government whose consent should be sought. Where this problem does not arise, there is the danger that the host Government may give its consent with the understanding that the United Nations or the OAU might be used to pressure the domestic opponents rather than to play a conciliatory role.[5] Unless a way can be found to obtain the consent or acquiescence of the contending factions for an interposition by an international organization and unless such an organization can inspire confidence that it would be immune from manipulation by one or the other side in the conflict, it would be difficult in most internal conflicts to avoid varying degrees of unilateral intervention and counter-intervention by foreign States.[6]

In both the Congo crisis (1964-65) and the Nigerian civil war, the OAU had to depend on the consent of Governments which were opposed to an intervention by the OAU in any manner that might enhance the status of the insurgent or secessionist regimes. In addition, the ideological aspect of the former conflict was so divisive for the African States that the OAU alone had little prospect of bringing about national reconciliation. Far from lending itself to impartial and effective mediation by the OAU, the Congo crisis together with the ideologically inspired tension between Nkrumah's Ghana and its West African neighbors threatened the very existence of that organization. On such divisive issues the diplomatic initiative of the United Nations Secretary-General would significantly complement the peace-making role of the OAU. If the OAU is unable to form a sufficiently impartial mediation committee or to designate a neutral African statesman to offer his good offices, it should encourage and, if possible, facilitate the exercise of good offices by the United Nations Secretary-General. In either case, insofar as an internal conflict has assumed civil war proportions, it would seem desirable, in the interest of restoring peace and preventing unilateral intervention by foreign Powers, for the Secretary-General to inform the parties, regardless of their legal status, of his readiness to offer good offices so that they may be encouraged to seek a political solution through negotiation.

If such an initiative is rejected by one or both parties and if there is no positive response to appeals for a cease-fire, it might be worthwhile for the political organs of both the OAU and the United Nations to consider the possibility of "neutralizing" the conflict area. Both organizations might find it desirable to collaborate in persuading African and non-African States to deny any political or military assistance to the two sides. This type of action, it should be recalled, was attempted unsuccessfully by the OAU Ad Hoc Commission on the Congo. It might work in the future if the OAU Assembly itself were to recommend this measure to Member States and if the United Nations organs were to build on it and obtain the consent of other States.

The OAU is hardly in a position at present to cope with the enormous problems arising from civil war or from protracted inter-State conflicts. It lacks sufficient military, financial, and personnel resources for such functions as border-sealing, truce observation, and restoring law and order, just as it lacks resources for large-scale relief operations. These tasks require close collaboration between the OAU and the United Nations. Though the establishment of a United Nations peace-keeping force does not seem to be imminent, some progress has been made in the deliberations of the United Nations Special Committee on Peace-Keeping Operations. If such a force is eventually established its African component (any stand-by forces earmarked by African States) might be utilized by the OAU for most of the above-mentioned tasks, with material assistance from and subject to review by the competent organs of the United Nations. But whenever such tasks necessitate large-scale military assistance from States and organizations outside Africa or require an international rather than an exclusively African peace force, the United Nations itself might consider undertaking the peace-keeping operation.

The role of the OAU in peaceful settlement could be strengthened at two points in the course of a dispute: before it develops into a crisis and after the crisis has subsided.

Since many of the internal conflicts of the African States are related to issues of ethnic, religious, or other fundamental human rights transcending national boundaries, the OAU could, with the help and encouragement of the United Nations, play a useful role in the promotion of human rights before hostilities break out. The creation of an OAU machinery for discussing and possibly investigating serious allegations of human rights violations within the OAU Member States might be desirable as a complement to the work of the United Nations in this field; it might indirectly contribute to the lessening of internal conflict and inter-State tension resulting from this problem. An important step has been made by the OAU with regard to the problems of refugees as a result of the conclusion of the OAU Convention relating to the status of refugees in Africa. A similar step with regard to human rights might be needed in the interest of the welfare of the African peoples in general as well as that of peace within the African States.

Some disputes and other differences between African States have been kept away from the OAU and other intergovernmental organizations and no bilateral or other forms of negotiation are in progress. The OAU might be able to provide an invaluable service if it were to encourage diplomatic initiatives before the situation deteriorates into a crisis. If a party to a dispute is reluctant to engage in bilateral negotiations or to seek a solution with the help of a third party, including the OAU, then it might be desirable for a representative of the OAU to try to persuade it to change its attitude. In this regard, the task of the OAU secretariat would be to collect adequate information on the evolution of potentially dangerous African disputes and other differences as well as on political developments affecting the prospects for negotiation. With the help of such information, the OAU representative would be able to engage in exploratory diplomatic contacts with the parties to a dispute in order to initiate a dialogue about the need for negotiation, either bilaterally or with the help of a third party, including the OAU Commission of Mediation, Conciliation and Arbitration.

Up to now neither the President of this Commission nor the OAU Administrative Secretary-General has been officially encouraged by the OAU to play such a role; and both seem to have been inhibited from taking independent diplomatic initiatives in this regard because of constitutional constraints. According to the Protocol of the Commission, the President and the two Vice-Presidents (the Bureau) of that body may consult the parties to a dispute to help them agree on the method of settlement to be applied, but only after the dispute has been brought before them and subject to both parties' acceptance of the Commission's jurisdiction. Since the OAU Assembly has so far refrained from utilizing the Commission and has now converted it from a body with a permanent Bureau to an ad hoc body, it might not be feasible any more to encourage the President of the Commission to assume the task that is being suggested here and to perform it on a continuing basis. As for the Administrative Secretary-General, the limitation of his diplomatic role stems from the fact that the OAU Charter does not confer upon him any prerogative for taking an independent political initiative. Perhaps the time has come for the OAU Assembly to recognize the need for building up his diplomatic role in order to enhance the effectiveness of the entire peaceful settlement machinery of the OAU. For the envisaged diplomatic task, it might not be necessary to amend the OAU Charter so long as he is encouraged to operate under the authority of the OAU Assembly.

With regard to the postcrisis phase of a dispute, the main weakness of the OAU role has been its lack of continuity beyond the point at which relations are normalized. Unless the substantive issues in a dispute are settled, tension may rise again to culminate in another crisis. Once the crisis is before the OAU, it should not be difficult to persuade the parties to accept mediatory services under the Protocol, as amended, in addition to any measures designed to remove the immediate crisis. Thus, when an extraordinary session of the OAU Assembly or of the Council of Ministers has brought the crisis under control by appeals alone or with the help of an ad hoc committee created for the emergency, the arduous task of finding a solution to the underlying problem should begin with the help of mediators or conciliators selected both from the members of the Commission of Mediation, Conciliation and Arbitration and, whenever necessary, from among African statesmen of higher stature. Drawing upon past experience, either deliberative organ might sometimes find it useful to designate a Head of State or another influential statesman to act as a mediator or as the chairman of a mediating body. If the latter course is followed, it might be advisable for the deliberative organ concerned to request the President of the Commission of Mediation, Conciliation and Arbitration to appoint the other members of the body from among his colleagues, in accordance with the provisions of the Protocol. This could be done in consultation with the Chairman of the mediating body. Since the factor of political prestige of a mediator or conciliator seems to be at least as important in the process of peaceful settlement in Africa as that of "recognized professional qualifications" required for membership in the Commission, it would be advisable to bear this in mind in utilizing that organ in its new form as an ad hoc body. It is hoped that the recent transformation should result not in downgrading the importance of its role but rather in making it more usable because of the flexibility that may be introduced in its manner of operation.

2. Problems of Southern Africa

The deteriorating situation in Southern Africa poses a serious challenge to the capacity of both the United Nations and the OAU to bring about peaceful adjustment of the situation in that area. The course of future relationships between the two organizations in the peace and security field would most likely be determined by the extent to which the United Nations is able to meet this challenge. Failure on the part of the United Nations in this regard could mean widespread disillusionment about the United Nations among those who believe that its greatest potential as an agent for peaceful settlement or adjustment lies in the area outside direct big Power confrontation.

The Security Council and the OAU have not been able to agree on an approach that could effectively resolve the situation in Southern Africa. This is largely because of the hitherto irreconcilable differences between the OAU demand for wide-ranging measures against the recalcitrant regimes and the insistence on the part of some other States, especially France, the U.K., and the U.S., that only methods of peaceful settlement should be applied.

These three permanent members of the Security Council have been opposed to the imposition of economic sanctions upon South Africa and Portugal on grounds of legality, practicality, and lopsidedness of the measures demanded by the OAU. Since they did not agree that the situations in South Africa, Namibia, and the Portuguese-administered Territories were already a threat to international peace and security, they have indicated that the application of Chapter VII of the United Nations Charter would be legally unjustifiable. They have maintained that it would be legally inappropriate for the Security Council to apply economic sanctions in order to force South Africa to change its racial policies and give up the administration of Namibia and to force Portugal to grant independence to its colonies. While agreeing that the principle of self-determination should be applied universally, the three Powers have warned that in the process of decolonization, the United Nations should refrain from substituting itself for the administering Power, if it is to avoid exceeding its powers under the Charter. With regard to practicality, they have stressed the possibility that non-white populations in Southern Africa might be the first to suffer from economic sanctions, that such measures might not be effectively carried out without a naval blockade, and that the United Nations might eventually bring about a major confrontation of military forces in Southern Africa rather than effecting peaceful change. An important factor in the assessment of sanctions is, of course, the extent of sacrifice to be made by the States imposing economic sanctions. In this regard, the main trading partners of South Africa—the three major Powers as well as the Federal Republic of Germany, Japan, Italy, and a few other States, including those in Africa whose economies are heavily dependent on South Africa—would be expected to make considerable economic sacrifices. Should it become necessary to introduce a blockade in Southern Africa, many of them would reasonably be expected to bear most of the military burden of preventing violations and to take measures against any of their citizens who fail to observe the boycott. Those of them that maintain mutual defense arrangements with South Africa or Portugal might also regard the blockade of Southern Africa as being detrimental to their strategic interests. From their perspective, resort to peaceful settlement of disputes would seem to be the most valid and realistic alternative.

But the OAU has been highly pessimistic about the possibility of peaceful settlement with the recalcitrant regimes, especially following the instant rejection by Portugal and South Africa of the Lusaka Manifesto's peaceful approach and South Africa's evasive response to the diplomatic efforts of the United Nations Secretary-General concerning Namibia. Its Members have indicated that while peaceful settlement is blocked by such a negative response and as long as the Security Council remains unable to take effective measures for peaceful progress in the area, they would have no alternative but to intensify their support for the activities of the liberation movements against the recalcitrant regimes. They have reached the conclusion that as long as the opposition to sanctions against those regimes continued, the only hope for a solution would lie in guerrilla warfare with moral and material support from the international community. They place special emphasis on the need for supportive action by friendly Governments and by non-governmental organizations and groups everywhere, as stressed in the proposals of the UN-OAU International Conference of Experts for the Support of Victims of Colonialism and Apartheid in Southern Africa (Oslo, April 1973) and the United Nations International Conference of Trade Unions against Apartheid (Geneva, June 1973).[7]

A course of action that aims both at preventing a generalized war in Southern Africa and at bringing about a solution based on racial equality and respect for the right of self-determination would seem to be the only one that could ensure the attainment of the objectives of both the United Nations and the OAU and could also cement relations between the two organizations. In view of the existing sharp differences between the strongly anti-colonial majority and other States—especially between the OAU Members and those Powers having significant economic or security ties with the white regimes in Southern Africa—regarding the feasibility, effectiveness, and implications of different kinds of collective measures against those regimes, it would be difficult for Government representatives (or experts) to chart such a course with any degree of certainty about its acceptability and effectiveness to attain the desired goal. However, it seems clear that there is no substitute for a persistent effort on the part of both the majority and the minority on the colonial issue to work out a strategy against the recalcitrant regimes which could bridge the gap between the

OAU request for far-reaching measures and the very modest response of those Powers having close ties with, and therefore more leverage on, those regimes. A meaningful context for the negotiation of a mutually agreed strategy might be the ideas and principles expressed in the Lusaka Manifesto which were welcomed by virtually all Governments, except the recalcitrant regimes, and whose potentialities for peaceful settlement in Southern Africa are currently being demonstrated with regard to the Portuguese-ruled Territories.

An intensification of the guerrilla warfare in Angola, Mozambique, and Guinea-Bissau in the past few years has exerted so much pressure on war-weary Portugal that it has significantly helped to bring about major political changes within that country. With the military overthrow of Premier Marcello Caetano's authoritarian colonialist regime in April 1974 and its replacement by a reformist regime under the leadership of General Antonio Sebastiao Ribeiro de Spinola, a veteran of the African colonial wars, Portugal has adopted for the first time a policy favorable to a negotiated settlement with the liberation movements in the three Territories. Having inherited a situation of virtual military defeat in Guinea-Bissau and major military setbacks in Angola and Mozambique, the new Portuguese Government has decided to recognize the right to self-determination and independence of all overseas Territories under its administration and has pledged full co-operation with the United Nations in the implementation of the Declaration on decolonization (General Assembly resolution 1514 (XV).[8] Contacts initiated by the new Government with the liberation movements in accord with earlier resolutions of OAU and United Nations organs have led to a cease-fire in Guinea-Bissau, Mozambique, and most of Angola and to negotiations with the African Independence Party of Guinea and Cape Verde (PAIGC) and the Front for the Liberation of Mozambique (FRELIMO). In addition, the Portuguese Government's contacts with the Chairman of the OAU Assembly and with the United Nations Secretary-General, which have culminated in the latter's special visit to Portugal in August 1974, have facilitated the evolution of Portuguese policy from one requiring a referendum prior to the granting of independence in Angola and Mozambique to one committed to taking immediate steps toward formal negotiations with FRELIMO and the liberation movements in Angola with a view to accelerating the process of independence in those Territories in accordance with United Nations resolutions. With regard to Guinea-Bissau, which had declared its independence in September 1973 under the leadership of PAIGC with recognition from over ninety States and had already become the 42nd member of the OAU, the Portuguese Government has accorded formal recognition to the Republic of Guinea-Bissau and has supported the application of Guinea-Bissau for membership in the United Nations. In concluding with PAIGC an agreement for the immediate transfer of the administration in Guinea-Bissau without the Cape Verde Islands, Portugal reaffirmed its recognition of the right of the people of those Islands to self-determination and independence and has undertaken to accelerate the process of decolonization through a referendum in close co-operation with the competent organs of the United Nations.

In view of this fruitful application of the ideas and principles of the Lusaka Manifesto and the United Nations Declaration on decolonization it might be possible to work out a "carrot-and-stick" method for solving the remaining problems of Southern Africa. On the positive side, it would seem to be indispensable to spell out the vague assurances to European settlers expressed in the Manifesto. For example, it would be useful to give a clearer indication of the type of guarantees to be given for safeguarding the rights and interests of European settlers in Southern Rhodesia under majority rule. As for South Africa, it might be worthwhile to stress on the basis of a thorough analysis the various economic and political reasons why apartheid cannot solve that country's complex problems and to try to persuade the Government to devise a more realistic and just policy—a policy based on the consent of all segments of the population rather than one maintained by force.

On the negative side, it might be possible to work out in the Security Council a combination of measures of pressure which could be refined with experience and, whenever necessary, expanded step by step with the consent of all members of the Security Council. The unanimous adoption of a policy of "progressive disengagement" of all Member States having ties with South Africa—a middle ground between OAU's request for the immediate imposition of sanctions and the policy of several members of the NATO alliance to agree to little more than verbal condemnation and a partial arms embargo—might have a significant psychological impact on that country. A logical first step might be to negotiate within the Security Council the suspension of any further economic aid, investment and emigration, the freezing of existing levels of trade, and the full and unconditional implementation of the existing arms embargo against the South African Government. If such initial measures are accepted and fully implemented by Member States, including the major NATO Powers, and if the door is left open for further economic steps of increasing intensity, any advice or words of caution given by those Powers to the South African Government might be expected to carry more weight.

The adoption of a policy of progressive disengagement would, of course, require a change of policy on the part of the main trading partners of South Africa. It would not be unreasonable to expect a change of policy in view of the fact that the suggested initial measures would hardly be burdensome for the States applying them and that any further steps that are required might be taken over a reasonable length of time to permit gradual diversion of trade. By demonstrating the determination of States to intensify economic pressure, this approach might induce the South African Government to engage in meaningful negotiations. However, it may be necessary to dispel first two fallacies that have been advocated by opponents of pressure: the contention that pressure only rigidifies the white regimes in their defiance; and the belief that, if pressure is relaxed, economic growth and the accompanying integration of more Africans into the modern economy may erode apartheid and eventually solve the problem of race relations.[9]

The adoption and implementation of this method of pressure and persuasion for the problems of Southern Africa would call for negotiations at four levels: within the Security Council; between the major Western Powers and those recalcitrant regimes in South Africa and Southern Rhodesia on whom they have some leverage; between the OAU and the liberation movements; and between the recalcitrant regimes and the liberation movements. First, within the Security Council, it would be necessary for the spokesman of the OAU and the three permanent members of the Council that hold the key to effective implementation of resolutions on Southern Africa—France, the U.K., and the U.S.—to negotiate patiently and adopt a workable strategy for the whole area, taking into account the sanctions that are already being taken against Southern Rhodesia. In view of the interrelated nature of the problems of the whole area, it might be advisable for the Security Council to establish a committee on Southern Africa, of which the Committee on Sanctions against Southern Rhodesia could become a major part. The new body would assist the Council in implementing diverse measures against the two recalcitrant regimes. Secondly, it might be useful if France, the U.K., and the U.S. were to take an initiative (individually or jointly, formally or informally) in holding consultations with the recalcitrant regimes with a view to persuading them to suspend any acts of violence and to seek a settlement through negotiation or popular consultation, as appropriate. It might then be feasible for the OAU to persuade the liberation movements to reciprocate by suspending their guerrilla activities and to seek a negotiated settlement. Finally, if the measures of pressure and persuasion are successful in creating suitable conditions for negotiation, the Security Council and, under its authority, the Secretary-General might be able to arrange appropriate mediation between South Africa and the political parties and liberation movements in South Africa and Namibia with a view to concluding agreement on the modalities for peaceful change. In Southern Rhodesia, the responsibility for such mediation might naturally fall upon the U.K. Depending upon the modalities for political change to be agreed upon, the Security Council or the General Assembly might have a useful role to play in all cases in performing tasks such as fact-finding and plebiscites.

Part 2
OAU-UN Relations in the Economic and Social Field

Chapter VI
OAU's Relations with Global
United Nations Bodies

A. INTRODUCTION

While the United Nations Charter provides specifically for relations with regional intergovernmental organizations in the peace and security field and even with international non-governmental organizations (Article 71), it includes no such provisions for relations with non-UN intergovernmental organizations in the economic and social field. Consequently, while the question of consultations with non-governmental organizations is dealt with at length in the rules of procedure of the Economic and Social Council (ECOSOC), no mention is made of non-UN intergovernmental bodies. However, as had been clarified by the Preparatory Commission of the United Nations Conference on International Organization and the Conference itself, the Charter provisions under Articles 57 and 63 about bringing the specialized agencies into relationships with the United Nations need not preclude ECOSOC from negotiating at its discretion relationship agreements with other types of intergovernmental organizations.

On the OAU side also, neither the Charter of the organization nor the rules of procedure of the main organs contain specific provisions concerning relations with the United Nations.

As was indicated in Chapter V, the over-all framework for UN-OAU relations in all fields of activity is provided by Resolution 2011(XX) of the General Assembly and Resolution AHG/Res. 33 (II) of the OAU Assembly of Heads of State and Government (texts in Appendix II). The General Assembly resolution provides specifically for UN-OAU relations at the level of the Assembly itself and that of the Secretariat and also serves as the basis for relations between ECOSOC and the OAU. In August 1951, ECOSOC had adopted Resolution 412B(XIII) whereby it decided to invite to its sessions, as observers, those intergovernmental organizations accorded similar privileges by the General Assembly; this decision became applicable to the OAU in 1965 when the General Assembly adopted Resolution 2011(XX). Similarly, the OAU resolution provides not only for United Nations representation at sessions of the OAU Assembly and the Council of Ministers but also at the meetings of the OAU specialized commissions.

In August 1967, ECOSOC reviewed its practice of relationship with major intergovernmental organizations and adopted resolution 1267B (XLIII) whereby, inter alia, it invited

(i) the United Nations Secretary-General to continue to maintain and to strengthen contacts at the secretariat level with major non-UN intergovernmental organizations in the economic and social field; and

(ii) its subsidiary bodies to make recommendations to it regarding the desirability of similar relationships between themselves and specific non-UN intergovernmental organizations active in the fields of concern to them, on the basis of proposals by the United Nations Secretary-General.

At the level of the principal economic and social organs of the United Nations, the provisions of the above-mentioned resolutions concerning reciprocal representation have been implemented through a method of standing invitations. The representatives of each organization at the sessions of the other's organs are entitled to participate in the debates, without the right to vote, upon the approval of the organs concerned. It is not clear from the terms of the resolution on UN-OAU relations whether attendance at meetings should include the right to submit written statements, but the two organizations are sufficiently well disposed toward each other to permit the circulation of such statements.

At the secretariat level, close relations have been established between the United Nations and the OAU in several fields of activity. In November 1965 in response to an aide mémoire from the OAU Administrative Secretary-General, the United Nations Secretariat agreed that relations between the two organizations should consist of "positive, dynamic cooperation and mutual assistance." Since the relations between the secretariats of the two organizations involve a number of departments, the Under Secretary-General for Inter-Agency Affairs and Co-ordination, is responsible for over-all co-ordination of relations between United Nations Headquarters and the OAU. Within this framework, each department is responsible for cooperation with the OAU in its fields of competence. In the economic and social field, such responsibility is borne by the Department of Economic and Social Affairs.

In the economic and social field, the major part of OAU's relations with the United Nations is carried out not at the level of the General Assembly and ECOSOC but at that of their subsidiary bodies. This part of the study will, therefore, focus mainly on relations at the latter level: first briefly in the present chapter on OAU's relations with the global subsidiary bodies concerned with African development and subsequently in more detail on OAU's relations with ECA.

Certain global bodies of the General Assembly and ECOSOC have had significant relations with the OAU: the Office of the United Nations High

Commissioner for Refugees (UNHCR), the United Nations Development Programme (UNDP), and the United Nations Conference on Trade and Development (UNCTAD). OAU's relations with the United Nations Industrial Development Organization (UNIDO), the United Nations Children's Fund (UNICEF), and the Commission on Human Rights have been more limited, but they are growing in importance.

B. RELATIONS WITH UNHCR

The problem of refugees in Africa comprises humanitarian, social, and economic aspects as well as important legal and political questions of concern to several African countries. Since 1961, the non-political aspects of the problem alone have been so serious that they have created a formidable task for several Governments, intergovernmental organizations, and non-governmental agencies. This has been due to the suddenness and magnitude of the flow of displaced people into neighboring African countries having pressing economic and social problems of their own. Moreover, the presence of such large groups of refugees across the borders of their countries of origin has created not only serious administrative problems but often also a situation of tension with the host countries.

1. Common Objectives and Respective Roles

In accordance with its Statute,[1] UNHCR has been engaged in tasks of a strictly humanitarian and non-political nature designed to help refugees. Its main objectives are: (i) to provide international protection for refugees defined as such in its Statute and for those whom it is called upon to assist under the terms of General Assembly resolutions; and (ii) to seek permanent solutions to their problems by assisting Governments and private organizations to facilitate voluntary repatriation or their assimilation within national communities in the country of asylum.[2] The aim of international protection is to safeguard the legitimate rights and interests of refugees and to encourage Governments to treat them as far as possible on a par with their own nationals. For this purpose, UNHCR promotes the conclusion of, and accession to, legal instruments concerning the status of refugees; the inclusion of clauses beneficial to refugees in more general legal instruments; and, within individual countries, the enactment of legislation and administrative regulations in favor of refugees. In order to attain a permanent solution to the problem, UNHCR provides emergency aid to refugees and, with the approval of its Executive Committee, assists those Governments which are burdened with large numbers of refugees.

The role of the OAU concerning refugees has been centered mainly on

three types of activity: (i) promoting diplomatic discussions and conciliation between countries of origin and asylum, with the help of field visits
by the Ad Hoc Commission on the Problem of Refugees[3] and secretariat
officials; (ii) preparing a convention on problems of African refugees; and
(iii) providing or channeling assistance for the education, placement, and
migration of refugees in collaboration with UNHCR and other members
of the United Nations family. The diplomatic role of the OAU regarding
the refugee problem has been considered in Chapter III; we shall, therefore, concentrate here on the second and third types of activity.

2. Refugee Conventions of the United Nations and the OAU

The drafting of the OAU Convention Governing the Specific Aspects
of Refugee Problems in Africa was a major area of UNHCR-OAU co-
operation. The goal was to ensure that the envisaged African legal instrument should become an effective regional complement to the 1951 United
Nations Convention on the Status of Refugees.[4] As a result of four revis-
ions of the OAU draft convention, the areas of possible incompatibility
were progressively reduced with the help of UNHCR whose regional representative in Africa actively participated in the drafting sessions of the
Legal Experts Committee of the OAU Ad Hoc Commission. The final
version was adopted by the OAU Assembly of Heads of State and Government at its sixth session in September 1969,[5] but the African States were
unduly slow in ratifying it: it entered into force on 27 November 1973
when the required fourteen States had ratified it.

A comparison between the OAU Convention and the 1951 United Nations Convention, which became applicable to African refugees in accordance with the 1967 Protocol on Refugees, would show the areas of complementarity and the points where certain differences of approach or
emphasis seem to exist between the OAU and UNHCR.

a. DEFINITION OF "REFUGEE"

Both the 1951 United Nations Convention and the Statute of UNHCR
define refugee as a person who,

> owing to well-founded fear of being persecuted for reasons of
> race, religion, nationality, membership of a particular social group
> or political opinion, is outside the country of his natonality and
> is unable or, owing to such fear, is unwilling to avail himself of
> the protection of that country; or who, not having a nationality
> and being outside the country of his former habitual residence as
> a result of such events, is unable or, owing to such fear, is un-
> willing to return to it.[6]

Such a person remains outside the mandate of UNHCR if he is already entitled to assistance from other United Nations bodies (such as the United Nations Relief and Works Agency for Palestine Refugees in the Near East—UNRWA) or has already acquired the same rights and obligations as nationals of his country of residence.[7]

The scope of the OAU definition of an African refugee is, however, somewhat broader. It includes also

> every person who, owing to external aggression, occupation, foreign domination or internal disorder affecting either part or the whole of his country of origin or nationality, is compelled to leave his place of habitual residence in order to seek refuge in another place outside his country of origin or nationality.[8]

In practice, the OAU addition may not constitute a major point of difference, since UNHCR has not been restrictive in its determination of eligibility for refugee status in Africa. Because of the vast numbers of the refugees and their location in several places over wide rural areas, it has been difficult to create an administrative machinery in Africa to determine eligibility on a individual basis. UNHCR has, therefore, found it necessary to consider any group displaying the general features of refugees as prima facie eligible.[9] Consequently, the groups that have been entitled for protection and assistance from UNHCR have been the same two groups that the OAU has been seeking to assist, namely: the refugees from Member States of the OAU facing political and social upheavals; and those from countries struggling against colonial rule or domination by a European minority. As regards the second category, there arises the problem of whether the members of the "liberation movements" struggling against colonial and European minority regimes in Africa should receive the benefit of refugee status and all assistance flowing from the acquisition of such a status. In view of the entirely non-political character of its mandate, UNHCR has not been in a position to consider such a group as refugees eligible for its material assistance.[10] The OAU, however, implicitly includes "freedom fighters" in its definition of the term "African refugee."[11]

b. REFUGEE RIGHTS AND SECURITY OF AFRICAN STATES

Both the OAU and UNHCR have been concerned with the question of how to protect and promote refugee rights and interests without in any way jeopardizing the security of any African State. However, while the main focus of the terms of reference of UNHCR is on the protection and promotion of the rights and interests of refugees, Article III of the OAU Convention gives special emphasis also to the protection of the security of signatory States from subversive activities. It requires a country of asylum "to prohibit refugees residing in [its territory] from attacking any Member State . . . either through press or radio, with arms, or through any other activities" and to settle them at a reasonable distance from the frontiers with their country of origin. This Article goes beyond the general requirement contained in the United Nations Convention that refugees should conform to the laws and regulations of the country of asylum as well as to any measures for the maintenance of public order. A notable omission in the OAU Convention is the stipulation contained in Article 26 of the United Nations Convention which accords refugees the right to choose their place of residence and to move freely within the country of asylum "subject to any regulations applicable to aliens generally in the same circumstances." Here also security considerations seem to have influenced the African States to leave the question of freedom of movement of refugees entirely to the discretion of the country of asylum.

C. THE QUESTION OF ASYLUM

If the OAU Convention appears to qualify some of the rights of refugees as stipulated in the 1951 United Nations Convention, its provisions on the right of asylum are a significant complement to the latter which affirms the principle of non-refoulment but contains no specific provisions on asylum. The provisions of the OAU Convention can in a sense be considered as an advance beyond the relevant provisions of the Universal Declaration of Human Rights and the General Assembly Declaration on Territorial Asylum adopted in December 1967.[12] The OAU Convention elevates the nature of the prescription, as regards the African States, from the stage of a mere declaration to that of a treaty obligation. Secondly, it advances the scope of the protection from a mere right "to seek and enjoy in other countries asylum from persecution"—as stipulated in Article 14 of the Universal Declaration of Human Rights—virtually to a *right to receive* such asylum. Article II of the OAU Convention states "no person shall be subjected by a Member State to measures such as rejection at the frontier, return or expulsion which would compel him to return or remain in a territory where his life, physical integrity or liberty would be threatened. . . ." In reaffirming this principle of non-refoulment, the OAU Convention omits the qualification made in the General Assembly Declaration (Article 3, para. 2) that "overriding reasons of national security" or the need "to safeguard the population" may justify an exception. In such circumstances, while this United Nations Declaration merely encourages the State concerned to "consider the possibility of granting the person concerned . . . an opportunity, whether by way of provisional asylum or otherwise, of going to another State," the OAU Convention requires African States to "use their best endeavours" to do so. Accordingly, a refugee "shall have a prior claim to temporary residence in any [African] country of asylum in which he first presented himself"; if the State concerned finds difficulty in continuing to grant asylum, it may appeal through the OAU and directly to the Member States who "shall in the spirit of African unity . . . take appropriate measures to lighten the burden" of the requesting State. Thus, though the duty of a particular Member State of the OAU to grant asylum is not absolute, the right of the refugees to receive such a grant from one or another African State with the help of the OAU seems to be an unqualified one.

It should be stressed that in spite of the foregoing differences in approach or emphasis between the legal instruments of the United Nations and the OAU on refugees, the OAU Convention has emphasized the intended harmony between them by requiring the African States to accept both instruments and to apply the African Convention as an effective regional complement of the 1951 United Nations Convention.

3. Procedures and Practices of Co-operation

The co-operation between UNHCR and the OAU has developed on the basis of, on the one hand, a general mandate contained in the Statute and the rules of procedure of the Executive Committee of UNHCR calling for close liaison with all organizations concerned with refugees[13] and, on the other, a specific mandate for collaboration contained in several resolutions of the OAU organs[14] and in the OAU Convention. The High Commissioner for Refugees and the OAU Administrative Secretary-General have pledged to maintain close relations, especially with regard to mutual consultations, reciprocal representation in meetings, exchange of information, and technical co-operation. These tasks have been facilitated by the existence of a UNHCR Regional Office in Addis Ababa and, more recently, an OAU office in Geneva.

A high point in the co-operation between the OAU and UNHCR was the 1967 Addis Ababa Conference on the Legal, Economic and Social Aspects of African Refugee Problems, which was convened by the two organizations together with ECA and the Dag Hammarskjöld Foundation. The Conference, which was attended by senior officials from 22 African Governments, 10 intergovernmental organizations, and several observers from non-African Governments and non-governmental organizations, has provided a comprehensive set of policies and measures to guide future collaboration among the participating organizations.[15] UNHCR's role was evident from its mandate as a United Nations body with over-all responsibility for refugee problems. The role of the OAU was recognized as being crucial because of the need to enlist the political support of the African States in the implementation of any resettlement plans. ECA was regarded as being well placed to estimate employment needs and placement possibilities in the various African States. Among the specialized agencies, the International Labour Organization (ILO) and the United Nations Educational, Scientific and Cultural Organization (UNESCO) were considered as having special roles to play in their respective fields of competence. Voluntary organizations were included for their valuable role in providing funds and supplies during emergencies, granting scholarships to individual refugees, and assisting them upon their arrival in their new homelands.

A major area selected for co-operation was the education and placement of individual refugees. Upon the recommendation of the Conference, a Bureau was established within the OAU for the purpose of promoting the resettlement and employment of refugees on an Africa-wide basis and for collecting and supplying information concerning opportunities in Africa.[16] An interagency committee advises the Bureau for Placement and Education of African Refugees and helps to co-ordinate the work of the Bureau with that of the component organizations—the OAU, UNHCR, ECA, the United Nations Secretariat at Headquarters, ILO, UNESCO, and the non-governmental organizations concerned. Since the UNHCR regards the OAU Bureau as an "operational partner," the High Commissioner has been helping to raise funds from voluntary sources for its operations[17] and has, in addition, undertaken to arrange grants for the transportation and resettlement of refugees helped by the Bureau.[18]

Distinct from the program of the OAU Bureau, the Department of Political and Security Council Affairs of the United Nations administers a special Training and Educational Program for persons from South Africa, Namibia, Southern Rhodesia, and the Portuguese-administered Territories.[19] As most of the beneficiaries of the Program are eligible for refugee status, this Department has found it essential to establish close working relations with UNHCR, the OAU, and other organizations assisting refugees from Southern Africa.[20]

In spite of the strong political implications of the question of refugees in Africa, especially that of the urban refugees, UNHCR with its strictly non-political objective and the OAU with its tendency to combine humanitarian and political objectives on the matter, have been able to develop close relationships.

C. RELATIONS WITH UNCTAD

The importance attached by the OAU to the work of UNCTAD is reflected in the fact that almost every ordinary session of the OAU Council of Ministers has devoted to it part of its deliberations and that the Economic and Social Commission of the OAU (OAU-ECOS) has set up a subsidiary body to co-ordinate the policies of the African States within the Trade and Development Board of UNCTAD. UNCTAD also has shown keen interest in the work of the OAU concerning trade and development.

1. Common Objectives, Policies, and Respective Roles

There has been no evidence of conflict of interest or wasteful duplication between UNCTAD and the OAU, largely because of the similarity of their basic objectives and the complementary nature of their roles.

The OAU objectives of seeking the restructuring of international trade and the establishment of an intra-African common market[21] is clearly compatible with the goal of UNCTAD "to promote international trade, especially with a view to accelerating economic development."[22] The OAU fully supports the UNCTAD objectives of formulating and implementing principles and policies of international trade and development, of initiating action for the negotiation and acceptance of multilateral agreements in the field of trade, and of providing a forum for the harmonization of the policies of Governments and regional economic groupings. Special significance has been attached by the OAU to UNCTAD's role of arranging conciliations on specific issues and proposals affecting the economic and financial interests of particular countries and to the good offices provided by the UNCTAD Secretary-General in this connection.[23] The OAU, being convinced that any reservations made by the developed countries could prevent effective implementation of majority recommendations adopted by the UNCTAD organs, has fully endorsed the procedure of conciliation prior to voting, as prescribed in the terms of reference of UNCTAD.

The OAU has described the role of the OAU in the field of trade and development as one of facilitating the formation of a "unified African stand" on all important issues and of assisting the African States and the other developing countries to secure effective implementation of the UNCTAD recommendations as well as new concessions from the developed countries.[24] The OAU plays this role through its Ad Hoc Committee on Trade and Development—most of whose members are also members of the Trade and Development Board of UNCTAD—and through meetings of the entire African membership of UNCTAD such as that which formulated the African Declaration of Algiers on Trade and Development (October 1967).[25] The Declaration became one of the bases for the Charter of Algiers[26] adopted on 24 October 1967 by the Ministerial Meeting of the Group of 77 (the group of developing countries within UNCTAD whose number actually exceeds 77).

The Secretary-General of UNCTAD has described the role of the Group of 77 and of the groupings within it, including the African Group, as "highly constructive" because they tend to facilitate the adoption of a common policy in all the subjects of common interest to the developing countries. In trying to demonstrate the complementary nature of the role of UNCTAD as a whole and that of the groups within it, he referred to the consensus, which he perceived among the developing countries, that their group meeting "should not constitute the basis for a confrontation with the developed countries . . . but rather an instrument for setting out the framework of an agreement of all countries."[27]

Though no clear-cut distinction has been made by the OAU between the notion of confrontation and that of presenting a framework for an agreement, the African Declaration of Algiers and the Charter of Algiers might, in the light of the contrasting positions of the developing and developed countries, be regarded more as pronouncements of the common stand of the developing countries than as a framework for a general agreement. Be that as it may, their role as an instrument of pressure for the modification of national trade and development policies seems to be helpful to the efforts of the UNCTAD secretariat. When the Group of 77 sent high-level goodwill missions to the major developed countries to seek acceptance of the principles of the Charter of Algiers, it was generally expected that a new incentive would be given to the consultations of the UNCTAD Secretary-General with various Governments concerning the implementation of the UNCTAD recommendations.[28] The OAU attached so much importance to the sending of such missions that its Council of Ministers urged the African States to participate in it actively and at a high level of representation.[29]

2. The OAU and Institutional Changes in UNCTAD

While there has been no basic incompatibility between the role of UNCTAD and that of the "Group of 77," or its regional groupings including the African Group, increasing concern has been expressed by the OAU about "the lack of political will on the part of the developed countries" to respond positively to the basic demands of the developing nations.[30] Thus, in order to enhance the influence of UNCTAD, the OAU Members and other developing countries have urged modification of its institutional machinery and its methods of work.

a. MACHINERY FOR NEGOTIATION AMONG STATES

A proposal for such improvement, prepared by a working party of the

"Group of 77" and strongly supported by the OAU Council of Ministers,[31] was submitted to the seventh session of the Trade and Development Board by its 31 members from developing countries.[32]

The OAU Members and other developing countries affirmed that UNCTAD should not be an organization for mere deliberation but also for attaining concrete results, that is, for influencing developed countries to adopt more favorable attitudes toward the trade problems of developing countries. This point of view was shared by the Secretary-General of UNCTAD who emphasized in his own report on institutional reforms[33] that there must be wider acceptance of the new dimension of the concept of negotiation, evolved since the creation of UNCTAD, which surpassed the traditional concept prevailing in the General Agreement on Tariffs and Trade (GATT). At the Trade and Development Board, these views prevailed over the contrasting notion expressed by the developed countries that UNCTAD should apply the traditional concept of negotiation in accordance with its function of providing a forum for the identification and discussion of issues with a view to making policy recommendations.[34] Thus, the Board decided unanimously that the process of negotiation at UNCTAD should have three components—exploration, consultation, and agreement—of which the third should be given special emphasis. In order to facilitate agreement, the Board decided that the Secretary-General of UNCTAD should take the necessary initiative in the negotiations and should intensify contacts with individuals or groups of countries in order "to stimulate their political will."[35]

b. NEW EMPHASIS ON OPERATIONAL ACTIVITIES

If one aspect of the institutional reforms deals with the strengthening of the UNCTAD machinery and procedures for conciliation, another equally important aspect concerns the intensification of UNCTAD activities with regard to technical assistance. The emphasis on technical assistance was also a response to the requests of the developing countries, especially the OAU members which are among the least developed, for technical assistance to promote their trade. Furthermore, in view of the paucity of achievements of UNCTAD in facilitating agreement between the developed and developing countries, the UNCTAD secretariat was keen to enhance its usefulness to the developing countries by spreading its domain to operational activities. In order to expand the technical assistance work of UNCTAD in these fields, which is largely performed by the newly created UNCTAD/GATT International Trade Centre, the General Assembly has decided, upon the recommendation of the Trade and Development Board;[36] that UNCTAD "shall" be a participating organization of the United Nations Development Program."[37]

These developments are of particular significance for the OAU because they are likely to facilitate the implementation of special measures to help the least developed among the developing countries, as recommended by the second Conference of UNCTAD,[38] largely in response to the persistent requests of the OAU. The OAU secretariat has welcomed UNCTAD's new emphasis on operational activities, which provides an opportunity for collaboration with the UNCTAD secretariat, that is, a possibility to make up for OAU's lack of expertise in this field and thereby strengthen its own role, which has been highly dependent on collaboration with the ECA secretariat.

3. Procedures and Practices of Co-operation

According to the terms of reference of UNCTAD, intergovernmental organizations such as the OAU whose activities are relevant to the functions of UNCTAD are given a status similar to that accorded to the United Nations specialized agencies to participate in the proceedings of the Conference, the Board, and their subsidiary bodies.

Paragraph 18 of the terms of reference of UNCTAD[39] states that the Trade and Development Board "shall, as required, make arrangements to obtain reports from and establish links with intergovernmental bodies whose activities are relevant to its functions"; paragraph 19 adds that the Board "may establish . . . [close and continuous] links with . . . relevant regional intergovernmental bodies." Moreover, according to paragraph 11, the Board "may make arrangements for representatives of . . . intergovernmental bodies . . . to participate, without vote, in its deliberations and in those of the subsidiary bodies and working groups established by it." The Conference and the Board have accordingly included in their respective rules of procedure provisions for the participation of representatives of selected intergovernmental organizations in their debates, upon the invitation of the President or Chairman of the organ or subsidiary body concerned. Any written statements of such organizations relating to items on the agenda of the Conference, the Board, or the subsidiary organs may be circulated by the secretariat to Member States.[40]

In the same way as the specialized agencies, intergovernmental organizations have been given the right to propose items for the provisional agenda of the Conference and the Board as well as to be notified in advance of a session and to receive the provisional agenda.[41]

Even before it was formally designated as an organization to be regularly invited to UNCTAD meetings,[42] the OAU attended, upon ad hoc invitations, the first two sessions of the Trade and Development Board together with certain other intergovernmental organizations. It has since been represented in most sessions of the Board and at the sessions of the Conference.

As regards the representation of UNCTAD in the relevant meetings of the OAU organs, the Secretary-General of UNCTAD himself has been invited, in the spirit of resolution AHG/Res. 33(II) of the OAU Assembly and resolutions of the OAU-ECOS, to participate in some of the joint meetings of the Ad Hoc Committee on Trade and Development and the ECA Working Party on Intra-African Trade. Not only has he attended those meetings but has also intervened in the discussions.

In addition to favorably responding to most of the recommendations of the ECA-OAU meetings, the UNCTAD secretariat extends some technical assistance to the ECA and OAU secretariats when they jointly organize meetings of African States in preparation for the Ministerial Meetings of the Group of 77.

From the procedural point of view, the relationship between UNCTAD and the OAU seems to have been satisfactory. But the present trend of UNCTAD activities in technical assistance is likely to call for the strengthening of working relations between, on the one hand, the UNCTAD secretariat and, on the other, the regional commissions and intergovernmental organizations outside the United Nations. In establishing day-to-day relations with the OAU secretariat, the UNCTAD secretariat may find the experience of other organs of the United Nations and some specialized agencies useful. Regardless of whether the UNCTAD secretariat decides to utilize for liaison with the OAU its staff members on loan to ECA or to establish a separate liaison office in Addis Ababa, the possibility of wasteful duplication of effort or possible organizational rivalry can be minimized if the emerging relations are conceived within a multi-organizational context (e.g., UNCTAD-ECA-OAU) rather than in sets of bilateral relations.

D. RELATIONS WITH UNIDO

UNIDO's relations with the OAU are based on specific provisions of its terms of reference[43] and the rules of procedure of the Industrial Development Board.[44] As in the case of UNCTAD, they provide for the establishment of working relationships with relevant intergovernmental organizations and for representation by observers in the meetings of the Board and its subsidiary organs. Upon being granted a standing invitation by the Board, the OAU has, since 1970, been able to attend several sessions of the Board.

As UNIDO intensifies its operational activities in Africa, separately as well as jointly with ECA in such matters as industrial planning, feasibility studies, training, and the establishment of centers for industrial information and promotion, it is likely that working relationships with the OAU will also be strengthened. As will be discussed in Chapter IX, ECA and the OAU are improving their relations in this field, especially following their first joint Ministerial Conference on Industry (May, 1971). In preparing the second Conference (December, 1973) UNIDO has joined ECA and the OAU as a co-sponsor and their intensive three-sided co-operation has facilitated the elaboration of a common position regarding Africa's global aid requirements in preparation for UNIDO's second general conference. In addition, the conference has facilitated progress toward the harmonization of policies concerning multi-national co-operation for the co-ordinated development or integration of specific industries.

It appears that OAU's growing relations with UNIDO will be placed on the same footing as those with UNCTAD, especially as regards Africa's requirements of external assistance for industrialization.

E. RELATIONS WITH UNICEF

UNICEF's relations with the OAU are based on ad hoc arrangements between the two secretariats rather than on specific provisions of the terms of reference concerned. The first session of the OAU Health, Sanitation and Nutrition Commission[45] had suggested that OAU-UNICEF relations should develop along formal lines. In June and July 1966 the Executive Director of UNICEF and the OAU Administrative Secretary-General discussed the possibility of concluding a formal agreement, but their consultations could not lead to a mutually acceptable arrangement for relationships.

Because of its concern with the problems of youth in Africa and its emerging activities in regard to nutrition and health, the OAU has often expressed special interest in the work of UNICEF. In May 1966, the OAU secretariat was able to attend, on the basis of an invitation from the Executive Director of UNICEF, two meetings organized by UNICEF in Addis Ababa, including a session of its Executive Board. But the OAU has rarely attended subsequent sessions and intersecretariat contacts have remained rather limited.

This is perhaps partly because the main concern of the OAU is with regional and multi-national activities while that of UNICEF is generally oriented to individual countries. Secondly, the present pattern of co-ordination of activities within each organization tends to make collaboration difficult. UNICEF's work in Africa is co-ordinated not by one regional office but by three area offices in sub-Saharan Africa (Lagos, Kampala, Abidjan), which report directly to UNICEF headquarters in New York, and by two offices in North Africa (Cairo and Algiers), which report, respectively, through the office for Eastern Mediterranean and that for Europe and North Africa. Although UNICEF's office in Addis Ababa (that for Ethiopia) maintains contact with the OAU secretariat there and its office in Lagos (that for Nigeria and Ghana) is in touch with the OAU office in the same city, there has been little or no contact between UNICEF headquarters and the OAU secretariat with regard to programs concerning most of the African countries.

F. RELATIONS WITH THE COMMISSION ON HUMAN RIGHTS

The OAU has attended some sessions of the Commission on Human Rights and its Sub-Commission on Prevention of Discrimination and Protection of Minorities in response to a standing invitation based on a resolution of ECOSOC.[46] The field of human rights has been an area where relations between the United Nations and the OAU have been constantly growing, especially since 1968 when the OAU participated actively in the International Conference on Human Rights held in Teheran.

The Commission on Human Rights has been encouraging the establishment or strengthening of regional institutions in the field of human rights. On the basis of a feasibility study by an ad hoc group, the Commission has recommended that regional human rights commissions should be established in those regions—such as Africa—where they do not exist upon the initiative of the States concerned. It was proposed that the relations between such commissions and other bodies dealing with human rights, whether they are United Nations organs or other regional bodies, should be determined by purely voluntary mutual agreements or arrangements.[47] It will be recalled that the urgent need for the establishment of a human rights commission for Africa under the auspices of the OAU has been emphasized in Chapter V of the present study.

G. RELATIONS WITH UNDP

As will become clear from the following chapters, OAU's serious shortage of financial and personnel resources for economic and social projects makes it necessary for it to look for assistance from organizations in the United Nations family. It has attached so much importance to the establishment of close co-operation with the specialized agencies that since 1965 it has concluded agreements with the ILO (1965), UNESCO (1967), FAO) (1967), IAEA (1967), and WHO (1969). But the volume of assistance so far received from these agencies for OAU-supported projects and for strengthening the OAU secretariat has been so limited that it has decided to establish direct links with UNDP, the organization which furnishes a large part of the agencies' project funds.

Intensive negotiations between the OAU secretariat and UNDP have produced an outline for an agreement which has been approved by both the OAU Council of Ministers and the Governing Council of UNDP.[48] It provides for

(i) technical assistance for strengthening the OAU secretariat—involving training, provision of fellowships, and equipment—with a financial ceiling of $50,000 a year;

(ii) financial and technical assistance for major projects arising from OAU decisions involving intercountry, subregional, or regional co-operation;

(iii) assistance for the education of persons displaced from African Territories under colonial rule or subject to racial discrimination; and

(iv) co-operation in the form of reciprocal representation at meetings (including those of the OAU Assembly and the Council of Ministers as well as the Governing Council of UNDP), mutual consultations, and exchange of information.

In all cases, the request for UNDP assistance is expected to be sponsored by the interested Governments, which should be willing to assume the normal counterpart responsibilities. It is understood that eventual UNDP assistance to the OAU should be channeled through Participating and Executing Agencies of UNDP.[49]

In spite of the concern expressed by some delegations to the UNDP Governing Council about the possibility that some of the activities referred to in the proposed agreement might overlap with or, perhaps, usurp a number of the functions of ECA,[50] the Governing Council has authorized the Administrator of UNDP to conclude an agreement with the OAU along the proposed lines. In doing so, it decided not to wait until the views of ECA were known; it was satisfied with the assurances given by the Assistant Administrator in charge of the UNDP Regional Bureau for Africa that UNDP would, as appropriate, try to associate ECA with the regional or sub-regional projects in question and would expect a subsequent session of ECA to formulate procedures that could ensure appropriate co-ordination of effort with UNDP and the OAU.[51] However, the existing rivalry between the secretariats of ECA and the OAU—which will be examined in the following chapters—would seem to suggest that there is a basic need for an agreed policy for co-operation among ECA, UNDP, and the OAU rather than mere procedures for co-ordination.

H. CONCLUSIONS

The non-representation or infrequent attendance of the OAU in the meetings of most of the United Nations bodies discussed above seems to be largely due to an OAU policy of limiting its participation only to the most relevant meetings of other bodies rather than to any procedural difficulties or restrictive policies followed by the United Nations bodies concerned. No public meetings of a United Nations body reporting to the General Assembly or ECOSOC would be closed to observers from the OAU secretariat if the latter expressed an interest to attend. The fact that most of the United Nations bodies have rarely participated directly in the meetings of the OAU specialized commissions is also hardly due to procedural difficulties or restrictive policies followed by the OAU. Within the framework of the standing invitations extended by the OAU Administrative Secretary-General to the United Nations Secretary-General, any secretariat unit servicing a United Nations body may request to attend a relevant OAU meeting either directly or through observers from ECA who normally represent the United Nations Secretariat as a whole. A routine exchange of provisional agenda of forthcoming meetings could, however, ensure that the various United Nations Secretariat units and the OAU secretariat are aware of any meetings that they may wish to attend directly or otherwise follow closely. The only problem has been with the meetings of the OAU Council of Ministers and its Economic and Technical Committee which have been generally closed to observers, including those from the Untied Nations. Since it is this Committee alone which presently considers economic and social matters, it would be particularly significant for the United Nations bodies concerned to have the opportunity to attend its meetings.

Where the OAU secretariat is unable to attend meetings of a relevant United Nations body for lack of time or because of the financial implication of such attendance, the African delegations to those meetings might be utilized as a link with the OAU. But the OAU secretariat would need to establish regular communication with each African group. The usefulness of such a machinery of co-ordination may be enhanced if, whenever possible, the African membership in a United Nations body is made to overlap with that of an existing OAU committee in a similar field of activity, as is the case with trade and development and the refugee question. In order to ensure a high degree of membership overlap, it might be necessary for the OAU to play a more active role in co-ordinating the selection of African candidates for posts in related bodies of the OAU and the United Nations.

Chapter VII
OAU's Relations with ECA:
Problem of Parallel Structures

The major part of the relations between the United Nations and the OAU in the economic and social field is carried out at the regional level. The remaining five chapters will, therefore, concentrate mainly on ECA-OAU relationships. Following an examination of the existing problem of parallel structures, we will, in subsequent chapters, analyze the resulting jurisdictional dispute and the problem of wasteful competition as well as the processes of co-operation and co-ordination between ECA and the OAU. An attempt will then be made to formulate suggestions for further improving the relationships of ECA and other United Nations bodies with the OAU.

A. THE ORGANIZATIONAL CONTEXT
OF OAU-ECA RELATIONS

Relations between ECA and the OAU are conducted in the context of a complex pattern of vertical and horizontal relationships. The vertical relations concern the respective links of ECA and the OAU specialized commissions with their superior organs. The horizontal relations concern the external links of each with the numerous intergovernmental organizations operating in Africa, which can be grouped into four categories: (i) functional bodies of the United Nations and the specialized agencies; (ii) institutions created by or having special links with ECA; (iii) institutions within the OAU orbit of operation; and (iv) African organizations that are independent of both the United Nations and the OAU.

All the United Nations bodies and agencies that operate in Africa are directly or indirectly concerned with problems of development. In recent years ECA has been seeking to provide, as far as possible, a framework for the co-ordination of economic and social activities carried out in Africa by all such bodies and agencies. It has tried to do so, for example, through the establishment of joint secretariat units in some cases or liaison arrangements and other forms of staff co-operation with others. Since 1967 ECA has taken the initiative to organize periodic consultative meetings among the regional offices of the United Nations family in Africa.

ECA also maintains special links with two regional institutions: the African Institute for Economic Development and Planning (IDEP), whose

Governing Council is a subsidiary body of ECA, and the African Development Bank (ADB), an independent intergovernmental organization which owes its origin to ECA's institution-building efforts.

On the OAU side, the principal organs have sought to establish their pre-eminence over all the less comprehensive African organizations on the basis of a decision of the OAU organs that all regional and sub-regional groupings of African States should be in keeping with the OAU Charter.[1] But they have so far not succeeded in doing so, except in the case of the Commission for Technical Co-operation in Africa South of the Sahara (CCTA) which was integrated into the OAU.[2]

The main sub-regional organizations that remain entirely outside the framework of both ECA and the OAU are: the African, Malagasy and Mauritian Common Organization (OCAM), a multi-purpose institution comprising most of the African States associated with the European Economic Community; and the sub-regional institutions for economic cooperation—the Central African Customs and Economic Union (UDEAC); the West African Economic Community (CEAO, formerly UDEAO); the Council of the Entente States (Conseil de l'Entente); the Conference of East and Central African States; the East African Community; and the Permanent Consultative Council of the Maghreb.[3] The various multinational institutions for the development of the basins of Lake Chad and the Rivers Niger and Senegal are also outside the framework of ECA and the OAU. Though the relations of ECA or the OAU with these independent organizations are as such beyond the scope of the present study, any aspects of the relations having direct bearing on the policies and programs of either organization will be examined as a factor in ECA-OAU relationships.

A second factor is the nature of the vertical links of ECA and the OAU specialized commissions with the superior organs. It should be noted that ECA and the OAU commissions have virtually identical membership (in addition to the 42 African Member States, ECA has non-voting associate members comprising Non-Self-Governing Territories in Africa and States other than Portugal responsible for the international relations of such Territories); but they differ in their sources of authority and control.

ECA, like its sister regional commissions, acts within the framework of the policies of the United Nations and is subject to the general supervision of its parent organ, ECOSOC. Though ECA may make recommendations on economic and social matters directly to its Member States, any proposals having important effects on the economy of the world as a whole require prior approval by ECOSOC; and its programs and priorities are subject to review by this organ. Furthermore, ECA's funds are financed from the regular budget of the United Nations, while its administrative machinery forms part of the United Nations Secretariat,[4] both under the control of the General Assembly.

On the OAU side also, the specialized commissions, which were established by the OAU Assembly in accordance with Article XX of the OAU Charter, are subject to the supervision of the political organs.[5] They operate in accordance with the directives of the OAU Assembly and submit their decisions and work programs to the Council of Ministers for review and endorsement. The Council's prior approval of a program is necessary only when a decision entails substantial financial or political consequences.[6] It is the Council of Ministers which decides upon budgetary and personnel matters. Not only does this organ supervise the work of the commissions, but it also considers any economic and social matters in the first instance whenever the commissions fail to meet.

This comparison of the vertical links suggests that in practice the economic and social programs of the OAU specialized commissions are subjected to greater political control by the higher organs than are the programs of ECA. Secondly, since the amount of financial and personnel resources at the disposal of the OAU is far less than that available to ECA, this inequality of means constitutes another element affecting the dynamics of ECA-OAU relationships.

In the light of the foregoing pattern of vertical and horizontal links affecting ECA-OAU relationships, an attempt will be made in this chapter to answer the following questions:

    (i)   What is the extent of overlapping of responsibilities between, on the one hand, the intergovernmental bodies and secretariat units of ECA and, on the other, those of the OAU? What is the rationale for the establishment of such bodies or units in certain sectors but not in others?

    (ii)   What is the implication of such establishment for the work of ECA and the OAU and for the relationship between them?

    (iii)   What effort is being made to reverse the trend of proliferation of such bodies?

B. OVERLAPPING OF RESPONSIBILITIES

In studying the problem of overlapping responsibilities, it is more significant to focus on the special policy-making bodies and their subsidiary bodies and on the substantive secretariat divisions than on higher organs with broader functions. The organizational structures of ECA and the OAU are shown in Charts IV and V.

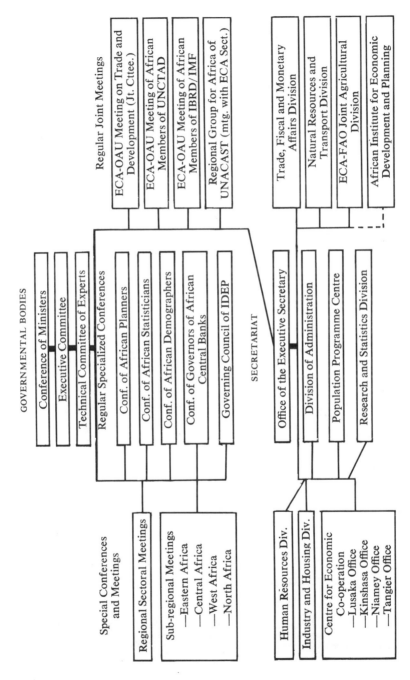

CHART IV
ECA ORGANIZATION CHART

CHART V
OAU ORGANIZATION CHART

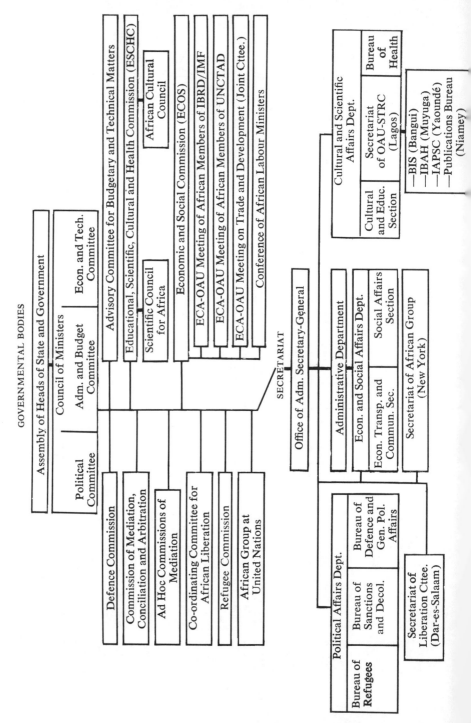

1. ECA and the OAU Specialized Commissions

The special policy-making bodies concerned are the Council of Ministers of ECA and the relevant specialized commissions of the OAU. The OAU bodies consist of the Economic and Social Commission (OAU-ECOS), of which the former Transport and Communications Commission (OAU-TRC) has become a part, and the Educational, Scientific, Cultural and Health Commission (OAU-ESCHC), which now combines the former Educational and Cultural Commission (OAU-EDC), the Scientific, Technical and Research Commission (OAU-STRC), and the Health, Sanitation and Nutrition Commission (OAU-HSNC).[7]

a. ECA AND THE OAU ECONOMIC AND SOCIAL COMMISSION (OAU-ECOS)

In May 1963, when the OAU was established, ECA had already been operating for five years. It was established by ECOSOC in response to a recommendation of the General Assembly and on the basis of Article 68 of the United Nations Charter[8] in order to:

"a) Initiate and participate in measures for facilitating concerted action for the economic and social development of Africa, including its social aspects, with a view to raising the level of economic activity and levels of living in Africa, and for maintaining and strengthening the economic relations of African countries, both among themselves and with other countries of the world;"

"b) Make or sponsor studies of economic and technological problems and developments within . . . Africa . . . and disseminate the results . . .;

"c) Undertake or sponsor the collection, evaluation and dissemination of economic, technological and statistical information . . .;"

"d) Perform . . . advisory services to the countries and territories of Africa . . . provided that such services do not overlap with those rendered by other bodies of the United Nations or by the specialized agencies;"

"e) Assist the [Economic and Social] Council at its request in discharging its functions [in Africa] in connexion with any economic problems, including problems in the field of technical asssitance;" and

"f) Assist in the formulation and development of co-ordinated policies as a basis for practical action in promoting economic and technological development in the region. . . ."

These functions were designed to be performed within the framework of the policies of the United Nations and, of course, within the limits of its resources; no action with respect to any country would be taken without the agreement of the Government of that country.

At its first session, ECA laid down certain principles to guide its work; it decided that it should undertake projects which individual countries by themselves would find difficult to handle and also those whose scope might extend beyond national frontiers.[9]

By the end of its fifth year, that is, by the time the OAU specialized commissions held their first round of sessions (December 1963-February 1964), ECA had not only completed building up its institutional structure including the secretariat but had also established or was completing the establishment of African institutions, notably the Annual Conference of African Statisticians, the African Institute for Economic Development and Planning, and the Conference of African Planners, as subsidiary bodies of ECA, and the African Development Bank as an independent organization. At the sub-regional level, ECA had established branch offices of its secretariat in North and West Africa to be soon followed by similar offices in other sub-regions. In addition to the building of institutions, its principal activities during this period comprised information gathering and research. Its operational activities such as training, the provision of advisory services to Governments, and co-ordination of national development plans, policies, and actions have, however, gained emphasis only since the beginning of the second five-year period.[10]

The OAU Economic and Social Commission, the body with the closest resemblance to ECA, was established to study problems relating to economic and social development, especially those concerning[11]—

(a) the creation of a free trade area among the African countries and the development of trade among them;

(b) the establishment of a common external tariff and a common fund for the stablization of raw material prices;

(c) the restructuring of international trade;

(d) the setting up of an African payments and clearing union and a Pan-African monetary zone following the progressive freeing of national currencies from all non-technical external attachments;

(e) the harmonization of existing and future national development plans;

(f) the raising of social standards and the strengthening of inter-African co-operation through the exchange of social and labor legislation, the organization of vocational training courses for African workers, and the establishment of an African Trade Union, an African youth organization, an African scouts union, and annual African sports.

In addition, the OAU-ECOS is charged with the co-ordination of means of transport and the establishment of inter-African transportation companies. By incorporating the Transport and Communications Commission, the OAU-ECOS has not only regained exclusive competence within the OAU over these matters but has also expanded its area of responsibility to include the co-ordination of African telecommunications and postal services.[12]

Since the terms of reference of ECA are far more general than those of the OAU-ECOS, the extent of overlapping of objectives becomes more apparent when activities of ECA are examined. In March 1963, just before the establishment of the OAU, ECA had instructed its Executive Secretary to undertake intensive studies on the major problems of an African common market, having particular regard to the balanced integration of economic development in various African countries. A preliminary paper on the subject was in fact submitted to the African Governments attending the Summit Conference that created the OAU. The concern of ECA with problems of stabilization of commodity prices and other aspects of international trade goes back to 1960 when these matters were included among the subjects to be given priority by the Executive Secretary. ECA's interest in the establishment of an African payments union was first expressed in March 1963 when the Commission requested the Executive Secretary to undertake a study on the subject. Its studies on the various monetary systems in Africa and their impact on intra-African trade go back to 1961; similarly with its activities in transport and communications. Moreover, ECA became actively engaged in the co-ordination of national development plans as early as March 1963.

In the social field also ECA's concern with social welfare, community development, and vocational training predates the establishment of the OAU, but its interest in youth mobilization was articulated later. The only subjects in the OAU-ECOS terms of reference which fall largely outside the ECA sphere of direct interest are those concerning African labor unions and sports. ECA had already become keenly interested in all the other subjects before the establishment of the OAU.

b. ECA AND THE OAU EDUCATIONAL, SCIENTIFIC, CULTURAL AND HEALTH COMMISSION (OAU-ESCHC)

The OAU-ESCHC combines all the objectives for which its predecessors—the OAU-STRC, the OAU-EDC, and the OAU-HSNC—had been separately established. Within the educational, scientific, and cultural fields, the OAU-ESCHC is concerned with developing effective means of co-operation among the African States in matters of science and technology relevant to the development of Africa. It has inherited the following responsibilities from the OAU-STRC: to formulate scientific policies; to conduct scientific surveys of Africa's natural resources; to execute multinational projects of scientific and technological research and promote effective utilization of the results by the African States; to promote training and exchange of scientific, technical, and research personnel and to provide facilities for the dissemination of scientific information to them; and to channel external aid for relevant OAU-sponsored projects.[13] The tasks derived from the OAU-EDC include the promotion of educational and cultural activities with relevance to both economic development and African unity. A major objective of the Commission in this regard is to help in the implementation of the UNESCO Plan for African Educational Development—the Addis Ababa Plan of 1961.[14]

All these areas of responsibility of the OAU-ESCHC, except those primarily concerned with cultural development, had been of direct interest to ECA long before the establishment of the OAU. In the field of education, the Addis Ababa Plan was the product of the first conference of African Ministers of Education which was convened jointly by UNESCO and ECA. ECA had also taken an active part in the implementation and review of this Plan within the overall framework of the economic and social development plans of the African countries. In the field of science and technology, ECA had long been engaged, in collaboration with other bodies in the United Nations family, in surveying natural resources in Africa as well as in disseminating technical information to the African Governments. It had also been concerned with the application of science and technology to the development of African agriculture, industry, transport, and telecommunications—a task which gained special emphasis following the establishment in 1964 of the United Nations Advisory Committee on the Application of Science and Technology to Development (UNACAST) and the subsequent setting up of regional groups of this Committee.

In the field of human and animal health, for which the OAU-ESCHC is now responsible, ECA's involvement has, until recently, been less direct than in other fields. However, since 1967, while continuing its regular programs on housing, social welfare, and community development, all of which have some health aspects, ECA became engaged in collaboration with WHO and FAO in projects dealing specifically with health problems.

C. RATIONALE FOR THE ESTABLISHMENT OF
THE OAU SPECIALIZED COMMISSIONS

Since the African States were presumably fully aware of the scope of ECA objectives and activities and since they had full control over the proceedings of the ECA sessions, it should be explained why they felt the need to create the OAU specialized commissions with objectives similar to those of ECA.

The African States appeared in 1963 to be somewhat disillusioned with ECA. They had come to realize that it was not quite the powerful African instrument that they had imagined it to be when, over the opposition of the colonial Powers, they won, with the help of other developing countries, majority support for a General Assembly resolution directing ECOSOC to establish ECA. ECA had a slow start—partly due to the prolonged debates on political issues at its sessions, especially that concerning the membership of the colonial Powers and South Africa.

Being primarily a research-oriented organization rather than an operational agency, it devoted most of its energy to data gathering and analysis while the African States were also expecting from it operational activities that could produce quick returns. In the view of many of them, its ambiguous relationship to the United Nations family of organizations had made it neither an effective channel for aid to Africa nor an instrument serving strictly African demands and priorities.[15]

Thus when the relevant provisions of the OAU Charter were drafted, the logic of creating specialized commissions in the economic, social, and related fields was hardly questioned by the African States. Indeed, all the Charters of previous African Summit Conferences—which were presented for consideration by the "founding fathers" of the OAU together with a new draft Charter proposed by Ethiopia—envisaged a comprehensive African organization, with the necessary institutions in the political, economic, social, and related fields.

When the various plans for an African organization were considered by the Preparatory Conference of Foreign Ministers, preceding the African Summit Conference of 1963, some delegations seemed to imply that the committees or commissions to be established should strengthen ECA by securing political consensus and support from the higher political organs, but without themselves engaging in operational activities.[16] Some of them even opposed a proposal, which was subsequently adopted, that the Summit Conference should appoint a committee of African experts to study in consultation with ECA various African economic and social problems, arguing that ECA with its adequate facilities and its vast experience in these subjects should be invited to accomplish the task.[17] However, the majority, while agreeing that the African States should give greater importance to their responsibilities within ECA than had been the case in the past, felt that ECA as a United Nations body could not be a substitute for the envisaged "genuinely African institutions" to guide African affairs. They insisted that new African institutions should be established even though they may "create the impression that they were duplicating in a way the work of international organs."[18]

The consensus reached at the Summit Conference was to establish four specialized commissions in the economic and related field (OAU Charter Articles XX-XXII) to co-ordinate and harmonize the general policies of the African States. It did not appear as if the commissions were intended for extensive technical operations. But it became increasingly clear during the first session of the OAU-ECOS that this Commission would embark on substantive duties in areas where ECA had already been engaged and not merely limit itself to considering the results of ECA's work with a view to making recommendations to its superior organs. The OAU-ECOS' general program of work implied that this body would be engaged, simultaneously with ECA, in studies concerning national development plans, intra-African trade, and transport and communications while, for the time being, leaving for ECA the tasks concerning natural resource development and the social aspects of economic development.[19]

Although some effort was made at the first session of the OAU-ECOS to minimize overlapping of responsibilities with ECA—the representative of ECA to the meeting was in fact invited to help in the drafting of the pertinent resolutions, including the ones on the work programs of the OAU-ECOS and on relations with ECA—the division of tasks between the two organizations remained far from clear. Since the resolution did not clarify the respective roles, the extent to which the OAU was to undertake programs of research, institution building, and various operational activities, such as those of ECA, depended on whether or not it was able to set up effective subsidiary bodies and corresponding secretariat units.

2. Overlapping Subsidiary Bodies and Secretariat Units

Charts IV and V showed that at the level of the subsidiary bodies of ECA and the OAU specialized commissions there are no OAU counterparts for ECA's Executive Committee and the Technical Committee of Experts or for ECA's periodic continental conferences in special fields and its sub-regional meetings on economic co-operation. A serious problem of parallel technical bodies occurred only in regard to certain OAU expert bodies and the working parties of ECA which have now been abolished. At the Secretariat level, the only substantive divisions of ECA whose activities are not covered by the OAU secretariat are the Research and Statistics Division and the Population Programme Centre.

Even though the problem of parallel technical bodies exists no longer, an examination here would elucidate the roots of the problem of competition between the two organizations. As is shown in Chart VI, during 1964 and 1965, ECA and the OAU specialized commissions decided to establish parallel or overlapping technical bodies dealing with various sectors of economic and social development. Of the technical bodies indicated in the chart, the following pairs were created with almost identical functions:

(i) the OAU Transport and Communications Commission and the ECA Working Party on Transport and Telecommunications;

(ii) the OAU Expert Group on Economic Integration and the ECA Working Party on Intra-African Trade; and

(iii) the OAU Expert Committee on Education and the ECA Working Party on Manpower and Training.

The other technical bodies of the OAU, though not constituting counterparts of particular ECA working parties, shared with the latter considerable areas of mutual interest.

Why were these rival technical bodies created? The interaction of three factors appears to have induced this development: intersecretariat competition, secretariat wish to create the impression of progress, and Member State desire to ensure joint ECA-OAU action. As the two secretariats were not genuinely co-operating, but rather competing for influence in the economic and social field, institutional duplication seemed to be a natural development. Secondly, as the two secretariats encountered serious obstacles in their efforts to induce the African Governments to move faster toward multi-national co-operation, while being constantly urged by the same Governments to show progress, they again seemed to face an almost irresistible temptation to resort to institution building. The third factor was paradoxical since the African delegations to the sessions of ECA and the OAU-ECOS appeared to be unconcerned about institutional duplication, as were the two secretariats.[20] A possible explanation was the expectation of many delegations that the existence of parallel bodies might eventually induce the two organizations to collaborate closely in those areas of deep mutual concern. This can be inferred from the ECA resolution establishing the working parties: that once those ECA bodies were constituted, the OAU might find it desirable and practical to collaborate with ECA in convening and servicing them, thereby in effect merging its own technical bodies with them.[21]

The lack of wisdom in the creation of such rival bodies became evident to the two secretariats when they encountered insurmountable difficulties in making such bodies operational. Only two working parties of ECA and one technical body of the OAU-ECOS could be convened. The ECA and OAU secretariats had to face the problem of persuading Member States to nominate experts for many technical bodies, established without much thought about the additional demands on the time of the relatively few,

CHART VI

PARALLEL TECHNICAL BODIES OF ECA AND OAU—1964-66

Field of Activity	Technical Bodies Envisaged in 1964-65 and Meetings Held				Remarks
	ECA Technical Body	Meetings	OAU Technical Body	Meetings	
Intra-African Trade	Working Party on Intra-African Trade (est. Feb. 1965)	Since May 1966	Expert Group on Economic Integration (est. Jan. 1965)	None	Since March 1966 the ECA Working Party and the OAU Ad Hoc Committee have held Joint Sessions
International	None		Ad Hoc Committee on Trade and Development (est. Jan. 1966)	Since April 1965	
Transport and Telecommunications	Working Party on Transport and Telecommunications	None	Transport and Communications Commission (OAU-TRC) (est. July 1964)	Oct./Nov. 1964	ECA and OAU convened a joint conference on telecommunication in Africa in March 1966; the OAU-TRC was merged into the OAU-ECOS
Human Resources Development	Working Party on Manpower and Training (est. Feb. 1965)	Sept./Oct. 1966 April 1967	1. Expert Committee on Education 2. Programming Committee of former OAU-EDC	None Jan. 1965	
Application of Science and Technology to Development	Joint Meetings of ECA Secretariat and African Regional Group of UNACAST (Jan. 1966)	Since Jan. 1966	1. Scientific Council for Africa (est. Feb. 1964) 2. Executive Committee of former OAU-STRC (est. Feb. 1964)	Since Dec. 1965 None	The Ad Hoc Programming Committee and the Panel of Scientists of the OAU-STRC met in Jan 1965 as an interim Exec Cmtee. of the OAU-STRC

hard-pressed experts.[22] The net result was that only when the OAU failed to convene most of its expert groups did it agree to organize in collaboration with the ECA secretariat joint meetings between its only functioning technical body, the OAU Ad Hoc Committee on Trade and Development, and the ECA Working Party on Intra-African Trade.

At the secretariat level, the problem of institutional overlapping was not serious from the outset. The OAU-ECOS had refrained from recommending the establishment of a separate secretariat for itself;[23] the general opinion of the African States was that the department dealing with general economic and social matters should be small. As regards the OAU-STRC, however, the Council of Ministers decided not only to maintain a small department for cultural and scientific affairs in Addis Ababa but also to convert the machinery of the CCTA in Lagos into a special OAU secretariat for scientific, technical, and research matters. But this special secretariat and its specialized bureaus in different African countries did not seem to raise a problem of wasteful overlapping with the ECA secretariat: the OAU-STRC's areas of operation were regarded as bearing lesser resemblance to the work of ECA than to that of such specialized United Nations bodies or agencies as UNACAST, UNESCO, and FAO, and in any case the former CCTA had already established a practice of collaboration with ECA.

The possibility of duplication of effort between the secretariats of ECA and the OAU has been further reduced by the fact that the latter has not been able to build its secretariat units to their authorized size, that is to about one-third the size of the corresponding divisions of the ECA secretariat.[24] Factors of finance and personnel have accounted for the weakness of the OAU secretariat. The relative smallness of the OAU budget (approximately $2.5 million per year covering all the OAU activities, including those in the political field, as compared with ECA's average yearly expenditure of over $4 million over the past five years) and the delays in the payment of assessments[25] have not only prevented the establishment of a sizable secretariat but have also made it difficult for that organization to offer conditions of employment that would attract highly qualified African candidates. However, although progress has been made toward raising the standards of employment to make them comparable to those prevailing in international organizations, especially ECA, and the diplomatic services of African Governments, the problem of recruitment still remains serious because of the shortage of qualified and experienced African experts in the economic and social field. Also, the fact that the OAU secretariat can recruit only Africans cuts it off from much of the expertise available to an international secretariat such as that of ECA.

C. CONSEQUENCES OF OVERLAPPING BODIES
AND EFFORTS AT STREAMLINING

The creation by ECA and the OAU of organs with parallel or over-lapping responsibilities seems to have had adverse effects on some aspects of the work of the two organizations.

There has been a tendency in both organizations to multiply the number of their meetings, which has entailed not only additional financial strain for the secretariats concerned and for the Member States but also an increase in the call upon hard-pressed African Ministers and other officials, with the result that the number as well as the quality of participants in meetings has been progressively declining. On the OAU side, many of the technical meetings envisaged by the specialized commissions could not be convened; for lack of quorum, the specialized commissions themselves have had to postpone repeatedly for over five years their scheduled third round of sessions.[26] Similarly, many meetings of ECA that had been pro-visionally scheduled had to be postponed or canceled partly due to diffi-culties in co-ordinating them with the meetings of other organizations, including the OAU, and partly to doubts concerning the degree of atten-dance. Even though ECA has begun holding biennial instead of annual sessions, the number of non-attending members has recently reached 13 in contrast to a maximum of 4 during the sessions prior to 1967.

The establishment of bodies with overlapping responsibilities seems also to have led ECA and the OAU to compete in inviting African experts, whose numbers are too limited to meet even the needs of the African Governments themselves, to serve in the technical bodies and secretariats of the two organizations. While the OAU has been anxiously trying to build up the core of its secretariat, ECA has been intensifying its efforts to raise the ratio of its African professional staff from the level of about 50 percent existing at the end of 1966 to a maximum of 75 percent in response to the demands of the African States and in accordance with a principle concerning regional recruitment laid down by the United Nations Secretary-General[27]

Even though the OAU specialized commissions had decided to establish only a few subsidiary bodies with close resemblance to certain technical bodies of ECA, considerations of finance, personnel, and time induced the OAU as well as ECA to seek remedial measures to the problem of wasteful overlapping, both within each organization and between them. The OAU Assembly found it necessary not only to limit the number of all technical meetings but, more significantly, also to reduce the number of the spe-cialized commissions and to make their sessions biennial rather than annual.[28] The regroupment of the five specialized commissions dealing with economic, social, educational, cultural, scientific, and health problems into two commissions—OAU-ECOS and OAU-ESCHC—became operative in November 1967 when the necessary amendment to the OAU Charter came into force. Similarly, ECA found it necessary first to limit the number of its meetings by organizing biennial instead of annual sessions of the Commission and arranging fewer but well-prepared technical meetings[29] and later to reorganize its subsidiary bodies by establishing the Executive Committee and the Technical Committee of Experts and abolishing all but one of its seven working parties.[30]

The institutional reforms carried out by ECA and the OAU have undoubtedly facilitated a more efficient use of scarce resources, but as each organization has continued to underline its policy-making function, the fundamental issue of respective roles has remained unresolved.

Chapter VIII

OAU-ECA: Jurisdictional Issues and Division of Labor

The establishment in ECA and the OAU of organs with overlapping responsibilities has raised jurisdictional issues as well as problems of co-operation and co-ordination in activities of mutual interest. These problems have led to a call for an agreement between the two organizations on principles governing their respective roles. Such principles could represent one or more of the following:

(i) acceptance of hierarchical relationships between the two organizations as regards decision-making on important issues;

(ii) division of roles between them based on the nature of the functions performed (assuming that a clear separation can be made between technical activities and the formulation of policy);

(iii) recognition of each other's spheres of special interest and of exclusive responsibility as regards subjects of economic development within the general areas of common concern;

(iv) acceptance, as a basis for co-operation, of the notion of equality of competence in all fields of mutual interest and at all stages of decision-making and implementation.

The question of respective roles and division of work between ECA and the OAU has been the subject of considerable debate at many meetings of the two organizations, especially during the two years preceding the conclusion in November 1965 of an agreement on co-operation.

The respective approaches of the two organizations can be examined in the light of the principles implied in the above four bases of relationships.

A. THE OAU APPROACH

The OAU approach seems to imply hierarchical relationships between ECA and the OAU and as such seems to call for a combination of (i) and (ii) above. The OAU secretariat has maintained that even though it did not doubt the ability of ECA to respond to the wishes and aspirations of the African Governments—they collectively form its policy-making body— the final policy decisions on economic issues with significant political implications, particularly those crucial to the objectives of African unity, should be taken by the highest political organ of the OAU, the Assembly of Heads of State and Government.[1] Accordingly, the role of the OAU in the economic field was to be defined in the light of the political nature

of that organization and its objective of bringing about "close co-operation . . . [and] unity of action and purpose among African Governments,
by deliberate and conscious efforts." In the view of its first Administrative
Secretary-General, the OAU was an organization with a built-in mechanism for the taking of decisions at the political level and specially suited
to deal with issues which were "half political and half economic which
ECA [was] not particularly suited to [handle] because of its nature as a
United Nations organ".[2] These arguments reflect a claim that the OAU
should have institutional pre-eminence over ECA because: (a) the African
States are represented in its highest organ by their Heads of State or Prime
Ministers, in contrast to the ministerial (or lower) representation in ECA,
and (b) OAU's capability as a politically oriented organization should
entitle it to play a special policy-making role in economic and social
development within the present political setting.

The OAU-ECOS adopted a resolution on the respective roles of the
two organizations on the basis of these arguments and also bearing in mind
the fact that ECA had already a well-established structure, a body of
experience, a wide range of projects in progress as well as technical and
financial resources far exceeding those of the OAU. This resolution notes
that

> the Economic and Social Commission of the Organization of Afri-
> can Unity is basically a policy-making and executive body while the
> role of the Economic Commission for Africa is generally limited
> to technical and advisory functions.[3]

Although there was very little difference between the subjects included
in the program of work accepted by the OAU-ECOS and the studies and
investigations which this OAU body requested ECA to continue, subsequent recommendations by the Administrative Secretary-General indicated
that among the political-economic issues which the OAU by its very
orientation was specially qualified to handle were the problem of economic
integration in Africa involving the creation of an African common market
and the harmonization of national and regional development plans and
policies.[4]

The OAU secretariat has argued that, irrespective of the number of
technical studies undertaken on the establishment of an African common
market, one has to recognize in the final analysis that its creation has to be
decided at the highest political level. On this basis, the following conclusion was drawn on the division of work between ECA and the OAU: ECA
would, in addition to undertaking a study of the technical problems, provide a technical forum while the OAU would provide a machinery to
consider "the political and other aspects of the problems" of economic

and social development, as well as co-ordinate the policies of the African States. Such an arrangement would not only promote intimate collaboration between the two secretariats but also permit the OAU to benefit from the large reservoir of expertise at the disposal of ECA. Moreover, by thus combining the efforts of the two organizations, it would ensure considerable saving in time for government officials dealing with this problem.[5]

Implied in this approach to relationships are not only organizational hierarchy between the two organizations/in decision-making and qualitative division of work in regard to specific fields of activity, but also a heavy reliance on ECA and other bodies of the United Nations for technical assistance. Arguing that the OAU by its very nature cannot be a suitable recipient of bilateral assistance, the OAU Secretary-General has indicated that much of the necessary assistance for the OAU economic and social programs would have to be obtained "through the medium of the United Nations and its Specialized Agencies."[6] The significance of this factor of international assistance has been such that the ninth ordinary session of the OAU Council of Ministers listed the maximization of such benefits as one of the cardinal principles guiding the OAU in its relations with the United Nations system.[7]

B. THE ECA APPROACH

In contrast to the OAU approach to the problem of respective roles, which is based on the premise that ECA and the OAU differ in the basic nature of their functions, in the nature and extent of their resources, and, therefore, in their relative suitability to take final policy decisions concerning Africa, ECA's approach tends to stress practical division of tasks and co-operation on the basis of formal equality and organizational independence. Thus, commenting on the OAU secretariat's assertion that there was a fundamental difference between the two organizations—namely, while the OAU was not subordinated to any higher authority ECA's decisions were subject to approval by ECOSOC—the ECA secretariat stressed that the Commission's constitutional position as an integral part of the United Nations could not adversely affect its African character since the orientation of its work was determined by its members, the African States. If, as suggested by the OAU secretariat, ECA should find it necessary to adapt its working methods to fit the new African context resulting from the creation of the OAU, such changes would have to be in accordance with its terms of reference, that is, "within the framework of the policies of the United Nations and subject to the general supervision of the Economic and Social Council." But ECA's claim that it was a genuinely African institution and the fact, pointed out by the OAU secretariat itself, that there had been no instances of action by ECOSOC making its supervisory functions over ECA distasteful to the African States, tended to reduce the significance of the issue of relative suitability of the two organizations for policy-making.[8]

As regards the related issue arising from the claim of basic differences in the functions and orientations of the two organizations, the ECA secretariat seems to distinguish between the consideration of the political aspects of economic problems and policy-making in the economic and social fields. Concerning the political aspects, it did not dispute the claim that it was for the OAU "to weigh their character and indicate how they should be dealt with."[9] But this was not to imply any hierarchical relationship because the OAU would be expected to provide recommendations rather than directives; on any matter of a political nature concerning ECA's work the final decision would have to be taken by the United Nations General Assembly. This issue was clarified at the ninth session of ECA in connection with the designation of representatives of the peoples of certain Non-Self-Governing Territories which were already associate members of ECA to participate in the proceedings of the Commission.[10]

On the function of policy-making and the implementation of economic and social programs, ECA felt that the OAU notion concerning respective roles would be inconsistent with ECA's terms of reference. Far from limiting its role to that of providing technical and advisory services, the relevant provisions in its terms of reference stipulate that the Commission may (i) "initiate and participate in measures for facilitating concerted action" for African economic and social development and (ii) "assist in the formulation . . . of co-ordinated policies as a basis for practical action."[11] These functions have been interpreted by the United Nations Secretary-General as involving not merely the provision of technical services for the study and exploration of African economic problems, but also as implying a role for ECA as a center for consultations where Governments can freely define and elaborate the form of their co-operation. In his view, ECA was conceived as a flexible institution which could "retain its value and usefulness through changes in political and constitutional patterns" in Africa.[12]

On the technical assistance aspect of ECA-OAU relationships envisaged by the OAU, there seem to be no significant differences between the two organizations. Upon the authorization of the United Nations Secretary-General, ECA has indicated its readiness to provide the OAU secretariat with as much technical assistance as its normal resources could permit.

It can be inferred from these considerations that ECA's approach to the problem of relationships was based not on any notion of "fundamental differences" between the two organizations but on the fact that the relevant

OAU specialized commissions, which like itself were subject to the supervision of higher political organs, were engaged in activities similar to its own. Arguing that it would not be feasible to divide responsibilities between them on the basis of fundamental principles, ECA has maintained that the tasks should be shared on pragmatic grounds; the two organizations could, for example, engage in joint programs or in complementary activities dealing with different aspects or phases of a problem.

Accordingly, rather than basing the relationships on an a priori definition of respective roles, the ECA approach relied on the application of agreed procedures to divide work between the two organizations in concrete cases and to co-ordinate their activities. This approach did not, of course, exclude the possibility that each organization might concentrate on those fields of activity in which it had a special interest and for which its orientation, experience, or expertise was appropriate so long as it did not claim exclusive jurisdiction.

C. THE COMPROMISE

The problem of guiding principles was not the only issue between ECA and the OAU during their two-year debate over the question of their mutual relationships which culminated in the 1965 Agreement on co-operation (see Appendix III). There was also disagreement over the degree of formality of the collaborative arrangements to be concluded. While the OAU advocated the conclusion of a formal agreement providing "a legal guarantee to every common action,"[13] the ECA secretariat preferred a "simple exchange of letters" between the two secretariats which would provide a framework "flexible enough to be immediately adapted."[14]

The 1965 Agreement on ECA-OAU co-operation is indeed a compromise between the two organizations as regards the above two issues.[15] As a formal legal instrument signed by the United Nations Secretary-General and the OAU Administrative Secretary-General, it meets the OAU demand for a binding arrangement defining precisely the framework of co-operation. On the more fundamental issue of respective roles, however, the concession was made by the OAU. The Agreement includes no provision that might imply functional differentiation or organizational hierarchy between them. In line with the pragmatic approach of ECA, consultations are to be held, when circumstances so require, between the Administrative Heads of ECA and the OAU to seek agreement on the most effective manner of undertaking specified activities.[16]

However, the absence of a definition of respective roles from the Agreement should not imply that the OAU has abandoned its claim of pre-eminence in policy-making. Even after the conclusion of the Agreement, representatives of the OAU secretariat continued to claim that the "OAU must be the sole forum for the drafting of decisions on economic policy, for the formulation of the most appropriate programmes and for the selection of projects best adapted to African realities." Not only have they stressed the shortcomings of the Agreement, but they have also suggested that it might be desirable to amend the terms of reference of ECA in order to ensure that this body would "limit its efforts to seeking the most effective technical and financial means" to implement the programs formulated by the OAU.[17] On the other hand, the ECA secretariat has maintained that since it has not proved impractical to apply the existing Agreement, there would be no immediate need to modify it. It would envisage no radical changes in the Agreement or the terms of reference since such changes could be detrimental to the effectiveness of ECA.[18]

D. EVALUATION

Although, in signing the 1965 Agreement, the two organizations had moved their contrasting positions toward a compromise solution, the problem of delineation of their respective functions has continued to be an issue between them. Whether or not the OAU will continue to press for acceptance by ECA of the former's approach—that of reserving for itself the role of policy and program formulation (or the power to approve ECA's policies and programs) as well as the main responsibility for fields such as trade, economic integration, and the harmonization of national development plans—might depend upon the extent of development of the OAU activities in the economic and social field. At present, the OAU preoccupation mainly with political problems and its inability hitherto to build up a strong machinery for economic and social programs seem to indicate that the need for a fundamental division of responsibilities may not be regarded as very urgent. The OAU position on the distribution of powers and areas of specialization, if adopted, might not only jeopardize the independence of ECA but also, in the short-run, reduce the latter's flexibility of action in attaining maximum impact from its diverse, inter-related programs, as well as adversely affect the continuity of some of them. In the long-run, however, if the OAU intensifies its activities in the economic and social field, it might be necessary, in order to avoid rivalry and wasteful duplication of effort, to agree upon extensive joint action or a fundamental distribution of work based on the orientation, experience, and resources of each organization. In the meantime, if the existing Agreement which provides procedures for mutual consultation and for co-operation in the planning and implementation of various projects is strengthened and applied more effectively than in the past, each organization might gradually develop areas for special concentration and for collaborative action.

It seems clear from the statements of the ECA secretariat that ECA would not accept a position of subordination vis-à-vis the OAU as regards the power of decision-making on matters that concern its work. However, resolution 190(IX) of the ninth session of ECA, which as will be shown later is a landmark in ECA-OAU relations, seems to have created a problem for the ECA secretariat. This resolution reiterates the OAU Assembly's view that this organ remains "the highest body for encouragement and orientation in matters of economic and social policy development on the African continent" and recommends that "reports on ECA's activities be presented regularly" for the consideration of the OAU Assembly. The ECA secretariat would have preferred the resolution to be phrased in such a way as to attract the support of African Heads of State for ECA's programs and their advice on any questions having political implications, but without any implication of "legislative control" over ECA.

Chapter IX

OAU-ECA: Policy Compatibility and Competition

The present chapter examines the policies and selected activities of ECA and the OAU in the economic and social field in order to assess, where possible, the extent of compatibility of policies and competition in carrying out projects. It is by examining any existing policy conflicts or competition between the two organizations that the jurisdictional issue discussed in the preceding chapter can acquire a concrete meaning. It is also in this light that the effectiveness of existing co-operative arrangements, the subject of the next chapter, can be properly evaluated.

A. NOTIONS ABOUT AN OVERALL APPROACH TO AFRICAN ECONOMIC DEVELOPMENT

The ECA secretariat has defined the primary objective of national and regional development for the 1970s as: (a) the mobilization of all sectors of population for participation in activities leading to the integration of the unproductive traditional sector with the modern dynamic sector; (b) the promotion of structural changes in order to reduce the almost exclusive dependence on external factors and initiate the processes of transformation and development; (c) the effective marshaling of national and external development factors.[1] After examining the implications of various strategies for attaining these objectives,[2] ECA has concluded that at present the problem facing the African States is one of properly combining different approaches. Thus, as regards priority between agricultural development and industrialization in Africa, it maintains that the real question is how to make them complement each other rather than which one to emphasize.[3] With regard to industrialization again, the problem is one of effectively combining rather than choosing between the following two approaches: (i) a resource-based approach involving the establishment of large industrial complexes, an approach which is oriented toward world markets; and (ii) one directed to the development of labor-intensive, small and medium-scale industries largely for the production of commodities (import substitutes) for local markets. It maintains that in the situation existing in Africa today "neither strategy can be pursued by member Governments exclusive of the other"[4] and has accordingly carried out with the approval of its Commission and ECOSOC projects in both these directions.

The OAU has not attempted to elaborate a development strategy of

its own, but it has, jointly with ECA and the ADB, enunciated basic principles in an "African Declaration on Co-operation, Development and
Economic Independence" ("Abidjan Declaration").[5] Those principles are
consistent with ECA's development strategy.

B. MULTI-NATIONAL ECONOMIC CO-OPERATION AND INTEGRATION

ECA and the OAU also agree that multi-national co-operation is essential if the African States, most of which are small and lacking in adequate
economic resources, are to benefit from economies of scale. By integrating
their economic plans and policies, the African States could remove wasteful
competition in agricultural production and avoid the establishment of a
host of small, inefficient industrial plants or the creation of a number of
underutilized plants with capacity in excess of the demands of a national
market. With this in mind, both ECA and the OAU have adopted a policy
of assisting the African States to establish African common markets.[6]
Economic integration may be regarded as the unifying concept for ECA's
activities; in fact, "there [is] no section in its secretariat in which the
objective of integration [is] not pursued."[7] As for the OAU, a resolution
of the OAU-ECOS has indicated that African economic integration should
be regarded not only as a means for bringing about rapid economic development but also as a major building block for African Unity.[8]

Initially, however, there was a difference in perspective between the
secretariats of ECA and the OAU, especially as regards the method and
geographical scope of economic co-operation and integration. The ECA
secretariat emphasized that it was essential to maintain a "pragmatic and
flexible approach to the entire question of economic integration" taking
into account both "the rate at which liberalization of trade should be
sought in common market areas and the groupings of countries that could
be regarded as reasonable for particular projects." This implied that "just
as some projects could be best carried out by groups of countries smaller
than the present sub-regional units, so would others need to be executed
for areas that were larger still, and indeed might embrace the entire continent."[9] In working toward the goal of pooling together the resources of
different parts of Africa and using them in a co-operative effort in economic development, the ECA secretariat has adopted a policy of moving in
stages. "The first is to bring together the economics of neighbouring countries in the different natural zones of the continent and install at the most
advantageous points within each zone multi-national enterprises" to supply
those countries with economic facilities and commodities for their common
market.[10] Accordingly, in the light of the physical and economic realities,

the ECA secretariat proposed first to divide the African continent into four sub-regional communities and later into seven more manageable sub-regions ranging in composition from five to eight countries.[11]

The approach of the OAU secretariat, which was less elaborate and concrete, was governed essentially by the desire to establish as early as possible a strong continental economy that could not only provide a higher standard of living for Africans but also consolidate and maintain [Africa's] political independence."[12] This approach, which was endorsed by the OAU Council of Ministers, regarded sub-regional integration as "a phase in the establishment of an expanded African market covering the entire continent";[13] it placed the emphasis on the transitory nature of such a phase. Concerned about the possibility of failure to extend sub-regional co-operation to the entire continent, the OAU secretariat has repeatedly warned at ECA's sub-regional meetings that

> it would serve no purpose to substitute for the old order [creation of so many small States] a new order, namely, sub-regional balkanization, because, being only a half measure, it is not calculated to give Africa its just place in the world today, in which every power including the liberating power of the economy belongs to blocs.[14]

Accordingly, it has stressed that all sub-regional economic activities should be planned and carried out with full knowledge of and in full harmony with what was being done in the other sub-regions.

In practice, the apparent difference between the OAU secretariat's politically oriented perspective on African economic integration and the economically oriented approach of the ECA secretariat has been almost negligible. Not only has the OAU secretariat accepted ECA's sub-regional approach as "a step in the realistic solution of the problem posed by the creation of an African common market" but it has also fully recognized that the ECA secretariat has demonstrated the technical feasibility of continental economic co-operation and eventual integration and has thus removed this goal from the realm of vague ideals. Moreover, the OAU Council of Ministers has encouraged the OAU secretariat to approach directly any existing sub-regional groupings[16] and explore with them possibilities for their expansion into larger sub-regional groupings without losing sight of "the final objective of integrating the continent."[17] Similarly, the ECA secretariat has sought increasingly to establish the largest possible sub-regional groupings transcending the relatively rigid older groupings based more on similarities of historical (colonial) and cultural background than on the potential for effective economic development. ECA has sought to co-ordinate national development plans and policies through continental institutions and has been able to assist in the establishment of economic institutions ranging in composition from a few fluvial States to all the States in a sub-region. It has also promoted transcontinental co-operation in fields such as transport and telecommunications.

A look at the relevant activities of the two organizations shows that the threat of competition and duplication of effort began to appear rather belatedly. Although the likelihood of parallel technical studies and surveys on the problems and prospects of an African common market (or markets) and on external trade has been removed through periodic joint meetings of the relevant technical bodies, there have been rival efforts between the two organizations with regard to the harmonization of national policies and the establishment of appropriate intergovernmental institutions. Parallel to ECA's efforts to establish new sub-regional groupings, with corresponding secretariats to promote economic co-operation at that level, the OAU has sought through its Administrative Secretary-General to persuade existing groupings not only to expand but also to associate themselves with the OAU. Claiming that it is "better equipped than the ECA secretariat to define a system and a technique by which divisions inherited from the colonial era (frontiers, currency, culture, etc.) [would] not dangerously counter the attainment of co-operation among neighboring States,"[18] the OAU secretariat has been actively participating in the meetings of various sub-regional and other multi-national groupings during the past few years at least to an equal extent as the ECA secretariat. Although it was ECA which convened the ministerial conferences in the four sub-regions of Africa taking place before May 1967, all except one of the major subsequent sub-regional conferences, including the conferences of Eastern African Heads of State (Kampala, December 1967 and Dar-es-Salaam, May 1968) were convened by the host States alone. The exception was the conference of West African Heads of State (Monrovia, April 1968) which was convened by the Liberian Government jointly with the OAU secretariat. As with the other conferences of Heads of State, the ECA secretariat had no part in convening the meetings; its role was formally limited to the submission of background papers, but its assistance was invariably called upon in servicing the meetings.

On the question of multi-national economic co-operation, therefore, the main problem of relationship between ECA and the OAU has been the competition between their secretariats for a more central role in the establishment and servicing of institutions for harmonizing divergent interests and policies of African States regarding multi-national integration. Apparently, the considerable narrowing of differences in their perspectives over the nature and scope of economic integration in Africa has not been accompanied by the avoidance of such competition.

So far, all attempts by the secretariats of ECA and the OAU respectively to promote sub-regional economic co-operation in Africa have encountered serious obstacles.[19] First, many African States have been concerned about the possibility that the creation of a common market in their area might lead to an unequal distribution of the gains—to the disadvantage of the poorer members. Secondly, the setting up of common external tariffs together with the freeing of internal trade might cost certain countries, especially the land-locked ones, tariff revenues unless arrangements are made to compensate them. Finally, since any scheme for a fair distribution of costs and gains, including the equitable location of new industrial plants, would necessitate a number of restrictions on the sovereignty of individual countries in deciding their economic future, the African States have tended to be reluctant to surrender any of their newly won freedoms. In spite of their solemn declarations in ECA and OAU meetings, African statesmen seem to be reluctant to commit themselves to fairly complex political and economic obligations which are based on imperfect economic data and projections. If any progress is to be made in overcoming this reluctance, concerted effort would have to be made by ECA and the political organs of the OAU. Obviously, the present competition between the secretariats of ECA and the OAU is detrimental to such an effort.

C. INTERNATIONAL TRADE

There has been no disagreement between ECA and the OAU about the fact that many of the new possibilities for development arising from sub-regional integration in Africa cannot be exploited without an increase in revenues from African external trade and without external financial and technical assistance.

African external trade is an area where close collaboration exists between ECA and the OAU. Through joint meetings, the two organizations have adopted broad common policies on all the major issues—policies contained in the "African Declaration of Algiers" on trade and development (1967) which became part of the "Algiers Charter" of the "Group of 77" within UNCTAD.[20] They agree that an appropriate strategy for the trade of African countries during the 1970s should have two basic objectives: (a) to generate structural changes by serving as a vehicle for transforming African economies from a traditional, almost exclusively primary producing basis, to a dynamic combination of agriculture and manufacturing industries; and (b) to provide foreign exchange earnings for the financing of development.[21] In order to increase the revenue earnings of the African countries while action is being taken to change the structure of African trade, the following steps have been jointly proposed as part of the strategy for the 1970s:

(i) an international commodity policy to secure remunerative, equitable, and stable prices for African exports of primary commodities;
(ii) improved access to the markets of developed countries through the removal of all barriers to the importation of primary commodities, semi-manufactures, and manufactures from developing countries and through the introduction of a general system of tariff preferences for the products of developing countries, especially the least developed.

The dominant position of the developed countries as customers of African products makes it necessary to pay special attention to those markets as sources of revenue in the short-run. But the long-term objective is to diversify the commodity composition of intra-African trade, especially in manufactures, and to increase the volume of the trade. The joint ECA-OAU plan for the 1970s is to encourage intra-African trade and payments and arrangements for a mutually beneficial preferential trade. ECA and the OAU have indicated that appropriate measures should be taken to prevent non-African States from claiming under the most-favored nation clause any concessions made among the African States; and in this regard they have recommended that the relevant provisions of GATT should be re-examined in order to determine the aspects which should be re-negotiated. As regards the problems arising from the special relations of groups of African States with extra-African economic blocs, they have proposed that all aspects detrimental to intra-African trade should be removed and that African States as a group should negotiate a new system of preferences which would provide at least equivalent advantages to those of developing countries presently enjoying special preferences.

D. DEVELOPMENT AID AND FINANCING

On the subject of development aid and financing, the respective policies and activities of ECA and the OAU seem to have been somewhat less harmonious than on the question of African international trade. Both organizations are concerned about how they can attract the maximum possible foreign assistance for African development with the minimum of political and economic costs to the African countries. Both of them expect that the machinery for sub-regional integration would provide a framework for the channeling and co-ordination of foreign assistance according to the developmental interests of the sub-region as a whole rather than the particularistic interests of individual States and would also minimize political and economic costs of foreign assistance by facilitating a common intergovernmental policy toward the donors of such assistance.[22]

Until recently, where the ECA and OAU secretariats seemed to have considerable disagreement was the range of sources of external aid and investment, particularly the question of whether, to what extent, and in what manner foreign bilateral assistance and private investment should be encouraged to contribute to African economic development. They also differed over the role that each should play in the field of development aid and financing.

The OAU secretariat has expressed the view that foreign technical assistance could be "politically dangerous" as it could be used as a means of "political pressure" against the African countries.[23] Accordingly, it warned against "affording the outside world a pretext for controlling [Africa's] future."[24] It has urged that foreign technical assistance should not be resorted to "unless the African personnel required cannot really be found on the continent."[25] Any necessary assistance from donor countries should acquire an international character, that is, should be channeled through the United Nations and its specialized agencies and, where that is not possible, through intergovernmental organizations of donor countries, before it reaches the development projects in Africa.[26] As for its own role, the OAU secretariat has maintained that it should act as an intermediary between aid-giving international organizations and African multi-national projects.

The ECA secretariat agrees that it is desirable to internationalize as much bilateral aid as possible but, since the bulk of foreign assistance today comes from bilateral sources, it has realistically adopted a flexible policy of inviting aid from individual donor countries, both public and private, to supplement the aid from international organizations. It has tended to regard its role as that of a "regional catalyst bringing together the independent African nations and the sources of capital and expertise available in the developed countries."[27]

The following example may illustrate the differences between the two secretariats in regard to development aid and financing in Africa. In 1967, the Executive Secretary of ECA convened a conference of industrialists and financiers from developed countries, with participants also from certain African countries, various United Nations bodies, and other organizations. The purpose was to obtain their views on measures to bridge the gap between pre-feasibility survey and the planning and implementation of sub-regional industrial projects.[28] More specifically, their advice was sought on how to identify bankable industrial projects, what sources and methods of finance to tap, how to develop an African cadre rapidly, and what kind of industrial promotion centers to establish. The OAU secretariat boycotted the conference, an act which seemed to indicate that it had serious reservations about the ECA secretariat's efforts to generate interest among foreign private enterprises and thereby attract investment to sub-regional projects in Africa.[29] In subsequent years, however, the differences have been virtually removed as emphasis was placed by both organizations on a policy of African "self-reliance" which stresses the vital importance of mobilizing domestic resources for development and the promotion of foreign investment strictly in accord with national and regional priorities. Such investment would be invited in conformity with an agreed investment code that would remove wasteful competition among the African countries as well as provide certain assurances to investors.[30]

E. STATE OF CO-OPERATION IN VARIOUS SECTORS

In addition to trade, the sectors of economic development in which both ECA and the OAU are specially interested include manufacturing industry, agriculture, transport and telecommunications, natural resources (minerals, water resources, and energy), and human resources (social development, manpower planning, education, and training). While ECA has had projects in all these sectors, the OAU has been fully active in an operational sense only in the field of agriculture. In the other fields, the involvement of the OAU has been mainly with respect to the harmonization of policies among the African States. While no significant policy differences can be discerned between ECA and the OAU in any of these sectors, co-operation between the two secretariats has been severely limited in some sectors by wasteful competition.

In the field of industry, intersecretariat competition had initially been a major problem especially as regards efforts to encourage negotiations among neighboring African countries to establish multi-national industries in mutually agreed locations. But a joint approach has been adopted since May 1971 as a result of the ECA-OAU Conference of Ministers of Industry which formulated the "Declaration on Industrialization in Africa in the 1970s."[31]

Relationships between the secretariats of ECA and the OAU in which specialized agencies are also involved tend to vary from close collaboration to keen competition, depending in large measure upon the perspective and the policies of a specialized agency regarding its role in Africa. Specialized agencies tend to view problems of economic and social development from both a global and sectoral standpoint. Within their respective sectors, they identify worldwide problems and formulate projects that would help to solve them. On the other hand, the perspectives of both ECA and the OAU are regional. Both organizations start by identifying Africa's development problems and try to design an order of priorities and projects based on African conditions. The difference between the global/sectoral outlook and the regional perspective is fundamental but some agencies have made long strides toward harmonizing the two perspectives. The policy of a specialized agency concerning its sectoral role in a region is, of course, an important factor in its relations with regional bodies such as ECA and the OAU. Thus, when a specialized agency is so jealous of its sectoral prerogatives in a region as to be reluctant to co-operate in joint projects over which it would not have primary control, the potential for harmonization of perspectives tends to be low and the chances for policy conflict and competition with regional bodies tend to be high. This situation is likely to compound the problem of regional bodies such as ECA and the OAU whose secretariats are already in competition.

The problems and prospects of a triangular relationship and their effects on ECA-OAU relationships can be illustrated by the following examples representing four types of cases, each in a different field of activity—telecommunications, agriculture, air transport, and scientific education.

The first example, which concerns relations among the secretariats of ECA, the OAU and the International Telecommunication Union (ITU), illustrates a situation where a three-sided collaborative arrangement has been most effective. In 1966 ECA and the OAU convened a joint meeting on telecommunications in Africa in order to elaborate a plan for implementing their common objective of developing a Pan-African telecommunications network which would be eventually linked with the networks of the other continents. This objective is fully shared with ITU, whose relations with ECA are so close that the two organizations have adopted a joint program to be carried out by a joint telecommunications team within the ECA secretariat. A pre-investment study on the development of telecommunications in Africa has been initiated in response to the recommendations of the ECA-OAU meeting.[32] Once ITU's Africa Plan Committee had prepared a "General Plan for the Development of the International Network in Africa" (February 1967), national experts carried out preliminary country surveys with technical assistance from ITU and ECA and with financial assistance from UNDP. The next phase is to undertake detailed pre-investment surveys, with assistance from the same sources and possibly from the IBRD, the ADB, and bilateral donors. The possibilities for financing are being explored by the ECA secretariat in consultation with the OAU secretariat. The activities of ECA, the OAU, and ITU have so far been free from competition. It seems that close collaboration among the three secretariats was made possible both by the complementary nature of the global and regional perspectives in this field and by the close relations already existing between the ECA and the ITU secretariats when the OAU entered the field.

The second example, which concerns relations among the secretariats of ECA, the OAU and FAO illustrates a situation where ECA maintains close relations with a specialized agency and, initially, very little contact with the OAU in the subject at hand; initially, the OAU had a competitive relationship with the same specialized agency. Since 1959, ECA and FAO have been jointly engaged in the development and co-ordination of applied research in all phases of food production, food processing, and marketing in Africa. They have also undertaken a number of projects of multi-national co-operation in this field.[33] The OAU projects which were inherited from the former CCTA deal with the development and application of vaccines against animal diseases; research on nutrition and on the improvement of cereal seeds; and assessment of the fishing potential of the West African continental shelf. They are normally scientifically oriented while the joint ECA-FAO projects tend to be economically oriented. As such, the OAU projects are somewhat similar to some of the separate projects of FAO and the World Health Organization (WHO), a fact which partly explains the competition between FAO and the OAU during 1965 and 1966.[34] However, with one or two exceptions, the non-technical newer projects of the OAU are quite distinct from FAO's separate projects or from the ECA-FAO projects since they tend to be legally oriented: they deal with the co-ordination of relevant legislation and the drafting of conventions on such subjects as plant protection and the conservation of nature and natural resources. Yet, even within this area, there was initially competition between the OAU and FAO,[35] one which did not affect the relations of either of them with the ECA secretariat. A new area of special interest for both ECA and the OAU is the establishment of sub-regional institutions such as the proposed centers for the storage of grain for emergencies. Gradually, close collaboration has been established between the OAU secretariat and the Joint ECA-FAO Agricultural Division, especially in assessing the feasibility of the proposal. It appears that the close relationship between ECA and FAO, as represented by their joint secretariat unit and their common program, was a significant factor in inducing the OAU secretariat in most cases to seek the co-operation of both of them together rather than separately. Though it may not be responsible for the improvement of relations between the OAU and FAO which culminated in the signing of an agreement in 1967, it seems to have made it possible to develop an effective three-sided collaborative arrangement for projects of common interest.

The third example, concerning relations among the secretariats of ECA, the OAU, and the International Civil Aviation Organization (ICAO), illustrates a situation where ECA and the OAU adopted a common stand against a specialized agency whose policy was at variance with their regional perspective. In November 1964, ECA and ICAO convened jointly an African air transport conference which recommended that the two organizations should, in consultation with the OAU, make the necessary arrangements for the establishment of an African Civil Aviation Organization. Subsequently, the secretariats of ECA and the OAU adopted a joint policy which was in sharp contrast with ICAO's policy, especially with regard to the relationship of the envisaged organization with each of the three secretariats. The secretariats of ECA and the OAU maintained that in order to promote the interests of the African States most effectively, the new body should be an organization with an African secretariat provided by ECA and the OAU, with technical assistance from ICAO and the International Air Traffic Association (IATA), and not one that would be, in effect, an ICAO regional office for Africa. Their point of view was emphatically endorsed by the OAU Council of Ministers when it stated that "ICAO's role . . . in Africa should be confined to the technical aspects of civil aviation, and the economic aspects and priorities should be worked out and handled by OAU and ECA so that the purely African interests are never lost sight of."[36]

The policy differences were such that, contrary to the spirit of the recommendation of the ECA-ICAO conference, ICAO circulated to the African States a draft statute for the envisaged organization prepared without consultations with the secretariats of ECA and the OAU, thus inducing them to prepare jointly and circulate an alternative draft to the same States. Subsequently, after intensive negotiations, the President of the ICAO Council accepted amendments to the ICAO draft proposed by the Executive Secretary of ECA and the OAU Administrative Secretary-General and thus cleared the way for an agreed draft for a conference of African States to be convened by the three organizations. But when the conference met in January 1969, the controversy over the links of the new body with the three organizations re-emerged, to be finally resolved in favor of the ICAO position. The new organization—the African Civil Aviation Commission (AFCAC)—was provisionally staffed by the ICAO secretariat and not by the secretariats of ECA and the OAU; however, AFCAC itself was expected to determine the rules governing recruitment and the conditions of service of the permanent staff.

This setback to the joint policy of the ECA and OAU secretariats might be explained by the fact that most of the African governmental representatives at the Conference were officials responsible for civil aviation whom one might regard as the natural allies of ICAO, an organization which is a major source of funds and technical assistance for their ministries' projects. Their reluctance to support the joint policy of ECA and the OAU on AFCAC's ties with those organizations might be explained by their desire not to jeopardize in any way AFCAC's ties with ICAO, the main potential source of technical and financial support for the new organization. It is possible that eventually AFCAC may establish an independent African secretariat, while welcoming technical assistance from ECA and ICAO and political advice and support from the OAU. With the removal of the main point of disagreement with ICAO, there may not be any need for ECA and the OAU to maintain a common stand against ICAO. Would they be able then to adopt a common policy toward the new autonomous body or would they be competing with ICAO and with each other in trying to influence AFCAC policy? The possibility of such competition cannot be ruled out, especially if ICAO improves its relations with either ECA or the OAU rather than with both.

The fourth example, which concerns ECA/OAU/UNESCO relationships with regard to the development of science-based education in Africa, may illustrate the point. It throws light on the effect of the interaction between ECA's deteriorating relations with a specialized agency and OAU's improving ties with the same agency. African educational development in general has been a field of common concern for ECA and UNESCO since the early 1960s when a jointly convened conference of African States (Addis Ababa, May 1961) adopted the "Outline Plan for African Educational Development" (the Addis Ababa Plan). Within the general framework of this plan, and as part of its manpower and training activities, ECA decided in 1965 to carry out a survey of existing African institutions for vocational training and to establish specialized training facilities in African universities and technical institutes.[37] The same year, the OAU-ECOS and the OAU-STRC decided to compile an inventory of such institutions, to prepare a roster of African scientists and technologists, and to establish training centers.[38] But even though the OAU secretariat was unable to carry out these tasks, the attitudes of both sides remained competitive. By this time the earlier co-operation between the secretariats of ECA and UNESCO had deteriorated as a result of competition, in marked contrast to the growing co-operation between the OAU and UNESCO. A case in point was the Conference of Education and Scientific and Technical Training in Relation to Development in Africa (Nairobi, July 1968) which was jointly convened by UNESCO and the OAU. The secretariats of ECA and the OAU had begun to co-operate in examining possibilities for the establishment in Africa of training and research institutions—"Centres of Excellence"—but their co-operation could not develop to such an extent as to convert the task of creating those institutions into a joint OAU-ECA project, as had been recommended by the OAU Council of Ministers.[39] The Nairobi conference was convened partly to consider possibilities for establishing such institutions. It was, according to the UNESCO General Conference of 1966, designed as a meeting to be organized jointly by UNESCO and the OAU, in close collaboration with ECA. ECA was thus meant to play a role not amounting to that of a co-sponsor of the meeting. The ECA secretariat was consulted by the secretariats of the OAU and UNESCO during the preparation of the conference and, upon their request, presented a basic document, but it was not encouraged to play an active role during the conference itself. The explanation perhaps lies in the fact that simultaneously with the deterioration of relations between the secretariats of ECA and UNESCO, the OAU secretariat was establishing close ties with the latter on the basis of an OAU-UNESCO agreement concluded in 1967. Subsequently, however, ECA's relations with UNESCO were improved as a result of intersecretariat meetings which led to further joint activities, including the ECA-UNESCO Regional Symposium on the Utilization of Science and Technology for Development in Africa (Addis Ababa, October 1970). But there has been little progress from the two sets of bilateral relations toward a triangular pattern of co-operation.

It is not surprising that a competition involving ECA, the OAU, and a specialized agency should arise, given the following factors: ECA's problem of establishing close relations with those specialized agencies which are particularly jealous of their sectoral prerogatives; the interest of such agencies to see in Africa a political counterweight to ECA which could help in safeguarding the autonomy of their programs; and the eagerness of the OAU secretariat to conclude agreements with the specialized agencies in order to remedy the dearth of material resources by obtaining agency funds and experts for its projects.

There may be some truth in the contention that the OAU secretariat's policy of concluding agreements with various specialized agencies and United Nations bodies is part of a plan to pre-empt the ECA secretariat in the spheres of interest of those agencies with which ECA has so far been unable to establish close links. The patterns of multi-organizational relationships discussed above seem to suggest that the key to a harmonious collaboration among ECA, the OAU, and a specialized agency is the establishment of close ties between ECA and the agency concerned, as in the case of the first two examples.

F. CONCLUSIONS

No serious differences of approach or policy can at present be observed between ECA and the OAU in any of their fields of mutual interest. Within the context of the constantly changing political environment in Africa, any differences of approach that had appeared in the earlier years seem to have been largely removed as a result of mutual influence between

ECA and the OAU. African economic integration and development financing were the only areas where there were marked differences of approach, but even there the gap has been virtually bridged. The OAU has been moving from a largely doctrinaire and all-embracing perspective to economic and social problems toward a pragmatic and selective approach; and ECA has been increasingly responding to OAU's evaluation of the political dimension of economic and social problems.

The problem of duplication of effort between ECA and the OAU has arisen mainly at the stage of program formulation. The OAU had initially adopted a number of projects resembling those of ECA, but it could not seriously attempt to implement most of them because of its small staff and meager financial resources and its primary preoccupation with political problems. Its relatively few attempts to implement certain duplicative tasks involving the preparation of surveys, inventories, and meetings were often frustrated by lack of adequate responses from several African Governments, while ECA's parallel efforts suffered less because of its more regular and direct channels of communication with the ministries concerned.

A more serious problem than duplication has been the lack of adequate collaboration between ECA and the OAU in formulating complementary programs designed for maximum impact upon the problems of African development. The projects of ECA and the OAU have not been parts of a mutually agreed master plan—a plan that would define the areas of priority, elaborate such areas into projects, and outline the respective roles of ECA and the OAU as well as other interested organizations in such projects. But considerable progress is being made in this direction, especially since the adoption of the various basic documents on African development, particularly ECA's "Strategy for Development in the 1970s" and the Abidjan "Declaration on Co-operation, Development and Economic Independence" adopted jointly by ECA, the OAU, and the ADB.

The lack of full complementarity between the programs and activities of ECA and the OAU is partly explained by the prevalence of competition between the two secretariats, especially with regard to the harmonization of African development policies and the creation of institutions for multinational co-operation and integration. Since certain Member States have also been taking an initiative in this regard, it has been rather difficult to sustain the momentum initially created by the ECA-sponsored conferences and to ensure continuity between those and other conferences organized by host States alone or jointly with the OAU. Although this problem may, to a large extent, be due to the fluid domestic and inter-State political situation in Africa, the lack or inadequacy of joint action by the ECA and

OAU secretariats may have contributed to the problem. The two secretariats may need to adopt a "common stand" not only against any adverse policies and actions of non-African States and groups of States, or of any specialized agencies and United Nations bodies, but also against any such policies or tendencies of individual African States.

Chapter X
OAU-ECA: Process of Co-operation
and Co-ordination

The organizational relationships between a body of the United Nations and any intergovernmental organization take place essentially at two levels:

(i) the level of the intergovernmental bodies where decisions on policies and programs are made; and

(ii) the level of the secretariats where programs are formulated and implemented.

At the former level, the relations concern interactions between the respective policy-making organs (as in the case of exchange of suggestions and recommendations) as well as between such organs of one organization and the secretariat of the other (as in the case of secretariat representation in each other's conferences). At the intersecretariat level, the relations range from exchange of relevant information and mutual consultation to assistance in personnel and other administrative matters.

In view of the virtually identical membership of ECA and the OAU, one might expect that existing difficulties of co-operation and co-ordination between the two organizations would be mainly located at the secretariat level. However, problems of collaboration between the two organizations seem to emerge also at the level of the decision-making bodies.

In examining the interorganizational relations of ECA and the OAU, the logical point of departure would be the legal framework of the relationships, consisting of the relevant provisions of the constituent instruments of each organization, as supplemented by rules of procedure and special resolutions, as well as the relationship agreements and arrangements concluded between the two organizations. After a brief description of the legal framework, there will be an examination of the procedures and practices of co-operation as applied or evolved during the past decade, to be followed by an examination of the machinery of co-ordination.

A. LEGAL BASES OF THE RELATIONS

Constituent and related instruments. In establishing the regional economic commissions, ECOSOC included in the terms of reference provisions concerning relations with relevant non-UN intergovernmental organizations, thus providing the basis for the conclusion of formal agreements or the establishment of informal working arrangements.

The terms of reference of ECA[1] state in paragraph 10 that the Commission "may invite observers from such . . . intergovernmental organizations as it may consider desirable, in accordance with the practices of the Economic and Social Council." In addition, they provide in paragraph 12 that the Commission "may establish such liaison as it deems appropriate with intergovernmental organizations in Africa operating in the same field."

On the OAU side, the relevant provisions on relations with organizations in the United Nations family are contained in special resolutions adopted by the relevant OAU specialized commissions themselves and later endorsed en bloc by higher political organs. Only the resolution adopted by the OAU-ECOS refers specifically to relations with ECA. It provides for the establishment of "close collaboration on the basis of complementarity [with] the Economic Commission for Africa and other specialized agencies of the UN."[2] The corresponding resolution of the OAU-ESCHC refers only to "collaboration with international scientific and technological organizations"[3] such as UNESCO, FAO, and WHO.

Agreement on ECA-OAU co-operation. The legal framework of relationships between ECA and the OAU consists of the above-mentioned constitutent and related instruments of the two organizations and the Agreement on ECA-OAU co-operation concluded between the United Nations and the OAU.

Since the informal working arrangements existing before 1965 were considered by both to be insufficient, the two organizations concluded the Agreement in accordance with parallel recommendations adopted by the OAU-ECOS and ECA.[4]

The relationship Agreement entered into force on 15 December 1965, upon the signing by the United Nations Secretary-General and the OAU Administrative Secretary-General, without requiring ratification by the deliberative organs of the two organizations (for text see Appendix III).

In its preamble it records the desire of the two organizations "within their respective spheres of responsibility" to establish "effective co-operation in the accomplishment of their common objectives . . . , in accordance more particularly with the Charter of the United Nations and the Terms of Reference of ECA on the one hand, and with the Charter of OAU and the Terms of Reference of its competent specialized commissions on the other." It defines in its operative articles methods and procedures for co-operation.

B. PROCEDURES AND PRACTICES OF CO-OPERATION

The procedures and practices of relationship between ECA and the OAU fall roughly into two main categories which correspond to the two

levels of interaction mentioned above. The first category consists of procedures and practices concerning relationships involving the intergovernmental bodies: reciprocal representation at meetings; reciprocal inscription
of items on the agenda; mutual provision of recommendations or comments
through resolutions; and joint activities of intergovernmental bodies. The
second category concerns co-operation at the secretariat level and it comprises mutual intersecretariat consultations; exchange of information and
documents; and intersecretariat administrative co-operation. All the items
in these two categories, except the one on joint activities of intergovernmental bodies, are examined individually in the following section. The
latter item will be considered under a subsequent section dealing with the
machinery of co-ordination.

Reciprocal representation and participation at meetings. Reciprocal invitation for representation by observers at the meetings of relevant organs of
ECA and the OAU has been provided for in Article III of the Agreement.
There is no evidence that either organization was denied an invitation to
a meeting of the other's commission or technical body that it had wished
to attend. But when economic and related matters are deliberated upon in
the OAU Council of Ministers—and this has been frequently the case
since 1965 when the last session of the OAU-ECOS was held—invitations
for ECA have not been forthcoming from the OAU secretariat as readily
and regularly as those for the meetings of the commissions. Moreover,
attendance by ECA representatives at Council of Ministers' sessions has
been largely limited to the relatively few public meetings but not to the
closed sessions. According to the OAU rules on the status of observers,
representatives of other organizations may attend private meetings of the
Council of Ministers only if they are "expressly invited."[5]

Consideration of subjects of mutual interest. Closely related to the question of reciprocal representation is the procedure for the study of questions
of common interest. According to Article II, the administrative heads of
ECA and the OAU are required to make all necessary arrangements compatible with the rules of procedure of the respective commissions in order
to submit to the latter agenda items proposed by the other organization.
In practice, however, there have been very few formal requests by either
of the two organizations to have an item inscribed in the provisional
agenda of the other. Each secretariat seems to be sufficiently aware of the
other's resolutions, recommendations, and suggestions as to reflect in its
draft agenda items that might potentially be brought up by the other.

*Reciprocal provision of suggestions, recommendations, and comments
through resolutions.* Although neither the terms of reference and other

relevant instruments of the two organizations nor the relationship agreement specifically provide for the reciprocal provision of suggestions, recommendations, or comments through resolutions, it has been the practice of both organizations to follow such a procedure. ECA and the OAU exchange suggestions or ideas either directly or indirectly by addressing them through their Member States.

ECA has on several occasions utilized the method of addressing suggestions directly to the OAU secretariat, but has sparingly used the method of communicating recommendations through the Member States. The OAU, on the other hand, has utilized the latter approach more often, while utilizing the direct approach at least as frequently as ECA. Typical examples of the application of the indirect method by the OAU are the resolutions of the OAU-ECOS requesting Member States to invite ECA to take account of the OAU work program and to request it to authorize its Executive Secretary to undertake a certain course of action.

Although the recommendations on economic and social matters addressed by ECA and the OAU specialized commissions to each other are normally phrased with due regard to the juridical equality of the two organizations, certain resolutions addressed by ECA to the OAU Assembly of Heads of State and Government have raised the issue of hierarchical relationships with regard to certain aspects of a political character. Thus, the resolution on the problem of granting associate membership in ECA to the peoples of Angola, Mozambique, Guinea (Bissau), and Namibia, recommended that the OAU should "determine the conditions under which the peoples of the countries concerned will be represented" (English version).[6] In a controversy created by the discrepancy between English and French versions of this resolution, the OAU Council of Ministers endorsed the more far-reaching wording of the French version which recommended that the OAU "désigne les representants des populations des pays interessés et en informe le Secrétaire Executif,"[7] while the ECA secretariat concurred with the legal opinion obtained from the United Nations Legal Counsel stating that the English version was closer to the constitutional position and the established United Nations practice.[8] The issue was resolved after two years of controversy when the ninth session of ECA adopted a resolution recommending that the OAU "should propose the names of representatives of the peoples of the countries in question and inform the Executive Secretary accordingly to enable him to bring the matter before the General Assembly."[9]

Having examined the procedures and practices of relationships at the level of intergovernmental bodies, we now turn to those concerning relations at the secretariat level.

Intersecretariat consultation. Article I of the Agreement prescribes that the two organizations "shall consult one another on all matters of common interest for the purpose of achieving their respective objectives and of co-ordinating . . . their activities." Accordingly, the Administrative Heads of the two organizations are required, whenever necessary, to arrange consultations to seek agreement on the most effective manner of undertaking specified activities within the limits authorized by the competent departments of the two bodies. Moreover, they are required according to Article VI to maintain effective liason and hold consultations regularly to examine their respective work programs with a view to avoiding wasteful overlapping of work.

Consultations have normally been held upon the initiatives of the two secretariats, but have also taken place, occasionally in response to specific requests from the respective policy-making organs. There have been frequent contacts between certain substantive divisions of the two secretariats—a situation facilitated by the fact that both are located in the same city—but consultations between the Executive Heads have been far less frequent. It seems that the Heads of the two secretariats have been inhibited from holding more regular and frequent contacts by the absence of mutual understanding on fundamental principles concerning the respective roles of the two organizations. A remedy for this state of affairs might be found if the policy-making bodies of ECA and the OAU were to urge the two secretariats more frequently than in the past to hold mutual consultations on specific subjects of mutual concern.

Exchange and joint use of information, documents, and working papers. The exchange of written information, which forms part of the process of intergovernmental consultation, has been provided for in Article V of the Agreement. With the exception of confidential information and documents, all relevant written materials of each organization concerning economic and social matters of common interest are supposed to be made available to the other. Moreover, in all matters of common interest, the Executive Secretary of ECA is empowered to convey to the Administrative Secretary-General of the OAU information in writing on ECA activities in Africa, accompanied where necessary by appropriate remarks. It is to be noted that the Article does not indicate whether the OAU Secretary-General is expected to reciprocate in this regard, thus giving the appearance of a one-way reporting procedure.

With regard to the exchange of documents the main difficulty seems to be the policy followed by the OAU to classify most of its documents, that is, all those submitted to the OAU Assembly and the Council of Ministers, irrespective of subject matter, as confidential. Thus, ECA and other outside organizations can acquire without difficulty only some of the documents which relate to their fields of interest. On the other hand, all the official documents of ECA have been regularly supplied to the OAU secretariat. The documentary collection of the ECA library has also been at the disposal of the OAU secretariat.

The procedures for exchange of written materials cover not only reports and general documents on activities but also working papers prepared for their joint or separate meetings. Accordingly, the two secretariats have, within the limits of their resources and at each other's request, prepared several such papers.

Administrative arrangements and assistance to OAU. ECA-OAU co-operation in administrative matters consists mainly of the sharing of administrative facilities and certain personnel arrangements, both for the strengthening of the OAU secretariat and the execution of specific activities of common interest. In such arrangements ECA is usually in the position of supplier of the relevant assistance.

The Agreement provides the legal framework for combined effort in the collection, analysis, publication, and dissemination of statistical information, with a view to making the most rational possible use of the available specialist staff and reducing to a minimum the tasks incumbent upon the African Governments. Because of the non-availability of such experts in the OAU secretariat, ECA continues to perform the tasks referred to while providing the OAU with staistical services.

Although not specifically provided for in the Agreement, ECA has been regularly providing the OAU with various administrative facilities and services. Both ECA and the OAU have been sharing the use of the conference rooms in Africa Hall (which is the property of the Ethiopian Government) for meetings taking place in Addis Ababa. In the early years of the OAU, such OAU meetings were partly serviced by the conference staff of ECA.

The personnel arrangements outlined in Article VI of the Agreement are of two kinds: assistance by ECA in the recruitment of staff for the OAU; and secondment of ECA staff for urgent assignments in the OAU secretariat, with the concurrence of the United Nations Secretary-General and the staff member concerned. The training of OAU staff by the United Nations was not specifically mentioned in the Agreement, but has actually become part of the personnel arrangements.

With the help of the European Office of the United Nations, ECA has assisted the OAU in the recruitment of conference personnel. In addition, ECA and the United Nations Secretariat at Headquarters have seconded for special duties at the OAU, a few administrative, conference, and general service staff, as well as a few experts on substantive subjects for periods ranging from a few days to one year. Moreover, due to the limited supply in Africa of qualified candidates for professional and other technical posts and of the expanding personnel needs of the ECA secretariat, the latter has found it difficult to meet fully the requests of the OAU. Indeed, its efforts to increase the African component of its own staff appear to have led to some recruitment competition with the OAU secretariat; the latter has been trying to establish an exclusively African secretariat of modest size.

The problem of scarcity of experienced African experts for service in the OAU secretariat has been somewhat mitigated by the training activities for new recruits arranged by organizations within the United Nations system, especially the United Nations Institute for Training and Research (UNITAR) and the ILO. A major technical assistance for the OAU secretariat is now expected from UNDP under the envisaged agreement on OAU-UNDP co-operation.

Financial arrangements. Expenditures incurred by the United Nations as a result of assistance provided to the OAU are, according to the Agreement, to be borne by the OAU. However, ECA has not always received financial compensation for all the services that it has rendered the OAU secretariat.[10]

No financial assistance has been directly given by ECA for the implementation of any OAU project. Requests of the OAU secretariat for financial assistance in connection with the convening of certain meetings, for example the second conference of the OAU Scientific Council for Africa (April 1967), could not be met by the ECA secretariat because, with a few exceptions, ECA is not permitted by the United Nations financial regulation to defray even the travel or per diem costs of delegates to its own conferences.[11] The ECA secretariat, however, has offered to consider the possibility of financing projects or consultancy services that may be carried out for ECA by organs of the OAU such as the Scientific Council for Africa, but not activities deriving entirely from OAU programs. It has also offered to help the OAU secretariat to secure grants and other forms of aid for its projects from international organizations and from bilateral and foundation sources once the development of the organs and programs of the OAU in the field of the application of science and technology has reached a more advanced stage.[12]

C. MACHINERY FOR CO-ORDINATION

The practical effect of the procedures and practices examined above

depends largely on the institutional arrangements through which co-ordination is to be carried out. These institutional arrangements consist of:

(i) national arrangements in various countries for ensuring consistency
of policy on the part of their representatives in different international organizations;
(ii) arrangements for securing internal co-ordination within each
international organization;
(iii) interorganizational machinery of co-ordination at three levels:
that of the secretariats, the expert bodies, and the decision-making
organs.

It is beyond the scope of this study to examine the arrangements made
by individual Governments to co-ordinate their policies and actions in
different international organizations. It suffices to mention that very few
of the African Governments have set up such a machinery. Moreover, the
majority of them do not even maintain continuity in the composition of
their delegations to international organizations dealing with similar problems. Lack of consistency in delegation composition is prevalent not only
as between the sessions of the ECA and the meetings of the OAU-ECOS,
the OAU counterpart of ECA, but also as between different sessions of
each of these bodies.

As regards internal co-ordination within each secretariat, the Executive
Secretary of ECA introduced in 1965 a method of co-ordination within
his secretariat whereby any questions concerning relations with the OAU
would be handled directly by his Office through his Special Assistant.[13]
This method was applied successfully in preventing unco-ordinated contacts
by different ECA division heads with OAU staff, but was unfortunately
discontinued after three years. On the OAU side, the Assistant Secretary-
General in charge of Economic and Social Affairs was designated liaison
officer with ECA, and still remains so.

More significant has been the machinery for interorganizational co-
ordination.

Intersecretariat machinery. In February 1969, the Executive Secretary
of ECA, the Administrative Secretary-General of the OAU, and the President of the ADB agreed on procedures that could lead to the establishment
of a tripartite machinery to help co-ordinate the policies and activities of
the three organizations. They agreed to meet at least twice a year in order
to exchange views on programs and activities, to evolve common positions
on all development problems in Africa, and to define jointly, where appropriate, a uniform African view in meetings of global organizations concerned with economic development. In addition, decisions of one organiza-

tion which were of interest to the other two were to be communicated to them for any comments and suggestions relevant to implementation. Since it has been difficult for the Executive Secretary of ECA and the Administrative Secretary-General of the OAU alone to hold regular mutual consultations, this tripartite arrangement may now provide an opportunity for more effective communication within a triangular system of co-operation.

Joint conferences and other meetings. Although no joint meetings have been convened at the level of the Commission of ECA and the OAU specialized commissions or at that of the ECA sub-regional conferences, the two institutions have, as mentioned previously, organized jointly ad hoc conferences in such subjects as telecommunications, trade, industry, and refugees in Africa. Those conferences have provided the participating organizations with an effective machinery for adopting common decisions and co-ordinating their programs of work on the subjects concerned.

In establishing its short-lived system of seven working parties of quasi-permanent governmental experts, the ECA secretariat expected to obtain help and guidance in bringing about effective implementation of ECA's program. It was ECA's intention that all of them would be serviced jointly by the secretariats of ECA and the OAU, if the latter so agreed. However, only in regard to trade did the OAU agree to such an arrangement, which was made possible by the merger of the OAU Ad Hoc Committee on Trade and Development and the ECA Working Party on Intra-African Trade. The abandonment of the system of sectoral working parties indicated that a new approach to co-ordination was called for.

Institutional reforms. In February 1969, the ninth session of ECA which marked the tenth anniversary of the Commission adopted a series of "commemorative resolutions" which sought to expand ECA's co-ordinative and operational functions and recommended the establishment of a new institutional machinery to carry out the expanded mission. Resolution 188(IX) recommended the convening of future biennial sessions of the Commission at the ministerial level in order to perform the policy-making function more effectively; and the creation of two new committes—the Technical Committee of Experts (a committee of the whole) and the Executive Committee. The Technical Committee of Experts, comprising principal civil servants concerned with economic and related matters, meets once a year to "ensure active contact" between the ECA secretariat and the "working level of competent officials" in Member States and to provide technical advice to the Conference of Ministers. The Executive Committee meets at least twice a year to assist the Executive Secretary in the implementation of resolutions and the work program of ECA and to foster closer co-operation between, on the one hand, the Bureau of the Council of Ministers and the Executive Secretary and, on the other, the States in each sub-region of Africa and the African groups in various United Nations bodies concerned with economic development in Africa.[14] To a lesser extent it is also meant to serve as a link with the secretariat of the OAU.

In establishing these new committees, there was a marked departure from the idea of joint ECA-OAU sponsorship underlying the creation of the defunct working parties of ECA. Though one of the functions of the Executive Committee is "to strengthen the cordial relations existing between the Commission and the political organs of the OAU . . . by means of regular consultations with the secretariat of the OAU," the OAU secretariat was not to act as co-sponsor of this Committee, but merely as an observer at the meetings. No organic links were established between this Committee and the relevant OAU specialized commissions or the OAU Council of Ministers' Economic and Technical Committee.

However, resolution 190(IX) established new and potentially significant forms of co-ordination between the ECA Council of Ministers and the policy-making organs of the OAU. It called upon African ministers and senior officials to co-ordinate closely their activities within the framework of the ECA Council of Ministers and the OAU-ECOS and to be constantly guided by decisions of the OAU Assembly of Heads of State and Government. In addition, it recommended that reports on ECA's activities should be presented regularly to the OAU Assembly in order that they may receive "the necessary political support."

D. CONCLUSIONS

There are essentially five forms of co-ordination between ECA and the OAU: (i) the procedures of co-operation contained in the 1965 Agreement; (ii) the tripartite arrangement of 1969 made by the Administrative Heads of ECA, the OAU, and the ADB; (iii) the Executive Committee of ECA; (iv) the African delegations to both the ECA Council of Ministers and the OAU-ECOS; and (v) the reporting procedure between ECA and the OAU Assembly of Heads of State and Government. Taken individually, these forms of co-ordination have certain elements which are regarded as shortcomings by one organization or the other. But, to a large extent, the weaknesses of each form of co-ordination are compensated for by certain elements of the other forms.

The main shortcoming of the 1965 Agreement is that it provides no guidelines for delineation of respective functions between ECA and the

OAU, nor does it specifically provide for systematic co-ordination of policies, programs, and priorities. However, the absence of specific provisions for co-ordination at the stage of policy and program formulation is now meant to be remedied by the tripartite arrangement for regular biannual meetings of the Administrative Heads of ECA, the OAU, and the ADB. The shortcoming of this arrangement lies in the fact that, being entirely based on the initiatives of the three Administrative Heads, it lacks the degree of institutionalization that could withstand the ups and downs of personal relationships.

The Executive Committee of ECA is an ingenious device for co-ordinating policies of African States in various intergovernmental organizations and for providing an influential pressure group for implementation of ECA programs. But the OAU secretariat's participation in this Committee is limited to attending as an observer, in spite of the OAU's active role in co-ordinating the policies of African groups in international organizations and its efforts to establish close links with sub-regional groups and organizations in Africa.

It appears that this shortcoming of the ECA Executive Committee was meant to be remedied by the expected role of the African Ministers and senior officials representing their countries in the sessions of ECA and the OAU-ECOS. But the OAU-ECOS has been dormant for several years and its raison d'etre has become questionable, especially following the 1969 reorganization in ECA. By transforming ECA's biennial sessions into ministerial conferences, the African States have given the Commission's policy-making role a special emphasis. In addition, they have sought to enhance the operational role of ECA by calling for the strengthening of its secretariat and for more decentralization of the activities of the United Nations system in Africa in favor of ECA. Yet, in spite of the confidence shown by the African States in ECA's future role, it appears that the main tasks of the non-functioning OAU-ECOS will most likely continue to be performed by the Economic and Technical Committee of the OAU Council of Ministers. The problem of co-ordination might thus continue to arise at the level of this Committee. It ought to be mentioned that most delegates in that Committee are often Foreign Ministry Officials and are usually not those who represent their countries in the sessions of ECA. Communication between this Committee and the ECA bodies could be made more effective if, as far as possible, the officials who attend ECA sessions were also to attend the meetings of the Committee.

No provision has been made in ECA resolution 190(IX) for co-ordination between ECA's Council of Ministers and the Economic and Technical Committee of the OAU Council of Ministers. What the resolution recommends is the submission of reports on ECA's activities to the OAU

Assembly of Heads of State and Government. It can be expected that when such reports are submitted to the OAU they would be studied first by the Economic and Technical Committee and then submitted through the Council of Ministers to the OAU Assembly. As was mentioned previously, this one-sided procedure of submitting reports might raise fears of undue control by the OAU over ECA, especially in the absence of effective co-ordination of policies and programs between ECA and the OAU bodies dealing with economic and social matters.

In the light of the foregoing, an attempt will be made in the next chapter to explore possibilities for overcoming the present obstacles to effective co-operation between ECA and the OAU.

Chapter XI

OAU-UN: Possibilities for Strengthening Co-operation in the Economic and Social Field

The purpose of this chapter is to formulate suggestions for improvement or modification of the relationship between the United Nations and the OAU in the economic and social field. Two sets of proposals are submitted as alternatives for strengthening co-operation between ECA and the OAU. The first is designed merely to improve existing forms of co-operation, in case that ECA and the OAU are not yet ready for more fundamental changes. If they are, the second set provides two alternatives for possible long-range solutions involving basic structural changes. As regards relationships involving other United Nations bodies concerned with economic and social development, it is proposed that the present trend toward multi-organizational co-operation should be accentuated.

A. CO-OPERATION BETWEEN OAU AND ECA

1. Strengthening Existing Forms

The existing forms of ECA-OAU co-operation may be strengthened at all three levels: that of the OAU political organs, the parallel commissions, and the secretariats.

a. ECA'S RELATIONS WITH THE OAU POLITICAL ORGANS

Since it is neither desirable nor feasible in the view of the United Nations and the majority of African States to establish any hierarchical relationships between the OAU and ECA,[1] a solution to the issue of respective roles in policymaking may have to be sought within the framework of the principle of organizational equality.

The ninth session of ECA seems to have pointed the way to a solution. Not only did it recommend in resolution 190(IX) that reports on the activities of ECA should be regularly presented to the OAU Assembly in order to obtain the necessary political support for them, but it also called upon African Ministers and senior officials working within the framework of ECA and the OAU-ECOS "to be constantly guided" by decisions of the OAU Assembly in economic and social matters. These recommendations, though not free from ambiguity, were designed to establish a more effective link between policies, programs, and activities of ECA and the policy guidelines adopted by the highest organ of the OAU, and were apparently not intended as an endorsement of the thesis of the OAU secretariat which would imply hierarchical relationships. Policy directives from the OAU Assembly are to be addressed not to ECA as a body but to the African Ministers who would attend meetings of both the OAU and ECA. As a result of these recommendations the influence of the OAU Assembly in the decision-making process of ECA may be enhanced, but the final decision on ECA's policies and programs would still remain with ECOSOC and the General Assembly (the latter as regards matters concerning administrative and financial questions as well as on any political aspects of ECA's work). By favorably responding to the general policies of the OAU concerning economic and social development in Africa, ECA might be able to attract OAU's political support for its projects. That ECA may invite advice and recommendation from the OAU but not directives on any matter, even on political issues, seems to have been established, especially as a result of ECA's resolutions concerning the representation of the peoples of Non-Self-Governing Territories in ECA conferences.[2]

There is, however, the problem of whether the right kind of advice and recommendation on specific economic and social action would be forthcoming from the OAU. So far, the OAU political organs and the OAU secretariat seem to have had neither the time nor the expertise to formulate proposals other than broad principles for economic and social co-operation, nor have they been able to demonstrate dedicated political support for any initiatives in these fields taken by the OAU secretariat itself, let alone those taken by the ECA secretariat. One is, therefore, tempted to conclude that at present most African States are perhaps not sufficiently committed to multi-national operational programs and are thus not yet inclined to give the two secretariats the required political support and guidance. If this is true, a more serious problem is conceivable in the worst of circumstances. If the OAU Assembly may not address policy directives to ECA, it may conceivably exercise a sort of veto on ECA activities by refusing to endorse them. Perhaps any danger from this form of "legislative control" might be kept at a minimum if sufficient effort is devoted to the co-ordination of policies and activities of ECA and the OAU prior to their submission to the OAU political organs.

b. ECA AND THE OAU-ECOS

Both the ECA and OAU secretariats have recognized the seriousness of the problem of collaboration arising at the level of the commissions of the two organizations. But they have not been in full agreement on the desirable form of relationship in this regard. Far from limiting itself, as had been proposed by the OAU secretariat, to technical and advisory functions while leaving the function of policy-making in the economic and social field for the OAU, ECA has in fact been strengthening its policy-making machinery: upon ECA's recommendation, ECOSOC has elevated the biennial sessions of the Commission to ministerial conferences. Since the OAU-ECOS is also designed to be a conference of ministers, the parallel with ECA is now complete.

Because of the absence of any delimitation of respective areas of special interest for ECA and the OAU in the 1965 Agreement, the OAU secretariat has been urging that its policy-making organs should indicate which of the subjects covered by ECA they would consider to be within their exclusive province. The ECA secretariat has maintained that the task of dividing work between the two organizations should be the responsibility not of one but of both organizations and that it should be carried out in accordance with the respective terms of reference and with due regard to the need for continuity of action in the existing projects.

However, ECA resolution 190(IX) has now called upon African Ministers and senior officials in charge of economic and social affairs "henceforth to co-ordinate closely their activities" within the framework of the Council of Ministers of ECA and the OAU-ECOS. Due emphasis has, therefore, been placed on the need for co-ordination at the national level. At this level each African State would need to determine which of the two organizations would be better equipped to deal with a specific task and accordingly give instructions to its delegations to the relevant meetings of ECA and the OAU. In addition to giving such instructions, the African States would need to maintain maximum consistency in the composition of their delegations to such parallel meetings. These considerations would, of course, apply only if the OAU Member States revive the OAU-ECOS.

In such an event, the process of co-ordination at the national level could be supplemented by procedures for co-operation between ECA and the OAU-ECOS. Hitherto, most of the resolutions of either body on its program of work have not even sought to acknowledge the existence of similar or related programs of the other. To remedy this state of affairs, it might be helpful to include in any revision of the 1965 Agreement a provision specifically encouraging direct exchange of comments, suggestions, and recommendations between ECA and the relevant commissions of the OAU.

c. INTERSECRETARIAT CO-OPERATION IN POLICY FORMULATION AND PROJECT IMPLEMENTATION

Apart from the absence of any reference to relations between the intergovernmental bodies of ECA and the OAU, a major weakness of the Agreement on ECA-OAU co-operation has been the omission of any specific reference to the need for systematic intersecretariat co-operation in the formulation of policy proposals and programs. The stress is merely on the need for co-operation in the implementation of "specified activities, within the limits authorized by the competent department of the two bodies." Intersecretariat co-operation in policy formulation, though still a subject of major controversy, remains essential for rational decisions by the intergovernmental bodies. It would, therefore, seem desirable to include in any revision of the Agreement a specific provision for intersecretariat consultations on the harmonization of policies, priorities, and work programs.

As regards co-operation in project implementation, the need has so far been less pressing than had been envisaged, largely because of the paucity of OAU projects that have actually reached the stage of implementation. Even so, close intersecretariat co-operation on specific projects has been largely limited to the relatively few cases where the intergovernmental bodies have requested such collaboration. Since little secretariat initiative for co-operation has been forthcoming with regard to other projects of mutual interest, it would be useful if the policy-making bodies were to encourage intersecretariat consultation or collaboration in such specific cases.

In policy formulation as well as project implementation, the prospect of closer co-operation between secretariats might be improved if the tripartite arrangement for periodic consultations among the Administrative Heads of ECA, the OAU, and the ADB were to acquire a more formal status as a result of endorsement by the appropriate policy-making bodies.

2. Possibilities for Fundamental Structural Changes

In view of the difficulties that have been faced by the OAU in making the OAU-ECOS fully operational and of the record of wasteful rivalry with ECA, the following new forms of ECA-OAU relationship might deserve serious consideration as alternatives to the maintenance of parallel commissions:

(a) the establishment of joint sessions of ECA and the OAU-ECOS; and
(b) the abolition of the OAU-ECOS, accompanied by the strengthening of ECA's relations with the OAU political organs.

The problems arising from the existence of ECA and the OAU-ECOS as parallel organs are mainly the following: duplication of conferences in spite of the limited financial and personnel resources and the constraints of time faced by the two secretariats and the ministries of African Governments; the resulting decline in the rate and level of attendance by African officials in the meetings of ECA and the difficulty of even attaining a quorum for the meetings of the OAU commissions; the difficulty in coordinating respective programs and activities; and the clash over issues of pre-eminence, jurisdiction, and respective roles.

a. JOINT SESSIONS OF ECA AND THE OAU-ECOS

If joint sessions could be arranged between the Council of Ministers of ECA and the OAU-ECOS, all of these problems might be solved. But to do so on a regular basis might require an amendment of the terms of reference of ECA and of the OAU-ECOS. Since there is no precedent for such joint sessions between any United Nations regional commission and non-UN intergovernmental organizations, acceptance of the idea by ECOSOC and by the competent organs of the OAU may not be easy. The legal, political, financial and administrative implications of the measure would first have to undergo a thorough examination. There would hardly be any problem concerning recommendations on any matter within the competence of ECA and the OAU-ECOS addressed by the joint session directly to the African States, but any resolution involving wider economic and social policies or having financial implications for either organization would need endorsement by the competent higher organs. Conceivably, a problem could arise if differences of policy or opinion emerge between such higher organs, particularly ECOSOC and the OAU Council of Ministers, when they consider the resolutions of the joint session. Since there seem to be no basic differences between the objectives and policies of the United Nations and the OAU in the economic and social field, the problem referred to is perhaps merely theoretical. The technique of joint conferences has been successfully carried out by ECA and the OAU with regard to certain specialized subjects, namely, trade and development, industry, telecommunications, and refugees. The fact that the recommendations of such conferences have been endorsed, on the one hand, by the sessions of ECA and by ECOSOC and, on the other, by the OAU Council of Ministers seems also to indicate that it is not unreasonable to expect similar treatment for the resolutions of joint sessions of ECA and the OAU-ECOS.

The financial and administrative implications of a joint session may be beneficial for both organizations, provided that agreement can be reached on the modalities of sharing conference expenses and distributing conference work between the two secretariats on an equitable basis. The joint session itself may decide on the extent of the programs and projects to be implemented jointly, as well as on those to be carried out either by the ECA or the OAU secretariat.

In view of the present legal and procedural obstacles to establishing joint sessions of ECA and the OAU-ECOS on a permanent basis, it might be worthwhile for ECA and the OAU to consider the possibility of convening a joint session on an experimental basis in accordance with parallel resolutions of the competent bodies of the two organizations. The experience gained from such an ad hoc arrangement would show whether it would be desirable to make it permanent through an amendment of the respective terms of reference and the rules of procedure.

b. ABOLITION OF THE OAU-ECOS

An alternative course of action worth considering is the abolition of the OAU-ECOS, simultaneously with the restructuring of the Executive Committee of ECA to permit greater participation by the OAU in the work of the Committee.

In view of the difficulties that the OAU has been facing in convening sessions of the OAU-ECOS and considering the useful role that the Council of Ministers' Economic and Technical Committee has been able to play since 1967, the Member States of the OAU might come to realize that there is no compelling need to retain the former body. The abolition of the OAU-ECOS would represent not a relinquishment by the OAU of its objectives in the economic and social field, but essentially a transfer of the functions of the Commission to the Economic and Technical Committee. However, since this Committee cannot be a substitute for the OAU-ECOS in all respects—its perspective is basically political rather than economic—abolition of the latter body might, on the one hand, necessitate greater OAU reliance on ECA with regard to the economic and social aspects of the problems concerned and might, on the other hand, call for greater harmonization of the differing perspectives of the two organizations.

Collaboration between ECA and the OAU could take place effectively at the level of the ECA Executive Committee if this body were to be converted into a joint body or were otherwise to establish special links with the Economic and Technical Committee of the OAU Council of Ministers. The Chairman of this OAU body as well as the Administrative Secretary-General might represent the OAU in the Executive Committee. Together with the existing joint ECA-OAU Committee on Trade and Development, a joint Executive Committee would not only ensure inter-secretariat co-operation in all relevant fields but also facilitate regular co-ordination of the policies and actions of African States in global, regional, and sub-regional intergovernmental bodies dealing with economic and social development in Africa. It could lay the foundation for a harmonious relationship between the economic perspective of ECA and other relevant United Nations bodies and the basically political perspective of the OAU with regard to issues of development in Africa.

With the abolition of the OAU-ECOS, ECA's Council of Ministers would provide the sole regional forum for considering the reports and recommendations of the joint committees. On the OAU side, the Council of Ministers, under the authority of the Assembly of Heads of State and Government, would provide a forum for the consideration of ECA's economic policies and plans within a political context. Once the policies and plans for African economic and social development have received the political support of the OAU they could be submitted to ECOSOC for adoption.

The abolition of the OAU-ECOS would involve drastic action on the part of the OAU, since it would require an amendment of the OAU Charter. However, it may not be unreasonable to expect such a course of action if ECA succeeds in building upon the measure of confidence in its potential role expressed by the African States during its ninth session. There have been some factors favoring a rise of confidence in ECA, namely: (a) the fact that through the ECA Executive Committee, representatives of African States are now more deeply involved in policy formulation and implementation; (b) the fact that the representation of African States in ECA's superior organ, ECOSOC, has now been increased following that organ's enlargement; and (c) the progress that is being made toward the "Africanization" (raising the ratio of African to non-African members of the staff) of the ECA secretariat. However, in order to induce the OAU Member States to abolish the OAU-ECOS through the time-consuming procedure of Charter amendment, ECA might need to transform its Executive Committee into an organ for more effective collaboration with the OAU.

For the OAU, the main advantage of abolishing the OAU-ECOS would be to enable it to concentrate on the co-ordination and harmonization of the economic and social policies of African States for which it is well suited and thus avoid dissipating its extremely scarce resources in trying to introduce its own projects or to take over the direction of existing ones. If the technical competence of the OAU Council of Ministers' Economic and Technical Committee is improved by involving in its work not only Foreign Ministers and their staff but also senior officials from ministries responsible for economic and related matters—as far as possible those who attend ECA meetings—then this Committee would be able to examine the work being done in Africa by ECA and a multitude of organizations, groupings, and Governments and to determine the nature and extent of the obstacles to progress. On the basis of the conclusions and recommendations of this Committee, the OAU Council of Ministers and the Assembly of Heads of State and Government would be able to urge Member States to give full support to all projects in high-priority areas and to change any policies that impede co-operation and development.

Furthermore, by abolishing the OAU-ECOS, the OAU would be able to devote greater effort to the work of the OAU-ESCHC and its subsidiary bodies. The OAU-ESCHC consitutes an integrated regional complement of the various United Nations specialized agencies active in Africa in the fields of education, science, culture, and health. As such, it serves a highly useful purpose and deserves to be strengthened. It would be most useful if the OAU would apply the financial assistance expected from UNDP under their envisaged agreement partly to enable the OAU-ESCHE to carry out its co-ordinative and operational tasks more effectively but not to revive the OAU-ECOS or its defunct projects.

B. MULTI-ORGANIZATIONAL CO-OPERATION

Important beginnings have been made toward multi-organizational co-operation for African economic and social development, especially in organizing joint conferences. Even when a conference is sponsored by only one or two organizations, the advice and assistance of other interested organizations is often indispensable for optimum results. In order to avoid duplicative or otherwise uncomplementary conferences on particular subjects, the different global and regional bodies of the United Nations system concerned with African development—the specialized agencies, UNDP, UNCTAD, UNIDO, UNICEF, UNHCR, and ECA—as well as the ADB and the OAU would need to engage in regular consultations in planning the subjects and focus of such conferences, the level of governmental representation, and the respective roles of the organizations concerned.

Since the ECA secretariat, which is a part of the United Nations Department of Economic and Social Affairs, maintains, on the one hand, joint divisions or otherwise close ties with the secretariats of various United Nations bodies and the specialized agencies and, on the other, co-operative links with the OAU secretariat, it occupies a pivotal position in any multi-organizational co-operation. The task of co-ordination would be greatly facilitated by ECOSOC's acceptance of the Secretary-General's recommendation that periodic interagency meetings should be held in each region by the representatives of interested United Nations organizations and agencies under the chairmanship of the Executive Secretary of the regional commission concerned. In Africa, the envisaged multi-organizational approach would be further strengthened if the proposed interagency meetings were broadened to include representatives from the major African organizations—the ADB and the OAU.

On the other hand, in those subjects for which the role of the OAU is more central than that of ECA—those covered by the OAU-ESCHC and such subjects as assistance to refugees and the promotion of human rights—the OAU secretariat is well placed to serve as the spearhead for multi-organizational co-operation.

Notes

Part I

OAU-UN Relations in the Peace and Security Field

I. AFRICAN REGIONALISM AND THE UNITED NATIONS

1. R. Emerson, "Pan-Africanism," in N.J. Padelford and R. Emerson (eds.), *Africa and World Order* (New York, London: F. A. Praeger, 1963), p. 7.
2. A. Quaison-Sackey, *Africa Unbound: Reflexions of an African Statesman* (New York: F. A. Praeger, 1963), pp. 91-97; N.J. Padelford, "The Organization of African Unity," *International Organization*, Vol. XVIII, No. 3 (1964), pp. 522-25.
3. Robert C. Good, "The Congo Crisis: A Study of Post-colonial Politics," in L. W. Martin (ed.), *Neutralism and Non-alignment—the New States in World Affairs* (New York: F. A. Praeger, 1962), pp. 55-56.
4. *General Assembly, Official Records (G.A.O.R.), 16th Session,* 1020th Plenary Meeting, 2 October 1961, p. 177 (A/PV.1020).
5. Of the fifteen Territories the following gained independence since 1964: Basutoland (Lesotho), Bechuanaland (Botswana), Equatorial Guinea, Gambia, Malawi, Mauritius, Guinea-Bissau, Swaziland, and Zambia. But the following still remain under colonial rule: The French Territory of the Afars and Issas, Namibia, South Rhodesia and Spanish Sahara. Following the military overthrow of the colonialist regime in Portugal in 1974, Mozambique and Angola became self-governing and will gain independence in June and November 1975, respectively.
6. OAU document CIAS/Plen.2/Rev.2, resolution A (Agenda Item 11: Decolonization), operative paragraph 6.
6a. For texts of the African Charter of the Casablanca Conference, as elaborated in the Protocol of 1961 and the Charter of the Inter-African and Malagasy Organization, adopted at the Lagos Conference of 1962, see Colin Legum, *Pan Africanism: A Short Political Guide,* Revised Edition (New York: Praeger, 1965), pp. 211–215.
6b. For text of the Ethiopian draft, see Summit Conference of Independent African States, *Proceedings of the Summit Conference of Independent African States,* Vol. I, section I, Addis Ababa, May 1963 (Publication of the Ethiopian Government), document COMM.I/EMPC/1, 17 May 1963.
6c. Text published in Z. Cervenka, *The Organisation of African Unity and its Charter* (London: C. Hurst and Co., 1969), Appendix B; and in Jon Woronoff, *Organizing African Unity* (Metuchen, N.J.: The Scarecrow Press Inc., 1970), Annex III.
7. The Casablanca and Monrovia Groups tended to disagree on a number of issues. Bearing in mind that there were some differences within each group, the differences between the two groups may be generalized as fol-

lows: most members of the Casablanca Group favored a "maximalist" approach to continental unity; maintained that independence could not be complete until colonial and "neo-colonial" ties were severed; backed Prime Minister Lumumba as against President Kasavubu in the Congo crisis and were highly critical of United Nations efforts in the Congo following the resolution of the constitutional crisis in favor of the latter leader; supported Morocco's border claims; staunchly advanced the position of Algeria versus France and permitted the Algerian National Liberation Front to be represented at Casablanca meetings by its "Provisional Government." In contrast, the Monrovia Powers referred to unity in only very general terms in their Lagos Charter, while stressing national sovereignty and non-interference in internal affairs; desired to maintain good relations with former metropoles; tended to support President Kasuvubu and the United Nations efforts in the Congo; and advocated that pre-existing colonial boundaries, though superimposed from without, were sacrosanct. The majority of the Monrovia Powers were much less militant in support of Algerian independence and would not permit full representation for the "Algerian Provisional Government" in African intergovernmental meetings such as the Lagos Conference of the Monrovia Group. See Good, op. cit., pp. 49–63.

8. OAU Council of Ministers resolution 5(I), 10 August 1963.

9. I. Wallerstein, *Africa—The Politics of Unity* (New York: Random House, 1967), pp. 121–26.

10. Articles II, paragraph 2(f), and XX of the OAU Charter.

11. Article 3 of the Inter-American Treaty of Reciprocal Assistance; and Articles 2-6 of the Joint Defense and Economic Co-operation Treaty Between the States of the Arab League, respectively.

12. Article III, paragraph 7, of the OAU Charter. Although there has been no clear official definition of non-alignment as a policy, one might conclude on the basis of the declarations of non-aligned conferences that for its adherents it represents (i) a deep concern about global problems, particularly those likely to endanger international peace and security; (ii) a tendency to "take a stand" on such problems, in contrast to an attitude of isolationism, a stand based not on an obligation to maintain equal diplomatic distance from the contrasting positions of the two sides in the cold war but on a flexible approach aspiring to treat every issue on its merits; and (iii) a minimum degree of co-operation and consensus in approaching critical international issues engendering tensions among nations.

13. For a full analysis of the relative capabilities and comparative performances of the OAU, the OAS, and the League of Arab States, see J. S. Nye, *Peace in Parts: Integration and Conflict in Regional Organization* (Boston: Little, Brown and Company, 1971), chapter 5; and E. B. Haas, R. L. Butterworth, and J. S. Nye, *Conflict Management by International Organizations* (Morristown, N.J.: General Learning Press, 1972), esp. pp. 48-55.

14. The main ones are the disputes between Algeria and Morocco; Somalia

and Ethiopia; Somalia and Kenya; Ghana and Upper Volta; Ghana and Togo; Ghana and Ivory Coast; Dahomey and Niger; and the conflicting claims of Somalia and Ethiopia to the French Territory of the Afars and the Issas; and of Morocco and Mauritania to Spanish Sahara. In an article entitled "On the Conflict Potential of Inherited Boundaries in Africa," Ravi L. Kapil contends that earlier predictions of a high incidence of conflict in Africa due to boundary disputes are not likely to be borne out, except in States where political power is exercised by leaders that represent either an indigenous national tradition transcending the colonial period or a culturally homogeneous political community. While this may be true of some of the cases listed above, Kapil seems to ignore the fact that inter-State differences over ideological or other political issues have tended to escalate the conflict potential of several boundary disputes. *World Politics,* Vol. 18 (1965-1966), pp. 656-673.

15. UN Charter, Art. 2:7.
16. OAU Charter, Art. IV:2; Article XII of the Protocol of the OAU Commission of Mediation, Conciliation and Arbitration states that the Commission "shall have jurisdiction over disputes between States only."
17. By 1965 the total number of African refugees exceeded half a million and by 1970 it virtually reached one million. See Reports of the United Nations High Commissioner for Refugees for 1965/66 and for 1969/70, *G.A.O.R., 21st Session, Supplement No. 11* (A/6311/Rev.1), pp. 8-9, and Ibid., *25th Session, Supplement No. 12* (A/8012), p. 46.
18. L. P. Bloomfield and A. C. Leiss, "Arms Control and the Developing Countries," *World Politics,* Vol. XVIII, No. 1 (Oct. 1965), pp. 5-6.
19. See General Assembly resolutions: 1652(XVI), 24 November 1961, and 2033(XX), 3 December 1965.
20. OAU resolutions: CIAS/Plen. 2/Rev. 2, resolution D (Agenda Item III: General Disarmament), 25 May 1963; CM/Res. 28(II), 29 February 1964; CM/Res. 38(III), 17 July 1964; and AHG/Res. 11(I), 21 July 1964.

II. THE OAU AND THE UN: OBJECTIVES, PRIORITIES, AND INSTITUTIONS

1. (Omitted)
2. T. O. Elias and Boutros Boutros Ghali, two African jurists who participated in the drafting of the OAU Charter, have analyzed the issue in detail and have reached the same conclusion. See T. O. Elias, "The Charter of the Organization of African Unity," *American Journal of International Law,* Vol. 59, No. 2 (1965), p. 247; B. Boutros Ghali, "The Addis Ababa Charter," *International Conciliation,* No. 546 (1964), pp. 25-26.
3. OAU document CIAS/Plen. 2/Rev. 2, resolutions B: Apartheid and Racial Discrimination; E: Areas of Co-operation—Economic Problems. And document CIAS/Plen. 3, resolutions: A: Labour Matters; B: Education and Culture; C: Health, Sanitation and Nutrition.
4. A count of the speeches of all major topics made by the African States at the fifteenth session of the General Assembly (1960) reveals that the

number of speeches on decolonization and apartheid was almost as high as the combined total of speeches made by the same States on all the other key issues; in the sixteenth session (1961), the former exceeded the latter by almost 40 percent. See David A. Kay, "The Impact of African States on the United Nations," *International Organization,* Vol. XXIII, No. 1, pp. 26-27.

5. The nine States were Australia, Belgium, Dominican Republic, France, Portugal, South Africa, Spain, the U.K., and the U.S.

6. General Assembly resolution 1654(XVI), 27 November 1961. The four States that abstained were France, South Africa, Spain, and the U.K. Portugal decided not to vote.

7. The impact of this notion is analyzed in Ali A. Mazrui, "The United Nations and African Political Attitudes," *International Organization,* Vol. XVIII, No. 3, p. 506.

8. OAU document CIAS/Plan.2/Rev.2, resolution A.

9. General Assembly resolution 2160(XXI), 30 November 1966. The vote was 98 to 2, with 8 abstentions. Significantly, of the permanent members of the Security Council, France, the U.S. and the USSR were among those voting in favor, while the U.K. voted against and China (Republic of) abstained. Of the other States, Portugal voted against and the following abstained: Australia, Belgium, Italy, Luxembourg, the Netherlands, New Zealand, and South Africa.

10. The Declaration, approved by and annexed to General Assembly resolution 2625(XXV), was the result of the work of the Special Committee on Principles of International Law concerning Friendly Relations and Co-operation among States, as reported in documents A/5746 (1964), A/6320 (1966), A/6799 (1967), A/7326 (1968), A/7619 (1969), and A/8018 (1970).

11. The U.K. abstained and Portugal and South Africa did not participate in the voting.

12. For an analysis of the relative powers of the General Assembly, see International Court of Justice, *Reports of Judgments, Advisory Opinions and Orders, Certain Expenses of the United Nations, Advisory Opinion of 20 July 1962,* pp. 163-172. (Hereinafter cited as I.C.J. *Reports.*)

13. Article XXVII of the OAU Charter.

14. Articles XIII, XXII, and XXIII of the OAU Charter.

15. See OAU document Inst./Rept. 1 and the decision of the OAU Assembly, AHG/Dec. 5, November 1966.

16. Z. Cervenka, *The Organization of African Unity and its Charter* (London: C. Hurst & Co., 1969), pp. 53-54.

17. Rule 5 of the OAU Assembly rules of procedure and rule 7 of the Council of Ministers rules of procedure, respectively.

18. Rule 36 of the rules of procedure of the OAU Assembly.

19. A detailed analysis of the Commission is given in T. O. Elias, "The Commission of Mediation, Conciliation and Arbitration of the OAU," *British*

Yearbook of International Law, Vol. XL, 1964, pp. 336-348.
20. Ibid., p. 343.

III. RELATIONSHIPS CONCERNING DISPUTES AMONG OAU MEMBERS

1. This designation was used in the relevant resolutions of the General Assembly but was not accepted by France which had sovereignty over Algeria until July 1962.
2. See *Le Monde,* 23 October 1963.
3. République algérienne démocratique et populaire, Ministère de l'orientation nationale, *De Bamako à Addis-Abéba,* p. 18.
4. Interviews.
5. *Keesing's Contemporary Archives, Weekly Diary of World Events,* Bristol: Keesing's Publications Ltd., Vol. XIV, 1963-1964 (7-14 March 1964), p. 19942.
6. *The New York Times,* 4 November 1963; *Le Monde,* 5 November 1963. *Le Monde* reported in addition that the Permanent Representative of Morocco to the United Nations had stated in a press conference on 3 November that "his government might request a meeting of the Security Council if Algeria's attacks against Figuig did not cease, but that it would first wait for the result of the contacts made by the President of Mali . . . and the Emperor of Ethiopia with [the President of Algeria] Mr. Ben Bella." [Unofficial translation] Both newspapers reported that Morocco had held consultations on the possibility of convening the Security Council but that it was encouraged to seek settlement within an African context. This, however, was not confirmed by Morocco.
7. OAU Council of Ministers resolution ECM/Res. 1(I), 15-18 November 1963.
8. The seven States were Ethiopia, Ivory Coast, Mali, Nigeria, Senegal, Sudan, and Tanganyika (later Tanzania).
9. OAU Council of Ministers resolution CM/Res. 18(II), 24-29 February 1964.
10. See *Le Monde,* 21 February and 10 March 1964.
11. Meeting at Tlemcen (Algeria) on 27 May 1970, the President of Algeria and the King of Morocco agreed to set up a joint commission to demarcate the frontier over the disputed area from Figuig to Tindouf, it being expected that the definitive line would follow the de facto border inherited from French rule. As a result, the Tindouf area with its rich iron deposits will remain in Algerian hands, but the two Heads of State agreed to set up a Moroccan-Algerian agency to study the joint exploitation of the mineral resources. See *Keesing's Contemporary Archives,* Vol. XVII, 1969-1970 (8-15 August 1970), p. 24125.
12. Somali Government, Ministry of Foreign Affairs, *The Somali People's Quest for Unity,* September 1965, pp. 10-11.
13. Ibid., p. 14. In December 1962, before Kenya became independent, a British fact-finding commission visited the Northern Frontier District of

Kenya and concluded that 87 percent of the population in the area were Somalis and that a majority of them would prefer to avoid assimilation into an independent Kenya. But the British Government decided that the area should remain an integral part of Kenya.

14. *Official Records of the Security Council* (S.C.O.R.), 19th Year, Supplement for January-March 1964, document S/5536, 9 February 1964, p. 60.
15. Ibid., documents S/5538 and S/5539, both of 13 February 1964, pp. 61-63.
16. Ibid., document S/5542, 14 February 1964, pp. 65-66.
17. Ibid., documents S/5557 and S/5558, both of 18 February 1964, pp. 77-83.
18. OAU Council of Ministers resolution ECM/Res. 3(II), 15 February 1964.
19. Ibid.
20. Ibid. and resolution ECM/Res. 4(II), 15 February 1964.
21. Summary Records of the Second Ordinary Session of the OAU Council of Ministers held in Lagos on 24-29 February 1964 (unpublished).
22. Somalia, Ethiopia, and Kenya agreed to the deletion of the item on the boundary disputes in the Horn of Africa from the provisional agenda. They also agreed that no action should be taken by any of them which could prejudice future bilateral talks. See Somali Government, Ministry of Foreign Affairs, *The Somali Republic and the Organization of African Unity* (Mogadishu, Somalia, 1964), pp. 39-40.
23. OAU Council of Ministers resolution CM/Res. 17(II), 24-29 February 1964.
24. OAU Assembly of Heads of State and Government resolution AHG/Res. 16(I), 17-21 July 1964.
25. "Declaration on Kenya-Somali Relations," OAU document AHG/ST. 2(IV), 11-14 September 1967.
26. In discussions held later in 1967 and 1968 at Addis Ababa and Mogadiscio, the two countries agreed to adhere to previous agreements about normalizing their relations and to convene the Joint Military Commission to investigate complaints about any violations. In addition, they agreed to undertake measures to eliminate tension between the two countries in the following manner: by according normal diplomatic treatment to each other's diplomats and fair treatment to each other's nationals residing in the territory of the other; by assuring safe repatriation for persons who had taken refuge in their country's embassy; by securing the release of each other's nationals detained against their will; and by exchanging territories occupied during the hostilities. They also agreed to set up a special joint commission to examine various claims to property acquired as a result of the hostilities; and to hold periodic consultations preferably every three months or whenever necessary at regional administrative levels in order to promote co-operation along the border. See "News in Brief: Somali Republic," *Africa Report,* November 1967, p. 31.

27. When President Kenyatta of Kenya and Prime Minister Egal of Somalia met in October 1967 at Arusha under the Chairmanship of President Kaunda of Zambia, they agreed to maintain good neighborly relations in accordance with the OAU Charter and to adhere to the Declaration of the OAU Conference at Kinshasa; to refrain from conducting hostile propaganda against each other and gradually suspend any emergency regulations imposed on either side of the border; to re-open diplomatic relations and encourage the development of economic and trade relations; and to appoint a working committe consisting of Somalia, Kenya, and Zambia to meet periodically to review the implementation of the agreement and also to examine ways and means of bringing about a satisfactory solution to major and minor differences between them. In February 1969, the three leaders met again in Nairobi and expressed their satisfaction at the progress made in the implementation of the Arusha Memorandum of Understanding. "Outstanding problems" were to be discussed at a future meeting. See OAU document AHG/ST.1, p. 2, and *Kenya News Agency Handout,* No. 26, February 1969.

28. The first referendum was held in 1958 when French Somaliland together with other African Territories under French administration, except Guinea, opted for greater self-government, rather than independence, by becoming members of a voluntary French Community with quasi-federal links between France and its overseas Territories. Subsequently, all the Territories in Africa, except French Somaliland were granted independence while remaining in the Community.

29. *The Somali People's Quest for Unity,* op. cit., p. 18.

30. Quoted from *Le Monde,* 18 and 19 September and 12 October 1966.

31. Ibid.

32. *Keesing's Contemporary Archives,* Vol. XVII, 1969-1970 (8-15 August 1970), p. 24125.

33. OAU Council of Ministers resolution CM/Res. 84(VII), 31 October-4 November 1966.

34. UN General Assembly resolution 2228(XXI), 20 December 1966.

35. Ibid. and General Assembly resolution 2356 (XXII), 19 December 1967; and OAU Council of Ministers resolution CM/Res. 144(X), 20-24 February 1968.

36. OAU Council of Ministers resolution CM/Res. 82(VII), 31 October-4 November 1966, and UN General Assembly resolution 2354(XXII), 19 December 1967.

37. *Keesing's Contemporary Archives,* Vol. XVII, 1969-1970 (8-15 August 1970), p. 24125.

38. The first ethnic conflict in Rwanda took place in 1959-61, before the two components of the Belgian Trust Territory of Rwanda-Urundi, which were separate countries before colonial times, regained their independence as separate States.

39. UN Press Release SG/SM/5, 7 February 1964.

NOTES

40. UN Press Release SG/SM/24, 3 March 1964.

41. UN Press Release SG/SM/24, 3 March 1964.

42. UN Press Release SG/SM/5, 7 February 1964.

43. *Keesing's Contemporary Archives,* Vol. XV, 1965-1966 (4-11 December 1965), p. 21113 and (12-19 February 1966), p. 21234.

40. UN Press Release SG/SM/24, 3 March 1964.
41. UN Press Release SG/SM/24, 3 March 1964.
42. UN Press Release SG/SM/5, 7 February 1964.
43. *Keesing's Contemporary Archives,* Vol. XV, 1965-1966 (4-11 December 1965), p. 21113 and (12-19 February 1966), p. 21234.
44. OAU document AHG/30, September 1967, p. 1.
45. Ibid.
46. Rwanda and Burundi agreed at Goma (Zaire) to apply the provisions of the Kinshasa Agreement on security; to take measures to prevent the traffic and possession of arms by political refugees in their respective countries; to appeal to all political refugees in possession of arms to surrender them to their host government within one month; to set up a Standing Tripartite Political Commission to study and suggest appropriate measures for repatriating refugees willing to go back; and to grant amnesty to refugees returning home as the result of this agreement.
47. Later, in October, Tshombé came to Cairo to attend the Second Conference of Heads of State or Government of Non-Aligned Countries, but was denied access to the meeting and was confined to his quarters in the palace for guests until he decided to return to his country.
48. OAU Council of Ministers resolution ECM/Res. 5(III), 5-10 September 1964.
49. Cameroon, Ethiopia, Ghana, Guinea, Kenya, Nigeria, Somalia, Tunisia, the UAR, and Upper Volta.
50. *Keesing's Contemporary Archives,* Vol. XIV, 1963-1964 (21-28 November 1964), p. 20425.
51. Press Communique of the OAU Ad Hoc Commission on the Congo, 28 November 1964.
52. These were Afghanistan, Algeria, Burundi, Cambodia, Central African Republic, Congo (Brazzaville), Dahomey, Ethiopia, Ghana, Guinea, Indonesia, Kenya, Malawi, Mali, Mauritania, Somalia, Sudan, Uganda, UAR, Tanzania, Yugoslavia, and Zambia.
53. *S.C.O.R., 19th Year, Supplement for October-December 1964,* document S/6076 and Add. 1-5, 1 December 1964, pp. 198-200.
54. Ibid., document S/6096, 9 December 1964, pp. 217-18.
55. *G.A.O.R., 20th Session, Supplement No. 2* (A/6002), "Report of the Security Council, 16 July 1964–15 July 1965," para. 483 (Ghana), 486 and 660 (Sudan), 499 and 501 (Mali), 505 and 672 (Algeria), 555 (UAR), 580-82 (Kenya), 590 (Central African Republic), 619 (Uganda), 652-53 (USSR), and 630 (Tanzania).
56. Ibid., para. 574-575 (the U.S.), 594 and 597 (Nigeria), 618 (Brazil), 624 (Republic of China), 465 and 542-43 (the Congo).
57. Ibid., para. 636 (Morocco) and 614 (Ivory Coast).
58. The vote was 10 in favor, none against, with one abstention (France).
59. *S.C.O.R., 19th Year,* 1186th Meeting, 28 December 1964, pp. 11-12.
60. Ibid., p. 9; *S.C.O.R., 19th Year,* 1187th Meeting, 29 December 1964, p. 8.

61. *S.C.O.R., 19th Year,* 1188th Meeting, 30 December 1964, p. 6.

62. See "Note Verbale" of 17 March 1965 from the OAU Administrative Secretary-General to the United Nations Secretary-General, circulated to the members of the Security Council: *Official Records of the Security Council, Twentieth Year, Supplement for January-March 1965,* document S/6257, 26 March 1965, pp. 255-258.

63. *S.C.O.R., 21st Year, Supplement for July-September 1966,* document S/7503, 21 September 1966, pp. 132-133.

64. *S.C.O.R., 22nd Year, Supplement for July-September 1967,* document S/8031, 5 July 1967, pp. 58-59.

65. UN Security Council resolution 239 (1967), 10 July 1967.

66. OAU Assembly resolution AHG/Res. 49(IV), 11-14 September 1967.

67. OAU Assembly decision AHG/Dec. 14(IV), 11-14 September 1967. The members of the Ad Hoc Committee were Burundi, Central African Republic, Congo (Brazzaville), the Congo (Zaire), Ethiopia, Rwanda, Sudan, Tanzania, Uganda, and Zambia.

68. UN Security Council resolution 241 (1967), 15 November 1967.

69. The members were Burundi, Uganda, Congo (Brazzaville), Tanzania, and Rwanda.

70. OAU document AHG/35, September 1968, pp. 2-3.

71. OAU document AHG/35, Annex 3, p. 5 and Annex 4, pp. 1-9.

72. These were Federal Prime Minister Sir Abubakar Tafawa Balewa, who was of northern origin; Sir Ahmadou Bello, Premier of the Northern Region and Sarduna of Sokoto; Chief Samuel Akintola, Premier of the Western Region; Chief Okotie-Eboh, Federal Minister of Finance, who was of midwestern origin.

73. These were the Heads of State of Cameroon, the Congo (Zaire), Ethiopia, Ghana, Liberia, and Niger.

74. OAU Assembly resolution AHG/Res. 51(IV), 11-14 September 1967.

75. OAU document AHG/34, Annex II, September 1968.

76. OAU Assembly resolution AHG/Res. 54(V), 13-16 September 1968.

77. Ibid.

78. "News in Brief," *Africa Report,* November 1968, p. 21.

79. At a press conference on 17 April 1969, the United Nations Secretary-General expressed the view that any attempt by a Member State to bring the Nigerian question before the Security Council or the General Assembly would not succeed because of the knowledge that the OAU was against the inscription of this question on the agenda of these organs. *UN Monthly Chronicle,* Vol. VI, No. 5 (May 1969), p. 78 (UN Press Release SG/SM/1092).

80. See the Summary of the fourth interim report of the observer representing the United Nations Secretary-General in *UN Monthly Chronicle,* Vol. VI, No. 2 (February 1969), pp. 7-8 (UN Press Release SG/1725, 17 January 1969), In November 1968, the observers from Canada, Poland, Sweden, and the U.K. issued a similar report entitled "International Ob-

server Team in the Nigerian Civil War, Comprehensive Report."
81. UN Press Release SG/SM/1531, 16 September 1971, p. 11.
82. UN Press Release SG/SM/998, 13 September 1968.
83. *UN Monthly Chronicle,* Vol. VI, No. 9 (October 1969), p. 46 (UN Press Release SG/SM/1151, 5 September 1969).
84. Tension between Togo and Ghana had been acute before the assassination of President Olympio of Togo in January 1963, but had subsided during the period in question.
85. *Keesing's Contemporary Archives,* Vol. XV, 1965-1966 (7-14 August 1965), pp. 20894-20895.
86. OAU Council of Ministers resolution ECM/Res. 9(V), 10-13 June 1965.
87. *Keesing's Contemporary Archives,* Vol. XV, 1965-1966 (6-13 November 1965), p. 21051.
88. OAU Assembly resolution AHG/Res. 27(II), 21-25 October 1965.
89. UN General Assembly resolution 2131(XX), 21 December 1965.
90. *Keesing's Contemporary Archives,* Vol. XV, 1965-1966 (12-19 March 1966), p. 21275.
91. *S.C.O.R., 21st Year, Supplements for April-June 1966,* documents S/7268 of 25 April and S/7270 of 27 April, pp. 55-57 and 58.
92. *Keesing's Contemporary Archives,* Vol. XV, 1965-1966 (26 November-3 December 1966), p. 21738.
93. Ibid.
94. *S.C.O.R., 22nd Year, Supplements for July-September 1967,* document S/8120 and Add. 1 and 2, 14 August 1967, pp. 176-177 (Annex IV).
95. Ibid., pp. 194-195 (Add. 2).
96. Ibid., p. 164.
97. Ibid., p. 166.
98. OAU Assembly decision AHG/Dec. 18(IV), 11-14 September 1967.
99. Ibid., pp, 178-182 (Annex VII).
100. Ibid., pp. 187-188 (Annex XII).
101. *S.C.O.R., 19th Year,* 1189th Meeting, 30 December 1964, p. 8.
102. *G.A.O.R., 26th Session, Supplement No. 1A,* document A/8401/Add. 1, para. 126.
103. Occasionally, such initiatives were taken within the framework of African organizations less comprehensive than the OAU, as in the case of the dispute between Niger and Dahomey (1965) for which the Conseil de l'Entente provided a forum for settlement. Before the creation of the OAU, the Union Africaine et Malgache had played a similar role in the dispute between Gabon and the Congo (Brazzaville).

IV. RELATIONSHIPS REGARDING COLONIAL AND RACIAL PROBLEMS IN AFRICA

1. The term "collective measures" is understood to have a broader connotation than the terms "action" or "enforcement action" referred to respectively in Chapters VII and VIII of the United Nations Charter.

2. See report of Committee 3 of Commission III on the Security Council, United Nations Conference on International Organization, *Documents,* Vol. 12 (Doc. 881, III/3/46, 10 June 1945), pp. 507-508. See also L. M. Goodrich, E. Hambro, and A. Simons, *Charter of the United Nations; Commentary and Documents,* Third and Revised Edition (New York and London: Columbia University Press, 1969), p. 365; H. Kelsen, *The Law of the United Nations* (New York: Praeger, 1950), p. 724; and I. L. Claude, Jr., *"The OAS, the UN and the United States," International Conciliation,* No. 547 (1964), p. 50.

3. For texts of relevant statements of the USSR, see *S.C.O.R., 15th Year,* 893rd Meeting, 8 September 1960, para. 22-26, and 894th ·Meeting, 9 December 1960, para. 51-56, 59, 66, 68-70, 74, and 76; also Ibid., *17th Year,* 991st Meeting, 27 February 1962, para. 31, 32, 34, 44, 47, and 48. Other States that agreed with the USSR were Poland, *Ibid., 15th Year,* 894th Meeting, para. 30 and 32-34; Romania, Ibid., *17th Year,* 991st Meeting, para. 79 and 80.

4. For texts of relevant statements, see the following:
   —the U.K.: *S.C.O.R., 15th Year,* 893rd Meeting, 8 September 1960, para. 94, 96, and 97, and Ibid., 991st Meeting, 27 February 1962, para. 8-11;
   —the U.S.: Ibid., 893rd Meeting, para. 49-54, and Ibid., 991st Meeting, para. 97-99;
   as well as the statements of:
   —Chile: Ibid., 17th Year, 991st Meeting, para. 12 and 18.
   —China (Rep. of): Ibid., 15th Year, 893rd Meeting, para. 102-104;
   —Italy: Ibid., 894th Meeting, para. 45-47;
   —Tunisia: Ibid., para 37;
   —Venezuela, Ibid., 893rd Meeting, para. 76, 77, and 80.
   France stated that it would not be in favor of an exclusive regional competence and could not maintain that the United Nations was necessarily competent in all cases; the Security Council "must decide in each particular case as to whether its intervention can in any way promote the purposes and principles of the Charter"; Ibid., 15th Year, 893rd Meeting, para. 86-90.

5. During the Security Council deliberations on the Dominican case in 1960, some members of the Council—Argentina, Ceylon, and Ecuador—had stated that the legal interpretation of Article 53 remained open to debate, but that the occasion was not propitious for a thorough consideration— *S.C.O.R., 15th Year,* 893rd Meeting, 8 September 1960, para. 32-34, 13-17, and 62-68. Without addressing itself to legal issues, the Council then merely took note of the OAS resolution concerning the application of certain diplomatic and economic measures by OAS Members against the Dominican Republic. But by March 1962, the issue of the powers of the Security Council with regard to diplomatic and economic measures taken by a regional organization was clarified and, as far as the majority

in the Council was concerned, settled. On 27 February 1962, the Council decided not to adopt an agenda concerning Cuba's complaint about certain political and economic measures applied against it by the OAS, thereby refraining from reopening the issue of the legal relations (only 4 delegations were in favor—Ghana, Romania, the UAR, and the USSR— while the remaining 7 abstained). Again, on 23 March 1962, a Cuban draft resolution (S/5095) for a Security Council request for an advisory opinion from the International Court of Justice on, inter alia, the interpretation of Article 53 and its application to the measures taken by the OAS, was rejected by 7 votes to 2 (Romania and USSR), with 1 abstention (UAR), and one not participating in the voting (Ghana). For the majority in the Council, therefore, "enforcement action" did not include measures not involving the use of force.

For an analytical summary of the practice of the Security Council with respect to the provisions of Article 53, see United Nations, *Repertory of Practice of United Nations Organs, Supplement No. 3,* Vol. II (Articles 23-72 of the Charter (New York, 1971), pp. 290-299. A detailed analysis of the issues is given in a UNITAR study by Aida L. Levin entitled "Relations between the Organization of American States and the United Nations (1973) (especially Chapter V).

6. The key provision in this resolution states: ". . . if the Security Council, because of lack of unanimity of the permanent members, fails to exercise its primary responsibility for the maintenance of international peace and security in any case . . . , the General Assembly shall consider the matter immediately with a view to making appropriate recommendations to Members for collective measures, including in the case of a breach of the peace or act of aggression the use of armed force when necessary, to maintain or restore international peace and security." General Assembly resolution 377(V), 3 November 1950.

7. I.C.J., *Reports, Certain Expenses of the United Nations, Advisory Opinion of 20 July 1962,* pp. 164-165, 206, and 217-219.

8. Statements made at the Sixth (Legal) Committee of the General Assembly during the twenty-fifth session of the Assembly, contained in summary records of 23-28 September 1970, UN documents A/C.6/SR.1178-A/C.6/SR.1184.

9. *G.A.O.R.,* 25th Session, Supplement No. 18 (A/8018), para. 151-152 (France); para. 234-235 (U.K.); para. 269-270 (the U.S.).

10. UN document A/C.6/SR.1182 and Corr. 1, 30 September and 8 October 1970, pp. 2-3 (mimeo.).

11. UN document A/C.6/SR.1184, 1 October 1970, pp. 4-5 (mimeo.).

12. A different point of view is given by a South African scholar who has addressed himself to the legal aspects of the issue of OAU support to liberation movement: C. J. R. Dugard, "The Organization of African Unity and Colonialism: An Inquiry into the Plea of Self-Defence as a Justification for the Use of Force in the Eradication of Colonialism," *The*

International and Comparative Law Quarterly, Vol. XVI, No. 1 (1967), pp. 162-176. He argues that the role of the OAU constitutes impermissible use of force which could not be justified as collective self-defense under Article 51. He explains that since no provision of the Charter or any other instrument (including the Declaration on Decolonization) envisages elimination of colonialism by the use of force, the OAU activites could not be regarded as legitimate measures against colonial domination or collective defense against what several States regard as "permanent aggression." But he fails to recognize that the principle of non-use of force contained in Article 2(4) of the Charter does not forbid civil strife or armed rebellion within a country and that the United Nations has, over the years, recognized the legitimacy of the struggle of dependent peoples against recalcitrant colonial rulers or illegal settler regimes and has encouraged external support for such struggle. He also fails to distinguish between the actual use of armed forces of States against colonial regimes and the mere encouragement and support of guerrilla fighters; while the former role would raise the issue of self-defense, the latter would hardly do so.

13. General Assembly resolution 1542(XV), 15 December 1960. Portugal claimed territorial sovereignty over Angola, Mozambique, Guinea (Bissau) and Cape Verde, São Tomé and Príncipe, Macao, and Timor. It also claimed sovereignty over the enclaves of São João Batista de Ajuda and Goa, but against its will, these Territories were united in 1961 with Dahomey and India, respectively. The Portuguese Constitution of 1951 had changed the status of these colonies to "overseas provinces" of Portugal, and the Portuguese Government had thus maintained that they were part of the metropole and were as such not Non-Self-Governing Territories in the meaning of Chapter XI of the United Nations Charter. It had thus consistently refused to report on the Territories as required by Article 73(e) of the United Nations Charter.

14. General Assembly resolution 1819(XVII), 18 December 1962, adopted by a vote of 57 to 14, with 18 abstentions. Those voting in favor included all East European Socialist States, most of the African and Asian States, and some Latin American States; voting against were Australia, Belgium, Canada, France, Italy, Luxembourg, the Netherlands, New Zealand, Portugal, South Africa, Spain, Turkey, the U.K., and the U.S.; and abstaining, Argentina, Austria, Brazil, Chile, China (Rep. of), Denmark, Dominican Republic, Finland, Greece, Honduras, Ireland, Japan, Mexico, Norway, Peru, Sweden, Thailand, and Uruguay.

15. *S.C.O.R., 20th Year,* 1267th Meeting, 22 November 1965, para. 50.

16. Ibid., para. 9 and 15. The Netherlands, the fourth State to abstain on the resolution, had other reservations not relevant in the present context.

17. *S.C.O.R., 18th Year, Supplement for October, November and December 1963* (S/5448), pp. 55-61.

18. See CIAS/Plen.2/Rev.2, Resolution A (Agenda Item II: Decolonization), adopted by the Summit Conference of Independent African States on 25

May 1963; OAU Assembly resolution AHG/Res. 9(I), 21 July 1964, AHG/Res. 45(II), 25 October 1965; and Council of Ministers resolutions CM/Res. 34(III), 17 July 1964, CM/Res. 49(IV), 9 March 1965.

19. Voting against: Argentina, Australia, Austria, Belgium, Bolivia, Brazil, Canada, Colombia, Costa Rica, El Salvador, Guatemala, Honduras, Italy, Luxembourg, Mexico, the Netherlands, New Zealand, Paraguay, Peru, Portugal, South Africa, Spain, the U.K., the U.S., Uruguay, and Venezuela. Abstaining: Chile, China (Rep. of), Denmark, Dominican Republic, Finland, France, Greece, Ireland, Japan, Laos, Norway, the Philippines, Sweden, Thailand, and Turkey.

20. Those States included, in addition to France, the U.K. and the U.S., Argentina, Bolivia, Brazil, Chile, Costa Rica, and Dominican Republic from Latin America; Denmark, Norway, and Sweden from Scandinavia; and some West European, Asian, and Pacific allies of the U.K. or the U.S. Further details given in United Nations Office of Public Information, *Yearbook of the United Nations, 1965*, p. 611.

21. *G.A.O.R., 20th Session, Plenary Meetings, 1407th Meeting,* 21 December 1965, para. 57-60 (France); Ibid., *Fourth Committee, 1592nd Meeting,* 18 December 1965, para. 24 (the U.K.) and para 10 (the U.S.).

22. In December 1966, the General Assembly adopted resolution 2184(XXI) by a vote of 70 to 13, with 22 abstentions (as against 66:26:15 for resolution 2107(XX). The following ten States shifted from opposition to abstention: Argentina, Bolivia, Colombia, El Salvador, Honduras, Italy, Mexico, Paraguay, Uruguay, and Venezuela; Guatemala, which had previously voted against, joined the following seven States, which had previously abstained, in voting for the resolution: Chile, China (Rep. of), Dominican Republic, Ireland, Japan, the Philippines, and Thailand.

    By November 1967, when the Assembly adopted resolution 2270(XXII) by a vote of 82:7:21, the following six States shifted from opposition to abstention: Australia, Belgium, Brazil, Canada, Luxembourg, and New Zealand; and three others, Colombia, Laos, and Venezuela, changed from abstention to affirmative.

23. Abstaining: Argentina, Australia, Belgium, Brazil, Cuba, Dominican Republic, France, Gabon, Italy, Ivory Coast, Luxembourg, Malawi, Mexico, Netherlands, New Zealand, Spain, the U.K., and the U.S.

24. OAU Assembly resolution AHG/Res. 9(I), 21 July 1964.

25. OAU Assembly resolution AHG/Res. 35(II), 25 October 1965; and OAU Council of Ministers resolutions: CM/Res. 83(VII), 4 November 1966, CM/Res. 137(X), 24 February 1968, and CM/Res. 151(XI), 12 September 1968.

26. On Senegal, Security Council resolutions: 273 (1969), adopted by 13:0, with Spain and the U.S. abstaining; 294 (1971), by 13:0, with the U.K. and the U.S. abstaining; 302 (1971), by 14:0, with the U.S. abstaining; and 321 (1972), by 12:0, with Belgium, the U.K., and the U.S. abstaining. On Guinea, resolutions: 275 (1969), adopted by 9:0, with China

(Rep. of), Colombia, France, Spain, the U.K., and the U.S. abstaining, and 290 (1970), by 11:0, with France, Spain, the U.K., and the U.S. abstaining. On Zambia, resolution 268 (1969), adopted by 11:0, with France, Spain, the U.K., and the U.S. abstaining.

27. Security Council resolutions 226, 14 October 1966, and 241, 15 November 1967.

28. Security Council resolution 290, 8 December 1970.

29. UN document S/PV.1563 (mimeo.), 8 December 1970.

30. General Assembly resolution 1747(XVI), 28 June 1962.

31. Under the 1923 Constitution, the Southern Rhodesian Parliament had full power to enact legislation on practically every domestic matter, subject only to the power of veto by the U.K. Government in cases of discriminating legislation, which it had never exercised. In the 1961 Constitution, this power of veto was replaced by the inclusion of a Declaration of Rights and other safeguards against violation of fundamental rights and freedoms, including review of all non-financial Bills by a multi-racial Constitutional Council before they were presented to the Governor for Royal assent. But the Southern Rhodesian Legislative Assembly could circumvent the safeguards by overruling an adverse opinion of the Council by a two-third majority, with little likelihood that Royal assent would be denied except when fundamental changes in the Constitution were proposed. However, any person could resort to the courts and eventually appeal to the Privy Council in the U.K.

The 1961 Constitution, which was drawn at a Constitutional Conference in Salisbury with the consent of the authorities in Southern Rhodesia, further expanded the local autonomy that the European settlers had been enjoying since 1923. The main element was the replacement of the British veto power over discriminatory legislation by a Declaration of Rights within the new Constitution purporting to provide equal enjoyment of fundamental rights and freedoms for all Rhodesians. An Assembly of 50 upper-roll and 15 lower-roll seats was introduced, but the high-income and property qualifications required for the upper-roll meant that, in practice, the 50 seats would be reserved for the European minority, thus limiting the representation of the African majority merely to the 15 seats. The franchise under the new Constitution had an element of multi-racialism, but the Africans were not to have parity of representation for another 30 years. By 1963, when the 10-year-old Central African Federation, consisting of Southern Rhodesia, Northern Rhodesia, and Nyasaland, was dissolved and the latter two Territories had gained their independence, the uncompromising, white suprematist party in power—the Rhodesia Front Party—began to intensify its demand for independence under a European settler regime.

For a fuller description of the U.K. constitutional position concerning Southern Rhodesia before 11 November 1965, see *G.A.O.R., 17th Session, Fourth Committee, 1360th Meeting,* 25 October 1962, para. 31-53.

32. OAU document CIAS/Plen.2/Rev.2—Resolution A, 25 May 1963.

33. The U.K. vetoed a draft resolution proposed by Ghana, Morocco, and the Philippines requesting it, inter alia, not to transfer any military force to a minority government in Southern Rhodesia. *S.C.O.R., 18th Year, Supplement for July, August and September 1963,* document S/5425/ Rev.1, 11 September 1963. The proposal was brought before the General Assembly and was adopted by a wide majority—90 to 2 (Portugal and South Africa), with 13 abstentions—as resolution 1883(XVIII), 14 October 1963.

34. Even though this resolution, 202 of 6 May 1965, avoided referring to the implications of the situation in Southern Rhodesia for peace and security and refrained from criticizing the U.K. for not implementing previous resolutions of the General Assembly and from demanding either the annulment of the 1961 Constitution or the cancellation of the scheduled elections, France, the U.K., and the U.S. abstained, the fisrt two contending that the matter concerned an already Self-Governing Territory outside the competence of the United Nations organs and the third maintaining that the demands on the U.K. were unrealistic. The fourth abstaining Power was the USSR which believed that the resolution did not go far enough. *S.C.O.R., 20th Year,* 1202nd Meeting, 6 May 1965, para. 89-95 (the U.K.), 96-98 (France), 99-104 (the U.S.), and 81-84 (USSR).

35. OAU Assembly resolution AHG/Res. 25/Rev.1(II), 25 October 1965.

36. General Assembly resolution 2022(XX), 5 November 1965, adopted by a vote of 82 to 9, with 18 abstentions. Voting against: Australia, Belgium, Canada, Luxembourg, the Netherlands, New Zealand, Portugal, South Africa, and the U.S.; abstaining: Australia, Brazil, Costa Rica, Denmark, Ecuador, El Salvador, Finland, France, Guatemala, Honduras, Iceland, Ireland, Italy, Mexico, Norway, Panama, Spain, and Sweden.

37. *Yearbook of the United Nations,* 1965, p. 123.

38. General Assembly resolution 2024(XX), 11 November 1965, adopted by a vote of 107 to 2 (Portugal and South Africa) with one abstention (France); the U.K. and Uruguay did not participate in the voting.

39. Security Council resolution 216, 12 November 1965 (10 votes to none, with France abstaining).

40. *S.C.O.R., 20th Year,* 1257th Meeting, 12 November 1965, para. 19-22.

41. For a lucid comparison of the British constitutional position regarding Southern Rhodesia before and after UDI, see Rosalyn Higgin's "Britain at the United Nations; A Demand for Results," in *The Round Table, A Quarterly Review of Commonwealth Affairs,* Vol. 56, No. 222 (March 1966), pp. 132-141.

42. OAU resolutions: AHG/Res. 25/Rev. 1(II) and AHG/Res. 39(b) (II), 25 October 1965; OAU Council of Ministers resolutions, ECM/Res. 13 (VI) and ECM/Res. 14(VI), 5 December 1965; CM/Res. 75(VI), 6 March 1966, and CM/Res. 78(VII), 4 November 1966. And General

Assembly resolutions: 2138(XXI), 22 October 1966, and 2151(XXI), 17 November 1966.

43. OAU Council of Ministers resolutions ECM/Res. 13(VI) and ECM/Res. 14(VI), 5 December 1965.

44. Algeria, Congo (Brazzaville), Ghana, Guinea, Mali, Mauritania, Sudan, Tanzania, and UAR. Somalia had previously broken off diplomatic relations, because of its dispute with the U.K. over the issue of the Northeastern province of Kenya.

45. By October 1968, the cost of the measures taken by Zambia to divert its trade and other economic relations away from Southern Rhodesia exceeded $241,000,000, of which just over $46,000,000 was repaid by the British Government (a net cost of over $195,000,000); Zambia's foreign exchange reserves were depleted and its development plans encountered a serious setback. See the section on Zambia in "Report of the Secretary-General in Pursuance of Resolution 253 (1968) adopted by the Security Council on 29 May 1968," document S/8786/Add. 2, 10 October 1968.

46. Security Council resolution 221, 9 April 1966. Bulgaria, France, Mali, USSR, and Uruguay abstained.

47. The first five principles are fully described in Great Britain, *Southern Rhodesia: Documents Relating to the Negotiations between the United Kingdom and Southern Rhodesian Governments, November 1963-November 1965,* Cmnd. 2807, pp. 65-68. The sixth principle was added by Prime Minister Wilson on 25 January 1966.

48. For the records of the talks in H.M.S. *Tiger,* see Great Britain, *Rhodesia: Documents Relating to Proposals for a Settlement, 1966,* Cmnd. 3171, Appendix J, pp. 38-103.

49. The proposed measures included action against non-compliance by Portugal and South Africa and use of force by the U.K. UN document S/7630 and Corr. 1 and Rev. 1, 15 December 1966; amendments to the U.K. draft resolution proposed by Mali, Nigeria, and Uganda.

50. The Committee was orginally composed of representatives of France, the USSR, the U.K., the U.S., Algeria, India, and Paraguay. As the terms of office of the last three States on the Security Council expired, the President of the Council designated the new members of the Council from the same regions to replace them on the Committee. Since October 1970, the Committee has been composed of the entire memebrship of the Council.

51. OAU Council of Ministers resolution CM/Res. 153(XI), 12 September 1968.

52. The vote was eight to none, with seven abstentions: the Republic of China, Hungary, and the USSR joined Algeria, Pakistan, Nepal, Senegal, and Zambia in voting for the resolution; while Colombia, Finland, Paraguay, and Spain abstained along with France, the U.K., and the U.S.

53. For the text of the agreed "Proposals for a Settlement," see *S.C.O.R.,*

Twenty-Sixth Year, Supplement for October, November and December 1971, document S/10405, Annex B, pp. 63-73. The proposals provided for acceptance of the 1969 Rhodesian "Constitution" (summarized in Annex A of document S/10405) as the basic governing instrument with appropriate modifications in order: (i) to allow for progress to African majority rule through the creation of an African higher roll, enrollment on which would be restricted to those Africans meeting the same educational and financial qualifications as the European electorate; (ii) to prevent retrogressive amendment of the modified constitution; and (iii) to confer a right of appeal to the High Court against violations of the anti-discrimination provisions contained in a new declaration of rights, which would be an entrenched provision of the modified constitution.

54. General Assembly resolution 2877(XXVI), 20 December 1971, adopted by a vote of 94 to 8, with 22 abstentions. Voting against: Australia, France, Luxembourg, the Netherlands, New Zealand, Portugal, South Africa, and the U.K.; abstaining: Argentina, Austria, Belgium, Brazil, Canada, Costa Rica, Denmark, Dominican Republic, Fiji, Finland, Greece, Ireland, Italy, Japan, Malawi, Nicaragua, Norway, Panama, Paraguay, Sweden, the U.S., and Uruguay.

55. UN documents S/10489, 30 December 1971, and S/10606, 2 February 1972. The votes were 9 in favor, 1 against, with 5 abstentions (Belgium, France, Italy, Japan, and the U.S.).

56. General Assembly resolutions 2765(XXVI) of 16 November 1971 and 2946(XXVII) of 7 December 1972; and Security Council resolutions 314 (1972) of 28 February, 318 (1972) of 28 July, and 320 (1972) of 29 September 1972.

57. UN document A/C.4/41, Statement by the Representative of South Africa, 4 November 1946.

58. I.C.J. *Reports, International Status of South West Africa: Advisory Opinion of 11 July 1950, p. 128; South West Africa—Voting Procedure: Advisory Opinion of 7 June 1955,* p. 67; and *Admissibility of Hearings of Petitioners by the Committee on South West Africa: Advisory Opinion of 1 June 1956,* p. 23.

59. I.C.J. *Reports, South West Africa Case: Second Phase, Judgment of 18 July 1966,* p. 51.

60. Ibid., pp. 10-13.

61. The vote was 114 to 2 (Portugal and South Africa), with 3 abstentions (France, Malawi, and the U.K.).

62. The members were Ethiopia, Nigeria, Senegal, and the UAR from Africa; Pakistan and Japan from Asia; Chile and Mexico from Latin America; Finland from Scandinavia; Czechoslovakia and the USSR from Eastern Europe; and Canada, Italy, and the U.S. from the North Atlantic area.

63. *G.A.O.R., Fifth Special Session, Annexes, Agenda Item 7,* document A/6640, Report of the Ad Hoc Committee for South West Africa, 7 April 1967, para. 102-107 and 113-122.

64. Ibid., para. 45, 52, 66, and 82.
65. Ibid., para. 84.
66. Ibid., para. 93 and 98.
67. OAU Council of Ministers resolution CM/Res. 97(VIII), 4 March 1967.
68. Those that abstained were Australia, Austria, Belgium, Botswana, Bulgaria, Byelorussian SSR, Canada, Cuba, Czechoslovakia, Denmark, Finland, France, Hungary, Iceland, Ireland, Italy, Luxembourg, Malawi, Malta, Mongolia, the Netherlands, New Zealand, Norway, Poland, Romania, Sweden, Ukrainian SSR, USSR, the U.K., and the U.S.
69. *G.A.O.R., 23rd Session, Agenda Item 64,* Report of the United Nations Council for Namibia, document A/7338, 1968, pp. 2-6.
70. UN documents S/PV.1464 (mimeo.), S/PV.1465 (mimeo.), 20 March 1969.
71. UN document S/PV.1496 (mimeo.), 11 August 1969.
72. UN document S/PV.1495 (mimeo.), 8 August 1969.
73. UN document S/PV.1494 (mimeo.), 6 August 1969.
74. Security Council resolutions: 276 (1970) of 30 January, 284 (1970) and 283 (1970) of 29 July.
75. The U.S. voted in favor of the moderately worded resolution 283 (1970) while the USSR and Poland abstained because they felt it was not strong enough.
76. I.C.J. *Reports, Legal Consequences for States of the Continued Presence of South Africa in Namibia (South West Africa) notwithstanding Security Council Resolution 276 (1970), Advisory Opinion of 21 June 1971,* para. 133.
77. OAU Assembly resolution AHG/Res. 65(VIII), 23 June 1971.
78. UN document S/PV.1598 (mimeo.), 20 October 1971.
79. UN documents: S/PV.1588 (mimeo.), 5 October 1971, and S/PV.1589 (mimeo.), 6 October 1971.
80. UN document S/PV.1593 (mimeo.), 13 October 1971.
81. Security Council resolution 323 (1972), 6 December 1973.
82. Report of the Secretary-General, UN document S/10921, 30 April 1973, para. 13, 14, and 19.
83. OAU Council of Ministers resolution CM/Res. 300(XXI), 17-24 May 1973 (subsequently endorsed by the OAU Assembly); and UN documents S/10930 (A/9066), Annex, 31 May 1973, and A/AC.109/425, 3 July 1973.
84. Voting against: Australia, Belgium, Canada, Greece, Ireland, Japan, Luxembourg, the Netherlands, New Zealand, Portugal, South Africa, Spain, Turkey, as well as France, the U.K., and the U.S.; abstaining: Argentina, Austria, Bolivia, Brazil, Chile, Colombia, Costa Rica, Denmark, Dominican Republic, El Salvador, Finland, Guatemala, Honduras, Iceland, Italy, Nicaragua, Norway, Panama, Peru, Sweden, Thailand, Uruguay, and Venezuela.
85. For the text of the resolution of the Conference of Independent African

States (1960), see Colin Legum, *Pan-Africanism—a Short Political Guide* (New York: Praeger, 1962), pp. 155-156.

86. France and the U.K. gave somewhat similar explanations for their abstention. France indicated that the measures proposed would constitute interference in matters falling within the domestic jurisdiction of a Member State. The U.K. pointed out that since there was no evidence that South Africa's actions threatened the territorial integrity or political independence of any State, these actions could not be said to pose a threat to international peace, and any action by the Security Council under Chapter VII of the United Nations Charter would be legally unjustifiable.

87. Though the resolution was adopted unanimously, France and the U.K. indicated that they would comply with the request only in regard to armaments which might be used to enforce apartheid.

88. France did not participate in any of the 38 meetings held by the Expert Committee.

89. Security Council resolution 191(1964), 18 June 1964; France, the USSR, and Czechoslovakia abstained.

90. *S.C.O.R., 20th Year, Special Supplement No. 2, Report of the Expert Committee.* Established in Pursuance of Security Council Resolution 191(1964), 2 March 1965 (document S/6210 and Add. 1).

91. By December 1972, the share in South Africa's foreign trade of the top ten trading partners was as follows:

	Imports from (million U.S. $)	*Exports to* (million U.S. $)
1. the U.K.	699,390	715,010
2. the U.S.	518,680	151,930
3. Germany (Fed. Rep.)	410,080	143,960
4. Japan	263,790	211,740
5. Italy	118,800	62,350
6. France	85,670	60,190
7. Belgium/Luxembourg	33,540	88,320
8. Canada	74,290	39,590
9. Netherlands	57,970	45,320
10. Australia	54,950	18,500

Source: United Nations, *Foreign Trade Statistics for Africa: Direction of Trade,* Series A, No. 19 (UN Publication, Sales No. E/F.72.11.K.9). The same ten States are identified, in UN document A/AC.115/L.2.2, as the main trading partners of South Africa as of 1969. The statistics do not provide details on South African trade with African countries, but it is known that Southern Rhodesia and, to a lesser extent, Zambia shared a major part of South Africa's $155,440,000 of imports and $357,450 of exports within Africa during 1972. (With an estimated export of $95,-000,000 to South Africa and an import of $170,000,000 during 1971, Southern Rhodesia would probably rank fifth in the above list. Recent figures for Zambia are not presently available.)

92. OAU Assembly resolution AHG/Res. 34(II), 25 October 1965.

93. The following States abstained: Australia, Austria, Belgium, Canada, Finland, France, Iceland, Ireland, Italy, Japan, Luxembourg, the Netherlands, New Zealand, Norway, the U.K., and the U.S.

94. Since no roll-call vote was taken in the General Assembly, an indication of the identity of the States that abstained can be obtained from the roll-call vote of the Special Political Committee on the draft resolution. In the Committee, the following 15 States abstained: Australia, Austria, Belgium, Canada, Colombia, Cuba, France, Italy, Japan, Luxembourg, Malawi, the Netherlands, New Zealand, the U.K., and the U.S.

95. *S.C.O.R., 18th Year,* 1078th Meeting, 4 December 1963, para. 16-20, and document S/PV. 1549 (mimeo.), 23 July 1970.

96. *S.C.O.R., 18th Year,* 1078th Meeting, 4 December 1963, para. 31, and document S/PV. 1547 (mimeo.), 21 July 1970.

97. For an analysis of South Africa's new "outward policy," see UN document A/AC. 115/L. 289, 18 March 1971; also L. B. Lowman, "South Africa's Southern Strategy and Its Implications for the United States," *International Affairs* (London), Vol. 47, No. 1 (January, 1971), pp. 19-30.

98. These projects were expected to provide opportunities for over a million European immigrants to settle in the two Territories and were thus meant to perpetuate Portuguese domination. In 1970, both the OAU Council of Ministers and the United Nations General Assembly condemned the Cabora Bassa project and called upon foreign governments and companies to desist from investments therein. See OAU resolution CM/Res. 209 (XIV), 6 March 1970, and General Assembly resolution 2703(XXV), 14 December 1970.

99. OAU Council of Ministers resolution CM/154(XI), 12 September 1968.

100. For the text of the Manifesto on Southern Africa, see UN document A/7754, 7 November 1969.

101. General Assembly resolution 2505(XXIV), 20 November 1969, adopted by a vote of 113 to 2 (Portugal and South Africa), with 2 abstentions (Cuba and Malawi).

102. UN document A/PV. 1814 (mimeo.), 20 November 1969.

103. UN document A/PV. 1815 (mimeo.), 20 November 1969.

104. For a list of such incursions, see UN document S/PV. 1590 (mimeo.), 8 October 1971.

105. OAU Council of Ministers document CM/ST. 5(XVII), 19 June 1971.

106. General Assembly resolution 2508(XXIV), 21 November 1969, adopted by a vote of 85 to 8, with 20 abstentions. Voting against: Australia, Belgium, the Netherlands, New Zealand, Portugal, South Africa, the U.K., and the U.S.; abstaining: Austria, Botswana, Brazil, Canada, Cuba, Denmark, Finland, France, Gabon, Honduras, Ireland, Italy, Ivory Coast, Japan, Lesotho, Malawi, Norway, Spain, Swaziland, and Sweden.

107. General Assembly resolution 2555(XXIV), 12 December 1969, adopted

by a vote of 76 to 45, with 22 abstentions. Voting against: Portugal, South Africa, the U.K., and the U.S.; abstaining: Argentina, Australia, Austria, Belgium, Bolivia, Botswana, Canada, Denmark, Finland, France, Iceland, Ireland, Italy, Ivory Coast, Japan, Luxembourg, the Netherlands, New Zealand, Norway, Spain, Swaziland, and Sweden.

108. The following programs of assistance have been established by the organizations in the United Nations family:

    (a) the United Nations Trust Fund for South Africa, established by the General Assembly in December 1965 (resolution 2054B(XX)) to provide legal assistance, relief, and education to victims of apartheid and their dependents;

    (b) the United Nations Educational and Training Programme for Southern Africa, established by the General Assembly in December 1967 (resolution 2349(XXII)) by integrating the separate training and education programs for South West Africa, the Territories under Portuguese administration, and South Africa;

    (c) the United Nations Fund for Namibia, established by the General Assembly in December 1970 (resolution 2679(XXV)) to finance a comprehensive program of assistance to Namibians in order to prepare them for self-government and independence;

    (d) the program of the United Nations High Commissioner for Refugees (UNHCR) for education, training, placement, and rural settlement of refugees from Southern Africa and for the protection of their legal rights; and

    (e) programs of the specialized agencies, especially UNESCO, ILO, WHO, and FAO, designed to assist in the implementation of the Declaration on the Granting of Independence to Colonial Countries and Peoples. (See UN document A/8314 and Add. 1-6 and A/8647.)

109. *G.A.O.R., 25th Session, Supplement 23B,* document A/8086, Annex 1, 5 October 1970.

110. Ibid., 1861st and 1862nd Plenary Meetings, 12 October 1970.

111. See OAU Council of Ministers resolution: CM/Res. 75(VI), 6 March 1966; CM/Res. 154(XI), 12 September 1968; and ECM/Res. 17(VII), 12 December 1970.

112. A/6356, Report of the Special Committee on the Policies of Apartheid, 29 June 1966. Also declining membership were Argentina, Australia, Austria, Belgium, Brazil, Ceylon, Japan, Mexico, the Netherlands, Norway, Spain, and Sweden. Canada did not reply, and Denmark and Italy replied conditionally.

113. Australia, which had withdrawn from the Special Committee of Twenty-Four in January 1969, rejoined the Committee in January 1973.

114. Resolution 974D III and IV(XXXVI) of the Economic and Social Council.

115. UN document A/8314, Implementation of the Declaration on the Granting of Independence to Colonial Countries and Peoples by the Specialized

Agencies and the International Institutions Associated with the United Nations: Report of the Secretary-General, 27 May 1971, pp. 9 and 13 (ILO); p. 21 (FAO); p. 36 (UNESCO); and pp. 60-62 (WHO).

116. Ibid., pp. 69-70 (UPU); and p. 77 (ITU).

117. The draft resolution, contained in UN document A/7383, was rejected by the General Assembly by a roll-call vote of 55 in favor, 33 against, and 28 abstentions.

118. UN document A/C. 2/L. 1030, Statement by the Legal Counsel Submitted Pursuant to a Request made at the 1236th Meeting of the Second Committee, 2 December 1968, p. 9.

V. POSSIBILITIES FOR STRENGTHENING RELATIONSHIPS IN THE PEACE AND SECURITY FIELD

1. J. N. Moore, "The Role of Regional Arrangements in the Maintenance of World Order," in C. E. Black and R. A. Falk (eds.), *The Future of the International Legal Order, Vol. III, Conflict Management* (Princeton, N.J.: Princeton University Press, 1971), pp. 135-140 and 162-164.

2. Aide Mémoire of the Administrative Secretary-General of the OAU addressed to the Secretary-General of the United Nations on 11 November 1965.

3. *G.A.O.R., 20th Session, Annexes, Agenda Item 108:* Co-operation between the United Nations and the Organization of African Unity, document A/6174, Report of the Secretary-General, 16 December 1965.

4. General Assembly resolution 2033(XX), 3 December 1965.

5. Oscar Schachter, "Intervention and the United Nations," in Richard A. Falk (ed.), *The Vietnam War and International Law,* Vol. II (Sponsored by the American Society of International Law; Princeton, N.J.: Princeton University Press, 1969), p. 279.

6. For perceptive analyses of the complex issues concerning the roles of international organizations in internal conflicts, see Ibid., pp. 237-288; Oscar Schachter, "The United Nations and Internal Conflict," in John N. Moore (ed.), *Law and Civil War in the Modern World* (Baltimore: The Johns Hopkins University Press, 1974), Chap. 16; Richard A. Falk, *Legal Order in a Violent World* (Princeton, N.J.: Princeton University Press, 1968), Chap. IV, esp. pp. 149-155; and Rosalyn Higgins, "Internal War and International Law," in Cyril E. Black and Richard A. Falk, *The Future of International Legal Order, Volume III, Conflict Management* (Princeton, N.J.: Princeton University Press, 1971), pp. 81-121.

7. *G.A.O.R., 28th Session, Annexes, Agenda Item 23,* International Conference of Experts for the Support of Victims of Colonialism and Apartheid in Southern Africa, Report of the Secretary-General, document A/9061, 7 May 1973; and Ibid., *Agenda Item 42,* International Conference of Trade Unions against Apartheid, Report of the Special Committee on Apartheid, document A/9169, 10 October 1973.

8. See Memorandum from the Government of Portugal, UN document A/9694 (S/11419), Annex, 6 August 1974.
9. The view that pressure only rigidifies the attitudes of the whites tends to overlook the following facts: the invention of the Bantustan Plan in South Africa and the Odendaal Plan in Namibia, both for the establishment of "self-governing homelands," was in part a response to external demands that Africans be given the right to vote. The response in the Portuguese-administered Territories were also largely a response to external pressure. The second fallacy—the idea that further industrialization and the accompanying integration of Africans into the modern economy will eventually solve the problem of race relations—had been demonstrated in a comparative study of *Industrialization and Race Relations,* sponsored by UNESCO and the Institute of Race Relations (London) and edited by Guy Hunter. The study "confirms overwhelmingly the subservience of the industrial to the racial pattern." A further discussion of the two fallacies is given in Vernon McKay, "Southern Africa and Its Implications for American Policy," in W. A. Hance (ed.), *Southern Africa and the United States* (New York and London: Columbia University Press), 1968, pp. 30-32.

Part II

OAU-UN Relations in the Economic and Social Field

VI. OAU'S RELATIONS WITH GLOBAL UNITED NATIONS BODIES

1. For the text, see Annex to General Assembly resolution 428(V), 14 December 1950.
2. Paragraph 1 of the Statute of UNHCR.
3. Established by the OAU Council of Ministers under resolution CM/Res. 19(II), 29 February 1964.
4. For the text, see United Nations, *Treaty Series*, Vol. 189, p. 137 ff.
5. For the text, see OAU document CM/267/Rev. 1, February 1969.
6. Article 1, A(2), of the United Nations Convention Relating to the Status of Refugees and paragraph 6 of the Statute of UNHCR.
7. Sub-paragraphs A and B of paragraph 6 of the Statute of UNHCR.
8. Article I, paragraph 8, of the OAU Convention Governing the Specific Aspects of the Problem of Refugees in Africa.
9. Document of the Conference on the Legal, Economic and Social Aspects of African Refugee Problems, AFR/Ref./Conf. 1967/No. 2, p. 11 (mimeo.).
10. Ibid., p. 10.
11. In prescribing the duties of an African refugee, Article III of the OAU Convention states that "he shall . . . abstain from any subversive activities against *any Member State of the OAU*" (emphasis added). The italicized words were substituted for the words "any State whatsoever" which were used in a previous draft, in order not to jeopardize the activities of the "freedom fighters." Cf. OAU document CM/267/Rev. 1 of February 1969 with CM/228, Annex I, of September 1968.
12. General Assembly resolution 217(III), 10 December 1948, and resolution 2312(XXII), 14 December 1967, respectively.
13. Paragraph 8(g) of the Statute of UNHCR and Rule 38 of the Executive Committee's Rules of Procedure.
14. Especially resolutions CM/Res. 52(IV), 9 March 1965, and AHG/Res. 26(II), 24 October 1965.
15. UN ECA document E/CN. 14/442, Report of the Conference on the Legal, Economic and Social Aspects of African Refugee Problems, 6 January 1969, pp. 91-118.
16. OAU Council of Ministers resolution CM/Res. 141(X), 24 February 1968.
17. The first $100,000 were raised in the Scandinavian countries and transferred to the OAU Bureau. UNHCR, *HCR Bulletin*, No. 4, Oct./Nov./Dec., 1968, p. 5.
18. UNHCR, *HCR Bulletin*, No. 2, April/May/June, 1968, p. 4.
19. General Assembly resolution 2349(XXII), 19 December 1967.

20. *G.A.O.R., 23rd Session, Annexes, Vol. I,* Agenda Item 70, document A/7284, 22 October 1968, pp. 3-4.
21. OAU document Summit CIAS/Plen.2/Rev.2, resolution E, 25 May 1963.
22. General Assembly resolution 1995(XIX), 30 December 1964.
23. OAU document ECOS/8(II), A Note on the Results of the United Nations Conference on Trade and Development, January 1965, pp. 8-9, and OAU-ECOS resolution ECOS/Res. 14(II), 22 January 1965.
24. OAU document ECOS/8(II), op. cit., and document CM/203, Trade and Development (Africa and UNCTAD), February 1967, p. 20.
25. Ibid., pp. 6-17.
26. Document of the Ministerial Meeting of the Group of 77, MN/77/I/20, 30 October 1967, reproduced as UNCTAD document TD/38, 3 November 1967.
27. UN-ECA document E/CN.14/361, Annex V: Address by the Secretary-General of UNCTAD before the Extraordinary Joint Meeting of the ECA Working Party on Intra-African Trade and the OAU Ad Hoc Committee of 14 on Trade and Development, August 1966.
28. The idea of the Goodwill Mission was welcomed by the Secretary-General of UNCTAD even before it reached formal endorsement by the Ministerial Meeting of the Group of 77—see ibid.
29. OAU Council of Ministers resolution CM/Res. 122(IX), 10 September 1967.
30. OAU Council of Ministers resolutions: CM/Res. 146(X), 24 February 1968 and CM/Res. 157(XI), 12 September 1968.
31. OAU Council of Ministers resolution CM/Res. 156(XI), 12 September 1968.
32. UNCTAD document TD/B/L. 126, 3 September 1968. (mimeo.)
33. UNCTAD document TD/B/173, 31 July 1968. (mimeo.)
34. For a summary of the positions of the UNCTAD secretariat, the developing and the developed countries, see UNCTAD Report of the Trade and Development Board, 10 September 1967—23 September 1968, G.A.O.R., *23rd Session, Suppl. No. 14* (A/7214), pp. 22-30.
35. UNCTAD Trade and Development Board decision 45(VII), 21 September 1968.
36. UNCTAD Trade and Development Board resolution 44(VII), 21 September 1968.
37. General Assembly resolution 2401(XXIII), 13 December 1968.
38. UNCTAD resolution 24(II), 26 March 1968.
39. General Assembly resolution 1995(XIX), 30 December 1964.
40. Rule 80 of the rules of procedure of UNCTAD (see UNCTAD document TD/63, 2 February 1968); and rule 78 of the rules of procedure of the Trade and Development Board (see UNCTAD document TD/B/16, 7 May 1965).
41. Rules 4 and 5 of the rules of procedure of UNCTAD and rules 4 and 5 of the rules of procedure of the Trade and Development Board.

42. The decision was made at the 32nd plenary meeting of the Trade and Development Board on 31 August 1965.
43. General Assembly resolution 2152(XXI), 17 November 1966, para. 35.
44. Rules 6, 8(h), 9, 10, 12, and 75 of the rules of procedure of the Industrial Development Board, UNIDO document ID/3/18, 7 June 1967.
45. Resolution of the first session of the OAU Health and Sanitation Commission, HSN/17/Res. 1, 14 January 1964.
46. ECOSOC resolution 1159(XLI), 5 August 1966.
47. UN Commission on Human Rights resolution 7(XXIV), 1 March 1968, and document E/CN.4/966 Report of the Ad Hoc Study Group Estabshed under Resolution 6(XXIII) of the Commission on Human Rights, 26 January 1968, pp. 15-16.
48. For the text of the proposed agreement, see UN document DP/L.214, 10 December 1971.
49. These agencies consist of the specialized agencies, the IAEA, GATT, UNCTAD, UNIDO, the United Nations Secretariat (Department of Economic and Social Affairs), and the three regional Development Banks.
50. UN document DP/SR.306, Summary Records of the 306th Session of the Governing Council of the UNDP, 28 January 1972, p. 4. (mimeo.)
51. Ibid., pp. 6-7.

VII. OAU'S RELATIONS WITH ECA: PROBLEM OF PARALLEL STRUCTURES

1. OAU Council of Ministers resolution 5(I), 10 August 1963. According to this resolution the only groupings encouraged by the OAU were those that met the following criteria: (a) geographical realities and economic, social, and cultural factors common to the States; (b) needs for co-ordination of economic, social, and cultural activities peculiar to the States concerned.
2. OAU Council of Ministers resolution 7(I), 10 August 1963. Earlier the Summit Conference of Independent African States that established the OAU had merely called for maintaining CCTA and for "reconsidering its role in order to bring it eventually within the scope" of the OAU; OAU document CIAS/Plen.2/Rev.2, resolution F, 25 May 1963.
3. The membership of these organizations is as follows:
   OCAM: Cameroon, Central African Republic, Chad, Dahomey, Gabon, Ivory Coast, Madagascar, Mauritius, Niger, Rwanda, Senegal, Togo, and Upper Volta. (Mauritania and Mali are members of some of the specialized institutions of OCAM; Zaire withdrew in 1972 and Congo (Brazzaville) in 1973; Cameroon, Chad, and Madagascar have announced their withdrawals effective in 1974.)
   UDEAC: Cameroon, Central African Republic, Congo (Brazzaville), and Gabon (Chad withdrew in 1968).
   CEAO: Dahomey, Ivory Coast, Mali, Mauritania, Niger, Senegal, and Upper Volta.
   Conseil de l'Entente: Dahomey, Ivory Coast, Niger, Togo, and Upper Volta.

CECAS: Burudi, Central African Republic, Chad, Congo (Brazzaville), Ethiopia, Kenya, Malawi, Somalia, Sudan, Tanzania, Uganda, Zaire, and Zambia (the Conference has no permanent secretariat).

East African Community: Kenya, Tanzania, and Uganda.

Permanent Consultative Committee of the Maghreb: Algeria, Morocco, and Tunisia (Libya withdrew in 1970).

4. ECA Terms of Reference, operative paragraphs 1, 2, 15, and 16, ECOSOC resolution 671A(XXV), 29 April 1958, as amended by the Council by resolution 974D(XXXVI), 5 July 1963, and resolution 1343(XLV), 18 July 1968. (See UN ECA document E/CN.14/111/Rev.4, 15 January 1971.)

5. Rules of procedure of the OAU Assembly, rule 3(iii) and rules of procedure of the Council of Ministers, rule 3(v). (Text in *Basic Documents of the Organization of African Unity,* published by the Provisional Secretariat of the Organization of African Unity.)

6. OAU document Inst./Rpt. 1, p. 4: Report of the Institutional Committee of the Assembly of Heads of State and Government, December 1965. The question of relations between the specialized commissions and the Council of Ministers was the subject of controversy during the drafting of the rules of procedure of the former. Although Article XXII of the OAU Charter prescribes that the functions of these commissions are to be carried out in accordance with the OAU Charter and the regulations approved by the Council of Ministers, the rules of the respective commissions reflected this provision in varying degrees. As a result of the study conducted in December 1965 by the Institutional Committee of the OAU Assembly, the long-debated question of whether the specialized commissions were to be answerable only to the Assembly or to both the Assembly and the Council of Ministers was resolved in favor of the latter alternative.

7. In response to the recommendations made by the Institutional Committee of the OAU Assembly in December 1965 concerning the regroupment of the specialized commissions, the Assembly recommended amendment to the relevant provisions of the OAU Charter; the amendment has been duly ratified.

8. General Assembly resolution 1155(XII), 26 November 1957, and ECOSOC resolution 671A(XXV), 29 April 1958.

9. UN document E/3864/Rev. 1 (E/CN. 14/290/Rev. 1): Statement by the Executive Secretary of ECA before the Sixth Session of the Commission, p. 175.

10. UN ECA document E/CN.14/294, Statement by the Executive Secretary on ECA Activities since the Sixth Session of the Commission, 27 January 1965, p. 1.

11. OAU-ECOS resolution ECOS/16/Res. 2(I), 13 December 1963.

12. For the Terms of Reference of the Transport and Communications Commission, see OAU Assembly resolution AHG/Res. 20(I), 21 July 1964.

13. OAU-STRC resolution STR/35/Res. 1(I), 7 February 1964.

14. OAU-EDC resolution EDC/28/res. 1(I), 8 January 1964.

15. J. S. Magee, "ECA and the Paradox of African Co-operation," *International Conciliation,* No. 580, November 1970, p. 7.

16. *Proceedings of the Summit Conference of Independent African States, Verbatim Records, Preparatory Conference of Foreign Ministers,* 15-25 May 1963, Committee I, second meeting, C-I-II, pp. 2, 5, 6, 9, 11, 12.

17. Ibid., Committee I, third meeting, C-I-III, pp. 34-38.

18. Ibid., pp. 35-36.

19. OAU-ECOS resolutions: ECOS/16/D/Res. 2(I) and ECOS/17/1/Res./ 3(I), 13 December 1963.

20. At the ECA session which created the working parties, hardly any objection was raised to the proposal of the ECA secretariat on the ground that there might be duplication with the OAU technical bodies. Although thirteen delegations had either abstained or voted against the proposal to set up the ECA working parties, their concern was largely based on other considerations. Some had reservations concerning the terms of reference of particular working parties and were concerned about duplication of effort within ECA itself, especially as regards the work of its sub-regional bodies; others had doubts about the advisability of having a small number of technical experts to represent the views of all African countries, while such experts might not even be qualified to represent the views of their respective Governments on semipolitical problems such as economic integration. UN ECA document E/CN.14/SR.114-127(VII): Summary Records of the seventh session of ECA, 9-23 February 1965, pp. 114-119, 120-125, 130-132.

21. UN ECA resolution 128(VII), 22 February 1965.

22. In explaining the reasons for the failure to convene most of the technical bodies, neither ECA nor the OAU stressed this crucial factor. The ECA secretariat explained that it refrained from convening most of its working parties because it wished (i) avoid duplicating the work of the numerous ad hoc continental conferences that it had planned to convene on the subjects concerned; (ii) to allow sufficient time for preparation in order to ensure effective meetings of the working parties; and (iii) to give priority to the work of ECA's sub-regional conferences. The OAU secretariat, on the other hand, explained that its difficulties were: (i) financial uncertainty caused by delays in the payment of OAU budgetary assessments; (ii) shortage of personnel to service the numerous meetings scheduled each year (then up to 40 in all fields of activity); and (iii) expectation that the whole system of subsidiary bodies of the OAU might have to undergo drastic reorganization. Though the reasons given by the two secretariats are valid, they do not provide a complete explanation. UN ECA document E/CN.14/377, Working Parties Established by Commission Resolution 128(VII), 15 December 1966, pp. 2-3, and ECA resolution 175(VIII),

24 February 1967; and OAU document CM/71, Report of the Administrative Secretary-General, October 1965, pp. 30-31.

23. The vast majority of the African States and the OAU secretariat were opposed to a proposal made in the second session of the OAU-ECOS by a few States (some of which had doubts about ECA's African vocation) to establish a separate secretariat for the Commission.

24. By February 1968, only 16 of the 31 professional posts authorized for all the substantive secretariat units of the OAU dealing exclusively with economic, social, scientific, and related problems had been filled (76 professional posts were authorized for the entire OAU secretariat, of which only 49 were filled). The 16 staff members were evenly divided between the OAU-STRC secretariat and the departments of the OAU General Secretariat dealing with economic and social matters. By contrast, ECA had at the disposal of its substantive divisions a total of 99 such personnel (the entire professional staff was 137). These figures show that as of that date not only were the relevant secretariat units of the OAU taken together less than one-third the size of the combined substantive departments of the ECA secretariat in terms of authorized posts, but also that in actual strength, i.e., in terms of posts already filled, the former were less than one-sixth of the latter. These ratios have not changed significantly since then. These figures were compiled from the OAU budget document for Fiscal Year 1968-69—document CM/180/Rev. 2—which also gives the relevant information for Fiscal Year 1967-68; and from UN document E/4463/Add. 30, pp. 6-8.

25. Even when the regular budget of the OAU was reduced from $4.5 million in fiscal year 1965-66 to approximately $2.5 million in subsequent years, delays in payments continued to pose a serious problem for the organization—see OAU document CM/109 (Part 2), pp. 18-19.

26. OAU document CM/71, op. cit., pp. 30-31, and OAU Council of Ministers resolution CM/Res. 126(IX), 10 September 1967.

27. See summary of statement by the Executive Secretary before the eighth session of ECA in UN ECA document E/CN. 14/SR. 128-139(VIII), Summary Records of the Eighth Session of ECA, 13-23 February 1967, p. 35.

28. OAU Assembly decision AHG/Dec. 5(III), November 1966, based on the recommendation of an ad hoc Institutional Committee of the Assembly, contained in OAU document CM/103 (INST/RPT.1) of December 1965.

29. UN ECA resolution 130(VII), 22 February 1965, concerning biennial sessions; resolution 175(VIII), 24 February 1967, authorizing the Executive Secretary to convene the working parties as necessary instead of at least once a year.

30. UN ECA resolution 188(IX), 10 February 1969; and decision of the tenth session of ECA, taken by its Council of Ministers on 13 February 1971.

VIII. OAU-ECA: JURISDICTIONAL ISSUES AND DIVISION OF LABOR

1. OAU document CM/71, Report of the Administrative Secretary-General October 1965, p. 44.
2. Ibid., pp. 43-44.
3. OAU-ECOS resolution ECOS/17/Res. 3(I), 13 December 1963.
4. OAU document CM/71, op. cit., pp. 19 and 44.
5. Ibid., pp. 44-46.
6. Ibid., p. 45.
7. OAU resolution CM/Res. 122(IX), 10 September 1967.
8. ECA document E/CN.14/L.298, Statement on Relations between ECA and OAU, 20 February 1965, pp. 3-5.
9. Ibid., p. 4.
10. UN ECA resolution 194(IX), 12 February 1969.
11. UN ECA Terms of Reference, para 1.
12. Quoted in the statement of the ECA secretariat before the Seventh Session of ECA, UN ECA document E/CM.14/L.298, pp. 4-5.
13. OAU document ECOS/13(II), January 1965, p. 2.
14. UN ECA document E/CN.14/L.298, p. 6.
15. Text of the Agreement is included as annex to UN document A/6174, December 1965.
16. Article I, paragraph 2, of the Agreement.
17. UN ECA document E/CN.14/SR.128-139(VIII), Summary Records of the Eighth Session of ECA, pp. 131-132.
18. Ibid., pp. 132-133.

IX. OAU-ECA: POLICY COMPATIBILITY AND COMPETITION

1. UN ECA resolution 218(X), "Africa's Strategy for Development in the 1970s," 13 February 1971, and resolution 238(XI), 22 February 1973.
2. See United Nations, *Economic Bulletin for Africa,* Vol. IV, January 1964, pp. 45-53; and UN document ID/Conf.1/REP/1, *Industrial Development in Africa,* pp. 20-22.
3. UN document E/4354, ECA Annual Report (24 February 1965–25 February 1967), *ECOSOC Official Records, 43rd session, Suppl. No. 5,* pp. 2-7.
4. Ibid., p. 3.
5. OAU Assembly Declaration CM/ST.11(XXI), 25 May 1973, endorsing the "African Declaration on Co-operation, Development and Economic Independence" which was adopted by the African Ministerial Conference on Trade, Development and Monetary Problems organized jointly by the OAU, ECA, and the ADB (Abidjan, 9-13 May 1973).
6. Ibid., section B.1.
7. UN document E/4004, ECA Annual Report (3 March 1964–23 February 1965), *ECOSOC Official Records, 39th Session, Suppl. No. 10,* pp. 55-56.
8. OAU-ECOS resolution 16(II), 22 January 1965.

9. UN document E/4004, op. cit., p. 56.

10. UN ECA document E/CN.14/346, Annex V, Statement by the Executive Secretary of ECA before the Sub-regional Meeting on Economic Co-operation in East Africa (26 October–2 November 1965), p. 2.

11. UN ECA document E/CN.14/462, Report of the Second Meeting of the Executive Committee, 17 November 1969, p. 50.

12. UN document E/CN.14/347, Annex VI, Statement by Assistant Secretary-General of the OAU at the Regional Symposium on Industrial Development in Africa (Cairo, 27 January–10 February 1966), p. 54.

13. OAU resolution CM/Res. 123(IX), 10 September 1967.

14. UN ECA documents: E/CN.14/351, Annex V, pp. 2-3; E/CN.14/366, Annex V, p. 7; E/CN.14/346, Annex VI, pp. 4-5—statements by OAU representatives at sub-regional meetings of ECA.

15. UN ECA document E/CN.14/366, op. cit., pp. 3-4.

16. Originally, the Council of Ministers had requested all existing sub-regional groupings to be associated with the OAU specialized commissions—resolution CM/Res. 5(I), 2-11 August 1963.

17. OAU Council of Ministers resolution CM/Res. 125(IX), 10 September 1967.

18. OAU document CM/168 (part 6), Regional Economic Groupings in Africa, September 1967, p. 11.

19. UN ECA, *Survey of Economic Conditions in Africa—1968*, (New York: United Nations Publication, Sales Number: E.71.II.K.1, 1972), pp. 94-96.

20. This Declaration was adopted by a Ministerial Meeting of African Members of UNCTAD, convened jointly by ECA and the OAU in October 1967, in preparation for the Ministerial Meeting of the Group of 77 which later adopted the "Algiers Charter" on trade and development—see OAU document CM/203, February 1968, and UN document A/C.2/237, 6 November 1967.

21. Further refinements of the joint ECA-OAU strategy for the trade of African countries can be found in UN ECA resolution 218(X), 13 February 1971, para. 8(7-14), and resolution 244(XI), 22 February 1973.

22. OAU Council of Ministers resolution CM/Res. 124(IX) and document CM/231 (part 2), Market Integration in Africa, September 1968, pp. 7 and 23; UN ECA resolution 153(VIII), 24 February 1967.

23. OAU document CM/204/Corr. 1, Inter-African Technical Assistance, February 1968, p. 11.

24. UN ECA document E/CN.14/347, Statement by the OAU representative at the Symposium on Industrialization in Africa, February 1966, p. 54.

25. OAU document CM/204/Corr.1, op. cit., p. 14.

26. OAU document MC/71, Report of the Administrative Secretary-General, October 1965, p. 45, and ECOS/4, May 1967, pp. 4-5.

27. UN ECA document E/CN.14/392, Annex II, Statement by the Executive Secretary of ECA at the Conference of Industrialists and Financiers, January 1967, p. 2.

28. UN ECA document E/CN.14/392, op. cit., pp. 1-9.
29. In a press interview the OAU Administrative Secretary-General explained that it would be inappropriate for him to participate in a meeting which was neither intergovernmental nor predominantly African in character. See *The Ethiopian Herald,* 19 January 1967.
30. OAU Assembly Declaration CM/ST.11(XXI), 25 May 1973, section B.3.
31. ECA document E/CN.14/525, Report of the ECA/OAU Conference of Ministers of Industry, 1971.
32. UN ECA document E/CN.14/357 (OAU document OAU/TEL 7), Report of the Joint ECA/OAU Meeting on Telecommunications in Africa, 7-12 March 1966, pp. 12-14.
33. It should be noted that the larger part of the FAO's projects for Africa are carried out independently of ECA and are co-ordinated by the FAO regional office in Accra, Ghana.
34. For example, in November 1966, FAO invited the OAU secretariat to participate merely as an observer in a forthcoming meeting of experts on contagious bovine-pneumonia, a meeting whose previous sessions were organized jointly by FAO and the former CCTA, with an official from the latter serving as Secretary. Because the OAU had taken over from the former CCTA, the OAU secretariat protested, thereby persuading FAO to accept it as a partner in organizing the meeting, with the OAU secretariat serving as Secretary. OAU document ESCHC/17 (1967), p. 3.
35. For example, in accordance with recommendations of the 1964 ECA/UNESCO conference on the development and utilization of Africa's natural resources, the OAU secretariat requested FAO to join UNESCO in assisting the International Union for Conservation of Nature and Natural Resources (IUCN) to draft for the OAU a revision of the 1933 London Convention on the flora and fauna of Africa. Though FAO had agreed to collaborate, it began to draft a separate African Convention on Wildlife. This led to some friction with the OAU secretariat which ended when FAO agreed to discontinue its separate effort.
36. OAU Council of Ministers resolution CM/Res. 130(IX), 10 September 1967.
37. See ECA projects Nos. 19, 89, 90, and 91 in the work-program for 1965-67, listed in UN document E/4004, pp. 88 ff.
38. OAU-ECOS resolution ECOS/Res. 9(II), 22 January 1965; and OAU document STR/P.CTE/1(II), Report of the Programming Committee, as adopted by the OAU-STRC in January 1965.
39. OAU Council of Ministers resolution CM/Res. 171(XI), 12 September 1968.

X. OAU-ECA: PROCESS OF CO-OPERATION AND CO-ORDINATION

1. ECOSOC resolution 671 A(XXV) as amended by ECOSOC resolutions 974 D(XXXVI) and 1343 (XLV).

2. OAU document ECOS/17/D/Res 3 (I), 13 December 1963.

3. OAU document STR/35/Res. I(I), February 1964.

4. OAU resolution ECOS/Res. 17(II), 22 January 1965, and UN ECA resolution 132(VII), 22 February 1965. These resolutions requested the respective secretariats to come to an agreement or arrangement defining precisely the framework of co-operation between them.

5. OAU document CM/162/Rev.1, Observer Status, September 1967.

6. UN ECA resolution 151(VIII), 21 February 1967.

7. OAU Council of Ministers resolution CM/Res. 143(X), 24 February 1968.

8. ECA Executive Secretary's circular letter of 13 December 1967 addressed to all Member States of ECA.

9. UN ECA resolution 194(IX), 12 February 1969.

10. Although the ECA and the OAU secretariats have made an arrangement to establish a fund out of which each organization would reimburse the other for services rendered, the OAU has not always kept a sufficient balance on hand to meet current commitments. In exceptional circumstances and particularly when it was not possible to secure a timely replenishment of funds from the OAU the "out-of-pocket" expenses have been met by the ECA secretariat itself. Such occurrences have not been frequent, but they have been criticized by United Nations auditors on the ground that providing "financial assistance" to the OAU secretariat was against the budgetry regulations of the United Nations. Information based on interviews.

11. General Assembly resolution 1798(XVII), sub-paragraph 2(b), 11 December 1962.

12. Interviews.

13. UN document ECA/ST/ORG/5, 4 June 1965—Organizational Directive No. 5.

14. The Executive Committee is composed of the Chairman, the two Vice-Chairmen and the Rapporteur of the sessions of the Conference of Ministers, the Executive Secretary of ECA, two representatives of each sub-region (each conference officer counting as a representative of his sub-region), two African members of ECOSOC (one English- and one French-speaking), and two African members of the Governing Council of UNDP (one English- and one French-speaking).

XI. OAU-UN: POSSIBILITIES FOR STRENGTHENING CO-OPERATION IN THE ECONOMIC AND SOCIAL FIELD

1. UN ECA document E/CN.14/SR.128-139(VIII), Summary Records of the Eighth Session of ECA (February 1967), pp. 114-116.

2. UN ECA resolutions 151(VIII), 21 February 1967, and 194(IX), 12 February 1969.

Appendices

Appendix I

Charter of the Organization of African Unity

We, the Heads of African States and Governments assembled in the City of Addis Ababa, Ethiopia;

CONVINCED that it is the inalienable right of all people to control their own destiny:

CONSCIOUS of the fact that freedom, equality, justice and dignity are essential objectives for the achievement of the legitimate aspirations of the African peoples;

CONSCIOUS of our responsibility to harness the natural and human resources of our continent for the total advancement of our peoples in spheres of human endeavour;

INSPIRED by a common determination to promote understanding among our peoples and co-operation among our States in response to the aspirations of our peoples for brotherhood and solidarity, in a larger unity transcending ethnic and national differences;

CONVINCED that, in order to translate this determination into a dynamic force in the cause of human progress, conditions for peace and security must be established and maintained;

DETERMINED to safeguard and consolidate the hard-won independence as well as the sovereignty and territorial integrity of our States, and to fight against neo-colonialism in all its forms;

DEDICATED to the general progress of Africa;

PERSUADED that the Charter of the United Nations and the Universal Declaration of Human Rights, to the principles of which we reaffirm our adherence, provide a solid foundation for peaceful and positive co-operation among States;

DESIROUS that all African States should henceforth unite so that the welfare and well-being of their peoples can be assured;

RESOLVED to reinforce the links between our states by establishing and strengthening common institutions;

HAVE agreed to the present Charter.

ESTABLISHMENT

Article I

1. The High Contracting Parties do by the present Charter establish an Organization to be known as the ORGANIZATION OF AFRICAN UNITY.
2. The Organization shall include the Continental African States, Madagascar and other Islands surrounding Africa.

PURPOSES

Article II

1. The Organization shall have the following purposes:
   a. to promote the unity and solidarity of the African States;
   b. to co-ordinate and intensify their co-operation and efforts to achieve a better life for the peoples of Africa;
   c. to defend their sovereignty, their territorial integrity and independence;
   d. to eradicate all forms of colonialism from Africa; and
      to promote international co-operation, having due regard to the Charter of the United Nations and the Universal Declaration of Human Rights.
2. To these ends, the Member States shall co-ordinate and harmonize their general policies, especially in the following fields:
   a. political and diplomatic co-operation;
   b. economic co-operation, including transport and communications;
   d. health, sanitation, and nutritional co-operation;
   e. scientific and technical co-operation; and
   f. co-operation for defense and security.

PRINCIPLES

ARTICLE III

The Member States, in pursuit of the purposes stated in Article II, solemnly affirm and declare their adherence to the following principles:
1. the sovereign equality of all Member States;
2. non-interference in the internal affairs of States;
3. respect for the sovereignty and territorial integrity of each State and for its inalienable right to independent existence;
4. peaceful settlement of disputes by negotiation, mediation, conciliation or arbitration;
5. unreserved condemnation, in all its forms, of political assassination as well as of subversive activities on the part of neighbouring States or any other State;
6. absolute dedication to the total emancipation of the African territories which are still dependent;
7. affirmation of a policy of non-alignment with regard to all blocs.

MEMBERSHIP

Article IV

Each independent sovereign African State shall be entitled to become a Member of the Organization.

RIGHTS AND DUTIES OF MEMBER STATES

Article V

All Member States shall enjoy equal rights and have equal duties.

Article VI

The Member States pledge themselves to observe scrupulously the principles enumerated in Article III of the present Charter.

INSTITUTIONS

Article VII

The Organization shall accomplish its purposes through the following principle institutions:

1. the Assembly of Heads of State and Government;
2. the Council of Ministers;
3. the General Secretariat;
4. the Commission of Mediation, Conciliation and Arbitration.

THE ASSEMBLY OF HEADS OF STATE AND GOVERNMENT

Article VIII

The Assembly of Heads of State and Government shall be the supreme organ of the Organization. It shall, subject to the provisions of this Charter, discuss matters of common concern to Africa with a view to co-ordinating and harmonizing the general policy of the Organization. It may in addition review the structure, functions and acts of all the organs and any specialized agencies which may be created in accordance with the present Charter.

Article IX

The Assembly shall be composed of the Heads of State and Government of their duly accredited representatives and it shall meet at least once a year. At the request of any Member State and on approval by a two-thirds majority of the Member States, the Assembly shall meet in extraordinary session.

Article X

1. Each Member State shall have one vote.
2. All resolutions shall be determined by a two-thirds majority of the Members of the Organization.

3. Questions of procedure shall require a simple majority. Whether or not a question is one of procedure shall be determined by a simple majority of all Member States of the Organization.
4. Two-thirds of the total membership of the Organization shall form a quorum at any meeting of the Assembly.

Article XI

The Assembly shall have the power to determine its own rules of procedure.

THE COUNCIL OF MINISTERS

Article XII

1. The Council of Ministers shall consist of Foreign Ministers or such other Ministers as are designated by the Governments of Member States.
2. The Council of Ministers shall meet at least twice a year. When requested by any Member State and approved by two-thirds of all Member States, it shall meet in extraordinary session.

Article XIII

1. The Council of Ministers shall be responsible to the Assembly of Heads of State and Government. It shall be entrusted with the responsibility of preparing conferences of the Assembly.
2. It shall take ˙cognisance of any matter referred to it by the Assembly. It shall be entrusted with the implementation of the decision of the Assembly of Heads of State, and Government. It shall co-ordinate inter-African co-operation in accordance with the instructions of the Assembly and in conformity with Article II(2) of the present Charter.

Article XIV

1. Each Member State shall have one vote.
2. All resolutions shall be determined by a simple majority of the members of the Council of Ministers.
3. Two-thirds of the total membership of the Council of Ministers shall form a quorum for any meeting of the Council.

Article XV

The Council shall have the power to determine its own rules of procedure.

GENERAL SECRETARIAT

Article XVI

There shall be an Administrative Secretary-General of the Organization, who shall be appointed by the Assembly of Heads of State and Government. The Administrative Secretary-General shall direct the affairs of the Secretariat.

Article XVII

There shall be one or more Assistant Secretaries-General of the Organization, who shall be appointed by the Assembly of Heads of State and Government.

Article XVIII

The functions and conditions of services of the Secretary-General, of the Assistant Secretaries-General and other employees of the Secretariat shall be governed by the provisions of this Charter and the regulations approved by the Assembly of Heads of State and Government.

1. In the performance of their duties the Administrative Secretary-General and the staff shall not seek or receive instructions from any government or from any other authority external to the Organization. They shall refrain from any action which might reflect on their position as international officials responsible only to the Organization.
2. Each member of the Organization undertakes to respect the exclusive character of the responsibilities of the Administrative Secretary-General and the staff and not to seek to influence them in the discharge of their responsibilities.

COMMISSION OF MEDIATION, CONCILIATION AND ARBITRATION

Article XIX

Member States pledge to settle all disputes among themselves by peaceful means and, to this end decide to establish a Commission of Mediation, Conciliation and Arbitration, the composition of which and conditions of service shall be defined by a separate Protocol to be approved by the Assembly of Heads of State and Government. Said Protocol shall be regarded as forming an integral part of the present Charter.

SPECIALIZED COMMISSIONS

Article XX

The Assembly shall establish such Specialized Commissions as it may deem necessary, including the following:

1. Economic and Social Commission;
2. Educational and Cultural Commission;

3. Health, Sanitation and Nutrition Commission;
4. Defence Commission;
5. Scientific, Technical and Research Commission.

Article XXI

Each Specialized Commission referred to in Article XX shall be composed of the Ministers concerned or other Ministers or Plenipotentiaries designated by the Governments of the Member States.

Article XXII

The functions of the Specialized Commissions shall be carried out in accordance with the provisions of the present Charter and of the regulations approved by the Council of Ministers.

THE BUDGET

Article XXIII

The budget of the Organization prepared by the Administrative Secretary-General shall be approved by the Council of Ministers. The budget shall be provided by contributions from Member States in accordance with the scale of assessment of the United Nations; provided, however, that no Member State shall be assessed an amount exceeding twenty percent of the yearly regular budget of the Organization. The Member States agree to pay their respective contribution regularly.

SIGNATURE AND RATIFICATION OF CHARTER

Article XXIV

1. This Charter shall be open for signature to all independent sovereign African States and shall be ratified by the signatory States in accordance with their respective constitutional processes.
2. The original instrument, done, if possible in African languages, in English and French, all texts being equally authentic, shall be deposited with the Government of Ethiopia which shall transmit certified copies thereof to all independent sovereign African States.
3. Instruments of ratification shall be deposited with the Government of Ethiopia, which shall notify all signatories of each such deposit.

ENTRY INTO FORCE

Article XXV

This Charter shall enter into force immediately upon receipt by the Government of Ethiopia of the instruments of ratification from two-thirds of the signatory States.

REGISTRATION OF THE CHARTER

Article XXVI

This Charter shall, after due ratification, be registered with the Secretariat of the United Nations through the Government of Ethiopia in conformity with Article 102 of the Charter of the United Nations.

INTERPRETATION OF THE CHARTER

Article XXVII

Any question which may arise concerning the interpretation of this Charter shall be decided by a vote of two-thirds of the Assembly of Heads of State and Government of the Organization.

ADHESION AND ACCESSION

Article XXVIII

1. Any independent sovereign African State may at any time notify the Administrative Secretary-General of its intention to adhere or accede to this Charter.
2. The Administrative Secretary-General shall, on receipt of such notification, communicate a copy of it to all the Member States. Admission shall be decided by a simple majority of the Member States. The decision of each Member State shall be transmitted to the Administrative Secretary-General, who shall, upon receipt of the required number of votes, communicate the decision to the State concerned.

MISCELLANEOUS

Article XXIX

The working languages of the Organization and all its institutions shall be, if possible African languages, English and French.

Article XXX

The Administrative Secretary-General may accept on behalf of the Organization gifts, bequests and other donations made to the Organization, provided that this is approved by the Council of Ministers.

Article XXXI

The Council of Ministers shall decide on the privileges and immunities to be accorded to the personnel of the Secretariat in the respective territories of the Member States.

CESSATION OF MEMBERSHIP

Article XXXII

Any State which desires to renounce its membership shall forward a written notification to the Administrative Secretary-General. At the end of one year from the date of such notification, if not withdrawn, the Charter shall cease to apply with respect to the renouncing State, which shall thereby cease to belong to the Organization.

AMENDMENT OF THE CHARTER

Article XXXIII

This Charter may be amended or revised if any Member State makes a written request to the Administrative Secretary-General to that effect; provided, however, that the proposed amendment is not submitted to the Assembly for consideration until all the Member States have been duly notified of it and a period of one year has elapsed. Such an amendment shall not be effective unless approved by at least two-thirds of all the Member States.

IN FAITH WHEREOF, We, the Heads of African State and Government have signed this Charter.

Done in the City of Addis Ababa, Ethiopia this 25th day of May, 1963.

ALGERIA	MALI
BURUNDI	MAURITANIA
CAMEROUN	MOROCCO
CENTRAL AFRICAN REPUBLIC	NIGER
CHAD	NIGERIA
CONGO (Brazzaville)	RWANDA
CONGO (Leopoldville)	SENEGAL
DAHOMEY	SIERRA LEONE
ETHIOPIA	SOMALIA
GABON	SUDAN
GHANA	TANGANYIKA
GUINEA	TOGO
IVORY COAST	TUNISIA
LIBERIA	UGANDA
LIBYA	UNITED ARAB REPUBLIC
MADAGASCAR	UPPER VOLTA

Appendix II
Resolutions on OAU-UN Relations

1. AFRICA AND THE UNITED NATIONS

Summit Conference of Independent African States, Agenda Item III: Resolution C, 25 May 1963.

The Summit Conference of Independent African States meeting in Addis Ababa, Ethiopia, from 22 May to 25 May 1963;

Believing that the United Nations is an important instrument for the maintenance of peace and security among nations and for the promotion of the economic and social advancement of all peoples;

Reiterating its desire to strengthen and support the United Nations;

Noting with regret that Africa as a region is not equitably represented in the principal organs of the United Nations;

Convinced of the need for closer co-operation and co-ordination among the African Member States of the United Nations;

1. *Reaffirms* its dedication to the purposes and principles of the United Nations Charter and its acceptance of all obligations contained in the Charter, including financial obligations;

2. *Insists* that Africa as a geographical region should have equitable representation in the principal organs of the United Nations, particularly the Security Council and the Economic and Social Council and its Specialized Agencies;

3. *Invites* African Governments to instruct their representatives in the United Nations to take all possible steps to achieve a more equitable representation of the African region;

4. *Further invites* African Governments to instruct their representatives in the United Nations, without prejudice to their membership in and collaboration with the African-Asian Group, to constitute a more effective African Group with a permanent secretariat so as to bring about closer co-operation and better co-ordination in matters of common concern.

2. RELATIONS BETWEEN THE ORGANIZATION OF AFRICAN UNITY AND THE UNITED NATIONS

OAU Resolution AHG/Res.33 (II), 25 October 1965

The Assembly of Heads of State and Government meeting in its Second Ordinary Session in Accra, Ghana, from 21 to 25 October 1965,

Considering that in 1965 there are thirty six African Members of the United Nations, representing almost one third of the membership of that organization,

Noting with satisfaction that, thanks to the efforts of the African Group at the United Nations, the Charter of the United Nations has just been amended in a way that will improve African representation on the Security Council and on the Economic and Social Council,

Noting also the decision taken at the twentieth session of the General Assembly of the United Nations to establish relations of co-operation with the Organization of African Unity,

1. *Expresses* its congratulations to the African Group for its efforts to achieve better representation of Africa in the United Nations and requests it to continue its action in the interests of Africa;

2. *Takes note* of the invitation sent to the OAU Administrative Secretary-General to follow the work of the General Assembly of the United Nations;

3. *Requests* the Administrative Secretary-General to invite the Secretary-General of the United Nations to follow the work of the Assembly of Heads of State and Government and the Council of Ministers as well as those of all the OAU Specialized Commissions as an observer;

4. *Welcomes* with satisfaction the establishment of relations of co-operation between the United Nations and the Organization of African Unity and requests the OAU Administrative Secretary-General to do his utmost to ensure that this co-operation be as close as possible and cover all fields that interest both organizations.

3. CO-OPERATION BETWEEN THE UNITED NATIONS AND THE ORGANIZATION OF AFRICAN UNITY

General Assembly Resolution 2011 (XX), 11 October 1965

The General Assembly,

Desiring to promote co-operation between the United Nations and the Organization of African Unity, in accordance with the purposes and principles of the charters of the two organizations,

1. *Requests* the Secretary-General of the United Nations to invite the Administrative Secretary-General of the Organization of African Unity to attend sessions of the General Assembly as an observer;

2. *Invites* the Secretary-General of the United Nations to explore, in consultation with the appropriate bodies of the Organization of African Unity, the means of promoting co-operation between the two organizations and to report to the General Assembly as appropriate.

Appendix III
Agreement Between the United Nations and the Organization of African Unity on Co-operation between the Latter and the United Nations Economic Commission for Africa, 1965

The United Nations and the Organization of African Unity,

Referring to the resolution of the Organization of African Unity, ECOS/RES.17 (II) (Cairo, January 1965), and to the resolution of the Economic Commission for Africa, E/CN.14/RES/132 (VII) (Nairobi, February 1965) whereby the Organization of African Unity (hereinafter referred to as OAU) and the United Nations Economic Commission for Africa (hereinafter referred to as ECA) requested their respective secretariats to come to an arrangement or agreement defining precisely the framework for co-operation between them,

Desirous of establishing, within their respective spheres of responsibility, effective co-operation in the accomplishment of their common objective for the economic and social development of Africa, in accordance more particularly with the Charter of the United Nations and the Terms of Reference of ECA on the one hand, and with the Charter of OAU and the Terms of Reference of its competent specialized commissions on the other hand,

Have agreed as follows:

ARTICLE I

Mutual Consultation

1. OAU and ECA shall consult one another on all matters of common interest for the purpose of achieving their respective objectives and of co-ordinating, so far as may be appropriate, their activities relating to the economic and social development of the African continent.

2. Accordingly, when circumstances so require, consultations shall be arranged between the Administrative Secretariat-General of OAU and the Executive Secretariat of ECA to seek agreement on the most effective manner of undertaking specified activities, within the limits authorized by the competent departments of the two bodies.

ARTICLE II

Study of Questions of Common Interest

Subject to preliminary consultations, the Administrative Secretary-General of OAU shall make all necessary arrangements compatible with the rules of procedure of the competent specialized commissions of OAU in order to submit to the latter items proposed by ECA or its subsidiary organs. ECA shall include on the provisional agenda of its sessions and the meetings of its subsidiary organs items proposed by the competent organs of OAU, in so far as is compatible with the Terms of Reference and Rules of Procedure of ECA.

ARTICLE III

Reciprocal Representation

1. OAU shall invite ECA to send representatives to attend as observers all meetings of OAU at which economic and social matters are considered—mainly meetings of the specialized commissions competent in the economic and social spheres coming within the terms of reference of ECA. ECA observers thus invited shall, if the competent organ so decides, be entitled to participate without voting rights in such deliberations of OAU.

2. ECA shall invite the Administrative Secretariat-General of OAU to attend the meetings of ECA and its subsidiary organs as observers. Representatives of the OAU secretariat thus invited shall, if the competent organ so decides, be entitled to participate without voting rights in such deliberations of ECA and its subsidiary organs.

ARTICLE IV

Statistical Services

OAU and ECA shall establish the closest co-operation between them with a view to avoiding as far as possible useless overlapping in their activities, so that each can make the most rational possible use of its specialist staff in the collection, analysis, publication and dissemination of statistical information.

They shall combine their efforts to secure the most efficient use of statistical information, to reduce to a minimum the tasks incumbent upon African Governments and to rationalize the various forms of assistance in this sphere.

ARTICLE V

Exchange and Joint Use of Information, Documents and Written Statements

Subject to such arrangements as may be necessary owing to the confidential nature of certain information and documents, the secretariats of OAU and ECA shall exchange and make joint use of information and documents concerning economic and social matters of common interest.

To this end, within the limits of its resources and at the request of the Executive Secretariat of ECA, the Administrative Secretary-General of OAU may prepare working papers for meetings of ECA.

In all matters of common interest, the Executive Secretary of ECA may convey to the Administrative Secretary-General of OAU information in writing on ECA activities in Africa, accompanied, where necessary, by appropriate remarks. Within the limits of its resources and at the request of the Secretariat-General of OAU, the Executive Secretariat of ECA may prepare working papers for meetings of OAU.

ARTICLE VI

Co-operation Between Secretariats and Assistance in Staffing

1. Discussions shall be held regularly between the Administrative Secretary-General of OAU and the Executive Secretary of ECA to ensure effective consultation and liaison between the secretariats of OAU and ECA. In particular, they shall examine their respective work programmes in the economic and social fields established by the competent organs of each institution with a view to avoiding useless overlapping of work and reaching agreement on measures of co-operation and co-ordination relating to specified projects or studies.

2. ECA may, when a request is received, and so far as its normal resources and those of the other competent services of the United Nations allow, lend its assistance to OAU in finding the staff or experts whom OAU might wish to employ. ECA may likewise, at the request of the Administrative Secretary-General of OAU, with the concurrence of the Secretary-General of the United Nations, and the agreement of the staff member concerned, make available to OAU specialist officials in the fields of administration, conferences, general services or economic and social questions, by seconding them for special duties of an urgent nature. Such seconding of personnel shall take place with full regard for the exclusively international status of the staffs of both organizations and for their obligations by virtue of their respective charters, and in conformity with the staff regulations and staff rules of each Organization. Expenditure incurred by the United Nations as a result of assistance provided for OAU shall be borne by OAU.

ARTICLE VII

Entry Into Force and Amendment

1. The present agreement shall enter into force on the date upon which it is signed by the authorized representatives of the Organization of African Unity and the United Nations.

2. This agreement may be amended by common consent of the two parties. The agreement may be terminated through notification by one of the parties, and shall lapse three months after the date of such notification.

DONE AT THE HEADQUARTERS OF THE UNITED NATIONS, NEW YORK, this fifteenth day of November, one thousand nine hundred and sixty-five, in two original copies in the English and French languages, one of which shall be deposited in the archives of the Secretariat of the United Nations and the other in the archives of the Administrative Secretariat-General of the Organization of African Unity.

For the United Nations:
U THANT
Secretary-General

For the Organization of African Unity:
DIALLO TELLI
Administrative Secretary-General

Selected Bibliography

Selected Bibliography

PUBLIC DOCUMENTS

United Nations*

Annual Reports of the Secretary-General on the Work of the Organization and Introduction to the Annual Reports.

International Court of Justice, *Reports of Judgments, Advisory Opinions and Orders.*

Official Records of the Economic and Social Council, Summary Records, Supplements, Annexes and Resolutions.

Official Records of the General Assembly, Verbatim Records of Meetings, Supplements, Annexes and Resolutions.

Official Records of the Security Council, Verbatim Records of Meetings, Supplements and Resolutions.

Repertory of Practice of United Nations Organs, Vol. II (1955), Supplement No. 3, Vol. II (1971).

United Nations Conference on International Organization, San Francisco, 1945. *Documents.* Vol. 12. New York and London: United Nations Information Organizations, 1945.

United Nations Preparatory Commission. *Report.* PC/20, 23 December 1945.

Organization of African Unity

Assembly of Heads of State and Government Resolutions, Decisions and Declarations of Ordinary and Extra-Ordinary Sessions (AHG/Res., AHG/Dec., and AHG/ST. series).

Basic Documents of the Organization of African Unity, Addis Ababa: Provisional Secretariat of the OAU, May 1963.

Council of Ministers Resolution and Declarations of Ordinary and Extra-Ordinary Sessions (CM/Res., ECM/Res., and CM/ST. series).

Documents of the Assembly of Heads of State and Government (AHG/series—mimeo.).

Documents of the Council of Ministers (CM/ series—mimeo.).

Documents and Resolutions of the OAU Specialized Commissions (ECOS/, EDC/, STR/, ESCHC/ series—mimeo.).

Reports of the Administrative Secretary-General (CM/ series—mimeo.).

Proceedings of the Summit Conference of Independent African States, Vols. I-V. Addis Ababa, May 1963. (Published by the Government of Ethiopia.)

---

* Since the specific relevant documents have been properly cited in the notes, only the broad categories are given in this bibliography.

307

Great Britain

Southern Rhodesia: Documents Relating to the Negotiations between the United Kingdom and Southern Rhodesian Governments, November 1963-November 1965. Presented to Parliament by Command of Her Majesty. London: H.M. Stationery Office, 1965. Cmnd. 2807.

Rhodesia: Documents Relating to Proposals for a Settlement, 1966. Cmnd. 3171 (December 1966).

Rhodesia: Report of the Commission on Rhodesian Opinion under the Chairmanship of the Right Honourable the Lord Pearce. Cmnd. 4964 (May 1972).

BOOKS AND ARTICLES

The United Nations and Regionalism

Aranha, O. "Regional Systems and the Future of the UN," *Foreign Affairs,* Vol. 26 (1948).

Bebr, G. "Regional Organizations: A United Nations Problem," *American Journal of International Law,* Vol. 49, No. 2 (April, 1955).

El-Ayouty, Y. and Brooks, H.C. (eds.). *Africa and International Organization.* The Hague: Martinus Nijhoff, 1973.

Etzioni, Minerva M. *The Majority of One: Towards a Theory of Regional Compatibility.* Beverly Hills, California: Sage Publications, 1970.

Frey-Wouters, E. "The Prospects for Regionalism in World Affairs," in R.A. Falk and C.E. Black (eds.). *The Future of the International Legal Order,* Vol. I. Princeton, N.J.: Princeton University Press, 1969.

Goodrich, L.M., Hambro, E. and Simons, A. *Charter of the United Nations; Commentary and Documents,* Third and Revised Edition. New York and London: Columbia University Press, 1969.

Haas, E.B., Butterworth, R.L., and Nye, J.S. *Conflict Management by International Organizations.* Morristown, N.J.: General Learning Press, 1972.

Iturriaga, J.A. de. "L'Organisation de l'unité africaine et les Nations Unies," *Revue générale de droit international public,* Vol. 69 (1965).

Levin, Aida L. *Relations Between the United Nations and the Organization of American States in the Peace and Security Field.* New York: UNITAR, 1974.

Miller, Linda. "Regional Organization and the Regulation of Internal Conflict," *World Politics,* Vol. XIX, No. 4 (July, 1967).

Miller, Lynn. "The Prospects for Regional Order through Regional Security," in R.A. Falk and C.E. Black (eds.). *The Future of the International Legal Order,* Vol. I. Princeton, N.J.: Princeton University Press, 1969.

Moore, J.N. "The Role of Regional Arrangements in the Maintenance of World Order," C.E. Black and R.A. Falk (eds.). *The Future of the International Legal Order, Vol. III, Conflict Management.* Princeton, N.J.: Princeton University Press, 1971.

Nye, J.S., Jr. *International Regionalism—Readings*. Boston: Little Brown and Co., 1968.

————. *Peace in Parts: Integration and Conflict in Regional Organization*. Boston: Little Brown and Co., 1971.

Padelford, N.J. "Regional Organization and United Nations," *International Organization*, Vol. VIII, No. 3 (1954).

Pechota, V. *The Quiet Approach: A Study of the Good Offices Exercised by the United Nations Secretary-General in the Cause of Peace*. (UNITAR PS No. 6.) New York: UNITAR, 1972.

Robertson, A.H. *The Relations Between the Council of Europe and the United Nations*. (A UNITAR Regional Study No. 1.) New York: UNITAR, 1972.

Russett, B.M. *International Regions and the International System*. Chicago: Rand McNally, 1967.

Smithers, Sir Peter. *Governmental Control: A Prerequisite for Effective Relations Between the United Nations and non-United Nations Regional Organizations*. (A UNITAR Regional Study No. 3.) New York: UNITAR, 1973.

Strauch, H. "Les relations entre l'Organisation de l'unité africaine et L'O.N.U.," *Revue française d'études politiques africaines* (October 1967).

Tharp, P.A., Jr. *Regional International Organizations: Structures and Functions*. New York: St. Martin's Press, 1971.

Wilcox, F.O. "Regionalism and the United Nations," *International Organization*, Vol. XIX, No. 3 (Summer 1965).

Yakemtchouk, R. *L'ONU, la sécurité régionale et le problème du régionalisme*. Paris: Editions Pedone, 1955.

African Diplomacy and the OAU

Borella, F. "Le système juridique de l'O.U.A.," *Annuaire française de droit international*, XVII (1971).

Boutros-Ghali, B. *L'Organisation de l'unité africaine*. Paris: Librairie Armand Colin, 1969.

————. "The Addis Ababa Charter," *International Conciliation*, No. 546 (January, 1965).

Cervenka, Z. *The Organization of African Unity and its Charter*. London: C. Hurst and Co., 1969.

Diallo, Telli. "The Organization of African Unity in Historical Perspective," *African Forum*, Vol. I, No. 2 (Fall 1965).

Elias, T.O. "The Charter of the Organization of African Unity," *American Journal of International Law*, Vol. 59, No. 2 (1965).

————. "The Commission of Mediation, Conciliation and Arbitration," *British Yearbook of International Law*, 1965.

Kay, David A. "The Impact of African States on the United Nations," *International Organization*, Vol. XXIII, No. 1 (1969).

Legum, C. *Pan-Africanism — a Short Political Guide.* Revised Edition. New
York: F.A. Praeger, 1965.
Markakis, J. "The Organization of African Unity: A Progress Report," *The
Journal of Modern African Studies,* Vol. 4, No. 2 (October, 1966).
Mazrui, A.A. *Towards a Pax Africana: A Study of Ideology and Ambition.*
Chicago: University of Chicago Press, 1967.
———. "The United Nations and African Political Attitudes," *International
Organization,* Vol. 18, No. 3.
McKay, V. (ed.). *African Diplomacy: Studies in the Determinants of Foreign
Policy.* New York: F.A. Praeger [For the School of International Studies,
Johns Hopkins University], 1966.
McKeon, Nora. "The African States and the OAU," *International Affairs*
(London), Vol. 42, No. 3 (July, 1966).
Nkrumah, Kwame. *Africa Must Unite.* New York: F.A. Praeger, 1963.
Padelford, N.J. "The Organization of African Unity," *International Organiza-
tion,* Vol. 18, No. 3 (Summer 1964).
——— and Emerson, R. (eds.). *Africa and World Order.* New York and
London: F.A. Praeger, 1963.
Quaison-Sackey, A. *Africa Unbound: Reflexions of an African Statesman,*
New York: F.A. Praeger, 1963.
Tevoedjre, A. *Pan-Africanism in Action: An Account of the UAM* (Occasional
paper No. 11). Cambridge, Mass.: Center for International Affairs, Har-
vard University, November, 1965.
Wallerstein, I. *Africa: The Politics of Unity.* New York: Random House, 1967.
———. "The Early Years of the OAU: the Search for Organizational Preemi-
nence," *International Organization,* Vol. XX, No. 4 (Autumn, 1966).
Woronoff, J. *Organizing African Unity.* Metuchen, N.J.: The Scarecrow Press,
Inc., 1970.
Zartman, I.W. *International Relations in Africa.* Englewood Cliffs, N.J.:
Prentice-Hall, 1966.

Boundary Disputes and Internal Conflicts

Anber, P. "Modernization and Political Disintegration: Nigeria and the Ibos,"
The Journal of Modern African Studies, Vol. 5, No. 2 (September, 1967).
Andemicael, Berhanykun. *Peaceful Settlement Among African States: Roles
of the United Nations and the Organization of African Unity.* (UNITAR
PS No. 5.) New York: UNITAR, 1972.
Ashford, D. "The Irredentist Appeal in Morocco and Mauritania," *Western
Political Quarterly,* Vol. 15, No. 4 (December, 1962).
Ayele, Negussay. "The Politics of the Somali-Ethiopia Boundary Problem,
1960-1967." Unpublished Ph. D. dissertation, University of California,
Los Angeles, 1971.
Bedjaoui, M. "Le règlement pacifique des différendes africains," *Annuaire
français de droit international,* XVIII (1972).

Brooks, H.C. and El-Ayouty, Y. (eds.). *Refugees South of the Sahara: An African Dilemma.* Westport, Conn.: Negro University Press, 1970.

Carrington, C.E. "Frontiers in Africa," *International Affairs* (London), Vol. 36, No. 4 (October, 1960).

Castagno, A.A. "The Somali Kenyan Controversy: Implications for the Future," *The Journal of Modern African Studies,* Vol. 2, No. 2 (July, 1964).

Chapal, Ph. "Le rôle de l'organisation de l'unite africaine dans le règlement des litiges entre Etats africains," *Revue algérienne des sciences juridiques, économiques, et politiques,* Vol. VIII, No. 4 (1971).

Charlier, T. "A propos des conflits de frontière entre la Somalie, l'Ethiopie, et le Kenya," *Revue française de science politique,* Vol. 16, No. 2 (April, 1966).

Dent, M. "Nigeria: the Task of Conflict Resolution," *The World Today,* Vol. 24, No. 7 (July, 1968).

Doob, L. (ed.). *Resolving Conflict in Africa—the Fermeda Workshop.* New Haven and London: Yale University Press, 1970.

Drysdale, J. *The Somali Dispute.* London: Pall Mall Press, 1964.

"Element du dossier relatif au différend entre la République du Congo et le Royaume du Burundi," *Travaux africains,* No. 39 (December, 1964).

Evans, J.D., Jr. "The Dilemma of the Horn: A Study of Conflict in Northeast Africa." Unpublished Ph. D. dissertation, Georgetown University, March 1967.

Feit, E. "Military Coups and Political Development: Some Lessons from Ghana and Nigeria," *World Politics,* Vol. 20, No. 2 (January, 1968).

Gallager, C.F. "Morocco and Its Neighbours, Part II: Morocco and Algeria," *American Universities Field Staff Reports* (North Africa Series), Vol. 13, No. 3 (March, 1967).

————. "Morocco and Its Neighbours, Part III, Morocco and Mauritania," *American Universities Field Staff Reports* (North Africa Series), Vol. 13, No. 4 (April, 1967).

Ghana. *Nkrumah's Subversion in Africa.* Accra: Ghana Information Services, 1966.

Good, R.C. "The Congo Crisis: A Study of Postcolonial Politics," in L.W. Martin (ed.). *Neutralism and Non-alignment—the New States in World Affairs.* New York: F.A. Praeger, 1962.

Hamrell, Sven (ed.). *Refugee Problems in Africa.* Uppsala: The Scandinavian Institute of African Studies, 1967.

Higgins, R. "Internal War and International Law," in C.E. Black and R.A. Falk (eds.). *The Future of the International Legal Order, Vol. III, Conflict Management.* Princeton, N.J.: Princeton University Press, 1971.

Kapil, R. "Of the Conflict Potential of Inherited Boundaries in Africa," *World Politics,* Vol. 18, No. 3 (July, 1966).

Lemarchand, R. *Rwanda and Burundi.* New York, Washington, London: Praeger Publishers, 1970.

Le problème des réfugiés en Afrique. Paris: Centre de hautes études administratives sur l'Afrique et l'Asie modernes, 1968.

Lewis, I.M. "The Problem of the Northern Frontier District of Kenya," *Race*, Vol. 5, No. 1 (July, 1963).

———. "The Referendum in French Somaliland: Aftermath and Prospects in the Somali Dispute," *The World Today*, Vol. 23, No. 7 (July, 1967).

Matthews, R.E. "Interstate Conflicts in Africa: A Review," *International Organization*, Vol. 24, No. 2 (Spring, 1970).

Mazrui, Ali. "Violent Contiguity and the Politics of Retribalization in Africa," *Journal of International Affairs*, Vol. 23, No. 1 (1969).

Miller, E.M. "Legal Aspects of the U.N. Action in the Congo," *American Journal of International Law*, Vol. 55 (1961).

Nkrumah, Kwame. *Challenge of the Congo: A Case Study of Foreign Pressures in an Independent State*. New York: International Publishers, 1967.

Nwankwo, A.G. and Ifejika, S.V. *The Making of a Nation: Biafra*. London: C. Hurst, 1969.

Panter-Brick, S.K. "The Right to Self-Determination: Its Applications to Nigeria [Biafra's Secession]," *International Affairs* (London), Vol. 44, No. 2 (April, 1968).

Perham, M. "Reflections on the Nigerian Civil War," *International Affairs* (London), Vol. 46, No. 2 (April, 1970).

Post, K.W.J. "Is There a Case for Biafra?" *International Affairs* (London), Vol. 44, No. 1 (January, 1968).

Reyner, A.S. "Morocco's International Boundaries: A Factual Background," *The Journal of Modern African Studies*, Vol. I, No. 3 (September, 1963).

Schachter, O. "The United Nations and Internal Conflict," in J.N. Moore (ed.). *Law and Civil War in the Modern World*. Baltimore: The Johns Hopkins Press, 1974.

Schwarz, W. *Nigeria*. New York: F.A. Praeger, 1968.

Segal, A. "Rwanda: The Underlying Cause," *Africa Report*, Vol. 9, No. 4 (April, 1964).

Singleton, F.S. "The African States and the Congo Affair, 1960 65." Unpublished Ph. D. Dissertation, Yale University, 1969.

Skurnik, W.A.E. "Ghana and Guinea, 1966—A Case Study in Inter-African Relations," *Journal of Modern African Studies*, Vol. 5, No. 3 (November, 1967).

Touval, S. *The Boundary Politics of Independent Africa*. Cambridge, Mass.: Harvard University Press, 1972.

———. "The Organization of African Unity and African Borders," *International Organization*, Vol. 21, No. 1 (Winter, 1967).

Verhaegen, B. *Rébellions au Congo*. Kinshasa: Institut de recherches économiques et sociales, 1967.

Whiteman, Kaye. "The OAU and the Nigerian Issue," *The World Today*, Vol. 24, No. 11 (November, 1968).

Widstrand, C.G. (ed.). *African Boundary Problems*. Uppsala: Scandinavian Institute of African Studies, 1969, esp.:

Chime, S. "The Organization of African Unity and Boundary Problems";

Zartman, I.W. "The Foreign and Military Politics of African Boundary Problems."

Wild, P.B. "The Organization of African Unity and the Algerian-Moroccan Border Conflict: A Study of New Machinery for Peacekeeping and for the Peaceful Settlement of Disputes among African States," *International Organization,* Vol. 20, No. 1 (Winter, 1966).

Wolde Mariam, M. "The Background of the Ethio-Somalian Boundary Dispute," *The Journal of Modern African Studies,* Vol. 2, No. 2 (July, 1964).

Young, C. *Politics in the Congo: Decolonization and Independence.* Princeton, N.J.: Princeton University Press, 1965.

Zartman, I.W. "The Politics of Boundaries in North and West Africa," *The Journal of Modern African Studies,* Vol. 3, No. 2 (August, 1965).

Colonial and Racial Problems

Adam, H. *Modernizing Racial Domination: The Dynamics of South African Politics.* Berkeley: University of California Press, 1971.

Akindele, R.A. "The Organization of African Unity and the United Nations: A Study of the Problems of Universal-Regional Relationships in the Organization and Maintenance of International Peace and Security," *The Canadian Yearbook of International Law—Annuaire canadien de Droit international,* Vol. IX (1971).

Barber, J. *Rhodesia: The Road to Rebellion.* London: Oxford University Press, 1967.

Barrie, G.N. "Rhodesian UDI—An Unruly Horse," *Comparative and International Law Journal of Southern Africa,* Vol. I, No. 1 (March, 1968).

Beza, S.J. "The Organization of African Unity and Rhodesia." Unpublished Dissertation, Southern Illinois University, Dept. of Government, Carbondale, Illinois, 1972.

Carter, M. (ed.). *South Africa's Transkei: Politics of Domestic Colonialism.* London: Heinemann, 1967.

Cefkin, J.L. "The Rhodesian Question at the United Nations," *International Organization,* Vol. 22, No. 3 (Summer, 1968).

Chilcote, R.H. *Emerging Nationalism in Portuguese Africa: Documents.* Stanford, California: Hoover Institution Press, 1972.

Doxey, M. "International Sanctions: A Framework for Analysis with Special Reference to the UN and Southern Africa," *International Organization,* Vol. 26, No. 3 (Summer, 1972).

Dugard, C.J.R. "The Organization of African Unity and Colonialism: An Inquiry into the Plea of Self-Defence as a Justification for the Use of Force in the Eradication of Colonialism," *The International and Comparative Law Quarterly,* Vol. 16, No. 1 (1967).

El-Ayouty, Y. *The United Nations and Decolonization: The Role of Afro-Asia.* The Hague: Martinus Nijhoff, 1971.

Falk, R.A. "The South West Africa Cases: An Appraisal," *International Organization*, Vol. XXI, No. 1 (Winter, 1967).

Finger, S.M. "A New Approach to Colonial Problems at the United Nations," *International Organization*, Vol. 26, No. 1 (Winter, 1972).

First, R., Steele, J. and Gurney, C. *The South African Connection: Western Investments in Apartheid*. London: Temple Smith, 1972.

Galtung, J. "On the Effects of International Economic Sanctions, with Examples from the Case of Rhodesia," *World Politics*, Vol. 19, No. 3 (April, 1967).

Gibson, R. *African Liberation Movements*. New York: Oxford University Press, 1972.

Goodwin, G. *Race Relations and the United Nations*. London: Pall Mall Press Ltd., 1966.

Grundy, K.W. *Confrontation and Accommodation in Southern Africa; the Limits of Independence*. Berkeley, Calif.: University of California Press, 1973.

————. *Guerrilla Struggle in Africa; an Analysis and Preview*. New York: Grossman Publishers, 1971.

Hance, W.A. et al. *Southern Africa and the United States*. New York and London: Columbia University Press, 1968.

Higgins, Rosalyn. "The Advisory Opinion on Namibia: Which UN Resolutions are Binding under Article 25 of the Charter?" *The International and Comparative Law Quarterly*, Vol. 21, No. 2 (April, 1972).

Hoagland, J. *South Africa: Civilizations in Conflict*. Boston: Houghton Mifflin Co., 1972.

Howe, R.W. "War in Southern Africa," *Foreign Affairs*, Vol. 48, No. 1 (October, 1969).

Kapungu, L.T. *The United Nations and Economic Sanctions Against Rhodesia*. Lexington, Mass.: D.C. Heath and Co., 1973.

Kay, D.A. "The Impact of African States on the United Nations," *International Organization*, Vol. XXIII, No. 1 (Winter, 1969).

Kennan, G.F. "Hazardous Courses in Southern Africa," *Foreign Affairs*, Vol. 49, No. 2 (January, 1971).

Legum, C. "The United Nations and Southern Africa," *ISIO Monographs*, First Series, Number Three. Brighton, Sussex: Institute for the Study of International Organization, University of Sussex, 1970.

Leiss, A.C. (ed.). *Apartheid and United Nations Collective Measures*. New York: Carnegie Endowment for International Peace, 1965.

Marcum, J. *The Angolan Revolution*. Cambridge, Mass.: M.I.T. Press, 1969.

McDougal, M.S. and Reisman, W.M. "Rhodesia and the United Nations: the Lawfulness of International Concern," *American Journal of International Law*, Vol. 62, No. 1 (January, 1968).

Minter, W. *Portuguese Africa and the West*. London: Penguin, 1972.

Mtshali, B.V. *Rhodesia: Background to Conflict*. London: Leslie Frewin, 1968.

Mudge, G.A. "Domestic Policies and U.N. Activities: the Cases of Rhodesia and the Republic of South Africa," *International Organization,* Vol. XXI, No. 1 (Winter, 1967).

Nyerere, Julius K. "Rhodesia in the Context of Southern Africa," *Foreign Affairs,* Vol. 44, No. 3 (April, 1966).

Potholm, C.P. and Dale, R. *Southern Africa in Perspective.* New York: Free Press, 1972.

Pratt, R.C. "African Reactions to the Rhodesian Crisis," *International Journal* (Toronto), Vol. XXI, No. 2 (Spring, 1966).

Segal, R. (ed.). *Sanctions against South Africa.* Harmondsworth, England: Penguin Books, 1964.

Taubenfeld, R.F. and Taubenfeld, H.J. *Race, Peace, Law and Southern Africa: Background Paper and Proceedings of the Tenth Hammarskjöld Forum.* Edited by John Carey. Dobbs Ferry, N.Y.: Oceana Publications, 1968.

Twitchett, K.J. "The Racial Issue at the United Nations: A Study of the African States' Reaction to the American-Belgian Congo Rescue Operation of November, 1964," *International Relations* (London), Vol. 2, No. 12 (October, 1965).

Regionalism for African Development

Abebe, Girma. "The Economic Commission for Africa: A Study of the Problems of the Geographic and Administrative Decentralization in the United Nations System." Unpublished Dissertation, New York University, Graduate School of Public Administration, New York, 1973.

Elisha, A. *Les Institutions internationales et le développement économique en Afrique.* Thése du 3ème cycle (Paris, 1969).

Ewing, A.F. Reflections from Afar on the Ninth Session of the U.N. Economic Commission for Africa," *The Journal of Modern African Studies,* Vol. 2, (July, 1969).

Gardiner, R.K.A., Anstee, M.J. and Patterson, C.L. *Africa and the World.* Addis Ababa: Oxford University Press, 1970.

———. *United Nations Regional Commissions and International Economic Cooperation.* Twenty-third Montague Burton Lecture on International Relations (5 March 1965). Leeds University Press, 1967.

Gregg, R.W. "The United Nations Regional Economic Commissions and Integration in the Underdeveloped Regions," *International Organization,* Vol. XX, No. 2 (Spring, 1966).

Hazlewood, A. (ed.). *African Integration and Disintegration: Case Studies in Economic and Political Union.* New York: Oxford University Press, 1968.

Hunter, Guy (ed.). *Industrialization and Race Relations; A Symposium* [sponsored by UNESCO and the Institute of Race Relations]. London: Oxford University Press, 1965.

Magee, J.S. "ECA and the Paradox of African Cooperation," *International Conciliation,* No. 580 (November, 1970).

———. "What Role for E.C.A.?–or Pan Africanism Revisited," *The Journal of Modern African Studies,* Vol. 9, No. 1 (1971).

Mangone, G.V. (ed.). *UN Administration of Economic and Social Programs.* New York and London: Columbia University Press, 1966.

Mutharika, B.W.T. *Toward Multinational Economic Co-operation in Africa.* New York: F.A. Praeger, 1972.

Robcock, S.H. and Solomon, L.M. *International Development—1965.* New York: Oceana Publications, Inc., 1966.

Sharp, W.R. *The United Nations Economic and Social Council.* New York and London: Columbia University Press, 1969.

United Nations, Economic Commission for Africa. *A Venture in Self-Reliance, Ten Years of ECA, 1958-1968.* (Doc. E/CN.14/424).

——. *Economic Bulletin for Africa,* Vols. I-X (1961-1970).

——. *Survey of Economic Conditions in Africa* (1970 and 1971).

Index

INDEX